PROLOG AND DATABASES
Implementations and New Directions

ELLIS HORWOOD SERIES IN ARTIFICIAL INTELLIGENCE

Joint Series Editors: Professor JOHN CAMPBELL, Department of Computer Science, University College London, and
Dr JEAN HAYES MICHIE, Knowledgelink Limited, Edinburgh

Andrew, A.M.	**Continuous Heuristics***
Bläsius, K.H. and Bürckert, H.-J.	**Deduction Systems in AI***
Boguraev, B.K.	**Natural Language Interfaces to Computational Systems***
Bramer, M.A. (editor)	**Computer Game Playing: Theory and Practice**
Campbell, J.A. (editor)	**Implementations of PROLOG**
Campbell, J.A., Forsyth, R., Narayanan, A. & Teague, M.	**Dictionary of Artificial Intelligence***
Campbell, J. A. & Cox, P.	**Implementations of PROLOG, Vol. 2***
Carter, D.	**Interpreting Anaphors in Natural Language Texts**
Davies, R. (editor)	**Intelligent Information Systems: Progress and Prospects**
Evans, J.B.	**Structures of Discrete Event Simulation**
Farreny, H.	**Artificial Intelligence Exercise Programs***
Forsyth, R. & Rada, R.	**Machine Learning: Applications in Expert Systems and Information Retrieval**
Gabbay, D.M.	**Programming in Pure Logic***
Gergely, T. & Futó, I.	**Artificial Intelligence in Simulation***
Glicksman, J.	**Image Understanding and Machine Vision***
Gottinger, H.W.	**Artificial Intelligence: The Commercialisation of Intelligent Systems***
Hawley, R. (editor)	**Artificial Intelligence Programming Environments***
Hayes, J.E. & Michie, D. (editors)	**Intelligent Systems: The Unprecedented Opportunity**
Hunter, J.R.W., Gotts, N.M. & Sinnhuber, R.K.E.W.	**Artificial Intelligence in Medicine***
Lopez de Mantaras, R.	**Approximate Reasoning and Knowledge Acquisition***
Łukaszewicz, W.	**Nonmonotonic Reasoning***
Mellish, C.	**Computer Interpretation of Natural Language Descriptions**
Michie, D.	**On Machine Intelligence, Second Edition**
Mortimer, H.	**The Logic of Induction**
Mozetic, I.	**Machine Learning of Qualitative Models***
Partridge, D.	**Artificial Intelligence: Applications in the Future of Software Engineering**
Ramsay, A. & Barrett, R.	**AI in Practice: Examples in POP-11**
Savory, S.E.	**Artificial Intelligence and Expert Systems**
Spacek, L.	**Advanced Programming in PROLOG***
Sparck Jones, K. & Wilks, Y. (editors)	**Automatic Natural Language Parsing**
Steels, L. & Campbell, J.A. (editors)	**Progress in Artificial Intelligence**
Torrance, S. (editor)	**The Mind and the Machine**
Turner, R.	**Logics for Artificial Intelligence**
Wallace, M.	**Communicating with Databases in Natural Language**
Wertz, H.	**Automatic Correction and Improvement of Programs**
Yazdani, M. (editor)	**New Horizons in Educational Computing**
Yazdani, M. & Narayanan, A. (editors)	**Artificial Intelligence: Human Effects**

* *In preparation*

PROLOG AND DATABASES
Implementations and New Directions

Editors:
PETER M. D. GRAY, M.A., D.Phil.
and
ROBERT J. LUCAS, B.Sc., M.Sc., Ph.D.
both of Department of Computing Science
University of Aberdeen

ELLIS HORWOOD LIMITED
Publishers · Chichester

Halsted Press: a division of
JOHN WILEY & SONS
New York · Chichester · Brisbane · Toronto

First published in 1988 by
ELLIS HORWOOD LIMITED
Market Cross House, Cooper Street,
Chichester, West Sussex, PO19 1EB, England
The publisher's colophon is reproduced from James Gillison's drawing of the ancient Market Cross, Chichester.

Distributors:
Australia and New Zealand:
JACARANDA WILEY LIMITED
GPO Box 859, Brisbane, Queensland 4001, Australia
Canada:
JOHN WILEY & SONS CANADA LIMITED
22 Worcester Road, Rexdale, Ontario, Canada
Europe and Africa:
JOHN WILEY & SONS LIMITED
Baffins Lane, Chichester, West Sussex, England
North and South America and the rest of the world:
Halsted Press: a division of
JOHN WILEY & SONS
605 Third Avenue, New York, NY 10158, USA
South-East Asia
JOHN WILEY & SONS (SEA) PTE LIMITED
37 Jalan Pemimpin # 05–04
Block B, Union Industrial Building, Singapore 2057
Indian Subcontinent
WILEY EASTERN LIMITED
4835/24 Ansari Road
Daryaganj, New Delhi 110002, India

British Library Cataloguing in Publication Data
Prolog and databases: implementations and applications. —
(Ellis Horwood series in artificial intelligence)
1. Artificial intelligence. Applications of computer systems. Programming languages. Prolog
I. Gray, Peter M. D. II. Lucas, Robert J. *1954–*
006.3′028′55133

Library of Congress Card No. 88–23083

ISBN 0–7458–0371–7 (Ellis Horwood Limited)
ISBN 0–470–21221–7 (Halsted Press)

Phototypeset by Ellis Horwood Limited
Printed in Great Britain by Hartnolls, Bodmin

Contents

Introduction

This collection opens up an exciting new area of computing: the use of Prolog in conjunction with databases. The availability of new implementations of Prolog which hold very large numbers of unit clauses compiled in memory and provide coupling to external databases has made possible a new kind of software architecture. This book collects together information on these new implementations, and shows how they are being used both in science and industry. It brings together a wealth of recent experience, much of it from the Alvey and ESPRIT research programs, and points to new directions.

The possibilities for this new architecture arise out of the nature of Prolog, which is unique among the programming languages in the way that it handles both data and procedures uniformly. In the case of procedures, unification is used to invoke a particular definition of the procedure by pattern-matching. Now, since data are represented by unit clauses, which are effectively just procedures without a body, the same method can be used to find facts matching a particular pattern. When there are very large numbers of such facts, we have the makings of a database, with unification being used for selection. Furthermore, a value found in a selected clause can be passed as a Prolog variable, and used to select a clause from another procedure. This is exactly the 'join' operation used to find matching tuples in a relational database. This correspondence was noted early on by van Emden and by Kowalski, and is at the root of much of the interest in Prolog and databases.

The chapters in this book show various directions that have been taken by researchers and implementers in pursuing this interest. In Part I, there are three chapters on the use of Prolog to implement various kinds of database query languages. The review by Mouta *et al.* shows how Prolog can be used to implement Query-by-Example, one of the earliest languages, and SQL, which is currently the most popular. Thus, being a full programming language, Prolog can be used to implement not just selections and joins, but all the operations originally defined by Codd. Howells *et al.* explore the use of Prolog to transform a query into an intermediate form and then into one of a number of target languages, for execution on another DBMS. With the growth in use of remote databases and distributed databases, this is becoming increasingly important. Lunn and Archibald explore the use of Prolog to implement an informal query language for end-users, which allows a terse natural language style, with words missed out. This is particularly important for making data available to unskilled operators and casual enquiry. Large amounts of data are locked up in databanks only accessible by programmers and experts, and techniques such as this, and the use of natural language as referred to by Imlah and Demoen, have great potential in industry.

Part II represents the beginnings of commercially available products that link Prolog to data stored in existing databases. The early work on query languages used a main-memory database of stored clauses, with the limited indexing facilities of current Prolog implementations. However, as the number of clauses grows very large and exceeds the size of physical memory, performance degrades quite dramatically, and it is necessary to use conventional database disk storage techniques and algorithms. The chapter by Bocca and Pearson and a later one by Freeston address these specific points. Even when the data are not so vast, it is equally important to have access to data that are being maintained and updated on a commercial database. The chapters by Lucas and Le Vine, and Irving show interfaces to MIMER and DBASE3, and describe the mechanisms for making clauses appear as though they were all in main memory. A crucial part of this is the facility for reclaiming space when the clauses are no longer needed; in particular, Lucas and Le Vine show how to reclaim the space taken by atoms, which can otherwise build up and exhaust that which is available. Venken and Mulkers describe the method used in BIM_Prolog, and Todd describes how IBM Prolog can be used with an 'entity-based' database using binary relations. This group of chapters forms the core of the book. It collects together material which is hard to find elsewhere.

Although the work described in this book mainly represents implementation and experimental tests of ideas whose theoretical basis is described in several books (Ullman [3 (page 133)], Gray [1 (page 51)]), we have included two chapters (Part III) on the theory of deductive databases and recursive queries, and the experience with such systems. The theory of these systems is still being developed. It takes us on from systems where the database is composed entirely of simple facts, in the form of ground unit clauses, to systems where the database also contains rules which can be used to generate facts (tuples) that are not stored explicitly. Clearly, such facts must be founded on sound rules of inference. Furthermore, the consequences of updates in such a system have profound consequences, and it is very necessary to enforce integrity constraints in order that the database remains consistent. This aspect is explored by Small. The second chapter, by Vieille, explains the theory of deductive databases that use recursive rules, as in the well-known problem of finding ancestors of a person. Simple-minded implementation of such rules can cause a system to behave very slowly, or even to loop endlessly, and Vielle's system shows how to overcome these problems.

Another very recent area of work concerns the use of new storage structures that are more appropriate to Prolog than those used in relational databases. There are five chapters in this group (Part IV). The chapter by Williams *et al.* sets up a collection of benchmark tests for those interested in evaluating Prolog used with large numbers of clauses. The tests have been used to evaluate main-memory (or virtual-memory) systems. They serve to show the crucial importance of indexing (or hashing) on the first argument when there are large numbers of clauses. This leads on to a chapter by Freeston on the BANG file (Balanced and Nested Grid File). This structure has many of the features of a B-tree, but it is also multi-dimensional, allowing one to locate just those tuples where combinations of keys lie in a given range. A major chapter by Ramamohanarao *et al.* describes the structures used in NU-Prolog, where a form of extensible hashing is used for the same purpose. This system has been developed over a number of years, and its performance, like that of the BANG file, is impressive. It also describes further solutions to the problems of recursive queries and updates to deductive databases that are discussed in Part III.

The last two chapters in Part IV describe an interface from Prolog to a database that supports not just atomic values held in unit clauses, but also complex term structures and lists. In relational terms these are 'non-normal form' databases and they are a development of the binary relational storage described by Todd. The chapter by Paton and Gray describes how such data can be organized into an object-oriented database, making use of class inheritance, and storing both procedures and data in classes. Thus, instead of seeing Prolog procedures as rules which infer clauses, they are seen as 'methods' to compute derived data, and the database becomes a way of sharing both methods and the facts to which they apply. The chapter by Moffat concludes this part by explaining how such a database can be organized in modules so that changes can be committed incrementally. This does not give one the fine granularity of locking used in a conventional database, but it may be quite suitable for design and CAD applications.

The final group of chapters (Part V) describes applications of systems of the kind described earlier. These are particularly interesting, since they point the way to a new kind of software architecture, which gets away from monolithic Fortran and Pascal programs reading and writing sequential files. Venken and Donner's chapter describes an exciting new architecture for commercial applications, based on the use of a spreadsheet-like view of the data. These data are updated by transactions, and verified by integrity constraints in Prolog. Another approach to transaction-handling is described by Nomura and Lunn; this uses a COBOL application program, running under a TP monitor, to set off Prolog goals which can access files. They also describe some more advanced architectures for Credit Control and Bid Estimation. This shows a way forward for commercial users who wish to gain experience of the flexibility of Prolog, without having to throw away their existing systems. A chapter by Williams reflects on experience gained in the Alvey TRACE Club, building a system for Travel Agents. This is a timely reminder of the inability of Prolog systems on small PCs to deal with substantial applications, and it shows what is required of Prolog systems in order to be more widely accepted in commerce. Fortunately, the newer systems with compilers for SUN, VAX and IBM workstations are becoming much more solid, and have the memory to cope with realistically large numbers of procedures and unit clauses.

The last two chapters discuss scientific applications. Imlah and Demoen describe a database for holding a lexicon to be used with a natural language system. Prolog was originally conceived by Colmerauer and others working in natural language, and the chapter by Lunn and Archibald shows how easy it is to develop a simple natural language front-end to a database. Imlah and Demoen's chapter is part of the LOQUI project, which aims to construct a full natural language enquiry system for databases; it is the forerunner of commercial systems which will make database information much more widely available. Another new area for database is for software engineering and configuration and version management. Singleton and Farris describe a Prolog system which they coupled to indexed external files in order to achieve this. These are not the only applications: the chapter by Todd also references application work on a molecular biology database, whilst Lucas and Le Vine reference applications in crime detection and scheduling for a conveyor system. It is clear that the range of database queries and search techniques possible with Prolog opens up a wide variety of future applications. This book is intended to create wider interest in the subject and to point the way. It is also intended as a companion volume to Campbell's *Implementations of Prolog*, which is published in the same series.

Most of the work described in this book has been supported either by the U.K. Alvey program, or by the European ESPRIT program. Thus it represents leading-edge research, but with a strong element of industrial participation. This was also reflected at the workshop at Chesford Grange, in December 1987, where many of the chapters were originally presented. We are very grateful to the Alvey Logic Programming Club for sponsoring the workshop, and to SERC for funding academic participants. We are also grateful to SCICON for helping to fund some of the visiting speakers. Finally, we wish to express our thanks to Coventry Polytechnic, for taking on the local organization of the workshop; to Professor Sleeman at Aberdeen University for his encouragement and support and to the two other members of the Program Commitee, Professor M. H. Williams (Heriot-Watt) and Dr K. Lunn (Shell Research), for their help in planning and refereeing.

P. M. D. Gray
R. J. Lucas

Part I
Query Languages

1

Implementing query languages in Prolog

Fernando Mouta
Departmento de Engenharia Electrotecnica e de Computadores, Faculdade de Engenharia da Universidade do Porto, Rua dos Bragas, 4099 Porto Codex, Portugal.
M. Howard Williams
Computer Science Department, Heriot-Watt University, 79 Grassmarket, Edinburgh EH1 2HJ, Scotland.
Jose Maia Neves
Area de Informatica e Controlo, Universidade do Minho, Largo do Paco, 4719 Codex, Portugal.

ABSTRACT

The close relationship between the query languages for relational database systems and logic programming languages facilitates translation between them. This chapter considers two different relational query languages, the tuple-oriented language SQL and the domain-oriented language QBE, and shows how queries in each of these languages can be mapped into the logic programming language Prolog. In both cases, query language processors have been constructed in Prolog to perform this translation and to execute the resulting queries

1. INTRODUCTION

First-order predicate logic plays an important role in relational database theory and can be used to express relational database formalisms and the functionalities normally associated with them [1]. Furthermore, it has been shown that Horn clause logic (a subset of first-order predicate logic) is sufficient for expressing the fundamental operations of the relational model [2]. Indeed, both first-order logic and Horn clause logic offer a deductive capability which considerably extends the relational model and provides a basis for more powerful database systems.

This chapter focuses on relational database systems and their relation to Horn clause logic in the form of the programming language Prolog. Two different relational query languages are considered — the tuple-oriented language SQL and the domain-oriented language QBE. In each case a query language processor was developed in Prolog to accept queries in the language, map them into Prolog, and execute them.

2. REPRESENTATION OF THE DATABASE

Each relation in a relational database comprises a set of tuples. In mapping these into Prolog, each tuple is represented as a ground unit clause, e.g.

```
emp(1,'Fernando',2,30,3).
emp(2,'Carlos',3,60,3).
emp(3,'Jose',1,25,4).
emp(4,'Luis', 2,20,5).
```

In addition, for each relation there is a clause, 'scheme', which defines the structure of the relation. This contains the name of the relation, the number of tuples in the relation, the number of attributes and a list of the attribute names. Although slightly different formats were used in the two systems, the differences are very minor and only one will be used here. For the above relation, the clause would be.

```
scheme(emp,4,5,[empno,name,dno,sal,mgr]).
```

Each query language processor (for SQL and for QBE) accepts a query in the query language concerned and maps it into equivalent Prolog clauses which, when executed, produce the effect of the query. In the process, the system builds up structures with the same name and arity as the clauses that represent the tuples of the relations concerned as well as structures representing conditions on attributes. These structures are transformed to produce a Prolog goal representing the query.

For example, the SQL instruction

```
SELECT name,sal
FROM emp
WHERE dno=2
```

and the QBE query

emp	empno	name	dno	sal	mgr
		P.X	Y	P.Z	

CONDITIONS
Y=2

can be transformed to the Prolog form

```
emp(_,X1,X2,X3,_),X2=2
```

or simply

```
emp(_,X1,2,X3_)
```

3. USER INTERFACE

Each system makes use of a special-purpose screen editor to assist users to compose queries. In the case of QBE a tabular format is used. At the beginning of a query the user is presented with a skeletal table of form

(1)	(2)
(3)	(4)

where the four areas are

(1) Table name field,
(2) Column name field,
(3) Tuple command field,
(4) Tuple entry field.

The four basic commands which are available are 'P.' (standing for PRINT), 'I.' (for INSERT), 'D.' (for DELETE) and 'U.' (for UPDATE). Using the screen editor, the cursor may be moved to any of the four areas. Starting with the table name field, if one of the basic commands is entered, it applies to the set of relations, e.g. print all relation names, insert a new relation, etc. On the other hand, one may enter the name of a relation, and if it already exists in the database, the system can generate the column names automatically. If the cursor is moved to the tuple command field and the command 'P.' is entered, it applies to whole tuples (i.e. print each tuple which satisfies some condition) whereas if it occurs in the tuple entry field, it applies only to the attribute concerned. For example,

emp	empno	name	dno	sal	mgr
P.			2		

will print all tuples from the relation emp which have the value 2 in the dno field whereas

emp	empno	name	dno	sal	mgr
		P.X	2	P.Y	

will print only the name and salary attributes of tuples for which dno is 2.

The user interface for SQL is rather different. It also uses a screen editor, but in this case a more conventional screen editor for text strings. This makes it easier for the user to enter a query, especially one which is long and complex.

Once a query has been entered, it is subjected to lexical analysis followed by syntax analysis to check that it is valid and to convert it to internal form. To assist the user further a spelling correction and abbreviation identification module is constructed. When the system analyses a query and encounters an incorrect word in the parse, this word together with information about the kind of word expected in that position of the query is passed to the correction module. The correction module attempts to match the characters of the word with those of possible correct words, checking for incorrect characters, missing characters, additional characters or permuted characters. It also checks for abbreviations of possible correct words. Thus if one were to enter the query

```
selact nmae
from emp
whre d=2
```

it would respond with the messages

LEXICAL ERROR — 1 letter of the word SELECT is wrong
LEXICAL ERROR — The name of the field name was written with 2 adjacent letters permuted
LEXICAL ERROR — 1 letter is missing in the word WHERE
LEXICAL ERROR — The name of the field dno has been abbreviated

and if the user accepted these corrections as valid, it would process the query as if the corrections had been made.

In each case the user interface was written in Prolog as part of the query language processor.

4. THE SQL SYSTEM

The overall structure of the SQL system is shown in Fig. 1. For this case a top-down parsing approach [3] was used, in which the nodes of the parse tree are created in pre-order starting from the root. The parser is implemented by building a procedure for each non-terminal node. As the BNF definition of SQL has left-recursive rules, these had to be rewritten to remove left recursion.

In the process of parsing, each attribute name that occurs in the query needs to be fully identified, checking the relation to which it belongs and its position in the list of attributes belonging to that relation. Each occurrence of an attribute name is mapped into a structure of form

[Relname,Lab,N,Attr]

where

Relname is the name of the relation to which the attribute belongs,
Lab represents a label name — if in the SQL query the relation to which

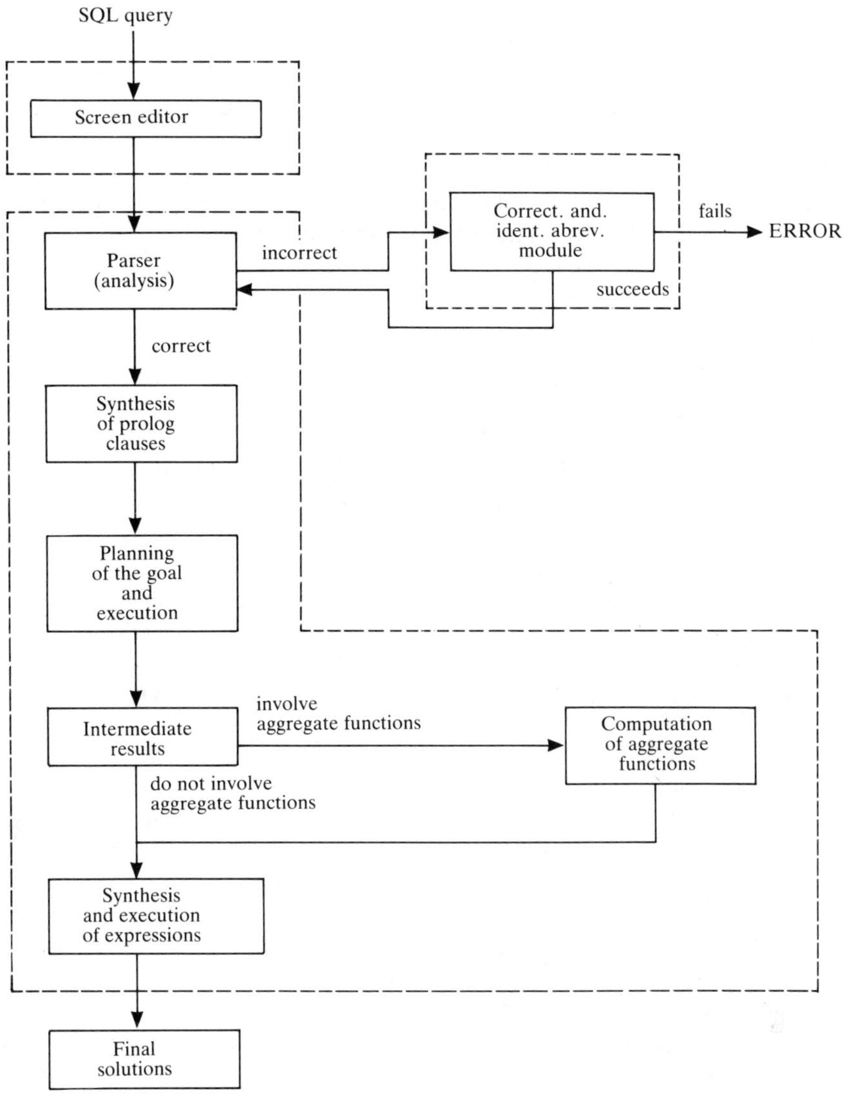

Fig. 1 — Structure of the SQL system.

the attribute belongs is referenced by a label, then Lab has that value, otherwide it is '*',
N is the position of the attribute in the list, and
Attr is the attribute name.

The aggregate functions are mapped into structures like

[Rel,Lab,N,setfn(AgrFn,Attr)]

where AgrFn is the name of an aggregate function ('count'. 'max','min',etc.).

In cases where these items appear in expressions, the evaluation of these expressions can only be performed after the appropriate tuples have been selected which satisfy the conditions in the 'WHERE' clause. In the case of aggregate functions, the computation can only be completed once all possible tuples have been selected.

From these attribute structures, a more complex structure is built, containing all the data necessary to construct a Prolog goal equivalent to the SQL query. This is a nested structure of form

str(N,Relname,Label,T,L.S,C,str(. . .))

where

N is the order number,
Relname is the relation name,
Label is the label name,
T is a term structure identical to the clauses that represent the tuples of the relation, with variables as arguments,
L is a list of the attributes of the relation,
S contains details of the selected items, and
C is a clause equivalent to the imposed conditions.

This structure will have a number of levels equal to the number of relation–label pairs. The innermost level has an anonymous variable as its last argument.

The argument S contains two lists of variables that stand for selected attributes. The first (SVar) contains variables which are used directly in the final Prolog goal to retrieve values of attributes for tuples which satisfy the query. The second is used for computing expressions and aggregate functions over the values retrieved by the goal.

The Prolog goal is constructed from the structure str, and is made up of the predicates representing the relations and those representing the conditions. Since execution of the Prolog goal can be inefficient, especially if the SQL query involves cartesian products of relations with many tuples, the planning of the Prolog goal attempts to minimize the total number of tuples considered during execution. The planning algorithm, described in [4], uses the following strategy:

(1) Divide the goal into independent parts that do not share uninstantiated variables, and add control information so that it will not be necessary to repeat them in different backtrack paths.
(2) Order the predicates (subgoals) of each independent part according to the size of the corresponding relations and the state of instantiation of the arguments. The planning algorithm selects the predicate with the least number of tuples that need to be considered, determines which variables will become instantiated as the result of its execution, and then repeats this whole strategy for the remaining subgoals of this part.

To illustrate this, consider the query which seeks the names of all employees who earn more than their managers. This may be represented in SQL as

```
SELECT X.name,Y.name
FROM emp X,emp Y
WHERE X.mgr=Y.empno AND X.sal>Y.sal
```

The attribute structures created will be

```
[emp,X,2,name]
[emp,Y,2,name]
[emp,X,5,mgr]
[emp,Y,1,empno]
[emp,X,4,sal]
[emp,Y,4,sal]
```

From this will be constructed the Prolog goal

```
(emp(_3B69,_3B6D,_3B71,_3B75,_3B79),
 emp(_3F11M,_3F15,_3F19,_3F1D,_3F21),true),
 cond((_3B79=_3F11,_3B75>_3F1D))
```

with the selected attributes

```
[name:_3B6D,name:_3F15]
```

5. THE QBE SYSTEM

The translation from QBE to Prolog is much simpler than the translation from SQL. Each line in a QBE query maps onto a Prolog goal in a very straightforward manner.

In order to collect together the attributes to be displayed, a separate predicate, 'solution', is introducted. Thus the query

emp	empno	name	dno	sal	mgr
P.			2		

can be translated into

```
solution (A,B,C,D,E):-emp(A,B,C,D,E),C=2.
?-solution(A,B,C,D,E).
```

whereas the query

emp	empno	name	dno	sal	mgr
		P.X	2	P.Y	

would be transformed into

```
solution(X,Y):-emp(_,X,2,Y,_).
?-solution(X,Y).
```

The SQL query from the previous section could be expressed as

emp	empno	name	dno	sal	mgr
	Z	P.Y		A	
		P.X		B	Z

CONDITIONS
B>A

which could be translated directly to

```
solution(X,Y):-emp(Z,Y,_,A,_),emp(_,X,_,B,Z),B>A.
```

Insertions and deletions of entries can be handled using the Prolog predicates assert and retract which, respectively, add clauses to and retract clauses from the database. For example, the QBE command

suppliers	sno	sname	status	city
U	X	Y	Z	10
	X	Y	Z	15

which instructs the system to update all entries with a status of 10 in the suppliers table to a status of 15, can be converted to a Prolog clause

```
?-retract(suppliers(X,Y,Z,10)),
 asserta(suppliers(X,Y,Z,15)),
 fail.
```

which will achieve the desired effect.

In this case the process of analysis is much simpler than for SQL, and this is described further in [5]. More examples of QBE and translation to Prolog, including the use of the GROUP-BY operator, are given in [6].

Other aspects such as the treatment of integrity constraints and authorization are described in [7].

6. CONCLUSION

This chapter has attempted to show how Prolog can be used to handle different relational query languages. Two query languages have been chosen for this study — the tuple-oriented language SQL and the domain-oriented language QBE. In each case a special-purpose screen editor was constructed to interface with the user.

The translation process for SQL is more complex than that for QBE since the system has to identify attributes occurring in the query, check these against the schema, and gradually build up a structure representing the query. This is then mapped into a Prolog query. In the case of QBE, the names and positions of attributes in a relation are handled automatically by the screen editor so that the translation process reduces to a much more straightforward mapping of the elements of the query into Prolog.

REFERENCES

[1] Gallaire, H., Minker, J., and Nicolas, J. M., Logic and Databases: a Deductive Approach, *ACM Computing Surveys,* **16**(2), 153–185, 1984.

[2] Kowalski, R. A., Logic as a Database Language, Research Report, Dept. of Computer Science, Imperial College, 1981

[3] Aho, A. V. and Ullman, J. D., *Principles of Compiler Design,* Addison-Wesley, Reading, MA, 1977.

[4] Warren, D. H. D., Efficient Processing of Interactive Relational Database Queries Expressed in Logic, *Proc. 7th Int. Conf. on VLDB,* 1981, 272–281.

[5] Neves, J. C. F. M., Anderson, S. O., and Williams, M. H., A Prolog Implementation of Query-by-Example, *Proc. 7th Int. Computing Symposium,* Teubner, Stuttgart, 1983, 318–332.

[6] Gray, P. M. D., *Logic, Algebra and Databases,* Ellis Horwood, Chichester, 1984, 145–153, 258.

[7] Williams, M. H., Neves, J. C. F. M., and Anderson, S. O., Security and Integrity in Logic Databases using Query-by-Example, *Proc. Logic Programming Workshop '83,* Albufeira, Ed. L. M. Pereira, 1983, 304–340.

2

A source-to-source meta-translation system for database query languages — implementation in Prolog

D. I. Howells, N. J. Fiddian, W. A. Gray
Department of Computing Mathematics, University College Cardiff, Cardiff, Wales.

ABSTRACT

The need of organizations to access data held in different database management systems is growing. This is stimulating the development of gateways between different database systems, and heterogeneous database systems which link several different databases together. An integral part of gateways and heterogeneous systems is the query language inter-translation system. This can take as input a query from one system and translate it into a suitable form to interrogate the relevant database of another system.

Using traditional approaches, such translators can be provided by either hand-coding or automatically generating their lexical and syntactical components, then augmenting the latter by additional complementary hand-coded progam fragments which define syntax-directed translation actions.

Translators produced in these ways take a considerable time to develop — expert estimates suggest a typical best time of 6 man months [1]. With the increasing need for such translators there is a requirement for a method of translator creation to be devised whereby such programs can be produced more rapidly from simple, concise specifications. Recently, progress has been made in this direction by developing specific translators [2] in Prolog [3]. This chapter describes the Prolog implementation of a source-to-source meta-translation system for database query languages [4] that generalizes the production of translators, allowing them to be developed far more efficiently than previously.

This source-to-source meta-translation system carries out translations via an intermediate relational algebra tree. In order to fully link a new query language into the system, two translators are required: source-input to tree and tree to source-output. The source-input to tree translator is specified by entering the syntax of the new query language in a Prolog-compatible BNF. This meta-language is augmented by a complementary meta-notation that allows the semantics of the query language to be easily specified. The tree to source-output translator is specified using a forms-based interface which prompts the user for syntactic constructs in the new query language that are equivalent to a given relational algebra operation or operations.

Each of these components is considered more fully in the following description, which surveys the design and operation of the complete meta-translation system first in external terms and then at a more detailed internal level. Special attention is paid throughout to the use of Prolog in implementing this system.

1. INTRODUCTION

The advantages of distributing data have been identified and acknowledged for quite some time [5]. At present the distribution of data in database systems may be modelled in one of four ways: homogeneous or heterogeneous variants of distributed or federated databases [5,6].

The increasing power of micro/mini computers has meant that a greater number of dispersed database user sites can afford local computers which have sufficient power and storage to meet many of their local requirements without recourse to a central mainframe installation. In such situations many different database management systems may be adopted locally. Dispersed data may be accessed remotely using computer networks, which are now capable of supporting the reliable transfer of information between sites. These factors have led to the development of the theory of heterogeneous distributed databases and to early prototypes of these systems [7,8]. More recently, the concept of building gateways between database systems has been proposed. An integral part of the gateways and heterogeneous systems is the query language inter-translation system. This can take as input a query from one system and translate it into a suitable form to interrogate the relevant database of another system.

In the PROTEUS heterogeneous distributed database project [8] some dozen specific inter-translators were produced. These were developed separately by traditional methods, translating via a common, intermediate, internal Network Query Language (NQL [8,9]). From this work it became evident that a more productive translator development technique was required for the future which would automate this production process. Thus the idea of a meta-translation system was conceived. The following sections investigate the external and internal architectures of the resultant system, beginning with a summary of traditional translator writing methods that influenced the choice of software technology for the meta-translation system.

2. TRANSLATOR WRITING METHODS

Two approaches are traditionally used to write translation systems. These are

(i) to write a hand-coded 'scanner' (lexical analyser) and 'parser' (syntax analyser) in a high-level language. This is not difficult — for example, the parser can be produced in a straightforward way by modelling its structure directly on the grammar of the subject language concerned — but it is nevertheless a lengthy and time-consuming exercise.

(ii) to use a scanner generator (e.g. LEX [10]) and an associated parser generator (e.g. YACC [11]) to produce the scanner and parser translator components automatically.

It should be noted that in both cases the parser *per se* has to be augmented with program fragments written in a high-level language (e.g. C [12] in the case of YACC) defining the translator action that is to be taken upon recognition of each case syntactic construct. This is a non-trivial development task which involves system programming expertise and takes an appreciable amount of time in its own right.

Query language inter-translators produced in these ways take a considerable time to develop — expert estimates suggest a typical best time of 6 man months [1]. Experience from the PROTEUS project led to the conclusion that it should be possible to build a meta-translation system that could substantially improve on this figure without severely impairing translation efficiency. It also led to an appreciation of the potential of certain newer programming systems, notably Prolog, for writing inter-translators, and, following some experiments in writing specific translators in this way [2], it was decided that Prolog would be a suitable implementation vehicle for the meta-translation system itself.

3. THE EXTERNAL ARCHITECTURE OF THE META-TRANSLATION SYSTEM

The external achitecture of the system and its interfaces are described in detail in the proceedings of the 13th VLDB conference [4]. This section will emphasize only those aspects of the external architecture that are relevant to the Prolog implementation of the system (see section 4).

3.1 Overview of the system

The system, depicted in Fig. 1, has at its heart the meta-translator module. This directs translation between source query languages via an intermediate, internal relational algebra tree (see Fig. 2). The system operates in two distinct phases. The specification phase accepts definitions of new query languages from which appropriate translation schemes are generated — for either input (RQL→Tree) or output (Tree→QL) query languages or both, as required. In the application phase a translation between a relational query language and either a relational or a CODASYL query language is invoked by selecting (cf. Fig. 2) an appropriate pairing of source-input and source-output translation schemes. In this phase the system needs to access a schema for the destination database.

Relational query language to internal tree translations are specified via

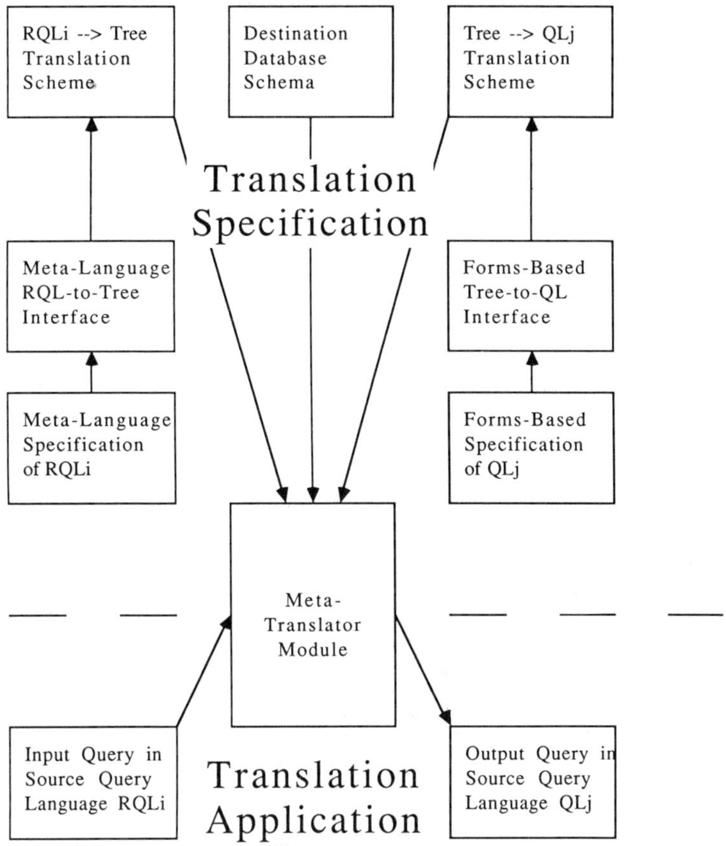

Fig. 1 — The external achitecture of the system.

the system's meta-language interface. Internal tree to output query language translations are specified via an interactive forms-based interface. Both interfaces elicit from the user a language definition which is used to generate an appropriate translation scheme. However, the two interfaces adopt different approaches to language specification owing to the dissimilar underlying translation problems. The source-input language to internal tree defining mechanism accepts as input a translation grammar (including an integrated semantic definition) unique to each language and produces a translation scheme whose range is a tree of pre-defined form. The internal tree to source-output language translation scheme generator must perform an opposite task.

3.2 Components of the system

3.2.1 The destination database schema

Inter-translation is possible without the use of a schema [2]. This does not allow semantic error checking though, as the necessary identifier attribute

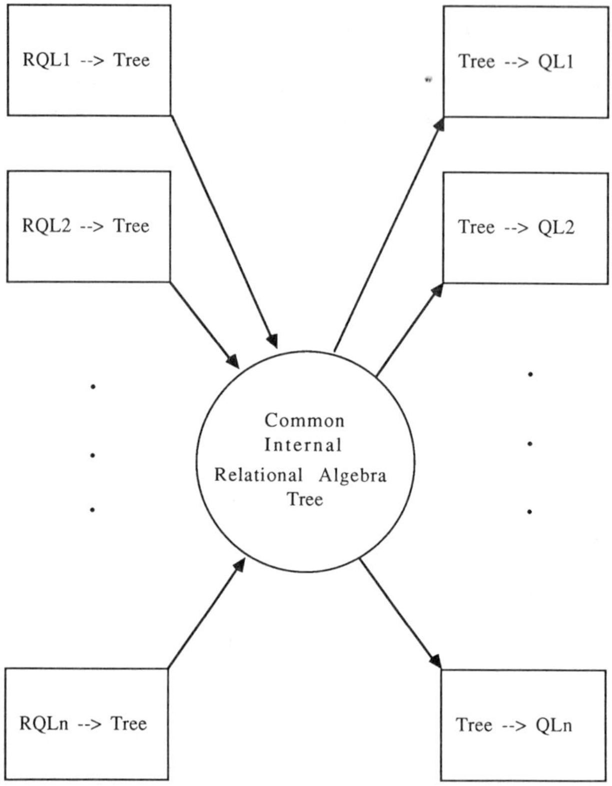

Fig. 2 — Multiple translation schemes.

information is not available. Semantic error checking in a source-to-source meta-translation system is very important. This is because if it is to be used in a distributed or federated context, errors must be trapped at source, since if they are not located until they reach their destination a great deal of communication effort will have been wasted. Therefore a schema is consulted within the meta-translation system.

A simple but adequate schema representation method is used that is capable of representing relational and CODASYL database structures. Information about temporary relations generated by input queries may also be stored within the schema.

The system can be directed to work either with a specific schema for a particular destination database cited at translation time or with a permanently resident global schema.

3.2.2 The internal relational algebra tree

When translating between source query languages, an intermediate query representation is often used (e.g. NQL in PROTEUS [8]). This offers the following advantages.

(i) The ability to generate good source-output code.
(ii) Partial translation between languages of differing retrieval power is facilitated.
(iii) The number of translation schemes required is reduced (for n languages, $2n$ schemes are needed as opposed to $n(n-1)$ when no intermediate language is used).

A tree-structured intermediate language based on relational algebra is employed within our system in this role. A typical example of an SQL [13] query and its tree representation is shown in Fig. 3. It should be noted that

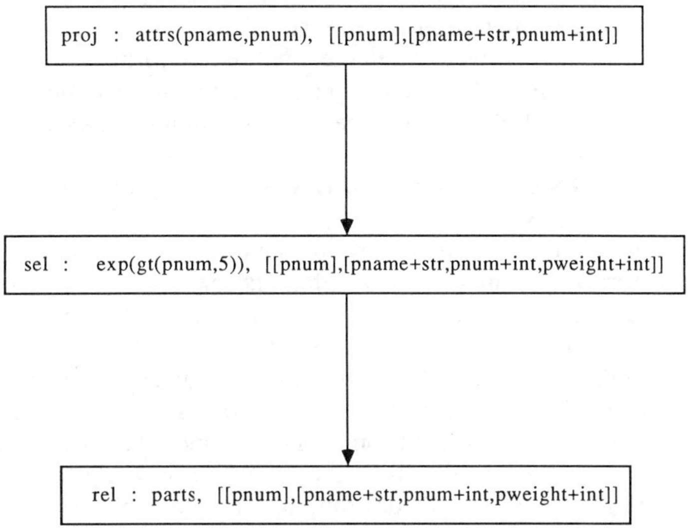

A Relational Algebra Tree

```
Select pname pnum
From parts
Where pnum > 5
```

The Equivalent SQL Query

```
schema(parts, [pnum], [pname+str, pnum+int, pweight+int]) .
```

Fig. 3 — The associated target schema.

the tree representation is totally self-contained. This offers a number of advantages.

(i) In the specification phase (see section 3.2.4) one can define translations from the internal tree form to a source-output language by reference to a set of node templates alone. No knowledge of, or reference to, a schema is needed. Hence output translation schemes are autonomous modules, conceptually independent from schemas and their various representations.

(ii) In the application phase, when translating from the tree form to a source-output language, no reference to the associated schema need be made.

(iii) Using traditional methods and data structures, when translating from an intermediate language to a source-output language, difficulties arise owing to the need to continually generate a list of current attributes after each algebra operation has been processed. In the source-to-source meta-translation system this is not necessary since this information is given within the internal tree form.

(iv) The internally held information can be used to aid the optimization of internal trees to produce efficient output queries.

3.2.3 The meta-language interface for specifying query language to tree translations

This interface facilitates the definition of any relational query language (source-input language) in relational agebra terms, giving the user the impression that he is describing the language as opposed to specifying a translator. This language description is used to generate a translation mapping between the relational query language in question and the internal tree form. It comprises lexical, syntactic and semantic specifications which are defined by a suite of complementary meta-languages. The syntax of the source-input language is defined in a Prolog-compatible BNF form, with lexical tokens embedded within this. The system's semantic meta-language augments the syntactic language, with each production being followed by a corresponding semantic definition. Communication within each meta-language and between the suite of meta-languages is vital. The semantic meta-language constructs define the meaning of individual syntactic components. The flow of communication between these constructs completes the semantic definition by specifying the appropriate sequencing of semantic applications.

The complete language definition is entered into a specification file. If necessary, extra semantic meta-language clauses particular to an input translation scheme can be added to the associated specification file and used as required. Very few additional clauses should be necessary, as the core set of semantic operations provided represents all of the functionality generally found in relational query languages. Extra clauses that are needed tend to be quite simple in their nature (e.g. in QUEL [14], to produce a list of relations used in a query, from the associated range statements).

Within the system environment, help about the semantic meta-language constructs can be requested by typing in a construct name. An explanation of the function of the cited construct, the input it expects and the output it produces is then provided.

The source-input translation schemes that are generated from their corresponding language definitions are capable of accepting as input a query that may be composed of a number of sub-queries. Each sub-query will have a tree generated to represent it that will be stored in the temporary schema. Only one tree — 'result tree' — is produced to represent the whole query. This may consist of a number of subtrees that represent intermediate relations, which have been stored in the temporary schema.

3.2.4 The forms-based interface for specifying tree to query language translations

This interface facilitates the definition of translations between the internal relational algebra tree form and any relational or high-level CODASYL query language (source-output language). Since the form of the tree is predefined, to produce a mapping between this and a source-output language one basically requires the specification of an equivalent output representation for each possible type of tree node. This implies a translation approach to semantic definition [15], where the internal tree form has its meaning defined in terms of an output language whose semantics are assumed to be well understood.

Such a translation can be realized by producing a traversing processor for internal trees that continually refers to a table for mapping information on how to perform a translation of the node it is currently processing. This table is generated by asking the user to follow a set of prompts which enumerate all possible single relational algebra nodes that can appear in the tree form. He is asked if each node is represented in the output query language in question. If it is, the system calls an editor so that the equivalent statement(s) in the output query language can be specified by completing a displayed form.

Since many query languages are able to perform more than one operation in a single statement, the system also allows the user to define composite node translations. An arbitrarily complex sequence of relational operations is entered by the user in prefix notation (e.g. proj sel), from which an appropriate form is generated to be completed in the same way as before.

4. THE META-TRANSLATION SYSTEM — A PROLOG IMPLEMENTATION

The architecture and interfaces used in the meta-translation system could have been implemented by using one or more traditional compiler writing languages and tools. However, from experience in writing specific inter-translators, Prolog was considered to be a suitable single technology with which to develop the whole system. This was because

(i) parsers may be simply generated in Prolog from a BNF-like specification,
(ii) Prolog's powerful pattern-matching facilities allow textual manipula-

tion functions to be easily encoded. This was evident in the dBASEII [16] to QUEL translator [2] developed in a pilot study into the use of Prolog. This capability pointed to Prolog being a suitable language with which to develop a semantic meta-language.

(iii) Prolog offers clear and comprehensive facilities for intra- and inter-meta-language (BNF and semantic meta-language) communication. Here the flow of communication between constructs in a language definition is obvious to the implementor, in contrast to systems that use such mechanisms as 'invisible' stacks to manipulate data.

The system has the internal architecture shown in Fig. 4. Here, circles

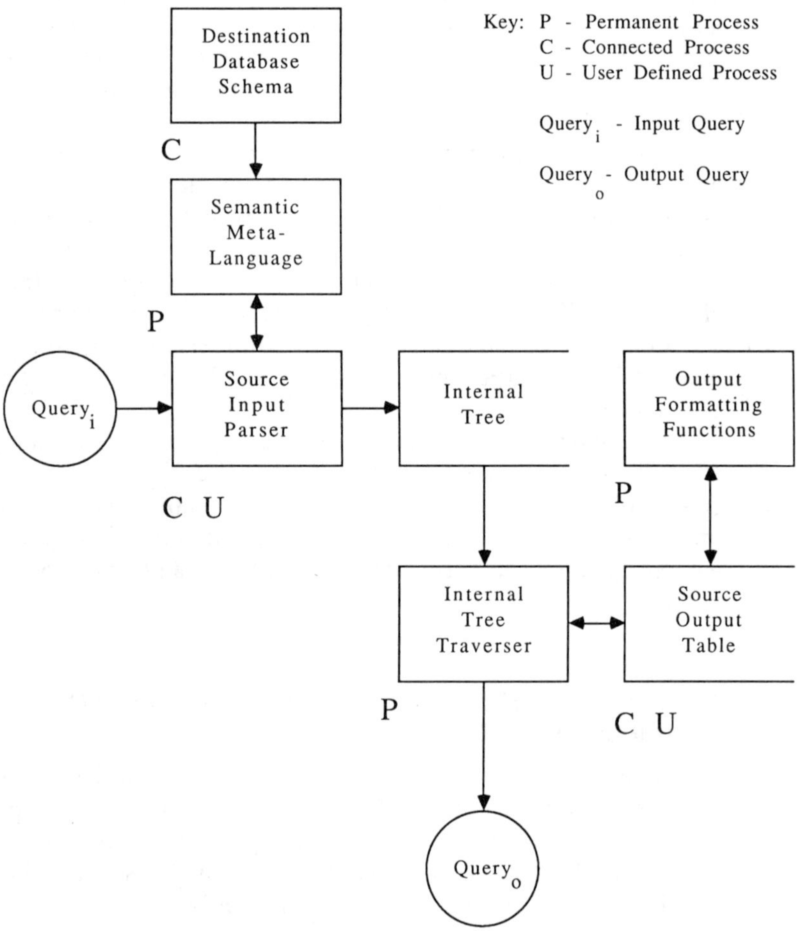

Fig. 4 — The internal architecture of the system.

indicate a source or recipient, rectangles a process, open-ended rectangles a data store and arrows a data-flow. The rectangles labelled with a 'P' are permanently resident within the system, those labelled with a 'C' are connected into the system at runtime, and those marked 'U' are generated from user-supplied definitions.

4.1 Translation between a relational query language and the internal tree form

This translation, which produces as output a representation of a source-input query in internal tree form, requires a parser for the relational query language concerned and access to the semantic meta-language and a destination database schema.

4.1.1 The source input parser

This parser is generated from the source-input language definition provided by the user. The supplied grammar is automatically converted to a system of Prolog clauses, that constitute the parser, when the language specification file is 'consulted'. As an example of the transformation, consider the following BNF definition of the dBASEII language 'display' command:

```
display_list(D)-->[display],[all],all_list(A),for_list(F).
```

which becomes

```
display_list(D,[display,all|I],T2) :- all_list(A,I,T1) ,for_list(F,T1,T2).
```

In this example, a value may be passed back within the grammar in D. The second parameter of display_list is the input to that clause. Since it is necessary for 'display' and 'all' to be parsed first for this clause to succeed, the input parameter starts with 'display, all'. The remaining input (variable I), after 'display, all' (which are removed by display_list), becomes the input to all_list. The last parameter of each grammar clause is what remains of the input stream after the clause has successfully parsed its part of the input.

The source-input parser communicates with relevant semantic meta-language constructs that were used in the language definition.

4.1.2 The semantic meta-language

This meta-language is represented by a set of Prolog clauses that may be fed information by the parser and return a transformation of their input. As an example of this, consider the following extract from a dBASEII language specification, consisting of a syntactic definition augmented by the associated semantic definition (in braces) for the dBASEII 'display' command:

```
display_list(D)-->[display],[all],all_list(A), for_list(F)
EC        {(inp_rels(L),
EC          get_inp_rels(L,[R]),
ML          mk_select_node(R,A,N1),
ML          mk_proj_node(N1,F,D),
ML          mk_rel(D,[]),
```

```
EC            abolish(inp_rels,1),
EC            asserta(inp_rels([])) )
          }.
```

Here, for expositional clarity, in the semantic definition section, extra clause invocations are labelled by the prefix EC and core meta-language construct applications by ML. The internal extra clauses determine the relation name (R) used in the query. Since all_list contains expressions that imply selection within a dBASEII query, this is semantically defined by associating mk_select_node with this construct via the variable A. Similarly, the fact that a for_list implies a projection is defined by the use of mk_proj_node and the use of the shared variable F. Conceptually, selection takes place before projection within a query. The flow of communication between the meta-language constructs defines the appropriate sequencing of semantic applications. This is shown in the example by the fact that the relation used in the query is first passed to a definition of selection (mk_select_node). After selection has been applied to the relation (R) a new relation (N1) is conceptually generated. This is passed to the projection definition which produces another conceptual relation (D). Mk_rel takes the data structure representing this conceptual relation and stores it either in the temporary schema or as a 'result tree' representing the whole query.

It should be noted that the conceptual form of the defined language (with projection being applied after selection) may not imply the optimal representation of a query. This does not matter since the system accepts conceptual definitions of language structures but internally produces more efficient equivalent representations where possible.

Semantic error checking is carried out implicitly by validating supplied expressions against information held in the destination database schema.

4.1.3 The internal destination database schema

A simple but adequate schema is used that is capable of representing relational and CODASYL database structures. Relational schemas are represented by a set of Prolog clauses and have the following internal composition:

schema(Base_Relation_Name,[Key_Attributes],[Attributes+Types]).

Here the first argument holds the name of the base relation, the second a list of all of the attributes that form its key, and the third a list of the attributes and their respective types. A typical example is

schema(parts,[pnum],[pname+str,pnum+int,pweight+int]).

CODASYL schemas may also be stored internally by adopting an approach similar to that used in the ASTRID [17] system. Here the CODASYL structure is mapped into a number of relations, each having an associated 'traversal'. This mapping is internally represented by the following general structure:

schema(Base_Relation_Name,[Key_Attributes,path,

Path_list],[Attributes+Types]).

This structure is identical to the aforementioned relational schema representation apart from the inclusion, after the key attributes, of the token 'path' followed by an 'ASTRID-like' pathlist that represents a traversal.

Temporary relations are also held within the overall schema as Prolog clauses and have the following general structure:

temp_schema(Result_Relation_Name,Tree).

Here, Tree stands for the internal representation of the query which generates the intermediate relation whose name is stored in the first argument (see next subsection for a detailed description of the internal form).

Prolog proved to be an ideal mechanism for representing schemas because of

(i) The concise storage-efficient structure with which schemas are held.
(ii) The ease with which Prolog is able to extract data from a schema.

For example, the key of the relation 'parts' may be retrieved by

schema(parts,[Key|Tail],_).

4.2 The internal tree form

Internal trees are stored in a linearized form — an example representing the tree shown in Fig. 3 follows:

```
proj(sel(rel(parts,[[pnum],[pname+str,pnum+int,pweight+int]]),
exp(gt(pnum,5)),[[pnum],[pname+str,pnum+int,pweight+int]]),
attrs(pname,pnum),[[pnum],[pname+str,pnum+int]]).
```

This form corresponds to a pre-order traversal of the tree in which each tree node has as its first argument an input relation and as its last argument a schema-like specification of the relation resulting from the application of the relational algebra function of the node.

The internal tree representation of a complete source-input query is stored as a 'result_tree' clause whose sole argument is the tree. Since the tree is represented as a Prolog structure it can easily be dismantled and its information accessed by Prolog's built-in predicates (e.g. functor, arg).

4.3 Translation between the internal tree form and a source output language

This translation, which takes as input a query represented in internal tree form and produces an equivalent source-output query, requires an 'internal tree traverser', a table to direct output generation and access to a set of output formatting functions.

4.3.1 The internal tree traverser

This recursively walks through a tree, looking at composite and single nodes. The traverser continually refers to a source-output table for mapping information on how to generate equivalent output language statement(s) for the node that it is currently processing.

Prolog proved to be very suitable language with which to write the traverser, as it allowed

(i) A recursive-descent traverser to be concisely and easily encoded.
(ii) Composite and single nodes to be easily inspected.

4.3.2 The source output table

This table is stored as a set of clauses with a standard name. They have the following structure:

tree(Node,Result_relation_name) :- Output_specification.

The first argument of this clause is a possible node that can be represented in the output language. The second is the name attached to the intermediate relation resulting from the node translation defined by the given 'Output_specification'. This output specification is generated from information in the associated source-output language forms definition.

Prolog proved suitable to store the table, as it provides the search mechanism required to find the relevant clause corresponding to each tree node for the traverser.

Output specification clauses may refer to output formatting functions.

4.3.3 The output formatting functions

The system contains a set of output formatting functions encoded in Prolog which transform expressions from their internal tree representation to the form expected in a source-output language. These functions fall into one of two categories:

(Class I) Functions that take an expression and transform it to a typical output format.
(Class II) Functions that take an expression and perform a transformation that is directed by a number of parameters.

For example, in response to the header

sel(rel(Rname,[Hr|Tr],exp(Sexp),[Hs|Ts]) into New_relname

a user might want the selection expression (Sexp) to be transformed from the internal prefix form to a standard infix representation and each attribute to be preceded by a relation name (held in the variable 'Rname') and a dot. This could be achieved by the use of the function call 'gen_sel_monadic (Rname, Sexp,Sexp_Out)' which would set 'Sexp_Out' to refer to the desired output. If a non-standard transformation was required (e.g. 'equals' instead of '=') then the function 'gen_sel_out_monadic_var' could be used. Such standard and variable monadic functions exist to manipulate expressions from each type of node. A suite of dyadic functions which operate on expressions that may refer to more than one relation also exists.

If translation is taking place to a CODASYL source-output language the system is connected to an internal schema representing the structure of a CODASYL database. The internal tree will contain information from this schema, and consequently 'path information' pertaining to the destination database is available. To facilitate translation to the source-output language, 'path generator' functions exist that are able to produce relevant paths for the source-output query. These functions can operate on one or more relations and use the 'join by overlap' method used in the ASTRID [17] system.

5. EVALUATION OF THE META-TRANSLATION SYSTEM

5.1 System exploitation

We have successfully developed input and output translation schemes for all the common types of relational query language, namely relational algebra (dBASEII), tuple-based relational calculus (QUEL), domain-based relational calculus (a line-oriented QBE [18]) and a relational algebra–calculus hybrid (SQL). An output translation scheme for a CODASYL query language (QRS of the MDBS system [19]) has also been developed.

In addition, the meta-translation system has been used to produce specific inter-intranslators by restricting the domain of the meta-translator module to a fixed translation scheme pairing.

Comprehensive testing of all translation schemes was carried out using a sample set of queries formulated for the purpose. This set was designed to contain a range of queries for testing all the common simple operations and most of the complex operations present in commercially available systems.

5.2 Performance measurements

To develop a translation mapping from a relational query language to the internal tree form took no more than a few days (at most a week). The specification input required varied between 50 and 120 Prolog clauses.

To develop a translation mapping from the internal tree form to a relational or CODASYL query language, specified via the forms-based interface, took a very short time — typically less than a day. The tree to dBASEII scheme took just over an hour to produce (including seven composite nodes)!

A typical complex query took approximately five-seconds to be translated between any pair of source query languages, using an interpretative version of Prolog (Edinburgh New Implementation of Prolog (NIP) on a VAX 8200). With the advent of new, fast versions of compiled Prolog, this time should be greatly reduced.

5.3 System assessment

The system is designed to be used by a person with a working knowledge of relational algebra, BNF, the relational query languages for which translators and a minimal amount of Prolog are required. There is very little difference in the required level of expertise between such a person and a person who could write translators in a traditional manner.

The advantages of using such a system are as follows.

(i) Translation schemes, and hence translators, can be very easily and quickly developed.
(ii) Relatively little input is needed to specify translation schemes.
(iii) The translation schemes produced are very manageable and easily maintainable. This is due to the conciseness of these schemes, their high level of abstraction and their applicative nature.
(iv) The system produces space- and time-efficient translations. Translation schemes are compact, and typical queries are translated in a few seconds. There is a potential to substantially reduce this time.
(v) Translation input is parsed in a top-down manner. This is a more readily understandable approach than bottom-up methods. This fact and Prolog's tracing facilities greatly aid the process of debugging translations during their development.
(vi) It is easy to learn to use the system. The semantic meta-language has only 17 simple constructs and often only a subset of these is needed. The forms-based interface is extremely easy to use and is quickly learnt.
(vii) The meta-translator produces efficient translations, since trees are built in as optimal a fashion as possible and composite nodes of abitrary complexity within a tree can be recognized.

6. CONCLUSIONS

Prolog proved to be an appropriate language for developing every part of the system (as was demonstrated in section 4), often enabling a far briefer program specification than would result from using more conventional languages.

One limitation in using Prolog occurred in the lexical analysis definition context, where strings and digits are specified in a production by using built-in meta-translation system functions. This approach proved to be perfectly adequate in every situation except in defining the SQL projection list (proj_list) shown in the following grammar (where the variables associated with each construct are omitted):

```
query --> [select] , proj_list , [from] , from_list , join_list
              group_list , have_list , order_expr
```

Proj_list is defined to be a list of projection attributes separated by spaces. Consequently when the input is parsed, the token 'from' is taken to be a projection attribute. This problem is overcome by defining within the grammer a projection attribute to be a string that is not 'from'. This situation did not arise with any other language definition because in other cases one or more of the following attribute distinction criteria were used.

(i) Attributes are prefixed by appropriate variables.
(ii) Projection attributes are separated by commas.
(iii) A delimiter, such as a bracket, signals the end of a projection list.

Development of the entire system in Prolog facilitated the production of each component and its integration into a unified translation system having closely coupled modules and encompassing different translation philosophies.

REFERENCES

[1] Hsiao, D., Panel Session: Hetereogeneous Distributed Databases — Past or Future?, *Proc. 13th VLDB Conf.*, England, September 1987.

[2] Howells, D. I., Fiddian, N. J., and Gray, W. A., A Comparison of Old and New Technologies for Translating between Relational Query Languages, *Proc. Third Int. Workshop on Statistical and Scientific Database Management*, Luxembourg, July 1986, 179–183.

[3] Clocksin, W. F. and Mellish, C. S., *Programming in Prolog*, Springer-Verlag, New York, 1981.

[4] Howells, D. I., Fiddian, N. J., and Gray, W. A., A Source-to-source Meta-translation System for Relational Query Languages, *Proc. 13th VLDB Conf.*, England, September 1987, 227–234.

[5] Ceri, S. and Pelagetti, P., *Distributed Databases: Principles and Systems*, McGraw-Hill, New York, 1984.

[6] Heimbigner, D. and Mcleod, D., Federated Information Bases — a Preliminary Report, Pergamon Infotech State of the Art Report on Databases, Series 9, No. 8, 1981.

[7] Smith, J. M., *et al.*, Multibase — Integrating Heterogeneous Distributed Database Systems, *Proc. AFIPS Conf.*, **50**, 1981, 487–499.

[8] Stocker, P. M., *et al.*, PROTEUS: a Heterogeneous Distributed Database Project, In: *Databases — Role and Structure*, Cambridge University Press, Cambridge, 1984, 125–151.

[9] Fiddian, N. J., *et al.*, First PROTEUS Queries Successfully Transmitted, *University Computing*, **6**, 177–182, 1984.

[10] Lesk, M. E., LEX — a Lexical Analyser Generator, Computing Science Technical Report No. 39, Bell Laboratories, Murray Hill, New Jersey, 1975.

[11] Johnson, S. C., YACC — Yet Another Compiler Compiler, Computing Science Technical Report No. 32, Bell Laboratories, Murray Hill, New Jersey, 1975.

[12] Kernighan, B. W. and Ritchie, D. M. *The C Programming Language*, Prentice-Hall, Englewood Cliffs, NJ, 1978.

[13] Chamberlin, D. D., *et al.*, SEQUEL 2: a Unified Approach to Data Definition, Manipulation, and Control, *IBM J. of Research and Development*, **20**, 560–575, 1976.

[14] Stonebraker, M., Wong, E., and Kreps, P., The Design and Implementation of INGRES, *ACM Trans. Database Systems*, **1**, 189–222, 1976.

[15] Aho, A. V. and Ullman, J. D., *Principles of Compiler Design*, Addison-Wesley, Reading, MA, 1977.

[16] dBASEII User Manual, Ashton-Tate, 1984.

[17] Gray, P. M. D., Implementing the Join Operation on Codasyl DBMS, in, *Databases: — Role and Structure,* Stocker, Gray and Atkinson (eds.), Cambridge University Press, 185–206, 1984.
[18] Zloof, M. M., Query-by-example: a Data Base Language, *IBM Sys. J.* **16**, No. 4, 1977.
[19] *MDBS User Manual*, Micro Data Base Systems, 1982.

3

TREQL (Thornton Research Easy Query Language): an intelligent front-end to a relational database

K. Lunn and **I. G. Archibald**
Shell Research Limited, Thornton Research Centre, P.O. Box 1, Chester, England, CH1 3SH

ABSTRACT

An easy-to-use query language has been implemented in Prolog to allow access to data held in a relational database; in particular, an interface has been constructed for a scientific database containing information on lubricating oils. With suitable development effort, a comprehensive query facility is possible for users with no detailed knowledge of a particular database structure. Complexities of retrieving data from multiple files are resolved using artificial intelligence search techniques and knowledge of the application domain.

The work is generic and it could be applied to any database system with a Prolog interface. The query language, schema extension and schema transformation possibilities are expected to be useful tools on any database where *ad hoc* querying of data by non-computing personnel is required.

1. INTRODUCTION

Despite the power and generality of relational database management systems, the relational representation of data and traditional query languages often prove hard to comprehend and use by non-experts. Even for experts, the expression of some queries in a standard query language can be difficult. Problems can also arise when, for historical or performance reasons, the database is structured so that it is difficult to extract data in the form the user would prefer to see it. Furthermore, the user may view the data in ways which are alien to traditional database representations.

A scientific database, containing information on additive packages for lubricating oils, is currently implemented in the RAPPORT† relational

† RAPPORT is a Logica trademark.

database management system. To validate Prolog as a database query language, increase our Prolog expertise and with some expectation of providing a better query facility for this database, a front-end (TREQL — Thornton Research Easy Query Language) has been developed which uses intelligent knowledge-based systems techniques to reduce the complexity of user queries so that any scientist should be able to extract data in a suitable form.

An interface between Prolog and RAPPORT has previously been developed at Thornton Research Centre in conjunction with Logica, the supplier of RAPPORT. This interface makes the relations in the database appear as Prolog procedures. Retrieval of individual tuples (or records) is implemented via normal Prolog matching. Prolog provides the expressive power of the relational algebra and hence is a viable query language for a relational database; moreover, it can be argued that the conciseness and clarity of Prolog are an advantage over traditional query languages such as SQL. Viewed as a general programming language, Prolog offers a completeness which traditional query languages cannot offer.

Prolog is a suitable language for implementation of many types of intelligent knowledge-based system. Therefore, it is an attractive means of implementing intelligent and/or natural language front-ends to relational database systems and database back-ends to expert systems.

Some of the features added by TREQL are available in existing database management facilities. However, there are many existing databases where the addition of such facilities would be useful and preferable to re-implementation of the database. Some features would be very difficult to implement using facilities in languages such as SQL.

This chapter introduces Prolog as a database query language, indicating some of its advantages. TREQL is then described, followed by a brief outline of its implementation. Some discussion of future work follows.

2. PROLOG AS A DATABASE QUERY LANGUAGE

Suppose we have the following relational database schema:

```
parts(part_no,part_name)
supplier(supplier_no,supplier_name,supplier_address)
supplies(supplier_no,part_no).
```

That is, there are three files (relations) called parts, supplier and supplies. The parts file has two fields (attributes) which are 'part_no' which is a number uniquely identifying a part, and 'part_name' which is the name of the part (in practice such a file would have many more fields). The supplier file contains 'supplier_no' which is a number uniquely identifying a supplier, 'supplier_name' which is the name of the supplier and 'supplier_address' which is the address of the supplier. The supplies file pairs 'supplier_no' and 'part_no' to indicate which parts are supplied by which supplier; a supplier may supply many parts, and a part may be supplied by many suppliers.

To access the database, a Prolog–database interface allows the user to think of each relation as if it is a Prolog procedure. The parts relation might appear thus:

```
parts(1,wheel).
parts(2,chain).
parts(3,handle_bar).
etc. . . .
```

2.1 Simple retrieval

To retrieve items from the parts relation, the user simply asks the Prolog question

```
?-parts(X,Y).
```

and the system will respond

```
X=1, Y=wheel
more?
```

By replying 'yes', the next item can be retrieved and so on through the file.

The user may know something about the item to be retrieved, and known values can be specified. For example,

```
?-parts(2,X).
```

will elicit the response

```
X=chain
more?
```

The user may ask more general questions. For example,

```
?-parts(X,Y), X>5, X<10.
```

would retrieve in turn the items where the part number is between 5 and 10, equivalent to a relational algebra selection operation.

2.2 Joining relations

Data from a number of relations can be retrieved very simply. For example, the query 'Give me the names of all suppliers who supply wheels' becomes

```
?-parts(P,wheel),supplies(S,P),supplier(S,NAME,ADDRESS).
```

The query 'Give me all suppliers who do not supply wheels' becomes

```
?-supplier(S,NAME,ADDRESS),
not (supplies(S,P),part(P,wheel)).
```

In relational algebra terms, the above queries are said to involve a join; that is, they merge data from two or more files.

2.3 Cataloguing queries

If a particular complex query is common, then one can create a Prolog procedure to implement that query and the user can call that procedure to retrieve the necessary data. For example,

```
supplies_part(PART,NAME,ADDRESS) :-
  part(P,PART), supplies(S,P), suppliers(S,NAME,ADDRESS).
```

would allow the user to ask

```
?-supplies_part(wheel,NAME,ADDRESS).
```

to find the names and addresses of all suppliers who supply wheels. Such a procedure is equivalent to a 'user view' or 'catalogued query' in many database management systems. In Prolog, such a procedure can be treated as if it were an actual relation and be included in complex queries, or as part of the definition of further Prolog procedures.

2.4 Transformation of relations

Prolog, however, permits quite complex processing of data. Suppose that the supplies relation is extended to include the suppliers price of that part:

```
supplies(supplier_no,part_no,price).
```

Consider the query 'For all known suppliers, what is the price of their wheels, frames and handlebars'. The following query would retrieve the necessary information:

```
query1(PART,NAME,PRICE) :-
  member(PART,wheel.frame.handlebar.nil),
  part(P,PART),supplies(P,S,PRICE),suppliers(S,NAME,ADDRESS).
```

From this query, one would be able to present a table such as

part	name	price	
wheel	bloggs & co.	9.25	
frame	bloggs & co.	17.90	
handlebar	bloggs & co.	5.40	
wheel	smiths ltd	8.90	
handlebar	smiths ltd	5.60	
...	...	...	...

This is the form that most query languages would allow one to produce. Suppose, however, that the user really wants

supplier	wheel	frame	handlebar
bloggs & co.	9.25	17.90	5.40
smiths ltd	8.90	unknown	5.60
...	...	...	...

which is a very reasonable request. The data are much more compact. This form is easier to read and does not repeat information unnecessarily. It is also possible to see who does not supply a particular part!

The user might want a further column which consists of the price of two wheels, a handlebar and a frame from that supplier. With Prolog, the problem can be overcome in the following way. First, a procedure is constructed which provides virtual relations with the schemata

```
wheelprice(supplier_no,wheelprice)
frameprice(supplier_no,frameprice)
handlebarprice(supplier_no,handlebarprice).
```

A new query can now be constructed:

```
query2(NAME,WHEEL,FRAME,HANDLEBAR) :-
    supplier(S,NAME,ADDRESS),
    wheelprice(S,WHEEL),
    frameprice(S,FRAME),
    handlebarprice(S,HANDLEBAR).
```

This allows one to retrieve the data in such a way that the second table above could be produced. To implement the extra column one would require

```
query2(NAME,WHEEL,FRAME,HANDLEBAR,TOTAL) :-
    supplier(S,NAME,ADDRESS),
    wheelprice(S,WHEEL),
    frameprice(S,FRAME),
    handlebarprice(S,HANDLEBAR),
    TOTAL is 2*WHEEL+FRAME+HANDLEBAR.
```

This is fine if WHEEL, FRAME and HANDLEBAR are instantiated to numbers. However, we wish to allow for any of them to be unknown. We can modify the above procedure to make TOTAL unknown if any of the constituents are unknown, as follows:

```
query2(NAME,WHEEL,FRAME,HANDLEBAR,TOTAL) :-
    supplier(S,NAME,ADDRESS),
    wheelprice(S,WHEEL),
    frameprice(S,FRAME),
    handlebarprice(S,HANDLEBAR),
    sumup(WHEEL.WHEEL.FRAME.HANDLEBAR.nil,TOTAL).
sumup(nil,0).
sumup(unknown._,unknown).
```

```
sumup(X.Y,N) :- sumup(Y,M),
                (M=unknown, !, N=unknown;
                N is M+X).
```

The implementation of the procedures wheelprice, frameprice and handlebarprice is carried out as follows.

To retrieve the data, one uses the rule

```
wheelprice(SUPPLIER,WHEEL) :-
        part(PARTNO,wheel),
        supplies(SUPPLIER,PARTNO,WHEEL).
```

This initially appears sufficient, but the above query would not then produce a result for anyone who did not supply a wheel. To overcome this, a second part of the rule must be

```
wheelprice(_,unknown).
```

and a cut is introduced into the above rule, producing a procedure

```
wheelprice(SUPPLIER,WHEEL) :-
        part(PARTNO,wheel),
        supplies(SUPPLIER,PARTNO,WHEEL), !.
wheelprice(_,unknown).
```

A further rule is introduced to cope with the query

```
?-wheelprice(S,W).
```

where S is unspecified. The above procedure would only report on the prices of wheels for suppliers who supply wheels. We thus end up with

```
wheelprice(SUPPLIER,WHEEL) :-
        SUPPLIER is_a var, !,
        supplier(SUPPLIER,_,_),
        wheelprice(SUPPLIER,WHEEL).
wheelprice(SUPPLIER,WHEEL) :-
        part(PARTNO,wheel),
        supplies(SUPPLIER,PARTNO,WHEEL), !.
wheelprice(_,unknown).
```

Finally, it is possible that the user may wish to ask a query such as

```
?-wheelprice(S,unknown).
```

The above procedure, unfortunately, will reply that every supplier has an unknown wheel price. To overcome this, a further rule is added, giving a final procedure

```
wheelprice(SUPPLIER,WHEEL) :-
        SUPPLIER is_a nonvar,
        WHEEL is_a nonvar,
        WHEEL=unknown, !,
        part(PARTNO,wheel),
```

```
                not supplies(SUPPLIER,PARTNO,_).
wheelprice(SUPPLIER,WHEEL) :-
                SUPPLIER is_a var, !,
                supplier(SUPPLIER,_,_),
                wheelprice(SUPPLIER,WHEEL).
wheelprice(SUPPLIER,WHEEL) :-
                part(PARTNO,wheel),
                supplies(SUPPLIER,PARTNO,WHEEL), !.
wheelprice(_,unknown).
```

Similar procedures can be constructed for handlebar price and frame price.

What can be concluded from this exercise? First, we have effectively invented new attributes for the relational schema, namely the prices for wheels, frames and handlebars. Where the price of a wheel before had to be identified by an attribute value, it can now be identified by an attribute name. This could have been achieved by redesigning the original database schema, but it would have led either to a lot of small binary relations, or to relations with a lot of null values. To add a new data item, say pedal price, then we simply add a new Prolog procedure, instead of having to modify the database schema. Secondly, we have introduced null values. Where a wheel price is unknown, we obtain the value 'unknown', instead of having to note the absence of a record. Many recent databases provide null-value handling, but often in a limited way. Using Prolog, we can add null values to any database. Finally, if we place a relation in the database which contains the set of all such similar attributes, we could generate the appropriate Prolog procedures automatically.

2.5 Recursive queries

One further advantage that Prolog has over traditional query languages is the direct support of recursion. Suppose we have a relation

```
partof(bike,wheel)
partof(bike,frame)
partof(wheel,spoke)
partof(wheel,rim)
partof(wheel,hub)
. . .
```

The query 'What are the basic parts of a bike?' can be expressed in Prolog as

```
basic_part(X) :- not partof(X,_).
/* X is a basic part if it has no sub-parts */

basic_partof(X,X) :- basic_part(X).
/* the basic part of X is X if X is a basic part */
basic_partof(X,Y) :- partof(X,Z), basic_partof(Z,Y).
/* Y is a basic part of X if Z is a part of X and
          Y is a basic part of Z */

?- basic_partof(bike,X).
```

```
/* what are the basic parts of a bike? */
```

An example of the practical use of recursion in scientific databases occurs where a component of a product may itself be a product, which in turn may contain a further product as a component, and so forth. Presently, an extra relation is often maintained within a database to provide details of the basic constituents of a product.

2.6 Other relevant Prolog features

Prolog includes input/output for terminals and files. It is thus possible to produce reports. For example, the procedure

```
bikeparts :- write('Basic Parts Of Bicycle'), nl,
             basic_partof(bike,X), write(X), nl,
             fail.
```

will produce a table on the screen of all the basic parts of a bicycle ('nl' throws a new line, 'write' outputs a data item), on asking

```
?- bikeparts.
```

Prolog also allows list processing. For example, suppose the list of bicycle parts is wanted in sorted order, one can compose a set of bicycle parts, sort them and then print out the set. For example:

```
sortedbikeparts :- setof(X,basic_partof(bike,X),Bikepartset),
                   sort(Bikepartset,Sbikepartset),
                   printlist(Sbikepartset).
?- sortedbikeparts.
```

Finally, there are various means of storing intermediate results. For relatively small relations, these could be asserted as Prolog procedures and accessed directly. For larger relations, these could be written to file and accessed as if they were Prolog procedures.

3. THE THORNTON RESEARCH EASY QUERY LANGUAGE (TREQL)

Although Prolog itself can be considered equivalent to existing query languages in terms of expressing queries on a relational database, it still requires the end user to have a fairly detailed knowledge of the schema and of the language in order to retrieve data. Many queries require complex joins and can require a substantial amount of effort to construct. To allow inexperienced users to query the database, a query language called TREQL (Thornton Research Easy Query Language) has been developed which does not require the user to understand the details of the database schema.

TREQL requires the user simply to list the attribute names of the items required from the database. These items may be from a number of relations. TREQL will determine the necessary joins, compose a Prolog query and extract the data.

For example, the TREQL query

supplier_name, supplier_no, wheelprice, frameprice.

would be (approximately) equivalent to the SQL query

```
SELECT supplier_name, supplier_no, part_name, price
FROM supplies, suppliers, parts
WHERE supplies.supplier_no=suppliers.supplier_no,
   AND supplies.part_no=parts.part_no
   AND ( parts.part_name=wheel
         OR parts.part_name=frame).
```

The first query produces a table with one entry for each supplier in the suppliers table, with the third and fourth columns giving the price of wheels and frames from that supplier; if a price is not available from the supplies relation, then 'unknown' will be entered for that price. The SQL query will produce zero, one or two entries for each supplier, depending on how many entries exist in the supplies relation for wheel and frame; if a supplier does not have an entry for a particular component, this will be indicated by there being no entry in the output table. The SQL query is harder to compose, requires a knowledge of the database schema, and presents data in a form which is less readable. The ability to introduce null (unknown) values to a relational database is seen to be one of the important aspects of TREQL.

TREQL also allows selection criteria. For example, to retrieve all suppliers with a wheel price less than five pounds, one would use

supplier_name, supplier_no, wheelprice < 5.00 .

which produces a table with three columns, the last one being the wheel price. Range specifications are possible. For example, to retrieve all suppliers with a wheel price between five and six pounds, one would use

supplier_name, supplier_no, wheelprice >= 5.00, wheelprice =< 6.00 .

The Prolog initially used to implement the query language and the Prolog–RAPPORT interface is MPROLOG running under VM/CMS on an IBM 4381. The Prolog–RAPPORT interface is written in a mixture of MPROLOG (approximately 400 lines) and FORTRAN (approximately 1000 lines). It allows complete access to the whole database, including update and transaction processing. The query language and extended schema are written entirely in MPROLOG (approximately 180 lines and 150 lines respectively). A version of TREQL now runs on a Symbolics workstation, running against a scientific database entirely compiled as a very large Prolog program.

3.1 Architecture

The architecture of the system is illustrated by the following diagram:

Query Language
Extended Schema
DBMS Schema

A query language statement is translated into a Prolog query which extracts the items from virtual relations provided in the extended schema. The technique is to find a minimal set of virtual relations which covers the data items required and to express a query which joins those relations. The query language is generic and could be used on any database management system supporting a suitable Prolog interface.

The relations in the extended schema either map directly into relations in the DBMS schema or are views of the data in the DBMS schema. The principal difference between the views provided here and in a traditional DBMS is that new data items may be introduced which are not derived from data items in the DBMS schema, but which are derived from data in the database. For example, 'wheelprice' may not be a discernible data item in the DBMS schema, but it may be in the extended schema and derived from data values present in the actual relationships. The extended schema is application-specific and contains knowledge of the application domain. However, its construction should be straightforward and concise; for a typical scientific database, it is approximately 150 lines.

The rest of this section will present some of the interesting details of the above system.

3.2 The query language layer

Finding the necessary relations

The relations used in the query are those which form the smallest set of relations which includes all the data items requested by the user. This should, in practice, be a unique set. For situations where more than one such set exists, strategies may have to be developed which cope with such ambiguities. One such strategy might be to report on the problem and to suggest that the database administrator should be consulted. Most database structures are simple enough to make this extremely unlikely, and we have ignored the problem. To improve search efficiency and to reduce the likelihood of ambiguous queries, only relations which contain at least two of the requested data items are considered.

From the list of data items presented, a minimal set of relations which covers the data items is derived using a breadth-first search. The extended schema contains facts which define the contents of all the actual and virtual relations which may be used by the query language. For example:

```
schema(supplies, supplier_no.part_no.price.nil).
```

Thus, 'supplies' is a relation which has 'supplier_no', 'part_no' and 'price' as attributes.

Optimizing the query

Clearly, the order of retrieval of data from any database is important in terms of efficiency. The more constraints on the values of the entries within a query on a single relation, the faster, in general, that retrieval will be, especially if an index is provided on a constrained value. As a first attempt at query optimization, the following simple trick was used:

```
optimise(Rels,Equalities,Relsopt) :-
  split(Rels,Equalities,Indexed,Nonindexed),
  append(Indexed,Nonindexed,Relsopt).

split(nil,_,nil,nil).
split(R.A,E,R.B,C) :-
  index(R,K),member((K=_),E)!,split(A,E,B,C).
split(R.A,E,B,R.C) :- split(A,E,B,C).
```

The set of relations used for retrieval is split into two; one set contains those relations where an indexed value is defined by an equality statement in the query, and the other set contains the rest. The relations in the first set are queried first. This should normally instantiate indexed values for the second set of relations. Much better optimization than this could take place, based on more knowledge of the database.

Further optimization could take place by allowing selection criteria to be passed down to the lower levels, reducing the number of tuples it is necessary to retrieve. For example,

```
p(A,B,C),C>3,C<4
```

could be written as

```
p(A,B,3<C<4)
```

and the indexing system underlying the retrieval could make use of the range on the third argument, reducing the number of records retrieved from disk. This technique has not been used within TREQL, but has been used successfully in other related work.

The generated query

The query

```
supplier_name, supplier_no, wheelprice < 5.00,
  frameprice < 12.00 .
```

would be translated into

```
query(A,B,C,D) :-
  supplier(B,A,_),
  wheelprice(A,C),
  frameprice(A,D),
  (C = unknown; not (C = unknown), C<5.00),
  (D = unknown; not (D = unknown), C<12.00).
```

where 'supplier' is in fact a relation in the DBMS schema, and 'wheelprice' and 'frameprice' are virtual relations in the extended schema. Note that unknown values are reported as meeting the selection criteria. The query reporting only those suppliers for which both 'wheelprice' and 'frameprice' are known is

```
supplier_name, supplier_no, wheelprice < 5.00,
  frameprice < 12.00, wheelprice \== unknown,
  frameprice \== unknown.
```

3.3 The extended schema layer

The extended schema layer implements the necessary virtual relations to improve the ease of querying (e.g. the 'wheelprice' relation described above). Depending on the application, these virtual relations may be quite elaborate.

There may be many virtual relations which could be constructed, and they may be generated automatically. In many instances a meta-relation will exist, or could be constructed, which contains the data values which are to be treated in this way, and hence the generation of virtual relations could proceed by querying that meta-relation. Alternatively, if access to the data dictionary is possible, much of the extended schema can be derived automatically from that.

Any set of relations in the schema or extended schema (or both) can be combined. Hence the extended schema can be used as a means of cataloguing user views or presenting specialized subschemata.

4. CONCLUSIONS

4.1 Further work

A number of themes has arisen from this work. The primary objective addressed by the research is the provision of front-ends to database systems. By using a language suitable for knowledge-based systems, we have been able to incorporate application-specific knowledge into an interface, at little expense, to make interrogation of that database a much simpler activity. Given that Prolog can interface with traditional procedural languages, we are investigating front-ends to other software packages such as mathematical or statistical packages.

A further line of enquiry may be the introduction of natural language front-ends to databases and software systems. Most Prolog systems include a parsing option, and Prolog has established itself as a useful tool for natural language processing.

The above work has introduced the problem of query optimization. This is a much studied area in database theory, and some of the work in that field could be incorporated. The interaction between Prolog and database retrieval introduces some novel problems.

Development of the query language into a product would require some work on man–machine interface. The user could well be assisted by selection of data items from a number of menus. Presentation of results on the screen and on printout must be improved. Some validation of queries before processing would also be necessary.

A final and important theme is that of Prolog as a unifying tool. Prolog can well be used as a means of providing a standard interface to a diverse range of databse systems, to file systems and to other software packages. The symbolic processing aspects of Prolog have much to offer in terms of general data processing as well as knowledge-based applications.

4.2 Conclusions

Prolog is a useful and powerful query language for a relational database. A Prolog interface to an existing database would be a useful means of integrating such a database into a knowledge-based system. Prolog provides the full power of a traditional query language, with interesting possibilities of extending the database through virtual relations and the handling of null values.

The query language TREQL introduces a useful technique which could be universally applied. Any database with a Prolog interface could be queried this way. The technique could be used to generate SQL instead of Prolog, but early attempts at this have indicated that the generation of equivalent SQL would be much more difficult than the generation of Prolog.

ACKNOWLEDGEMENTS

Many thanks are due to Steven Death, John Redfearn and Allan Robinson of Shell Research, and Peter Gray of Aberdeen University for their comments, advice and constructive criticism.

REFERENCES

[1] Gray, P., *Logic, Algebra and Databases,* Ellis Horwood, Chichester, 1984.
[2] Bratko, I., *Prolog Programming for Artificial Intelligence,* Addison-Wesley, Reading, MA, 1986.
[3] Product Formulation Expert System — Report to the Alvey Directorate, ALV/PRJ/IKBS/052, available from A. Robinson, Shell Research Limited, Thornton Research Centre, EMT/6, P.O. Box 1, Chester, England, CH1 3SH.

Part II

Database interfacing and implementation

4

On Prolog-DBMS connections: a step forward from Educe

J. Bocca and **P. J. Pearson**
European Computer-Industry Research Centre GmbH†,
Arabellastr. 17, D-8000 Muenchen 81, West Germany

ABSTRACT

Following the implementation of Educe — a logic programming system based on the coupling and integration of Prolog and relational DBMSs — we wished to assess the relative importance of a number of factors which contribute to performance and usability of systems of the Educe type. Early applications of Educe provided us with the preliminary information about candidate factors to be studied in isolation. In this chapter, we present a detailed case study of an application of Educe. We performed tests on the relative importance of performance and usability factors; then we analysed the results and derived the elements of design for Educe*. This new system is a follow-up system to Educe, and it relies on compiled code to be maintained by the external storage subsystem, instead of the classical solution based on the interpretation of source code managed by the external DBMS.

1. INTRODUCTION

In the context of designing a system for constructing large knowledge-based systems, based on Prolog and relational database management technology, we wished to determine the need to compile Prolog clauses/procedures which will be maintained by the external database.

Although relational systems have come of age, they still appear to present some significant performance problems. When they are front-ended to Prolog, the problem can be made worse by a naive interface. Some time ago we implemented a system that integrates Prolog with a relational DBMS — Educe [1] — and since then we have been studying the performance aspects of such an integration [2]. Also, at the user level we have been

† The European Computer-Industry Research Centre is a joint research centre established by Bull, ICL and Siemens in January 1984.

looking at the problems encountered in using such systems. It is no surprise to find that many of the user's problems are induced by performance issues.

In Educe, we both loosely coupled and integrated a Prolog interpreter and a relational DBMS. This makes sense in principle, since both relational DBMS and Prolog itself are (in appearance) geared for interactive use. An interpreter was used, as — at the time — there was no suitable Prolog compiler for this task. This integration demonstrated its capabilities in practical terms with the implementation of the prototype knowledge-based system — KB2 [3]. However, it is our feeling that although on the retrieval of facts the performance of the current Educe system is satisfactory, even in large relations, the retrieval of rules and its consequent usage can lead to major performance problems.

Toward achieving the above goals, we considered the possibility of storing compiled code in the relational DBMS. Our preliminary studies showed that three factors contributed to adverse performance whenever rules stored in the external database were in use: the use of an interpreter instead of a compiler for Prolog, poor selectivity on the retrieval of rules stored in the external database and the frequent assertation (and erasure) in the main memory of rules stored in the external database.

Since Prolog compilation in the WAM is directed to produce code for one Prolog term at a time, while the retrieval engine of relational DBMSs is goal oriented, we wished to examine closely the possible interaction of the two (candidate) components to construct a new system based on compilation rather than on interpretation. For this purpose, we undertook a case study which incorporated a sufficiently large number of rules and facts as to make the results meaningful. We wanted a large variety of procedures types, e.g. deterministic and non-deterministic procedures, facts, clauses with one goal, clauses with several goals, etc. In particular we were interested in determining the amount of processing time needed by parsing (during assertions), the quality of present filters to retrieve in the case of general Prolog terms (the structured terms), amount of backtracking as opposed to environment allocation, etc.

The application itself is based on the Munich public transport system, and involves a database of a size sufficient (1 Mbyte data) for obtaining significant results. The program implementing the algorithms to solve the problems in the application uses all of the procedure types mentioned in the previous paragraph.

From this case study, we determined the relative importance of a number of parameters which could have an effect in the performance and usability of Educe. This is a newly designed system that follows in the footsteps of Educe. As expected, it is based on the compilation of Prolog terms. This code is stored in the external relational manager.

This chapter describes the results of our case study and its impact on the design of Educe*. The chapter is divided into six sections. The next section describes the application to be used as a case study; the third section describes the tests performed and the reasons for doing them; the fourth section discusses the results of the tests; the fifth section describes the process of compilation using external storage, and the associated problems are discussed; the sixth section presents the current state of work, offers conclusions, and discusses future work.

2. CASE STUDY

2.1 Overview

It is our belief that the principles behind Educe provide a system for the solution of many problems where the amount of data is large, and a logic programming language would be the most natural way of expressing the algorithm. For this reason, after Educe was implemented, we used it to prototype the knowledge-based system, KB2 [3]. This implementation revealed a number of potential problem areas in the approach taken to integrate the logic language and DBMS. One of these areas was in the storage and retrieval of rules in the external database. Towards a better identification and solution of the specific problems of this area as well as the more general problems of deductive databases, we decided on the provision of a controlled system with which to experiment. To this end an application was sought to be solved using Educe. It was necessary that the problem was a 'real world' problem, that it contained a significantly large amount of data and that the program provided a variety of procedure types in order that the method of rule storage and retrieval could be tested. For this purpose, we chose as our target application a public transport system. This application was chosen because of the potentially large numbers of facts and rules as well as the varying degrees of complexity of the rules.

2.2 Other related work

The problem approached here was also used to demonstrate parallel programming techniques at ECRC. This work is complementary to the current exercise; a system that could run on a parallel machine would have the benefits provided by both systems, and would be more powerful than each system. Given the nature of the algorithm it would also seem to fit a constraint programming approach; see, for example [4].

On a less specific level it is interesting to compare the modelling here of the public transport system with simulation problems generally. It has been said [5] that the provision of database technology with the programming language would be a desirable objective in the field of simulation. When one considers the amount of data and associated organization and manipulation involved in simulating 'real life' situations, this is hardly surprising. Thus it was recognized that providing only appropriate programming languages may not be sufficient and that they need to be supported by data-handling systems. With Educe it is hoped to demonstrate various problems that can be tackled.

2.3 The application

The MVV public transport system (the transport system in operation in Munich, West Germany) was chosen as a problem suitable to meet the requirement mentioned above. An automatic solution to the problem of how to get from one part of the city to another using a system which, though efficient, is undoubtedly complex is desirable both to the operators and to the users.

The MVV network can be considered as a number of (unique) named nodes (the transport stops of the system) and links (the transports used) between them. The problem of getting from one part of the city to another is constrained not only by the links in the system but by the timetables that are associated with them. In an implementation that is to be in any way useful, the solution provided should be optimal from some point of view of the system. (Although, in this problem, optimality is somewhat subjective, a good approximation would be that the journey should take as short a time as possible and involve as few changes as possible, this being a compromise between minimizing the time and minimizing the number of changes. In the Munich transport system, because of the way it has developed, one often finds that with more changes one can arrive at the destination more quickly than with taking a route involving fewer changes).

The algorithm used in the current implementation was quite straightforward and, undoubtedly, other solutions exist. It was based on an algorithm used to solve the same problem in a parallel Prolog environment. The resulting program is small, in the region of 200 clauses, and would present no problems in any logic programming environment. Now consider the data on which this program must draw in order to construct a valid path. They must be able to use the information contained in the timetable for the network, which is estimated to contain 300 nodes and 240 different transports. The number of tuples stored and the size of the resulting database are, of course, dependent on the format used to store the information in that database. The format used in this implementation enables the information to be condensed, albeit at the cost of a slight oversimplification. Using this condensed format the estimated number of tuples of the database needed to cover the complete MVV system is 23 000. The current implementation covering the 200 sq km of Munich city contains approximately 16K tuples, and the total size of the database is approximately 3/4 Mbytes. This is not large for a database (a medium-sized KB could be expected to have in the region of 30 Mbytes of data), but it would be large if it had to be held in an internal database of a Prolog system.

In the following subsections the approach is described in more detail.

2.3.1 Data

For implementation purposes the information can be classified as follows:

1. Nodes (the halts of the transport system).
2. Links (the transport between nodes).
3. Timetables.

Nodes can be subdivided into the following:

1. Major nodes: at which a change of transport is possible.
2. Minor nodes: at which no transport change is possible.
3. Places: which do not lie on the MVV network but are desirable starting points or destinations nevertheless, e.g. ECRC, home.

The information relevant to these nodes consists of coordinates, transport types major nodes on either side of a minor node and the nearest network nodes to a place, with the times to go between them.

Transports are simply identified by the type and number, e.g. bus(44), s(3), tram(20).

The timetable contains such information as depart time, halts, frequency, etc.

2.3.2 Algorithm

The problem reduces to one of finding a path between two major nodes, since any minor node or place start/end point may be considered as start/end modifications to a path between major nodes lying nearby.

The main part of the algorithm advances between major nodes, finding possible advances and choosing the next node from among these possibilities.

The program takes as input the start point, the start time, and the destination, and provides a table of changes, departure and arrival times necessary to traverse between them.

Prolog provides a good programming language with which to formulate the process of finding a path through the network, and the backtracking enables exploration of routes.

2.3.3 Database

The data were stored externally on the Educe database (for those familiar with Educe — see [2] the integrated system (tight integration) was used, making the underlying database transparent to the Prolog program). The storage of the database externally on a DBMS enables it to be maintained easily, as one would expect from a DBMS. A further advantage gained was that once a path had been calculated it could also be stored in the external database. As far as the DBMS is concerned, this is not much of an overhead and enables even faster retrieval of paths in some cases. If this information were to be held internally, on the other hand, it would add significantly to the process time as the information collected grew. In the results below, a table provides some of the associated figures.

2.3.4 Example

In the following example, let

p=place, M=major node, m=minor node, s=start and d=destination.
Given the simple network

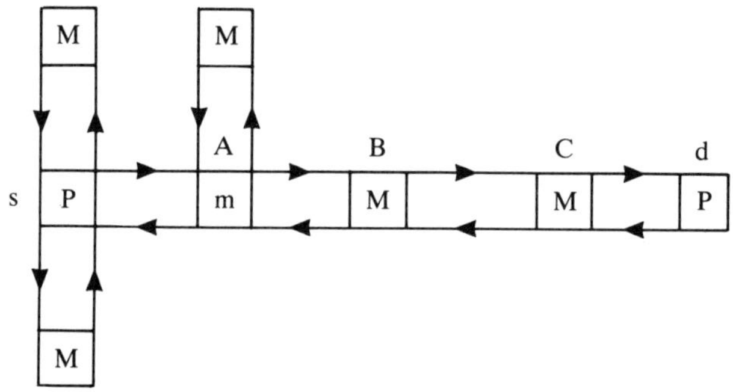

this reduces to four steps:

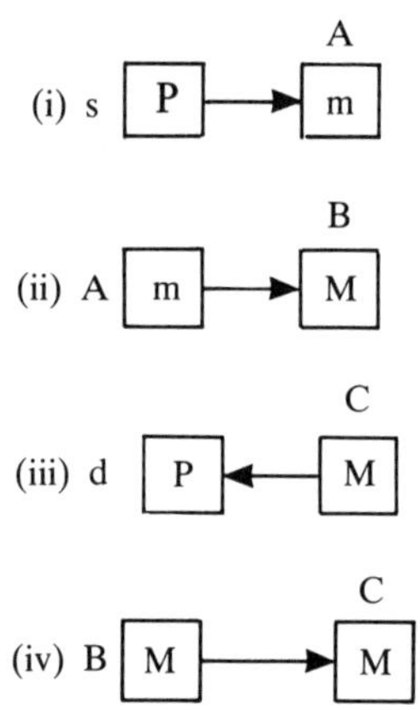

3. THE TESTS

The experiments performed on the application had two main purposes: first, to compare the performances of different types of system, in order to determine the gains and losses in performances using the different approaches, and, secondly, to see how much effect the use of stored rules had on the system when the rules were stored in a way requiring them to be asserted into the internal database and interpreted instead of their already being in the internal database. Ideally the comparison should also be made with a system allowing the storage of the compiled rules in the external database, but, since such a system was not available at the time of these experiments, no such comparisons were made.

The queries used to test the system were divided into four classes.

1. Very simple queries involving travel between adjacent major nodes with minimal choice of transport involved.
2. More involved quieries involving travel between major nodes (not involving more than one change) with many transports to choose between.
3. Travel between minor nodes (with only one or two major nodes between) with many available transports.
4. Complex queries involving travel between remote nodes (that is, with many intermediate nodes), and hence with many available transports.

In the first series of experiments, the application was run under three different system configurations.

1. The normal Educe system. The details for this can be found in, for example, [1]. All the program rules and all the data were held in external storage, i.e. in Ingres files.
2. The Educe system, but with the rules for the program now held in internal storage, i.e. as a Prolog program would be in, for example, Mu-Prolog. The data for experiments were still held in external storage as in the configuration described above.
3. The normal Mu-Prolog system. All the program rules and data for the application were held in internal storage. No external file accesses were necessary to run the application in this node.

In order to obtain the results, a sample of ten queries from each class was run on the application for each system configuration, and the average of the times achieved was taken. The times given are in cpu seconds spent in obtaining the answer, and are taken from profiles run using gprof under UNIX running on a SUN computer (see Table 1)

Table 1—Comparison of times in cpu seconds between three configurations

System	1	2	3
Query Class			
1	14.87	10.91	3.54
2	23.10	18.64	8.46
3	24.93	20.52	8.62
4	337.15	308.98	(i)

Notes.
(i) The Muprolog system ran out of internal memory space trying to process this query.

The second series of tests was run to see the effects of having the rules for the application program stored on backing store. The Educe system stores the rules in such a way that in order to be executed they first have to be asserted temporarily into internal storage and then interpreted. The following results provide a comparison of the relative times spent in two contributory processes.

For these experiments, classes 2 and 4 of the query types were used. These provide a sufficiently rich use of the program rules to see the effects and, at the same time, a significant difference in the program execution time.

The tests were not run on the third system configuration mentioned above, as, this time, we were only interested in the differences due to the method of holding the rules.

The two processes considered were

(1) assert — each call to a rule held in external store and not present in internal store requires an assert of the clause into internal memory.
(2) retrieve — this is the opening of the file, the reading of the data, and the closing of the file when complete.

The two figures in each box in Table 2 are, first, the figure obtained from

Table 2 — Comparison of proportion of times spent in two processes

	assert	retrieve
System		
1	2.95/0.04	45.15/53.87
2	1.28/0.01	51.66/56.44

class 2 queries and, secondly, the figure obtained from class 4 queries. All figures give the percentage of the time spent in the process to the total time of the query to run.

Table 3 shows the timings when the paths are found to have already been

Table 3

System	1	2	3
Query Class			
1	0.36	0.32	0.37
4	0.41	0.35	(i)

Notes
(i) Since the path could not be calculated, it could not be saved and thus not retrieved.

stored, in the external database for classes 1 and 2 and in the internal database for class 3.

In Table 3, the figures provided must just be considered as giving an idea of the performance. All systems seemed to perform at about the same level, for most of the time. The Mu-Prolog version, however, encountered some problems when data were asserted into memory to save the solutions. In some cases where the path had been calculated, the growth in size of the internal database caused by saving solutions would mean that the system would be unable, after a while, to calculate even simple paths without running out of internal memory. Erratic behaviour near the limits of the size of Mu-Prolog's internal store was also observed, which could have been due to the fact that since there is no garbage collection in this system the internal memory was invisibly decreasing.

4. DISCUSSION OF RESULTS

For the purpose of this discussion, we refer to the Prolog interpreter, without the external DBMS, as the *Prolog interpreter*, and to the Educe system with facts and rules in the external DBMS as *Educe with rules*, and to the Educe system with facts in the external DBMS but with rules in main memory as *Educe without rules*. The main points to notice in the above tests are the following.

1. On simple queries, the Prolog interpreter performed on average better by a factor of four.
2. On more complex queries the Prolog interpreter could not cope with the amount of data and soon ran out of memory.
3. The use of compound terms was biased against Educe, in general, and against Educe with rules, in particular.
4. The use of interpreted stored rules in Educe with rules had one of the worst effects in performance, as Educe with rules spent four times as long in asserts and retracts.
5. The Prolog interpreter showed severe memory space problems and unpredictable results because of this.
6. The use of Educe allowed the storage and re-use of results from previous queries. Owing to the expansion in size of the associated database, this was not practical in the Prolog interpreter system.
7. Given the size of the database, there would be huge problems with maintenance on the Prolog interpreter's implementation of the application.
8. It is not clear from the timings above, but from the analysis traces, that backtracking has an impact on performance which is much greater than procedure calling in these sorts of application. Backtracking is the counterpart of an inner loop in a nesting of loops in conventional deterministic languages.

From the above points and to confirm our early conceptions, the need for the storage of compiled code in the external DBMS is very clear. Parsing, asserting interpretation and erasing of transient rules normally maintained by the external DBMS represents one of the highest costs in cpu time.

Other areas of considerable impact on performance are: dealing with recursive programs in the external DBMS, backtracking, treatment of compound terms, filtering the retrieval of clauses and the physical representation of compiled rules in the external DBMS.

5. COMPILATION IN THE EXTERNAL DBMS

The above results and considerations have led to the design and implementation of Educe*, a follow-up system to Educe. This is a purpose-built system for interactive use, and is designed to support continuous operation over a long period. The user interface is still Prolog, but in addition it supports pure database modules. The query sublanguage supported in these modules is purely declarative.

In order to support the above features the Warren Abstract Machine [6] was chosen as the basis on which to develop a model for compilation of logic terms to be maintained in external storage. In addition, facilities to support a strongly typed language at the lowest possible level were added. This is to avoid the unnecessary use of base and derived relations purely to handle type information. An example of this in our case study is provided by tests needed to be performed on the type of public transport to use: bus, train, underground train, etc.

To provide continuous operation over long periods, it was necessary to develop a memory management system capable of being fully garbage collected. It should be noted at this point that current technology of Prolog compilers normally supports the garbage collection of stacks but not of the internal atom dictionary nor the memory used by code. This is a very important consideration because of the large difference in orders of magnitude between the space required by a Prolog compiler running purely in main memory and that of a logic language, say Prolog again, supporting an external DBMS. Potentially, millions of atoms might need to occupy temporary dictionary space when evaluating a query involving externally stored relations. The same amount of transient information is never required during the running of a Prolog program in main memory and without access to external storage.

Because of the interactive nature of the system, the requirement is for an incremental garbage collection mechanism. It should also be appreciated that sometimes garbage collection alone is not going to provide all the memory needed for the evaluation of certain queries. In such cases, the basic memory areas in use must be able to expand and, once satisfied, the space returned to the host operating system. This avoids penalties imposed by the host operating system on processes requiring excessive resources.

Also in connection with gabage collection, it should be noted that it would be extremely expensive to perform garbage collection over compiled code maintained in external storage, particularly if this were done during the normal running time of the system. To avoid this problem, we have developed a system in Educe* to perform dynamic loading of the code. This allows for the storage of compiled code in external storage, but only with associative addresses in the code. Naturally, there is a small cost incurred in resolving addresses at run time. Fortunately, this cost is less than 10% of the time that normal interpretation of source code would require.

Another important area that affects performance significantly, as detected by this case study, is the lack of a better filtering mechanism in the retrieval of compound terms. This clearly affects performance of queries over base relations supporting compound terms, e.g. bus(45), tram(18), undergr(u3), etc. More significantly, this has an effect in the retrieval of rules. Because of this, we use compilation for external storage as a mechanism to support a form of pre-unification of terms in the external database retrieval engine.

A detailed description of motivations, design and implementation issues of the compiler for Educe* can be found in [7]. In this section, we have only attempted to highlight its most important features.

6. CURRENT STATE OF DEVELOPMENT, CONCLUSIONS AND FUTURE WORK

6.1 Current state of development

At the time of writing, we have completed the implementation of the kernel Prolog compiler and all its internal machinery to support inferences in external storage. We are now in the process of defining interfaces for the integration of the Bang file described in Chapter 12. Bang is a low-level file management system, specially designed for deductive usage where key specification by the user is a practical impossibility.

6.2 Conclusions

The differences in performance between compilation and interpretation have been clearly stated, with the relatively recent appearance of Prolog compilers. It is not unusual to have performance increased by a factor of more than 20–30 times when moving from an interpreter to a compiler generating native code (for the host machine, as opposed to some virtual machine). However, in the context of an integrated Prolog–Relational DBMS system, this sort of compilation is not possible because of the need for garbage collection of externally stored compiled code. More realistically, one could consider the possibility of storing code for a specially adapted virtual machine based on a well known and proven design, such as WAM [6], which must be able to handle associative addresses to avoid garbage collection of external storage. Typical improvements from interpreted Prolog code to compiled code for a virtual machine are of the order of 10–20 times. This type of compilation is also attractive because of the ease with which the interpretation mechanism of relational DBMS would fit with the emulator for the virtual machine (and its resolution of associative addresses).

In a system such as Educe, the obvious way of storing rules in the external DBMS is to store them in source form. In addition, Educe stored some extra information to make rule selection more selective. In a system using a compiler for Prolog, it is possible to use the compiler itself to collect all sorts of information to help in the latter process of retrieval, so improving its selectivity.

Assertion of prolog clauses, whether rules or facts, is a very expensive operation in terms of cpu time. Compiled code stored externally could make this activity almost completely unnecessary. The parsing of Prolog terms would not be required at all when loading from the external DBMS.

To conclude, this chapter has highlighted those aspects that greatly affect the performance of deductive systems based on logic and capable of supporting large knowledge bases. From the successful solution of these problems depends the future and acceptability of very large knowledge-based systems to be implemented using this technology. More specific solutions are discussed in [7].

6.3 Future work

In the near future, the details of design and the implementation in general of Educe will be completed. This includes the integration to Bang, the strong type system (the weak typing of Prolog is part of the compiler), tuning of memory management and garbage collection, and a debugger specifically for use in large knowledge-based systems.

REFERENCES

[1] Bocca, J., On the Evaluation Strategy of EDUCE, In Zaniolo, C. (ed.), *Proc. 1986 ACM–SIGMOD Int. Conf. on Management of Data*, ACM, Washington, D.C., USA, May 1986.

[2] Bocca, J., EDUCE — A Marriage of Convenience: Prolog and a Relational DBMS, In Keller, P. (ed.), *Proc. '86 SLP Third IEEE Symp. on Logic Programming*, IEEE, Salt Lake City, Utah, USA, September 1986.

[3] Wallace, M., *KB2: a Knowledge Based System Embedded in Prolog*, Technical Report TR-KB-12, European Computer-Industry Research Centre, Munich, Aug. 1986.

[4] Dincbas, M. and Vanhentenryck, P., *Constraints and Logic Programming*, Technical Report TR-LP-09, ECRC, February 1986.

[5] Standridge, C. R. and Prisher, A. A. B., Using Data Base Capabilities in Simulation, *Progress in Modelling and Simulation*, Academic Press, New York, 1982, pp. 347–365.

[6] Warren, D. H. D., *An Abstract Prolog Instruction Set*, Technical Report tn309, SRI, October 1983.

[7] Bocca, J., *Compilation of Logic Programs in Very Large Knowledge Base Systems*, Technical Report KB-19, ECRC, October 1987.

5

A Prolog–relational database interface

Robert J. Lucas
Department of Computing Science, King's College,
Old Aberdeen AB9 2UB, Scotland
Gabriel A. Le Vine
Computer Science Dept., Coventry Polytechnic, Priory Street,
Coventry CV1 5FB, England

ABSTRACT

A Prolog interpreter has been written and interfaced to the Mimer commercial database system. The interface tightly couples the database to the Prolog front-end, making its existence virtually transparent to the user. Records are retrieved from tables with little loss of efficiency over normal application programs. Records can also be added, deleted and amended from Prolog. The 'cut' of Prolog works on table searches as well as on the internal database. Rules may be stored in the database, which is structured by the existence of automatically updated system tables.

The system has been used to create several expert systems processing extensive databases — in particular a burglar detection system has been piloted for the Devon and Cornwall Police and tested live over a period of months on real data.

The design and implementation of the interface are described in this chapter. Performance aspects of the system are also discussed.

1. OVERVIEW

The system as described here was implemented on a VAX 11-750 under UNIX 4.2. It has also since been ported to a VAX 11/730 under VMS 4.3.

Mimer is a relational database system. The database is split into any number of databanks, each databank being a logically connected and coherent set of data tables. Facilities have been provided from the Prolog environment for

(1) opening a databank;
(2) associating predicate names with table names;
(3) accessing table entries through the associated predicate name;

(4) using 'cut' over table accesses;
(5) saving rules in, and loading rules from, a databank;
(6) structuring the rule-base;
(7) adding, deleting and amending records in a databank table;
(8) creating and removing databank tables;
(9) loading databank tables with Prolog files.

The Mimer system comes with a Fortran library of general access routines. The interface to call these routines was coded in Fortran and this was linked to the interpreter, written in Pascal, via a thin band of 'C' code. At the Prolog end there is a set of Mimer oriented routines written in Pascal.

The entire system with the interface looks like

```
Internal D.B.                                                      DB1
    |                                                             /
Prolog _ mimerpreds _ C-band _ Main interface _ Mimer DB lib /
interp     Pascal      'C'       Fortran          Fortran      - DB2
    |
user
```

The Mimer system was experimentally interfaced to a Prolog interpreter written in Lisp, and the use of Prolog as an extended query language demonstrated [1]. The current work is an attempt to provide a Prolog interface as a tool for database users to implement expert systems operating on existing data. The system has been used to prototype several expert systems. Examples of these are for fault processing on a large-scale network [2], scheduling objects on a conveyor for paint spraying [3] and the filtering of suspects for burglary [4,5].

2. THE OPTIONS FOR AN INTERFACE

There are basically two types of interface possible: a loose coupling and a tight coupling. Jarke and Vassiliou [6] have defined these terms in the context of expert systems and databases as: *loose*, the ES does all its work before the DBMS is called; *tight*, deduction in the ES is interleaved with partial search in the DBMS. In the context of coupling a database to a Prolog system, these definitions become: loose coupling, where it is necessary to download selectively extracted parts of the external database into Prolog's internal database; tight coupling, where external records are retrieved from the database and unified with Prolog terms as and when required. Perhaps it is sensible to define a third category of coupling — transparent tight coupling — which is tight coupling with the external database accesses behaving in an identical fashion to internal Prolog unit ground clause accesses. This definition is helpful because, although some systems are tightly coupled, they do not offer transparency, which is of major significance to the application developer.

Loose coupling has the following disadvantages:

(1) it requires the data to be read into Prolog before they can be processed; this may take a considerable time;
(2) it loses an important advantage of being able to use a database which is constantly updated by external processes;
(3) database indexing cannot be assumed;
(4) it does not solve the problem of there being some practical upper limit to Prolog's internal database, whilst a good database system will have virtually unlimited storage facilities.

Tight coupling without transparency overcomes these problems and creates a few more:

(1) some form of efficient garbage collection is needed to prevent the Prolog system becoming full with discarded records;
(2) Prolog applications cannot be tested on small unit clause sets which can then be applied to large external datasets without significant alteration.

Tight coupling with transparency overcomes all of the problems associated with loose coupling, but has the same problem with garbage collection as the non-transparent tight coupling. The requirement for transparency introduces the following problems:

(1) Prolog's search mechanism must be duplicated for the external database;
(2) metalogical features must explicitly be provided for.

The options for implementing a tightly coupled system are to go to the datafiles directly and write the necessary code for interpreting their contents. This can be done in a straightforward manner for simple database systems such as dBASE III, where the file structures are straightforward, although, taking advantage of existing indexes may not be trivial. The alternative is to use a 'call interface' (also known as 'call library'). This provides the necessary 'hooks' into the database with the added advantage that database protocols are automatically observed and any existing indexes are used automatically. Unfortunately not all database systems supply a call interface. Mimer, the database system used here, has an extensive range of well documented subroutines. Some examples of these are

(1) BEGIN2 — begin Mimer session;
(2) OPENT2 — open table cursor;
(3) PROJE2 — project column;
(4) SELEC2 — select rows;
(5) SET2 — set table cursor.

Other relational database systems, such as Oracle, Adabas, Datacom and Empress, have similar call interfaces.

The additional features required for transparency are that

(1) table cursors, or their equivalent, must be available for manipulation from the 'call interface'. This will allow the depth first search strategy to be implemented;

(2) the data dictionary must be accessible so that Prolog can ignore column names and refer to fields by position.

The interface described here is a transparent tight coupling. Although it provides most of the problems in terms of software engineering, it also provides the best possible functionality.

3. THE PROLOG–MIMER PREDICATES

3.1 Initiating a Prolog–Mimer session

In order to use an external database from Prolog, a few protocols imposed by the external database must be observed. A session is initiated by means of two system predicates: 'startmimer' and 'accessdb'. The first identifies the user to the database system by means of a username and password; the second tells the system which databank he will be using. These allow the system to identify the user's access privileges and prevent any violation. They are called by the user in the following way:

```
?-startmimer('USERNAME','PASSWORD').
?-accessb('DRUGDB','X').
```

where 'DRUGDB' is a Mimer databank and the 'X' indicates that exclusive access to the databank is required. The password can be hidden from view if required by using a Prolog rule which prompts for the password, having made the appropriate system call to turn off keyboard echo.

3.2 Accessing table entries

3.2.1 The external predicate

There is a natural mapping between entries in a relational database table and facts in Prolog. This is implemented by the 'external' predicate, which tells Prolog which particular predicates are to be associated with tables in the databank and what these tables are called.

For example, in the databank DRUGDB there is a table called MANUFACT. it has two columns called MANID and MNAME. Here are the first few entries:

MANUFACT	
MANID	MNAME
T1	MILES LAB INC
T2	IMPERIAL CHEMICAL IND
T3	HOFFMAN LA ROCHE

If we declare the table to be external in the following fashion:

```
?-external(manufact,'MANUFACT').
```

it is as though the table now exists in Prolog in the following form:

```
manufact('T1','MILES LAB INC').
manufact('T2','IMPERIAL CHEMICAL IND').
manufact('T3','HOFFMAN LA ROCHE').
```

The first parameter to external is not in quotes, as it refers to a Prolog atom and cannot be confused with anything else.

What the external predicate does is to tell Prolog that every time it wishes to solve a goal which is named as the first parameter then this is going to be done by an access to the Mimer table which is given as the second parameter. For example, the following simple query will write the values of the columns in the first row to the screen:

```
?-manufact(X,Y),writeln(X,Y).
```

An array in the interpreter called 'firstused' stores the first position of the first occurrence of every functor in the internal database to increase search speeds. The 'firstused' entry for a predicate that has been defined as external is set to a negative value. The absolute value points to the occurrence of the Mimer table name in the 'stringpool' where the original strings for all atoms are kept.

Joins across tables may be made as though the tables were present as facts in Prolog's database; select conditions are set simply by the values of in-line constants or variables. The following query will give a product of the manufacturer 'HOFFMANN LA ROCHE', given that the 'product' table has the columns *manufacturer code* and *product*. All of this manufacturer's products could be obtained by backtracking.

```
?-manufact(M,'HOFFMAN LA ROCHE'),product(M,P).
```

3.2.2 Solving a query involving a Mimer table

The principal routine for solving a goal in the interpreter is called 'solve'. When the predicate for a table access is being solved it is an easy matter to determine that it is not going to be satisfied by the internal database, by inspection of the 'firstused' entry for the predicate, and to recover the necessary table name.

Once 'solve' has established that the predicate is associated with a Mimer table name, 'accesstab' is called. The object of this routine is to access the next relevant table entry that fits the current unifications. To this end it builds a template of what the next entry required will look like, leaving blanks for the unknown fields. The template is then passed to the Fortran routine 'accesstable' which fills in the blank entries from the next suitable table entry. Once the template has been returned, the fields are parsed and substitutions for the previously unknown values are made in the normal way. Thus the entire unification procedure is bypassed, allowing the fastest possible retrieval of the data items to Prolog. The template is a singly dimensioned character array. It may be thought of as having an indefinite number of slots into which values of table fields may be stored in character format. The total number of available slots is such that the sum of the lengths of the fields plus a one character overhead is equal to or just less than the total length of the template. The ability for the template to work in a paging mode has been implemented for storing and retrieving rules and could easily be extended to data record access, but so far the need has not arisen. If all the elements in the template are blank, i.e. there are no 'select' conditions, then the first (or next) row is retrieved from the table. A 'switch' is passed to 'accesstable' to indicate whether the search is an initial search (i.e. starting at the first row in the table) or a continued search (starting from where the previous search finished). Where the template has non-blank elements, unless the first two positions of such elements contain a relational operator, 'accesstable' will search the Mimer table looking for columns in positions matching the positions of the non-blank template elements, containing data matching (the same as) those within the template, and will fill in the blank elements of the template with corresponding column data from the table. For example, consider a Mimer table TABNAMES containing the following names in columns NAME1 to NAME5:

TABNAMES				
NAME1	NAME2	NAME3	NAME4	NAME5
FRED	JOE	BILL	JIM	JOHN
MARY	JOE	ANN	JIM	ROB

If 'accesstable' is passed an input template containing JOE in the second element and JIM in the fourth, e.g.

?-tabnames(X,'JOE',Y,'JIM',Z),writeln(X,Y,Z).

an initial search would fill in the blank elements 1, 3 and 5 with FRED, BILL and JOHN respectively. if this was followed by a continued search (i.e. the above query was followed by ',fail') those elements would be filled with MARY, ANN and ROB. A second continued search would return a flag to Prolog indicating that there were no (more) records matching the template.

The method of operation of 'accesstable' can be described by the following pseudocode:

```
begin
  if initial search then
    if first ever search on this table then
      get column names, types and lengths
    end if
    get a new table cursor
    set up variables to project into
    set selection conditions from template
    set table cursor to relevant row
    project values into variables
  else
    pop cursor
```

```
    end if
    get matching row
    if successful then
      fill template 'gaps' from variables
      push the cursor {this is so a continued search may be
      peformed}
      flag=0
    else
      flag=−1 {table access has not be successful}
    end if
  end
```

At the Prolog end, a table access involves the creation of a backtrack point. This is in every respect like a normal backtrack point arising from a choice. Backtracking to this point will cause the popping of the relevant table cursor and retrieval of the next matching record in the table: the template containing the select conditions does not need to be rebuilt, as these were set at the time of the first access.

The method of accessing rows from the database tables as and when they are needed is the essential feature of a 'tightly coupled' system [6]. The Prolog used here differs from many implementations, in that strings are tokenized so that unification can compare tokens rather than every character. This is desirable because strings are used extensively when interfacing with external databases; it is not uncommon for the contents of a database to be entirely in upper case. This forces us to treat the table entries as strings to avoid confusion with variables. The Prolog used here also recovers space taken by strings; this is essential, as there is the potential for virtually unlimited access to external strings. Most Prolog systems will not reclaim this space and can cause severe problems if allowed to run for long periods whilst accessing external files. Quintus Prolog will carry on claiming memory on disk (to page to) from the operating system, finally bringing the entire system to a grinding halt. The strategy for recovering this space is very simple and allows for rapid tokenizing of the strings whilst catering for the dangling pointers that arise from this. It is only necessary to stack pointers to the various heaps for the strings, integers and floating-point values at the choice points and unstack them upon backtracking to reclaim dynamically all the space used by the data items. Obviously an 'assert' executed in the middle of a series of table accesses might cause problems as might 'bagof', but these devices are unnecessary, as tables can and should be used for the storage of any intermediate result or set of results. The rapid tokenizing of the strings is done by a simple hashing on the length and first character of each string into the stringpool token array. Any pointers in the hash table that point beyond the end of the stringpool are dangling (and correspond to garbaged values) and can safely be ignored. This simple strategy works efficiently because at any one time the number of external fields active in the interpreter corresponds exactly to the sum of the arities of the active external database goals. A join does not require all the data from the first table to be brought into Prolog and then for the second table in the join to be processed. One record from the first table is processed and then the second table is processed until backtracking forces the search back to the first table. Hence, all space recovery can be done on-the-fly just by resetting pointers from the backtrack stack; dangling pointers in the hash table are harmless, and tokenizing is rapid because the number of external fields is kept to a minimum.

The cursor-stacking mechanism means that recursive searches on the same table are possible.

3.2.3 The cut as applied to the database

When a cut is performed in Prolog, all backtrack points as far back as the parent goal are removed from the backtrack stack. This stack holds current search information and other housekeeping parameters to allow Prolog to continue from the choice point. If the cut invoked has subgoals at the same level or deeper in the solution tree that involve Mimer accesses then the search information is not available to Prolog but rather resides in a static memory area of the interface routines. The relevant values are the cursors associated with each open table. Prolog must communicate to the interface that a cut has taken place and the relevant cursors are to be discarded ('popped').

The solution to this was to count all discarded subgoals caused by the cut that involved Mimer accesses and to keep the count value global in order that any subsequent routine that used the interface could pass the value to the interface. The interface routine then only has to pop the given count of disused cursors before performing the required table access.

3.2.4 'Call' and 'not' as applied to the database

It may not be immediately apparent that there is a problem here. The fact that Prolog's depth-first strategy is mimicked in the interface by a LIFO stack of table cursors has the consequence that whenever there is a Prolog construct that defies this search mechanism then some way must be found to communicate the necessary information to the interface to manage the cursors. We have such a case with both 'call' and 'not'. If a 'called' predicate creates a backtrack point, this should be discarded upon completion of the 'call'. If a 'notted' goal succeeds and hence fails owing to the 'not' it must not leave any backtrack points 'inside' the 'not'. Both 'call' and 'not' are implemented in similar ways — the basic goal-solving routine 'solve' is called recursively for the new goal sequence generating a new set of local variables. At the end of a goal sequence, space is recovered from the backtrack stack by simulating backtracking where there is no backtracking. In addition to this it is necessary to count any cursors that may have been opened in the current invocation of 'solve' so that this number can be given to the interface at the next table access or update. A simple loop is used to examine the heads of the goals in the current active portion of the backtrack stack and sum those that involve table accesses, and this is passed to the interface at the next table access as the number of cursors to discard in a similar fashion to 'cut'.

3.2.5 Optimization with simple search restrictions

If there is a simple restriction on the value of a field being accessed of the form: X<, >, >=, <=, +, − Value, then this can be included directly in the goal representing the access, and the database search will be restricted by the criteria given. The keyword 'opt' is used by the interpreter to identify the occurrence of the optimizing term which will take the form: opt(Var relational operator Value). For example, the following query would retrieve and write, from the table associated with the predicate 'tab', all the first column values which begin with the letter 'J':

```
?-tab(opt(A+'J')),writeln(A),fail.
```

The restriction operator is passed via the template followed by the Value. This is then interpreted by the relevant interface routine (accesstable, delrec or updaterec) as a select condition.

3.3 Storing and loading rules from Mimer tables

Primitive functions are provided for storing the source code of rules to tables and retrieving them. These facilities cause automatic updates of system tables that record what rules are in each table and what application each table is associated with. These features provide the application developer with the tools to aid the modularity and structure of his rule base. Further tables can be defined for documentation reasons and rules defined to interact with various tables give unlimited potential for tailoring the development environment. These features are more fully described in [5].

3.4 Adding, deleting and amending rows in database tables

Records may be added to a table using the predicate 'addrec'. Assuming the table TABNAMES has been associated, via an 'external' directive, with the predicate 'tab', a record (row) could be added thus:

```
?-addrec(tab('MATTHEW','MARK','LUKE','JOHN','PETER')).
```

Similarly, records may be deleted by means of the 'delrec' predicate:

```
?-delrec(tab('MATTHEW')).
```

This would delete the first row in the table 'tab' whose first column value is MATTHEW. Note that even though the table has five columns, only one 'match' field is given: the interface will work on just the amount of information with which it is provided. Both of these systems predicates use the template for passing the fields of the record. A choice point is created for 'delrec' but not for 'addrec'. This is because the latter must identify the key completely.

To change a table row, the predicate 'updaterec' is used. This uses two templates: the first contains the 'matching' information which will enable the interface to access the required row, and the second contains the new values for the columns which are to be updated; for example,

```
?-updaterec(tab('MATTHEW'),tab(_,_,'SIMON')).
```

would change the value of the third column to SIMON of the first row in the table 'tab' whose first column has the value MATTHEW.

3.5 Creating and removing databank tables

3.5.1 Creating databank tables

New tables may be created in a databank using the predicate 'create_table'. Its parameters are the table name, followed by, for each column required in the table, the column name, type (character, integer or floating point), length (in bytes) and whether or not it forms part of the primary key. For example:

```
?-create_table('NEWTAB','COL1',c,5,k,'COL2',i,4,n,'COL3',f,4,n).
```

will create a table called 'NEWTAB' in the current databank with three columns: COL1 which is of type character, length 5 bytes, forming (part of) the primary key; COL2 which is of type integer, length 4 bytes, non-key; COL3 which is floating point, length 4 bytes, non-key.

3.5.2 Removing databank tables

Tables may be removed from a databank using the predicate 'delete_table'. It has one parameter: the table name. The table will be removed irrespective of whether or not it contains data.

4. PERFORMANCE CONSIDERATIONS

In order to assess performance, several tests on retrieval times were made and compared to application programs created by Mimer's program generator, PG (for Fortran) and Mimer's query language, QL. The tests were to retrieve all rows from a single table, to 'join' two tables using keys, and to join two and three tables without using keys. No 'select' conditions were given in any case.

The tests were conducted using three tables, 'TEST1', 'TEST2' and 'TEST3'. All had two columns 'COL1' and 'COL2', COL1 being the key. Tables TEST1 and TEST3 had the integers from 0 upwards in COL1 (integer length 4) and their character representations (in words, character length 30) in COL2. Table TEST2 simply had the two columns transposed, i.e.

TEST1	
COL1	COL2
0	zero
1	one
2	two
up to	up to
197	one hundred and ninety seven
198	one hundred and ninety eight
199	one hundred and ninety nine

TEST2	
COL1	COL2
eight	8
eighteen	18
eighty	80
up to	
twenty two	22
two	2
zero	0

SINGLE TABLE			
No. of records	QL	PG	Prolog
5	1	5	1
20	2	6	2
50	3	8	5
100	6	11	8
200	12	20	21

The commands were

Single table:

```
QL    : get test1.*;
PG    : program test1-get test1.*;
Prolog: ?-test1(A,B),writeln(A,B),fail.
```

Join on 2 tables using key:

```
QL    : get test2.* whe test2.col1 eq test1.col2
```

```
        and test2.col2 eq test1.col1;
PG    : program test2=get unsorted test2.* where
        test2.col1 eq test1.col2 and test2.col2 eq test1.col1;
Prolog: ?-test1(A,B),test2(B,A),writeln(B,A),fail.
```

Join on 2 tables not using key:

```
QL    : get test2.* whe test2.col2 eq test1.col1;
PG    : program test3=get unsorted test2.* where
        test2.col2 eq test1.col1;
Prolog: ?-test1(A,B),test2(C,A),writeln(C,A),fail.
```

Join on 3 tables not using keys:

```
QL    : get test3.* whe test2.col2 eq test1.col1
        and test3.col2 eq test2.col1;
PG    : program test4=get unsorted test3.* where
        test2.col2 eq test1.col1 and test3.col2 eq test2.col1;
Prolog: ?-test1(A,B),test2(C,A),test3(D,C),writeln(D,C),fail.
```

The results were as follows:

SINGLE TABLE

No. of records	QL	PG	Prolog
5	1	5	1
20	2	6	2
50	3	8	5
100	6	11	8
200	12	20	21

JOIN ON 2 TABLES: USING KEY

No. of records	QL	PG	Prolog
5	2	5	2
20	4	7	5
50	8	10	14
100	13	17	27
200	24	28	59

JOIN ON 2 TABLES: USING NON-KEY

No. of records	QL	PG	Prolog
5	2	5	2
20	7	10	7
50	31	34	33
100	108	110	111
200	424	421	442

JOIN ON 3 TABLES: USING NON-KEY

No. of records	QL	PG	Prolog
5	12	16	12
20	46	50	46
50	126	131	129
100	302	318	307
200	805	817	888

All times are in seconds of real time on a VAX 11/730 under VMS 4.3 using Mimer PG version 3.2.12 and Mimer QL version 3.2.7c.

The tests clearly indicate that Prolog's speed is comparable to that of both QL and PG except where keys are used. This is thought to be due to the fact that QL and PG read the index to a table into main memory and pin it there until the entire query has been solved. This facility is not available to Prolog, and it is thought that the index is being read into memory as each row is retrieved. It should be clear, from a consideration of the software solution, that the access time for each record is a constant (caused by creating and dismembering the template) plus whatever function is caused by the database library routines. The constant is because the interpreter is virtually in the same state before every access, because of the on-the-fly recovery of space taken by unreferenced strings. There are slight differences due to the current contents of the hash table, but these do not affect any particular access more than another except for the random element of some strings from a record just happening to already be hashed because they have occurred elsewhere in the program.

It is clear that, except in the very simplest cases, Prolog's queries are more concise. This is even more apparent where select conditions are used: the more complex the query, the more concise Prolog is compared to QL or PG.

It is not known why the program generators performs so badly. Not only is it slower than QL in most cases and quicker than Prolog in only a few cases, but no account has been taken of the overhead in generating, compiling and linking code: even in the simple examples above, this was in the region of four minutes in each case.

5. CONCLUSIONS

We have prototyped several applications which have fully demonstrated the advantages of this system. As well as the usually expected virtues of programming in Prolog, the following additional features are available.

(1) The ability to process large datasets. The Prolog–Mimer system can access virtually unlimited amounts of data without incurring the need for garbage collection.
(2) The ability to build rule-based expert systems 'sitting on top of' existing databases.
(3) An extremely succinct query language.
(4) The suitability for real-time applications. The tight coupling allows the Prolog rule base to interact with a database that is being updated by simultaneous processes.
(5) Access times approaching those achieved with standard database tools.

It remains to develop Prolog tools to enhance the system to a complete database programming environment.

ACKNOWLEDGEMENT

We would like to thank the Savant Institute of Carnforth, Lancashire, for providing funding to undertake this research.

REFERENCES

[1] Risch, T., *A Data Base Extension of Prolog and its Implementation,* Upsalla Programming Methodology and Artificial Intelligence Laboratory, Department of Computer Science, University of Uppsala, 750 02, Uppsala, Sweden. 18 Aug., 1982.
[2] Lucas, R. J., Expert system modelling using a logic language and a relational database, in *4th Int. Conf. on Systems Engineeing,* Coventry Polytechnic, 1985, 10–12 Sept.
[3] Farris, C. D. and Lucas, R. J., The batch selection by a Prolog rule-base of objects on a conveyor for paint spraying, pp. 215–224 in *Systems Fault Diagnostics, Reliability and Related Knowledge-based Approaches,* D. Reidel, 1987.
[4] Lucas, R. J., An expert system to detect burglars using a logic language and relational database, in *5th Brit. Nat. Conf. on Databases,* CUP, 1986.
[5] Lucas, R. J., *Database applications using Prolog,* Ellis Horwood, 1988.
[6] Jarke, M. and Vassiliou, Y., Databases and expert systems: opportunities and architectures for integration, in *New Applications of Databases,* Academic Press, 1984.

6

A generalized interface between Prolog and relational databases

Tim Irving
Managing Director, Quintec Systems Limited

ABSTRACT

The objective of this chapter is to define a minimum specification for an interface between a logic programming language, Prolog, and a relational database system. The functional requirements and practical uses for such an interface are discussed. A generalized implementation scheme for such a database is defined in terms of both Prolog and the underlying database system. This scheme is related to the various implementation techniques and interfaces provided by the main commercial database systems. A commercial interface between SD-Prolog and dBASE/III is described as a working example.

1. INTRODUCTION

Recent years have seen considerable growth in the research, development and commercial application of artificial intelligence (AI) techniques. Much of this activity has been concerned with the development of knowledge-based systems aimed at reproducing or complementing the expert reasoning capabilities of scarce or expensive human specialists. Many blue-chip industrial companies are now actively engaged in evaluating the technology of AI and in applying it to such tasks as process control, fault diagnosis, planning and resource management.

AI is now showing some signs of becoming a mature technology, and an ever increasing range of AI products and tools is available to the commercial developer. Many of these products fall into the category of 'shells', where the user is forced to model his application in terms of an often rather restricted set of representation and interference techniques.

For anything more than relatively trivial applications, the developer needs the power, flexibility and richness provided by lower-level AI languages such as LISP or Prolog. For historical reasons, LISP has until recently been the dominant tool in this field and was used to implement most of the early American expert systems (MYCIN, DENDRAL, and others).

However, the announcement in 1981 of the Japanese 'Fifth Generation Computer Project' has caused considerable growth in the use of logic programming as a general-purpose tool for AI and expert systems development. The logic programming language, Prolog, is now well established as a powerful research and implementation tool, and the number and sophistication of commercial Prolog systems is increasing rapidly.

As Prolog begins to be used for more ambitious projects where the size of the internal database (roughly proportional to the number of Prolog clauses) exceeds a few magabytes or so, then the developer becomes aware of a number of problems inherent to large Prolog databases. Very often these are the classical problems of performance and data management which have already been successfully addressed by the designers of relational database systems. The representation of at least part of the internal Prolog clause store using a commercial database tool therefore has many advantages.

This chapter discusses some of the limitations of current Prolog systems in dealing with large databases, and shows how external database systems can be used to overcome these problems. In addition, interaction between Prolog and a commercial database system provides many other advantages, particularly in complex multi-tasking environments.

The ultimate promise of Prolog will only be fulfilled when the powerful inferencing and selection capabilities of Prolog are allowed to interact with real-world data rather than the restricted closed world of the internal clause store. Towards this goal, the specification for a generalized database interface is discussed, including the design and implementation of a fast interface between a compiled Prolog system and dBASE/III.

2. PROBLEMS INHERENT TO THE INTERNAL PROLOG DATABASE

A Prolog program consists of a set of facts and rules expressed in a variant of first-order predicate logic. Each logical statement in a Prolog program is represented by a 'clause' which may be unconditionally true (a 'fact') or true provided some sequence of sub-goals can be shown to be true (a 'rule'). A single complex relation (a 'predicate') may be expressed as a set of related clauses which together correspond to a procedure in conventional computing terms. Prolog uses the Resolution Principle of Robinson (1965) to solve problems in a goal-directed manner. Given a goal to be proved against the database, Prolog searches the clauses using a left–right depth-first strategy to match the current goal against one or more clauses (using unification as the matching algorithm).

Most Prolog systems represent the set of clauses for a program in primary memory, either as literal representations of the Prolog source clause (in interpretive systems) or as executable machine code (in compiled systems). The Prolog database is usually organized as a heap, with clauses dynamically allocated (asserted) and deleted as records within a network of linked lists.

Such a representation works very well where the number of clauses and relations is less than a few thousand, but begins to degrade as the size of the system increases. There are a number of reasons for this.

2.1 Memory constraints

Because the Prolog clauses are held in main memory, there are severe constraints on the maximum size of the system. Many Prolog systems make use of virtual memory techniques to page sections of the database to and from backing storage. However, the nature of most Prolog programs means that database access is often very random in nature, causing much paging of the virtual memory system, leading to poor performance. Most hardware virtual memory systems operate optimally where there is a high degree of locality of reference, as is usually the case with conventional procedural languages.

2.2 Clause indexing

Almost all Prolog systems use hashing techniques to identify the set of clauses for the relation corresponding to the current goal (i.e. having the same functor). Early Prolog systems searched this subset of clauses in a simple sequential manner. Where a large declarative relation is represented as many unit clauses (a table) this technique is slow and inefficient, particularly in relations where only one or two clauses match and most of the clauses must be tried fruitlessly.

More advanced compiler-based Prolog systems extend the hashing mechanism within predicates so that one or more arguments of the goal can be used to select a further more restricted subset of candidate clauses which must then be tried sequentially using unification and backtracking. This scheme works very well for the relatively static clauses representing the procedural part of the program but often does not allow indexed predicates to be modified by the addition or deletion of component clauses, as is often the case with declarative predicates representing dynamic information.

What is needed is a more general clause indexing scheme which allows fast selection of a small group of candidate clauses which are most likely to unify with the selection goal and which also allows dynamic modification of the clause store without extensive re-compilation and re-hashing. The associative lookup techniques based on B-trees and other structures used in conventional databases often provide a suitable mechanism.

2.3 Integration with other systems

The Prolog database represents a closed world within which the program reasons. In using Prolog to solve real-world problems it is obviously necessary to represent external concepts and objects in terms of the clauses and relations manipulated directly by Prolog. This is adequate for stand-alone systems where Prolog is the sole operator on the data of the application and where a direct clausal representation is optimal. Increasingly the need is being seen to bring the high-level reasoning typical of Prolog-based systems to bear upon volumes of existing data represented in some non-

Prolog manner — often in the form of a relational database. Such external databases will typically be created and maintained by other programs within a multi-tasking environment. In such an environment it is essential that all participating systems have shared access to the database, and this precludes its direct representation in terms of Prolog clauses.

3. THE INTEGRATION OF PROLOG AND RDBMS

The integration of Prolog with an external relational database management system (RDBMS) both solves most of the technical limitations of the memory-based internal Prolog database and provides a powerful new tool for use in database management.

By representing some subset of the Prolog database as a disk-based database, the limitations of size are immediately removed. Furthermore the problems of effective indexing of large databases in the presence of frequent transactions have already been largely solved in the best commercial RDBMSs.

The powerful pattern-matching and reasoning capabilities of Prolog make it an ideal tool for the implementation of appropriate high-level facilities sitting on top of conventional DBMSs. For example, Prolog can be used to apply expert-system rules or other heuristics to the analysis of databases — producing trend reports, predictions or management recommendations.

4. PROLOG/DBMS INTERFACE: A MINIMUM SPECIFICATION

Given the desirability for the interfacing of Prolog to a conventional RDBMS, what should the minimum functionality of such an interface include? The following points are certainly not meant as an exhaustive list but cover the key features to be considered.

4.1 Generality of representation

Within a conventional database record, each field is typically a scalar unstructured object (string or number). In contrast, the expressive power of Prolog allows for complex tree-like data structures and lists to be constructed and used in pattern matching. Any database interference must ideally support the mapping of complex Prolog terms into linear database records in a way which is transparent to the unification and backtracking mechanisms of Prolog.

Furthermore Prolog implements the concept of the logical variable — a feature largely unexploited in conventional database technology. The ideal database interface should allow the unrestricted representation of free variables within externally held clauses.

4.2 Uniform syntax

Clauses held in the external RDBMS should be represented at the Prolog source level in exactly the same form as standard clauses held within Prolog's internal database. This allows flexibility in coding and testing where the exact representation of a particular set of clauses need not be hard-wired at the design stage. A uniform syntax allows clauses to be transferred between internal and external databases very easily and transparently.

4.3 Transparent unification

Unification is the key operation used by Prolog to select clauses from the database. Any database interface where the clauses are represented by external database records must also allow the purely generalized use of unification in matching the current goal against external records.

4.4 Transparent backtracking

Backtracking is the key control mechanism used by Prolog in searching the database for matching clauses. Whenever the current goal cannot be proved because no unifiable clause exists, then Prolog invokes backtracking to retry the most recently matching predicate and explores an alternative search path. In addition to its role in exploring the search tree, backtracking is also used as a procedural technique to give the effect of iteration.

Any database interface must fully support the use of backtracking in searching an external database. This requires the Prolog system to record references to external 'choice points' where further external database clauses remain to be tried. Where internal Prolog choice points contain a reference to the next alternative clause (usually its address), external choice points must contain an implementation-dependent database reference to the next alternative record(s).

Furthermore, the use of the Prolog 'cut' mechanism must also be fully supported for external databases. The effect of the 'cut' is to selectively remove choice points back to some specified point in the search tree, thereby rendering part of the program deterministic.

4.5 Transparent assert/retract

Prolog allows dynamic modification of its internal database through the built-in functions **assert** and **retract**. This capability should also be supported for clauses held externally where practical. Where shared access to the external database is supported, modifications will usually involve some form of database 'locking' protocol.

4.6 Low-performance overhead

An obvious requirement is that the database interface does not impose an unacceptable overhead when accessing clauses held on an external RDMBS. For standard sequential clause lookup, external access will always be much slower than that for internal clauses, particularly in compiler-based Prolog systems where the internal clauses are actually executed directly as machine code. However, indexed access, using one or more arguments in the query to select subsets of potentially matching records, can be expected to be acceptably fast using an external DBMS.

In designing the detailed interface, the following maxim should be borne in mind: 'Never put off till run-time that which can be done at compile-time'. This implies that, as far as possible, the mapping from external DBMS format onto internal Prolog form should be compiled and not interpreted at run-time. Given a definition of the structure of the external database records for a particular external predicate, the Prolog support system is able to compile an access predicate which performs both the database access and the format mapping with the minimum overhead.

5. A GENERALIZED PROLOG/RDBMS INTERFACE SCHEME

The construction of a practical interface between Prolog and some external database system conforming to the above specification requires

(a) that the host Prolog system supports the basic scalar data types found in databases record fields: strings, integer and floating-point numbers,
(b) that the host Prolog system supports the creation and invocation of low-level sub-programs written in some suitable systems programming language such as 'C',
(c) that the host Prolog system is sufficiently well integrated with such external languages to allow for the creation and unification of Prolog data structures (variables, atoms, strings, numbers and tuples) directly within the low-level language,
(d) the scheme described within this chapter assumes that Prolog data structures can be destructively assigned to from the low-level support language. Where this act of scarilege is prohibited then the effect can be simulated using global Prolog 'states' or even assert/retract as a last resort.

The outline implementation of a generalized interface will be described in terms of

(i) the high-level Prolog support code which is very largely independent of the particular external database adopted,
(ii) the low-level database access code which must interact directly with the database software. Although specific to a particular database, this code will be functionally similar for most commercial systems.

The basic interface described below makes the following important design assumptions.

(a) All external predicates consist only of unit clauses.
(b) All external clauses contain only ground terms, i.e. terms containing no uninstantiated variables.

5.1 The high-level Prolog interface

The most efficient and flexible technique for constructing a database interface to Prolog is to create an access predicate for each external database predicate (corresponding to a single database table or relation in the RDBMS). Each access predicate is in fact a standard internal Prolog predicate which performs the following tasks.

(i) mapping the current goal format onto the external database record format.
(ii) Performing successive unifications with external database records, instantiating Prolog variables where necessary.
(iii) Creating a choice point where more than one external database record matches (unifies with) the current query.

The general form for an external access predicate is as follows:

```
(1)     <clause head in internal Prolog format> :-
(2)         <initialize external database for access>,
(3)         <initialize internal index to [1] >,
            repeat,
            (
(4)         <unify next database record from index [I]>
            ;
(5)         <test index for last record marker>, !,fail
            ).
```

where

(1) The clause head performs the unification with the current goal, instantiating variables appropriately.
(2) This goal is an implementation-dependent call to the low-level database support code which prepares the external database for access. For many database systems this may not be required.
(3) This goal creates a local Prolog data structure which holds the current index into the database for the predicate concerned. For simplicity, integer indices may be used with the first record for the predicate having a conceptual index of 1. The low-level database access code can easily map this index onto whatever indexing scheme is actually used by the host RDBMS.
(4) This goal invokes the low-level support code and passes the set of Prolog terms to be unified with the corresponding fields of the next record retrieved from the database (starting at the specified index position). If a matching record exists then the Prolog index is updated accordingly to be used as the starting point for the next access for this invocation, and the access succeeds. If no matching record exists than the Prolog index is set to some special marker such as 'end_of_table', and the low-level access call fails.
(5) This goal examines the index to determine whether it has been set to the marker for 'end_of_table'. If this test succeeds the following **!,fail** will cause the entire access predicate to fail, corresponding to the usual Prolog semantics. Normally, where further records exist, this goal fails, causing the next record to be accessed using the low-level access goal (4).

The predicate index is normally represented as the Prolog term **[Index]**, i.e. a list containing the integer **Index**. By holding the index as a list (or a tuple), the term is allocated global storage on Prolog's term stack and will thus survive popping of the environment stack on success of the predicate. This technique ensures that the database reference is preserved between successive calls of the predicate on backtracking, allowing the next matching record to be retrieved.

The low-level database access and unification procedure, **unify_external**, must be coded in the low-level support language and usually has the following calling pattern:

unify_external(Relation(Field1,Field2, . . Fieldn), [Index])

where

Relation is the name of the external relation (database table) to be accessed, passed as the functor of a term.

Fieldi is unified with the *i*th field of the record in the database table specified by **Relation**.

Index is the integer index (passed within a list) used to specify the point from which the database table should be searched.

The internal details of **unify_external** are described in the next section.

The creation (compilation) of correct access functions for external predicates should be made a responsibility of the host Prolog system. This is best achieved by providing the system user with a set of system primitives which allow for the declaration of external predicates and the specification of the mapping form internal Prolog to external database formats.

For example, the directive

external <Prolog Template> : <Database Template>.

declares that <**Prolog Template**> is to be held on an external database in a format defined by <**Database Template**>. The correspondance of variable names between the two templates provides the detailed mapping information.

The **external** directive performs the following actions:

(i) Extracts name and arity of the internal predicate and the external database table.
(ii) Initializes and interrogates the host database system to determine that the specified table exists.
(iii) Generates and compiles (asserts) a suitable access function into the internal Prolog database.
(iv) Asserts a declaration into the system symbol table identifying the predicate as 'external'. This fact is used by system meta predicates such as **assert**, **retract** and **clause** to ensure that database modification is transparent.

Once an external predicate has been declared **external** it may be accessed immediately and transparently as a standard Prolog predicate.

Example

Suppose that a set of simple personnel records is to be held as a table within an external database and accessed as Prolog unit clauses of the general form

```
person( name(Surname, Initials),
        Employee_No,
        address( A1,A2,A3,A4 ),
        dept( Dept,Manager ),
        grade( Class,Salary )
      )
```

The above clause is to be mapped onto a linear database record having the structure

```
person( Surname,Initials, Employee_No, A1,A2,A3,A4,
        Dept,Manager, Class,Salary )
```

where each of the above fields is to be mapped onto an atomic Prolog data type (atom, integer or real).

The following **external** declaration will perform the required consistency checking and generate the required access function:

```
external    person( name(Surname,Initials),
                    Employee_No,
                    address( A1,A2,A3,A4 ),
                    dept( Dept,Manager ),
                    grade( Class, Salary ) )
            :
            person( Surname, Initials,
                    Employee_No, A1,A2,A3,A4,
                    Dept.Manager,
                    Class,Salary ).
```

The above declaration will generate the following access function to perform the required database access and unification:

```
person( name(Surname, Initials),
        Employee_No,
        address( A1,A2,A3,A4 ),
        dept( Dept,Manager ),
        grade( Class, Salary ) ) :-
            Reference = [1],
            repeat,
            (
            unify_external( person( Surname,Initials,
                    Employee_No, A1,A2,A3,A4,
                    Dept,Manager,Class,Salary),
                            Reference )
```

```
;
Reference = [end_of_table], !,fail
).
```

5.2 The low level database support code

This section will concentrate on the functionality of the low level support function **unify_external** to be implemented in a language such as 'C'. Low-level details of the implementation are dependent upon both the external database access mechanism and the parameter-passing mechanism provided by the host Prolog system.

The sophistication and complexity of the access function will largely depend upon the level of access provided by the host database system.

(i) Direct low-level access at the binary byte level where all record access and decoding must be explicitly hand-coded.
Example: dBASE/III from Ashton-Tate.

(ii) Intermediate-level access where a set of library functions is provided to implement the database management functions (e.g. retrieve the next record).
Example: INGRES.

(iii) High-level query language based access where each database access must dynamically generate and submit a query phrased in a language such as SQL.
Example: Oracle.

The function **unify_external** can be summarized in pseudo-code as follows:

```
unify_external(          Record,Index)
    PARAMETERS: Record:  A Prolog tuple defining the record
                Record:  name and fields.
                Index:   A Prolog list containing the
                         integer index for the next record.
    BEGIN
        Extract the functor and arity from 'Record'. Consult the
        data dictionary to identify the relation and to obtain its
        internal structure.

        Extract the index number from 'Index' and map this onto
        an internal database index into the relation.

        IF the end of the table is not reached THEN
            Read the next record from the relation into local
            storage using the index reference.

            Assign the index to the following record to the Prolog
            index number ( by destructive assignment rather
            than unification ).

            FOR each field in the local record DO
```

```
                SWITCH on the type of the ithe field:
                    CASE text:
                        Encode the field text as a Prolog atom (
                        or string ) and unify with the ith argu-
                        ment of tuple 'Record'.
                    CASE integer:
                        Encode the field text as a Prolog integer
                        number and unify with the ith argu-
                        ment of tuple 'Record'.
                    CASE float:
                        Encode the field text as a Prolog float-
                        ing number and unify with the ith
                        argument of tuple 'Record'.
                    Other data types to be handled here.
                ENDSWITCH
            ENDDO
        ELSE
            Assign the marker 'end_of_table' to the Prolog index
            number and fail.
        ENDIF
    END
```

The above scheme will require access to the data dictionary for each and every external clause retrieved. If this is expensive then the data dictionary can be accessed once only at the time that the predicate is declared **external** and used to build a local definition of the external record structure used directly by **unify_external**. This is the approach adopted in the dBASE/III interface described in the following section.

5.3 Representation of non-ground clauses

External database representation can be made far more generalized and powerful where external clauses are allowed to contain free Prolog variables.

The implementation of the Prolog variable requires that the database is able to represent a special data type — the LINK. Within a database record, a LINK field contains a reference (pointer or offset) to a field within the same record.

The first or only occurrence of a variable is represented externally by a LINK field refers to itself. Subsequent occurrences of the variable are represented by LINKs to the first occurring field of the variable.

For example, the clause **fact(equal, X,X, =, X)** could be represented by an external record of the format

```
RECORD:
    Field 1:    Text 'equal'
    Field 2:    Link (2)
    Field 3:    Link (3)
    Field 4:    Text '='
```

Field 5: Link (2)

To support LINK fields, the unification of the access template with the current database record must be extended. If the *i*th field is a LINK to itself then simply ignore it and proceed to unify the $(i+1)$th field. If the *i*th field is a LINK to the *j*th field (where $j<i$ always) then unify the *j*th and *i*th arguments in the access template.

6. AN EXAMPLE OF A COMMERCIAL PROLOG INTERFACE TO dBASE/III

The techniques described in this chapter have been used commercially to implement PROLOG/dBASE, a transport interface between SD-Prolog and dBASE/III on the IBM PC/XT/AT.

SD-Prolog is a high-performance multi-windowing Prolog environment based upon an incremental compiler. SD-Prolog provides a very flexible interface to 'C', allowing both 'C' and Prolog to call each other with the unrestricted passing of Prolog arguments between languages. The 'C' programmer is fully supported with tools to access and create Prolog data structures and to invoke the Prolog unification and backtracking systems.

dBASE/III is a very popular database system for PCs, and provides relatively rudimentary database functions using its own proprietary query language. Database relations are held in text form in indexed files, one file per relation. The low-level programmer is not supported (at the time of writing) with any high-level database access library, and all access from 'C' must decode the binary disk files explicity. In addition, the system provides no data dictionary as such. The structure of each relation is encoded in an obscure binary format in the header of each database file, and it is the responsibility of the Prolog interface to access and decode these headers and to read and decode successive records.

PROLOG/dBASE allows dBASE II/III database files (.DBF) to be accessed directly from programs written in SD-Prolog. Using PROLOG/dBASE, dBASE II/III records appear as standard Prolog facts and can be selected using the powerful mechanisms of pattern matching (unification) and backtracking.

PROLOG/dBASE provides the following interface predicates callable from SD-Prolog.

open_database(Name)

Opens the named dBASE II/III database (.DBF file) as a Prolog stream and creates an access procedure for the records of the database with functor 'Name'. The arity of the predicate is determined by inspection of the database file header. Unlike standard dBASE II/III, PROLOG/dBASE buffers all database access. For sequential un-indexed access, this buffered approach leads to access speed several times better than dBASE/III itself (doing a 'join' between two databases, for example).

In the absence of a data dictionary for dBASE/III, the **open_database** predicate reads the database header and builds an internal description of the format of database records for use by the **record** facility shown below.

For example,

open_database(person)

will open the dBASE/III database file PERSON.DBF, allocate suitable buffer space, inspect the file format and create an access function for predicate **person** with the correct arity.

close_database(Name)
Closes a currently active database file and releases all storage buffers associated with the database.

record(Record,Ref)
Unifies 'Record' with the first/next matching record with reference number 'Ref' from the relevant active database. The record is specified as a Prolog tuple whose functor defines the database name. The reference 'Ref' may be used in two ways: if uninstantiated, 'Ref' is instantiated to the reference number of 'Record'; if instantiated to the positive integer, record number 'Ref' is retrieved from the database. Thus, this predicate may be used either within a backtracking loop to read successive matching records or to read a specific record by reference number.

Normally **record** is not called directly but is hidden within the access predicate for each external predicate created by **open_database**. For example,

person(A1,A2, . . An) :– record(person(A1,A2, . . An), Ref).

update(Record, Ref)
Updates the record with reference number 'Ref' with the specified data. Thus **update** may be used to perform in-place editing/update of dBASE records and could be hidden within the standard system predicate **assert**.

append(Record)
Appends the specified 'Record' to the end of the relevant active database.

delete(Record, Ref)
Marks the first/next matching record from the relevant database for deletion. This predicate works identically to **record** so that the record can also be read as well as marked for deletion.

recall(Record, Ref)
Unmarks the first/next matching record from the relevant database for deletion. This allows previously deleted records to be 're-called'.

PROLOG/dBASE supports all the standard data types of dBASE II/III, mapping onto standard SD-Prolog data types as follows.

— Type 'C': Character strings.
Unifiable with Prolog strings.

— Type 'N': Numeric fields, either integer or floating point.
Unifiable with Prolog integers or floats.

— Type 'L': Logical fields, .T. or .F.
Unifiable with atoms **true** or **false**.

— Type 'M': Memo text fields (dBASE/III only).
Unifiable with Prolog strings.

— Type 'D': date dd/mm/yyyy fields (dBASE/III only).
Unifiable with terms of the form DD/MM/YYYY.

7. CONCLUSION

This chapter has highlighted the desirability of coupling the high-level reasoning features of Prolog with the efficient mass-storage and retrieval capabilities of commercial RDBMSs. The basic requirements of such an interface in terms of its constraints on the Prolog programmer are in general straightforward to implement.

The conciseness of Prolog means that the implementation of a transparent interface supporting syntax transformations, unification and non-determinism is very straightforward. The effort required to implement the low-level access procedures will vary considerably with the facilities provided by the host database and Prolog systems.

Commercial interfaces between Prolog and large-scale relational databases are becoming increasingly available, and the next few years can expect to see Prolog-based tools in widespread use within conventional data-processing environments.

REFERENCES

[1] Moffat, D. S. and Gray, P. M. D., Interfacing Prolog to a Persistent Data Store, *3rd Int. Conf. on Logic Programming*, London, 1986.

[2] Gray, P. M. D., *Logic, Algebra and Databases*, Ellis Horwood, Chichester, 1984.

[3] Codd, E. F., A Relational Model of Data for Large Shared Data Banks, *Comm. ACM*, **13** No 6, pp. 377–387.

[4] *SD-Prolog Programmers Reference Manual*, Systems Designers plc, Camberley, 1986.

7

The interaction between BIM_Prolog and relational databases

Raf Venken
BIM R&D, Kwikstraat 4, 3078 Everberg, Belgium
Anne Mulkers
Catholic University Leuven, Dept. of Computer Science, Celestijnenlaan 200 A, 3030 Heverlee, Belgium

ABSTRACT

This chapter summarizes the results of the study of the different compilation techniques to transform Prolog queries in conjuctions of database calls and the investigation of the different ways and techniques to effectively integrate an existing Prolog system and a relational database system.

We describe a few extensions that have been made to BIM_Prolog in order to enable the efficient implementation of database couplings.

We further describe the results of an effective integration between BIM_Prolog and Unify. This interface and the interface with Ingres and SunUnify are available from BIM.

1. INTRODUCTION

We will not elaborate the rationale for an extension of a Prolog system with a secondary storage system, but we rather restrict ourselves by quoting the main motivations: access to very large amounts of elementary facts, need to share data between different users, and access to operational data already residing in existing databases.

One approach to extending Prolog with an external storage is to integrate a suitable file system into the Prolog interpreter. The advantage of this approach is that the access to elementary facts can be realized very efficiently by implementing a dedicated retrieval scheme for the Prolog partial match queries. The manipulation of the facts on secondary storage is invisible to the user; the access and manipulation of elementary facts is translated automatically by the dedicated Prolog system in a series of elementary manipulations of the underlying dedicated file system. Examples of this approach are described in [1], where Prolog is extended with a multi-level B+ tree mechanism, in [2] and [3] where a multi-key hashing method for dynamic file access into MU-Prolog is incorporated, and in [4] where a balanced and nested GRID filestructure is described.

The disadvantage of these approaches, however, is that the file system is dedicated to the Prolog type of data access and is not necessarily suited to access by other software. On the other hand, the only way to access the data residing in existing, and possibly huge, databases is to convert them into the dedicated file system, which can be as impractical and also time consuming.

The alternative solution, which we adopted in BIM_Prolog, is to use a conventional relational database system which solves the fact storage and retrieval problem as well as sharing data between different users, and to integrate it, as a 'back-end', with the deductive part (the inference mechanism of Prolog).

2. TRANSFORMING PROLOG QUERIES INTO DATABASE CALLS

There are essentially two ways to transform a Prolog query into a conjunction of database calls. The first is the so-called 'compiled approach' (see the work of Reiter, Kellogs *et al.* and Chang in [5]), the second the 'interpretive approach' (see [1] or [6]). In this section we also describe the partial evaluation technique and show how it can be used as a compromise between the former two methods.

2.1 The compiled approach

In the compiled approach it is assumed that the procedural statements are non-recursive. The technique consists of applying procedural statements until all goal statements consist of relations that are known to be stored in the database. The result is then a conjunction of database calls which is passed to the database for processing. There are two methods to realize this approach: one requires some modifications to be made to the Prolog system, which essentially consist of delaying database calls until one has one conjunction of database calls that can be handled by the relational database; the second method avoids these changes to the Prolog system by the construction of a Prolog metasystem, a Prolog system written in Prolog, that simulates the behaviour of the former system.

The advantage of the compiled approach is that the calls to the database are clustered together in a conjunction which can be subject to some more or less elaborated optimization process (see e.g. [7]). One great disadvantage of the compiled approach is the restriction to non-recursive rules. This problem has been partially solved in [8] where it is shown how recursive queries can be compiled into iterative programs. Further investigation in [9] points out how an extension of this technique can be exploited in a deductive database.

2.2 The interpretive approach

In the interpretive approach one interleaves searches of the database with deductive steps. Each time a database call is encountered by the Prolog system, this call is sent to the database for evaluation; the Prolog system resumes execution with values obtained from the first resulting tuple, and the remaining tuples of the solution of the query are consumed one by one on backtracking.

One possibility of implementing this scheme is to change the database system in such a way that it always gives the first tuple which answers the query to the Prolog system. The next tuples are provided on demand of the backtracking mechanism of the Prolog system. This approach can be implemented with a stack, all tuples being stored on a stack and consumed one by one by the Prolog system on backtracking. It appears that one only needs one stack for storing the resulting tuples of consecutive database calls. Furher details concerning this approach can be found in [1]. In this chapter we will describe an implementation of such an interface between BIM_ Prolog and Unify.

A variant of this approach is the so-called set-oriented approach [6]. In contrast with the previous approach, which typically generates the search tree one node at a time, the set-oriented approach manages the entire unification set at each node. The Prolog system has a set of substitutions instead of a single substitution at each node, and the operations are performed on the whole set. The task of generating and manipulating, including intersection and union, of unification sets is delegated to the database system which can handle it in an efficient way. This approach requires a considerable change in the Prolog system and a special database system which can take advantage of some parallel processing.

The former approach seems to be the closest to the logic programming philosophy. In the context of interactive systems for querying databases though, it seems appropriate to consider an alternative method which, as the compiled approach, could permit an optimization process on the database calls. The partial evaluation technique adapted for database manipulation seems a possible alternative.

2.3 Partial evaluation

The initial goal of partial evaluation [10] is to transform Prolog programs into more efficient ones. This optimization is accomplished by mainly three techniques: instantiate the parameters of a program by propagating values for top-level arguments through the program (perform the unification process at compile time); reduce the number of logical inferences by opening calls; and by evaluating builtin predicates ('builtins' for short) whenever possible. Partial evaluation can be seen as a compile-time application of the basic mechanisms, which are normally applied at run-time. A Prolog program is converted to a semantically equivalent Prolog program, where unification and evaluation are already partially done, thus requiring fewer logical inferences at run-time. A description of the building of a partial evaluation system starting from a Prolog meta-interpreter is given in [11].

The effect of the partial evaluation on a program interacting with a relational database [12] is very similar to that of the compiled approach: the transformed program consists of a conjunction of builtins (which were not evaluatable at compile time), calls to recursive rules and database calls. Each recursive rule is partially evaluated to a similar conjunction of calls. As in the compiled approach, the calls to the database are clustered together and can be optimized using statistical [7] or semantic information [13,14].

The evaluation of the resulting programs, however, is very similar to the interpretive approach. A normal Prolog system can be used to solve the builtins and recursive rules; the conjunctions of database calls are transferred to the database system; the results, a set of tuples, are again consumed one by one on backtracking of the Prolog system. This approach can therefore exploit an integration like the stack-oriented one described above.

Another effective integration, exploiting partial evaluation in a slightly different way, has been realized in the context of the Epsilon Esprit project 530; see [15] for details.

3. INTEGRATION OF A PROLOG SYSTEM AND A RELATIONAL DATABASE SYSTEM

A number of Prolog systems provide access to existing databases. They use different interface methods. The BIM_Prolog strategy will be compared with the choices made by other similar projects. Important aspects of such an interface are of course the efficiency of the data access, the buffer space management needed for intermediate results, and the flexibility to access other database systems.

In [16] an interface to the INGRES database is described that requires access to, and modifications of, the INGRES system source code. The implementation provides access to a specific database system only. In [17] an interface is described that would be portable to all SQL database systems (like UNIFY), but it also requires some modifications to the user interface normally aupplied by those database systems (for example, the format in which answers are returned).

The C-interface of BIM_Prolog provides an easy way of implementing interfaces with different external databases such as INGRES, UNIFY ORACLE and other relational subsystems such as the one described in [1], without modifying the database systems, provided that they have an interface with a general-purpose programming language such as C (Pascal or Fortran).

3.1 Level of access

On the functional level there are different ways to access a relational database system:

On the upper layer we could think of a system that translates Prolog database queries into a SQL-type of query language. These queries could be answered by a standard database system, which only requires a very simple interface that fits in the scheme of the compiled approach.

In the compiled or partial evaluation approach one could also think of a lower layer of access which solves a conjunction of database queries. The standard optimization of the database system can then be used or can be replaced by a more domain dependent or application dependent optimization scheme residing in the Prolog system.

Even lower levels of access can be useful in the context of the development of information systems in Prolog. Primitives to query single relations, or even to manipulate filepointers and individual tuples, should be available then. In this case the responsibility for the optimization process is shifted towards the application programmer. It is feasible to implement the higher levels of access in terms of this last one.

The ways to effectively integrate an existing Prolog system and a commercial database system evolve in a natural way from this scheme. BIM_Prolog provides the necessary functions for integrations at all these levels.

3.2 Prolog and SQL

Since a database query, as stated in Prolog, is essentially a conjunction of calls to elementary relations, it is evident that any relational query language can express them. Thus a simple way to couple a Prolog system and a relational database is to use the compiled approach or the partial evaluation approach and translate the resulting conjunctions of database queries into the available database query language. On execution of the program the query is translated into the query language and transmitted to the database system; the answers, on the other hand, have to be translated in the internal Prolog format.

We studied this approach for the SQL/SEQUEL-type of languages. The results of this investigation can be summarized as follows.

- The form of the conjunctions of database calls as they appear in Prolog correspond with the following SQL-type of query:

  SELECT <variables>
  FROM <union of relations>
  WHERE <set of equalities>

  This type of query is general enough to express all queries that can be expressed in the framework of Prolog. The transformaion to be made is rather simple and straightforward.
- However, in this case one does not use the full power of the SQL-like languages; these generally provide special constructs for special types of queries, but when these special queries are expressed in the unique Prolog form, it is not always evident how to make the conversion to the appropriate SQL-query.
- When using this kind of interaction, it is not possible to control the process of optimization; in general it is not possible to switch off the optimization process, or even to recognize (on reading the reference manual) whether there is any optimization at all. In particular it is not clear whether the order of relations in the union or conditions in the set of equalities has an impact on the response time of the database system.

- The response of the database system to the query is usually very human oriented and not machine nor Prolog oriented; this implies that a transformation has to be applied to the resulting tables to convert them into the internal Prolog format.
- A better result can be obtained when the database system can be invoked from a procedural language, while results of queries can be collected within that language. This technique has been tested with the integration of Ingres (which offers the possibility of embedding QUEL statements between the language statements) and SunUnify (embedding of SQL), and BIM_Prolog.

3.3 Prolog and a conjunction of database calls

Another way to realize an integration between Prolog and relational database systems is offered by the partial evaluation variant of the compiled approach. The Prolog program as stated by the user is converted into a number of rules, each consisting of a conjunction of calls to builtins, calls to recursive rules and conjunctions of database calls. This technique requires a slight modification to be made to the Prolog system.

The modifications to be made to the Prolog system are similar to those of the interpretive approach: when the system, during the normal evaluation of the transformed Prolog program, encounters a conjunction of database calls, the system transfers it for evaluation to the database system, and the results of the global query are delivered to the Prolog system one by one which consumes them on backtracking. The details of an effective implementation are described below.

3.4 Primitive database actions

Depending on the application to be written in Prolog, it may be necessary to provide the Prolog programmer with access to the low-level primitives of the relational database. For example, if one writes a query optimization module in Prolog (which is a reasonable choice), the programmer needs access to some kind of data dictionary containing statistical or meta-information, which is stored in the same way as the raw data. Access to this kind of information has to be structured and optimized by the programmer himself, using a more primitive kind of interaction, which is similar to the approach proposed in [18] (however, van de Riet *et al.* argue that this should be the unique approach in the overall interaction between a programming language and a database system).

The level of interaction in such an approach is of the following kind: positioning and moving filepointers, extracting records from files, manipulating buffers and values, etc., which are generally offered in a conventional language interface by the relational database and can be accessed as desired through the external language interface of the Prolog system.

3.5 Loose versus tight coupling

It is not always clear what different authors mean by these terms. In [16] and [17] a loose coupling is said to be one that uses UNIX pipes and forks, and requires substantial modifications to the database system. A tight coupling (or integration) is said to imply that the Prolog and database system be compiled together to have a direct access to the C-language interface, or to the database access methods. Following these criteria, BIM_Prolog could be called a tightly coupled system.

4. AN EFFECTIVE IMPLEMENTATION OF A DATABASE INTERFACE WITH BIM_PROLOG

The dynamic or static linking facility of BIM_Prolog to procedural languages allows for an easy integration with the interface modules, which can be developed and compiled completely independently of the Prolog system. To facilitate an efficient implementation, in particular to allow the BIM_Prolog programmer to define backtracking C-functions, a number of control builtins were added to the BIM_Prolog system.

The BIM_Prolog interface to external databases also makes use of the external language interface supplied by the different database systems. UNIFY provides a low-level C-language interface to the UNIFY database manager. SUN's version of UNIFY also supplies direct access from C to the SQL processor. INGRES provides access to the QUEL processor from C.

Using dynamic or static linking and the relational language processor directly has the advantage of providing access to the optimizations performed by the language processor and avoiding the inefficiencies of communication between separate processes otherwise needed. A requirement for the database language interface is that it should support nested queries. This is the case for the SUN UNIFY database. In the INGRES coupling, the problem is solved by using buffering to allow the Prolog programs to have more than one database access open simultaneously. A serious disadvantage of buffering is that it introduces an unacceptable user response time and involves excessive storage requirements for real database applications. It can only be an acceptable solution for small applications. Writing the intermediate results to files will solve the storage problem but not the response-time problem. Another solution, chosen by MU-Prolog (Melbourne University), and also described in [17], uses a pair of UNIX pipes and a separate database process for each database call. This has serious drawbacks, because it causes large overheads and moreover UNIX permits only a limited number of pipes per process. The depth of a recursive program querying the database is thus restricted to the maximum number of pairs of pipes. If the database system supports multiple queries only one pair of pipes and one process would be needed.

In this section we describe the coupling between BIM_Prolog and Unify, which uses a stack-oriented approach: the different solutions of a query are stored on a stack and provided to BIM_Prolog on backtracking. This stack mechanism is implemented in C and takes advantage of the builtin functions for backtracking.

4.1 BIM_Prolog control builtins for interface modules

This subsection describes the builtins of the BIM_Prolog system designed to provide users of the C-interface with a more efficient way of defining external backtracking predicates, and to detect and control the interactions with the cut operation. These builtins were used to implement the interface with the database [19].

mark_repeat/2

arg1 : in : term
arg2 : in : atom

A backtracking builtin predicate that succeeds repeatedly. The second argument is a user-chosen identification for the corresponding backtrackpoint. The term saved in the first argument will be the information returned by the recent_mrepeat/2 builtin for the most recent still-active backtrackpoint created by this predicate.

recent_mrepeat/2
arg1 : out : term
arg2 : in : atom

arg1 returns the first argument of the most recently executed mark_repeat/2 call still active (not removed by a cut), and identified by arg2. The call fails if there is no such backtrackpoint.

There are some C-routines that can be called from the C-modules of an interface. To remove (cut) the most recent marked backtrackpoint (respectively all marked backtrackpoints) identified by 'string'.

Declarations in C:

```
BIM_Prolog_rm_mrepeat( string )
  char * string;

BIM_Prolog_rm_all_mrepeat( string )
  char * string;
```

The builtin mark_repeat/2 makes a backtrackpoint that causes a repeated execution of all the goals that follow it, unless a cut or a call of one of the mentioned C-procedures removes that particular backtrackpoint.

The recent_mrepeat/2 builtin can be used, for example, to detect which space, allocated by external routines, can be reallocated or deallocated, when a cut has removed some database backtrackpoints.

4.2 Unify C-language interface

The implementation uses the following selection functions of Unify [20]:

entsitm

Enters a selection criterion (i.e. a comparison involving a database field) in the selection table.

mtchitm

Enters a match item in the selection table. The next selection will select the child records of the parent records, selected in a previous selection. The relationship between parent and child relations is established with so-called reference fields in the database schema. This is equivalent to an equi-join with a common field.

A selection file can be created using a selection table. A selection file is a bitmap which refers to the tuples selected. To access records, using these selection files, the functions **frstsel**, **nextsel** and **prevsel** can be used, to access respectively the first, the next, or the previous tuple.

4.3 The BIM_Prolog database predicates

A number of database manipulation predicates were implemented (see [21]) using the above-mentioned functions. A partial list follows; for a complete list and more details about their use, refer to [22].

openUNIFYdb/0

The UNIFY database (given by the UNIX environment variable DBPATH) is made accessible to the user. At most one database can be open at a time.

closeUNIFYdb/0

The UNIFY database is no longer accessible.

schema/0

Prints a list of all the database relations on standard output

schema/1

arg1 : any : database relation name

Prints the schema of the relation (if ground) or all relations (if free) on standard output.

printr/1

arg1 : ground : atom : database relation name

Prints a listing of the database relation on standard output

retrieve/1

arg1 : partial : term : a database goal

Accesses the UNIFY database to resolve the goal.

insert/1

arg1 : ground : term : a database fact

The fact is added to the UNIFY database relation

delete/1

arg1 : partial : term : a database goal

The facts that unify with the goal are retracted from the UNIFY database relation

referencejoin/1

arg1 : partial : conjunction of two database facts

Accesses the UNIFY database to resolve the conjunction. If possible, explicit references between the records are used.

4.4 Example BIM_Prolog session

```
> ?-openUNIFYdb.

> ?-schema.

node(_6,_7,_8,_9)
orders(_6,_7,_8)
customer(_6,_7,_8,_9,_10,_11,_12)
item(_6,_7,_8,_9,_10,_11)
model(_6,_7)
manf(_6,_7,_8,_9,_10,_11)

> ?-schema(manf).

Record Type : manf/6
```

KEY POS FIELD	TYPE	LENGTH(BYTE) REF
* 1 mano	Integer (short	2
2 mname	String (char *)	35
3 madd	String (char *)	35
4 mcity	String (char *)	20
5 mstate	String (char *)	2
6 mzip	String (char *)	5

```
> ?–printr(manf).

manf(100,RH Smith Manufacturing,523 Galveston Ave.,
  Centerville,CA,95923)
manf(101,Precision Tool Co.,2600 West 16th Stree,San
  Francisco.CA,94109
manf(102,A & H Industries, Inc.,2434 Evergreen Ave.,Eagan,MN,55122)
manf(103,Grover Parts and Supplies,9462 Jackson Road,Rancho
  Cordova,CA,95670)
manf(104,The Tool Depot,7562 Orange Dr.,Tucson,AZ,85745)
manf(105,BHP Ltd.,17385 Weatherby Rd.,New York,NY,10022)
manf(106,John Gallagher, Norderstedt,Hamburg,Ha,2000)

> ?-insert(manf(107,BIM,Kwikstraat,Everberg,Be,'1000')),write(ok)

ok

> ?-printr(manf).
```

```
manf(100,RH Smith Manufacturing,523 Galveston Ave.,Centerville,
  CA,95923)
manf(101,Precision Tool Co.,2600 West 16th Street,San
Francisco,CA,94109)
manf(102,A & H Industries, Inc.,2434 Evergreen Ave.,Eagan,MN,55122)
manf(103,Grover Parts and Supplies,9462 Jackson Road,Rancho
  Cordova,CA,95670)
manf(104,The Tool Depot,7562 Orange Dr.,Tucson,AZ,85745)
manf(105,BHP Ltd.,17385 Weatherby Rd.,New York,NT,10022)
manf(106,John Callagher,Norderstedt,Hamburg,Ha,2000)
manf(107,BIM,Kwikstraat,Everberg,Be,1000)

> ?-retrieve((mand(_x,_y,_,_,_z,_),_x>=101,_z==CA)),write(_y),nl.

Precision Tool Co.
Grover Parts and Supplies

> ?-retrieve((manf(_x,_y,_,_,_,_),_y=='*Tool*')),write((_x,_y)),nl.

101 , Precision Tool Co.
104 , The Tool Depot

> ?-closeUNIFYdb.
```

5. CONCLUSION

We have described the different ways of transforming a Prolog program in conjunctions of database calls and the mechanisms to integrate a Prolog system and an existing database system effectively. We have indicated how the interface between BIM_Prolog and a commercial database system can be realized. Note that the performance of the interaction is only 10 to 40 times less performant than using an in-core Prolog database. Appropriate caching could still improve this situation.

Apart from this connection with Unify, the interface has also been realized with Ingres and SunUnify. Moreover the BIM_Prolog user disposes of all primitives to implement other interfaces. An integration with Sybase is planned as well.

ACKNOWLEDGEMENTS

The research has been done partly under contract KBAR/SOFT/1 (a grant from the Belgian Ministry of Science Policy) and partly in the context of the ESPRIT Pilot Project 107 (sponsored by the Commission to European Communities). The work reported upon was realised thanks to substantial contributions from: Ralph Meyer and John Callagher (SCS, Hamburg), Bart Demoen, Jose Cotta and Erik Pieters (BIM) and Gerda Janssens (KUL).

REFERENCES

[1] Venken, R., A Simple Relational Database as an Extension for Prolog, in Dutch, Undergraduate Student Thesis, June 81, K. U. Leuven.

[2] Lloyd, J. W., An Introduction to Deductive Database Systems, *Australian Computer J.*, **15**, No. 2, May 1983.

[3] Ramamohanarao, K., Lloyd, J. W. and Thom, J. A., Partial Match Retrieval Using Hashing and Descriptors, *ACM Trans. on Database Systems,* **8**, No. 8, 552–576, 1983.

[4] Freston, M., The Bang File: A New Kind of Grid File, ECRC, Muenchen, 1986, and this book.

[5] Gallaire, H., and Minker, J., Eds., *Logic and Data Bases*, Plenum Press, New York, 1978.

[6] Chakravarthy, U. S., Minker, J., and Tran, C., Interfacing Predicate Logic Languages and Relational Databases, *Proc. First Int. Logic Programming Conf.*, Marseille, 1982.

[7] Warren, D. H. D., Efficient Processing of Interactive Relational Database Queries Expressed in Logic, *Proc. 7th Int. Conf. on Very Large Databases*, Cannes, 1981.

[8] Henschen, L. and Shanim, A. N., On Compiling Queries in Recursive First-order Databases, *J. Assoc. for Computing Machinery,* **31**, No. 1, 1984.

[9] Vieille, L., Recursive Query Processing: Fundamental Algorithms for the DedGin System. ECRC, Muenchen, 1987, and this book.

[10] Komorowski, H. J., A Specification of An Abstract Prolog Machine and its Application to Partial Evaluation, Linköping studies in Science and Technology Dissertations, No. 69, Software Systems Research Center, Linköping University, 1981.

[11] Venken, R., A Prolog Meta-interpreter for Partial Evaluation and its Application to Source to Source Transformation and Query Optimisation, *Proc. ECAI '84*, Pisa, September 1984.

[12] Venken, R., Query Optimisation and Partial Evaluation, *Proc. Workshop on Coupling Prolog and Databases*, Venice, 1986.

[13] King, J., Quist: A System for Semantic Query Optimisation in Relational Databases, *Proc. 7th Int. Conf. on Very Large Databases*, Cannes, 1981.

[14] Hammer, M., and Zdonik, S., Knowledge Based Query Processing, *Proc. 6th Int. Conf. on Very Large Databases*, Montreal, 1980.

[15] Kouloumdjian, J., Epsilon 36th Month Progress Report, University of Lyon, 1987.

[16] Bocca, J., On the Evaluation Strategy of EDUCE, SIGMOD '86, Washington, D.C., June 1986.

[17] Zobel, J., and Ramamohanarao, K., Accessing Existing Databases from Prolog, Technical Report 86/17, Department of Computer Science, University of Melbourne, 1986.

[18] van de Riet, R. P., Wasserman, A. I., Kerstens, M. L., and de Jonghe, W., High Level Programming Features Improving the Efficiency of a

Relational Database System, *ACM Trans. on Database Systems,* **6**, No. 3, pp. 464–485, 1981.

[19] Mulkers, A., Accessing Existing Relational Databases from BIM_Prolog, KUL Internal Report, Leuven, 1987.

[20] *Reference Manual UNIFY Release 3.1*, Chapter 10, Unify Corporation, Oregon, 1985.

[21] Meyer, R., *Prolog–Unify Interface Version 1.2 Manual*, SCS-Tas, Hamburg, 1987.

[22] *BIM–Prolog Version 2.2 Manual*, BIM, Everberg, 1987.

[23] Gallaire, H., Minker, J., and Nicolas, J. M., Logic and Databases: An Overview and Survey, Report CERT/CGE, University of Maryland, 1983.

[24] Naish, L., Thom, J. A., and Ramamohanarao, K., Concurrent Database Updates in Prolog, Technical Report 86/12, Department of Computer Science, University of Melbourne, 1986.

8

An interface from Prolog to a binary relational database

Stephen Todd
IBM United Kingdom Scientific Centre, Athelstan House, St Clement St., Winchester, England

ABSTRACT

This chapter describes an interface from Prolog to the binary relational database NDB. The pure entity oriented nature of NDB makes it particularly suitable for integration with Prolog. The interface was developed for application with database and graphics to the exploration of scientific data.

The interface is designed at three levels. The lowest level makes NDB's PLI call interface available to Prolog. The second provides a convenient way for Prolog programs to navigate NDB databases. The top level extracts the schema from the NDB database and compiles it into Prolog rules. This permits the Prolog program to read data from the database as if it were stored as Prolog predicates.

1. INTRODUCTION

There has recently been much interest in the integration of Prolog with conventional databases. This chapter describes an experimental implementation of VM/PROLOG [1] to the Data Mapping Program (DMP) [2,3], commonly known as NDB [4]. The work was done as a small feasibility study, and was mainly concerned with local implementation details. This chapter does not cover these details, but focuses on features that distinguish an NDB interface to Prolog from other database interfaces.

The implementation was part of a project looking into the use of graphics for data exploration. This work involved the use of a relational database for the storage of scientific data, and close integration with graphics to help the user visualize those data [5]. Applications include molecular chemistry [6,7] and archaeology [8]. Similar applications in molecular chemistry are described elsewhere in this book [9].

Most of the work was based on the Peterlee Relational Test Vehicle (PRTV). Even though PRTV has greater data manipulation power than most databases, it became clear that yet more power was needed, especially in queries involving closure and sequence matching. Experiments with Prolog [11,12] showed that it had much of the required power, and that it could easily be integrated with graphics.

Lack of large volume data storage on Prolog led to the need for a Prolog database integration. This route has been followed by many other researchers [13–18]. In many integrations there has been a bad match between the facilities offered by the database and those required by Prolog: both systems try to be too clever. Most relational databases present a high-level, set-oriented interface, exemplified by the join operation. When accessed on a record level they cannot make good use of optimization and internal indexing. On the other hand, it is natural for Prolog to request data at the record level. This is especially true when Prolog performs operations such as closure (parts explosion); and these are the very operations for which Prolog interfaces will be used, as relational databases handle them so badly.

The entity orientation and relatively low level of NDB made it particularly suitable as a data store for Prolog. Most of the query power lies in Prolog, but it passes basic indexed data searches to NDB. NDB is just clever enough to integrate well with Prolog.

The problems of badly matched interface levels are highlighted elsewhere in this book [9,14]. In both cases the authors consider what form of database is required to support Prolog, rather than considering the problem of using Prolog to extract data from an existing database.

Our implementation is at three levels. The lowest level makes the PLI interface of NDB available to Prolog. The next level provides simple Prolog use of NDB sets and relations. The top level makes NDB sets and relations appear to the Prolog programmer as Prolog predicates. It is the top level interface that we consider most important, as it provides both efficient and convenient access to database data.

The rest of this chapter is in two main parts. The first outlines NDB, and the second discusses the implementation.

2. NDB

This section gives an introduction to NDB. NDB is a binary relation database. It is based on the entity set model [19,20]. Each entity has a unique surrogate (entity identifier). Each entity is associated with a value: this association has a special role in the NDB implementation. Entities are collected into named entity sets.

Entities are associated via binary relations, which may be many-many relations. They are directional in the sense that we distinguish between father(fred,bill) and father(bill,fred); but the system can equally easily answer the queries father(fred,Son) and father(Father,bill).

NDB is similar to the object-oriented database whose Prolog integration is described by Paton *et al.* [9]. The main difference is that NDB does not implement methods and modules: that is why we call it entity oriented rather than object oriented.

Throughout this chapter we use capitalization to indicate a value that will be set as a result of calling a predicate. We use lower case for values that will be input, even where these values are expected to be integers and not atoms.

In Prolog terms, we may consider an NDB database as a set of facts of the forms

```
entity(entity_id, type, value)
relation(relation_id(from_entity_id,to_entity_id))
```

The schema [4], which holds information such as the from-type and to-type of a relation, is itself held in the database. Thus relations and types are themselves entities, and there are relations that define the from-type and the to-type for each relation. The exact constraints imposed in the schema, and the details of how relation names are used, are not important to this chapter.

The implementation of NDB is based on entities, with sets of related entities radiating from them. NDB can easily answer an entity-oriented query with an unbound functor, of the type

```
relation(Relation_id(fred,Related_entity_id))
```

that is: tell me all you know about fred. It cannot directly answer a relation-oriented query of the type

```
relation(father(Father_id,Son_id))
```

To implement this we must find the entity that represents the set of people, find all the people, and then find their father.

NDB provides an indexed search, which exposes itself in two forms. The first finds entities within a given entity set associated with a given value.

```
entity(Entity_id, type_id, value)
```

The second navigates from a given entity via a given relation to an entity with a given value.

```
relation(relation_id(from_entity_id, To_entity_id)),
entity(To_entity_id, _, value)
```

All relations in NDB are binary, and they are always indexed in both directions. This simplicity in the storage schema can cause unnecessary overheads on certain updates and in storage use. However, it makes the Prolog interface much simpler, as the storage schema is implied by the conceptual schema, so the Prolog interface does not have to worry about access path selection.

NDB can be used at two levels. The lower interface, which we use from Prolog, is a set of 40 PLI calls. A couple of these return the identifiers of the set of sets entity and the set of relations entity, giving the program a route into the database. A few perform controls such as opening the database. The remainder provide basic navigational tools, such as

DBR given identifiers for an entity and a relation, find the list of related entities.

DBCN given an element in a list, find the next element.
DBFIND given a list and a string, find the first element in the list whose value is equal to the string. This is the programmer interface to the indexing mechanism of NDB.

The higher level of NDB is a language designed to be used from the terminal. A typical command to look for all people and check if their telephone number is 1234 is

list set 'PERSON' rel 'TEL#' eq '1234'

We will use this example to illustrate the Prolog interface. The equivalent

list set 'TEL#' eq '1234' rel 'PERSON'

is more efficient, but the first example better illustrates the Prolog interface.

The lower interface guarantees internal consistency of the NDB interface. However, certain constraints such as a relation being many-one are only checked at the higher level. The low-level programmer must thus be very careful when updating the database.

3. THE IMPLEMENTATION

The implementation is at three levels. The first makes the PLI calls available to the Prolog programmer. The second provides convenient navigation of the NDB structures to the Prolog programmer. The third makes the database available to the programmer as a Prolog predicate.

3.1 The low level

The low level is implemented using a general utility to interface VM/PROLOG to program suites written in PLI and other conventional languages. The input to this utility is a set of PLI ENTRY declarations. The outputs are an assembler interface program that is linked with the program suite, and a set Prolog declarations to make it available to Prolog.

Here is an example of a Prolog program to find all people and check if their telephone number is 1234. It is intended to give a flavour of the NDB facilities at this level.

```
lowtest:—
/* compile stage, to look into schema
   dbusers(D)                  /* find root of sets
   dbmem(D, 'PERSON', P),      /* find id P for set PERSON
   dbmem(D, 'TEL#', T),        /* find id T for set TEL#

/* execution stage, to search database
   dbr(P, P, R),               /* find root R for list of people
   dbc(R, C_id1),              /* find first element C_id1 of list
   clist(C_id1, C_id),         /* loop on list for all elements C_id
   dbe(C_id, P_id),            /* find person P_id for C_id
   dbr(P_id, T, R1),           /* find list R1 of P_id's tel#s
```

```
dbfind(R1, '1234',V_id1),    /* findfirst entity for '1234'
ne(V_id1,0),                 /* check there
dbv(P_id, Name),             /* ok, we have found a person
write(Name),
fail.
```

The main body of the program is in two parts. The first 'compiles' the program by extracting the internal identifiers for the set and relations required. The second navigates the database. This program is very similar to an equivalent PLI program.

This uses a simple sub-program CLIST to walk NDB lists.

```
/* clist goes through a list
/* the first parameter is input, and defines the head of the list
/* the second walks each element of the list
clist(0, _) :- / , fail.            /*end of list
clist(C_id, C_id) :- true.          /* first element of list
clist(C_id1, C_id) :-
        dbcn(C_id1, C_id2),         /* get the tail of the list
        clist(C_id2, C_id).         /* and walk it
```

CLIST holds NDB cursors as Prolog integers, and uses Prolog recursion and backtrack. It would operate very inefficiently in storage for large retrieval lists. For those it should be replaced by an external predicate which holds cursor stacks and performs its own backtrack, as implemented in [16].

3.2 The second level

The second level of the interface provides the Prolog user with more convenient tools for navigating the database and following NDB lists. Some of these could have been provided in a similar manner to PLI programmers, but many rely on the loop implicit in executing a backtracking Prolog predicate. This is the 'transparent backtracking' of Irving [15]. The second level is written in Prolog directly on top of the first level. The program CLIST in the example above is part of the second-level code.

The facilities offered by the second level are as below.

CSET compile the identifier for a named set
CSET(setname, Set_id)

CREL compile the identifier for a named relation
CREL(relname, Rel_id)

WSET walk all identifiers in a given set
WSET(set_id, Id)

WREL walk all entities linked to a given entity by a given relation
WREL(from_id, rel_id, To_id)

WREL walk all entities linked to a given entity by any relation
WREL(from_id, Rel_id, To_id)

ESET walk all entities with a given value in a given set

ESET(set_id, value, Id)

EREL walk all entities with a given value and linked to a given entity by a given relation

EREL(from_id, rel_id, tovalue, To_id)

TREL test if entity connects by relation to v-ele

TREL(from_id, rel_id, to_id)

OUT writes a list. Elements of the list that represent entities are converted to their value (optionally tagged by entity identifier).

OUT(list)

Here is our sample query coded in the level-two interface.

```
midtest:-
    cset('PERSON', P),
    cset('TEL#',T),
    wset(P, P_id),
    erel(P_id, T, '1234', T_id),
    out( ['Person ', P_id, ' has tel: ', T_id] ),
    fail.
```

3.3 Top-level interface

The top-level interface presents the NDB database to Prolog as a set of predicates. At setup time, the entire NDB schema is scanned and converted to Prolog axioms. These are close to the 'obvious' Prolog form, with extra predicates to take advantage of NDB indexing.

Wherever possible, we use entities (strictly entity identifiers) rather than values. Values must be specified to take advantage of NDB index search. Apart from this, a value is usually only required on output. In this case the predicate OUT performs an automatic lookup. Where the value of an identifier is required internally to a query, the low-level NDB function DBV is used (see namesake example below).

The decision to use entities wherever possible was based on data modelling considerations, not implementation ones. However, it also reduces the problem (raised during the workshop) that some Prolog implementations have with garbage collection of string and atoms.

Database values are held in Prolog as strings, and identifiers as integers. We use this to distinguish them internally. This is not very formal, and relies on the fact that NDB stores and transmits all values as strings, but it is convenient in practice for simple examples. In a more complete system it would be better to use tagged terms,

The forms of predicate generated for a set PERSON are

person(Person_id) find all entities in the set PERSON.

PERSON('value',Person_id) find all entities with the specified value in the set PERSON.

new(person('name',Person_id)) create a new person with given name and return his identifier.
delete(person(person_id)) delete a given person.

For a relation (FATHER say) we have the following possibilities:
father(son,Father) find (all!) father(s) of the specified son. Son is specified as an identifier, and father returned as one.
father(son,'name',Father) find all fathers with value 'name' of the specified son.
father(Son,father) find all sons of a given father.
father(Son,Father) find all father–son pairs (implemented by following the set of people).
father('name',Son,father) find all sons with value 'name' of a given father.
father(Son,Father) find all father–son pairs.
addcon(father(son,father)) assert a father–son relationship.
delcon(father(son,father)) retract a father–son relationship.

This level provides the 'transparent unification' of Irving [15]. There is a slight irregularity in the interface where we take advantage of the NBD indexing. The example

FATHER(son,'name',Father)

is more efficient but less regular than the equivalent

FATHER(son,Father) , dbv(Father, 'name')

At this level our sample query is coded as below.

```
hightest:-
    person(P),            /* find all people
    tel#(P, '1234', T),   /* and telephones with number '1234'
    out( ['Person ', P_id, ' has tel: ', T_id] ),
    fail.
```

An example of a query where names are internally important is

"Find Bill's father's namesakes"

```
sillytest :-
    person('Bill',B),     /* find Bill's identifier
                          /* (strictly identifiers for all Bills)
    father(B,F),          /* find his father's id (fathers' ids!)
    dbv(F,Name),          /* and thus his fathers name
    person(Name,O),       /* and identifiers for namesakes
    write( ['The internal id for a namesake is',O] ),
    fail.
```

The top-level interface has one significant performance implication. When the schema is read and the Prolog axioms are generated, the identifiers for the named sets and relations get coded into the Prolog axioms. This means that when the rules are used, there is no futher database compilation to be performed.

The top-level interface does not have a construct equivalent to

WREL(from_id, Rel_id, To_id)

Such a construct would be unnatural to Prolog.

4. PERFORMANCE

To estimate the speed of the NDB interface, we have performed some simple retrievals based on the database described by Lucas [16]. This consists of two entity sets: one consists of the numbers from 1 up to 200, the other of their names one up to twozerozero. We have two relations TEST1 and TEST2 connecting them one to one: e.g. test1(12,onetwo), test2(onetwo,12).

All timings are virtual cpu times in seconds and milliseconds for an IBM 4341, which is *very roughly* five times the speed of a VAX 11/730. They include the time to access the data but not to perform any output. The results are shown below.

		table size				
		5	20	50	100	200
single table	test1(A, B) , fail	0.010	0.033	0.082	0.169	0.321
join on two tables first column key	test1(A, B) , test2(B,C), fail	0.014	0.054	0.132	0.282	0.534
join on two tables second column key	test1(A, B) , test2(C,A) , fail	0.015	0.057	0.142	0.307	0.575
join on two table no key	test1(A, B) , test2(C,D) , eq(B,C) , fail	0.055	0.702	4.270	17.025	68.308

We see that in every case except the non-key join, the timings are linear with relation size. For the non-key join, the timings are quadratic. As NDB indexes everything in both directions, we see that there is very little difference in the timings with first and second columns of the second relation used to join. We had to code a rather artificial query to force a non-key join.

Comparing the timings with those of Lucas, and allowing for the machine differences, we see that the non-key join case is comparable. Other timings are better for NDB. This is probably due to the tight integration of NDB with Prolog, to NDB's entity-based indexing, and to its efficient buffer handling. The improvement is especially noticeable in the two key join examples. This is due to NDB's entity-oriented as opposed to relation-oriented index handling.

We were only able to measure elapsed time reliably for the slowest queries. On a lightly loaded machine they were about 20% higher than the cpu figures given.

5. SUMMARY

We have described an interface from Prolog to the entity-based relational database NDB. The interface is at three levels: the lowest provides basic NDB calls; the highest makes the database look like Prolog predicates.

NDB and Prolog coexist very happily. The integration was easy to program and is easy to use. This is mainly because of the very clean nature of the NDB database and of its low-level interface.

The interface is efficient: many queries run as quickly with Prolog as with PLI. This is because of the very tight coupling, and the fact that the low-level NDB interface is designed for the many extractions of single data items rather than a few extractions of large ones. The efficiency is helped when the high-level interface is used. In this case the NDB schema is compiled into the Prolog axioms, and does not have to be checked during program execution.

REFERENCES

[1] *VM/Programming in Logic, Program Description and Operations Manual,* IBM Manual SB11-6374.

[2] *Data Mapping Program User's Guide,* IBM Manual SB11-5340.

[3] *Data Mapping Program Program Description and Operations Manual,* IBM Manual SB11-5339.

[4] Winterbottom, N. and Sharman, G. C. H., The Data Dictionary Facilities of NDB, *Fourth Conf. on Very Large Databases,* IEEE, West Berlin, Sept. 1978.

[5] Burridge, J. M., Morffew, A. J., Quarendon, P., and Todd, S. J. P., WGS: A Flexible Combination of Interactive and Solid Molecular Modelling, UCLA–GENEX Symp. on Protein Structure, Folding and Design, March 1985.

[6] Morffew, A. J., Todd, S. J. P., and Snelgrove, M. J., The Use of a Relational Database for Holding Molecule Data in a Molecular Graphics System, *Computers and Chemistry,* **7**, 1, 9–16, 1983.

[7] Burridge, J., Morrfew, A., and Todd, S., Application of Relational Database and Graphics to the Molecular Sciences, British National Conference on Databases, July 1984.

[8] Colley, S., Todd, S., and Campling, N., 3d Computer Graphics for Archaeological Data Exploration: An Example from Saxon Southampton. *J. Archaeological Sci.* **15**, 99–106, 1988.

[9] Paton, N. W. and Gray, P. M. D., An Object-Oriented Database for Storage and Analysis of Protein Structure Data, see Chapter 14 of this book.

[10] Todd, S. J. P., The Peterlee Relational Test Vehicle — A System Overview, *IBM Systems J.,* **15**, 285–308, 1976.

[11] Burridge, J. M., Morffew, A. J., and Todd, S. J. P., Experiments in the Use of PROLOG for Protein Querying (abstract only), *J. Molecular Graphics,* **3**, 109, 1985.

[12] Morffew, A. J. and Todd, S. J. P., The Use of PROLOG as a Protein Querying Language, *Computers and Chemistry,* **10**, 9–14, 1986.

[13] Bocca, J., EDUCE — A Marriage of Convenience: PROLOG and a Relational DBMS, *Proc. 1986 ACM–SIGMOD Int. Conf. on Management of Data* (ed. Zaniolo, C.), ACM, Washington DC, USA, May 1986.

[14] Bocca, J. and Pearson, P. J., On PROLOG–DBMS Connections: A Step Forward from EDUCE, see Chapter 4 of this book.

[15] Irving, T. A Generalized Interface between Prolog and Relational Databases, see Chapter 6 of this book.

[16] Lucas, R. J. and Le Vine, G. A., A Prolog–Relational Database Interface, see Chapter 5 of this book.

[17] Risch, T., A Database Extension of PROLOG and its Implementation, Uppsala Programming Methodology and Artificial Intelligence Laboratory, Department of Computer Science, University of Uppsala, 750 02, Uppsala, Sweden, Aug. 1982.

[18] Jarke, M. and Vassiliou, Y., Databases and Expert Systems: Opportunities and Architectures for Integration, *New Applications of Databases,* Academic Press, New York, 1984.

[19] Senko, M. E., Altman, E. B., Astrahan, M. M., and Fehder, P. L., Data Structures and Accessing in Database Systems, *IBM Systems J.* **17**, 30–93, 1973.

[20] Chen, P. P-S., The Entity-relationship Model: Towards a Unified View of Data, *ACM Trans. on Database Systems,* **1**, 9–36, 1976.

[21] Hall, P. A. V., Owlett, J., and Todd, S. J. P., Relations and Entities, *Modelling in Data Base Management Systems* (ed. G. M. Nijssen), North-Holland, Amsterdam, 1976.

Part III
Deductive databases

9

Guarded default databases: a prototype implementation

Carol Small
Knowledge System Group, Department of Computer Science, University of Reading, Whiteknights, Reading, Berkshire, RG6 2AX, England

ABSTRACT

A guarded default database (GDDB) comprises a set of base facts, a set of derivation rules, a set of default rules, and a set of integrity constraints. The default rules define the assumptions to be made about information not implied by the derivation rules and base facts, and are used to create a less incomplete extension. The integrity constraints define valid database states, and are used to prevent transactions which would otherwise result in the database being changed from a valid to an invalid state.

We define the structure of a GDDB, show how the default rules define a less incomplete extension, and also how the integrity constraints define valid database states. We then describe a prototype implementation of a system which supports GDDBs, and finally draw some conclusions regarding the implementation.

1. INTRODUCTION

A guarded default database (GDDB) comprises a set of base facts, a set of derivation rules, a set of default rules, and a set of integrity constraints. The default rules define the assumptions to be made about information not implied by the derivation rules and base facts, and are used to create a less incomplete† extension. The integrity constraints define valid database states, and are used to prevent transactions which would otherwise result in the database being changed from a valid to an invalid state. In this chapter

† A database is incomplete if for some formula F neither F nor ~F is implied by the database. In general a database will be incomplete unless an inference rule such as the negation as failure rule [1] is employed.

we describe a prototype implementation of a system which supports guarded default databases.

The structure of this chapter is as follows. The base facts and derivation rules of a GDDB are defined in terms of function-free causal form formulae, and consequently in section 2 we review briefly the syntax of such formulae. In section 3 we define the structure of a GDDB, show how the default rules define a less incomplete extension, and show how the integrity constraints define valid database states. In section 4 we describe a prototype implementation of a system called Exegesis which supports GDDBs. Finally, in section 5 we draw some conclusions regarding the implementation.

2. CLAUSAL FORM FORMULAE

A *term* is either a *constant* or a *variable*. An *atom* consists of an *n*-ary *predicate* followed by *n* terms. Throughout this chapter we use upper case letters for variables, strings starting with lower case letters as constants, and place the terms of an atom within brackets, separated by commas. A *literal* is either an atom or its negation. A *clause* is a disjunction of literals; the variables of a clause are implicitly universally quantified. A clause consisting of a single literal is termed a *unit* clause. A literal or clause is *ground* if it contains no variables. Two literals are of opposite *polarity* if one is an atom and the other a negated atom; otherwise they are of the same polarity.

A set of *substitutions*, *S*, is a set of ordered pairs:

$$S = \{ \nu_1/\tau_1, \nu_2/\tau_2, \ldots \nu_n/\tau_n \}$$

where the ν_i are distinct variables and the τ_i are terms, not necessarily distinct. The result of applying a set of substitutions to a clause is a new clause in which each ν_i is replaced by the corresponding τ_i. For example, the result of applying { P / mikhail } to the clause

~ Reads(P,herald_tribune) v ~ Reads(P,pravda)

is the clause

~ Reads(mikhail, herald_tribune) v ~ Reads(mikhail,pravda)

Throughout this chapter we denote the application of a set of substitutions, S, to a clause, C, as $C^{(S)}$. Finally, a set of substitutions, S, *unifies* atoms A_0 and A_1 if $A_0^{(S)}$ is identical to $A_1^{(S)}$.

3. GUARDED DEFAULT DATABASES — DESCRIPTION

3.1 Default databases

A default database (DDB) consists of a set of base facts, a set of derivation rules and a set of default rules (i.e. it is a GDDB without integrity constraints). A *base fact* is a ground unit clause. A *derivation rule* is a non-ground or non-unit clause (i.e. a clause which is not a base fact). A *default rule* is a formula of the form

$$L_0 \leftarrow L_1 \ \& \ \ldots \ \& \ L_n \ \& \ \mathrm{M}L_0$$

in which L_0 to L_n are literals and the operator M may for the moment be read as 'it is consistent to believe', or more briefly as 'maybe'. L_1 *to* L_n are termed the preprequisite literals and L_0 the assumption literal of the rule. A default rule contains only free variables. We read informally such a rule as

> 'if L_1 and . . . and L_n are true and it is consistent to believe L_0 then infer L_0'

Definition 1. Let Δ be a default database and let

$$E_0, E_1, \ldots$$

be a series of sets of clauses such that

1. E_0 consists of the base facts and derivation rules of Δ;
2. For each odd i, E_i is the deductive closure of E_{i-1}; and
3. For each even i, $i > 0$, let D_i be the set of all unit clauses which result from the application of the default rules to E_{i-1}. That is, D_i consists of all unit clauses $L_0^{(S)}$ such that

   — there is a default rule

   $$L_0 \leftarrow L_1 \ \& \ \ldots \ \& \ L_n \ \& \ \mathrm{M}L_0 \ ;$$

   — a set of substitutions, S;
   — $L_1^{(S)}$ to $L_n^{(S)}$ are contained in E_{i-1};
   — neither $L_0^{(S)}$ nor $\sim L_0^{(S)}$ is contained in E_{i-1}; and
   — $L_0^{(S)}$ to $L_n^{(S)}$ are ground.

   If D_i is empty then E_i consists of E_{i-1}; otherwise E_i consists of E_{i-1} together with a non-deterministically selected clause of D_i.

When no further unit clauses result from invoking the default rules then we have an extension of Δ, i.e. E_j is an *extension* of Δ if j is the least *even* integer such that $E_j = E_{j-1}$.

Example 1. Consider the following DDB:

F1 Read(mikhail,pravda)

R1 ~Capitalist(X) v ~Socialist(X)

D1 Capitalist(X) ← Reads(X,wall_street_journal) & M Capitalist(X)
D2 Socialist(X) ← Reads(X,pravda) & M Socialist(X)

This DDB possesses an extension containing the following clauses:

Socialist(mikhail)
~Capitalist(Mikhail)

An extension is a set of facts derived from the default rules, derivation rules and base facts, and is consistent iff the set of base facts and derivation rules are consistent [2]. This factor is essential since we do not want the default rules to 'introduce inconsistency' into the extension. In general, however, a DDB may not have more than one extension, as can be seen by adding the following base fact to the DDB of Example 1:

F2 Reads(mikhail,wall_street_journal)

Facts from two extensions cannot be used simultaneously without risk of inconsistency. However, we believe that in general the user will require a DDB to maintain only one extension, and will believe a DDB to be in error if it supports more than one extension. Consequently we say that a DDB is safe† if the derivation and default rules can support only one extension for any given set of base facts. For example, the DDB of Example 1 can be made safe by giving a 'lower priority' to one of the default rules, such as

D1′ Capitalist(X) ← Reads(X,wall_street_journal) &
~Reads(X,pravda) & M Capitalist(X)

The ability to characterize a DDB as safe by examination of the derivation and default rules only is important for two reasons. First, it is likely that the DDB will contain many more base facts than derivation and default rules, and hence ensuring that the DDB is safe would seem to be much less costly. More importantly, however, the set of base facts is likely to be far more volatile than the set of derivation and default rules, and consequently the DDB need be checked less frequently for safety. The way in which the safety of a DDB can be ascertained is beyond the scope of this chapter, but can be found in [2]. Throughout the remainder of this chapter we consider only safe default databases with a consistent set of base facts and derivation rules.

3.2 Integrity constraints

An *M-literal* is a literal preceded by the operator M; a *Non-M-literal* is a literal which is not preceded by the operator M.

An *integrity constraint* is a formula of the form

$$\leftarrow \mathrm{D}$$

where D is a conjunction of M- and Non-M-literals. Thus an integrity constraint is typically of the form

$$\leftarrow L_0 \ \& \ \ldots \ \& \ L_{n-1} \ \& \ \mathrm{M}L_n \ \& \ \ldots \ \& \ \mathrm{M}L_{n+m}$$

We read informally such a constraint as

† The concept of a safe default database should not be confused with safe or range restricted formulae (as considered by Ullman [3], for example).

'it is not the case that L_0 and ... and L_{n-1} is true and ... and maybe L_{n+m} is true'

In other words, if L_0 to L_{n-1} are true then at least one of L_n to L_{n+m} are false.

Definition 2. Let Δ be a default database and IC a set of integrity constraints. Δ is said to *violate* ic ∈ IC iff there are substitutions for the variables of ic such that:

1. each Non-M-literal is contained in the extension of Δ; and
2. the negation of each M-literal is not contained in the extension of Δ.

The extension of Δ is said to be *invalid* with respect to IC if there is a constraint of IC which is violated by Δ, and is said to be *valid* otherwise. If Δ is a DDB and IC a set of integrity constraints, then Γ = (Δ,IC) is a guarded default database if the extension of Δ is valid with respect to IC.

Example 2. Consider a GDDB comprising DDB:

F1 Reads(mikhail,pravda)
D1 Capitalist(X) ← Reads(X,wall_street_journal) & M Capitalist(X)
D2 Socialist(X) ← Reads(X,pravda) & M Socialist(X)

and IC:

I1 ← Socialist(X) & Capitalist(X)

Constraint I1 is not violated by DDB since Capitalist(mikhail) is not contained in the extension of DDB. However, consider the same GDDB with I1 replaced by

I1′ ← M Socialist(X) M Capitalist(X)

Constraint I1′ *is* violated by DDB, since neither ~ Socialist(mikhail) nor ~ Capitalist(mikhail) is not contained in the extension. Hence the extension of this GDDB is invalid.

4. GUARDED DEFAULT DATABASES — AN IMPLEMENTATION

4.1 Overview

This section decribes the implementation of a prototype system called Exegesis† which supports GDDBs. The base facts are stored in the *fact base*, the derivation and default rules (which we generally term *deduction rules*) are stored in the *rule base*, and the integrity constraints are stored in the *constraint base*.

Fig. 1 shows in broad outline the principle components of the Exegesis system, and the access paths between them. It indicates that the rule, fact, and constraint bases can be updated, that the completion of a transaction will trigger the constraint enforcer, and that queries are processed by the proof procedure.

† Εξηγησιζ: explanation or critical interpretation of a text, esp. of the Bible.

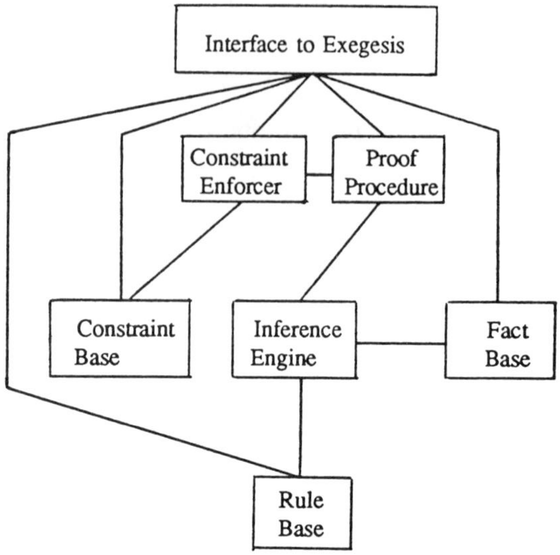

Fig. 1 — The structure of the Exegesis system.

A transaction may consist of any sequence of insertions, deletions, and retrievals of deduction rules, integrity constraints, and base facts. Thus 'schema' type information (deduction rules and integrity constraints) can be inserted and deleted in the same way as 'non-schema' type information (base facts). The integrity constraints are enforced when a transaction is committed. Throughout a transaction, two lists, called the Possible Deletions (PD) and Possible Insertions (PI), are maintained for the purpose of optimizing the constraint enforcement process. Both lists are 'empty' at the start of a transaction. If the database is closed when a transaction is in progress it is first rolled back.

The remainder of this section is structured as follows. In section 4.2 we show how information may be retrieved from a GDDB. In section 4.3 we consider the actions undertaken when an update to a GDDB is made. Then in section 4.4 we show how the PD and PI lists are maintained throughout the transaction. Finally in section 4.5 we show how the integrity constraints are selected and validated when the transaction is committed.

4.2 Retrieval operations

A query against the database is regarded as a proposition to be proved with the database itself regarded as a set of axioms. To prove a proposition the proof procedure shows that the negation of the proposition is inconsistent with the database, and hence that the proposition is implied by the database. A *denial* is a formula of the form

$$\leftarrow Q$$

in which Q is a (possibly empty) conjunction of M- and Non-M-literals. A denial states that there are no substitutions for the variables such that each Non-M-literal is contained in the extension and that the negation of each M-literal is not contained in the extension. For example, the denial

← Politician(P) & M Socialist(P) & M Capitalist(P)

states that there is no substitution, p, for P, such that the extension contains Politician(p) but neither ~ Socialist(p) nor ~ Capitalist(p).

A set of substitutions is an *answer* to a denial if the extension and the denial, with those substitutions, are inconsistent. If the denial and the extension can be shown to be inconsistent then we say that there is a *refutation* of that denial.

Description of the proof procedure

To attempt to derive a *refutation of a denial* we use the following proof procedure. There are two phases in the derivation of a refutation of a denial, corresponding to the processing of the non-M- and the M-literals of the denial respectively.

In the first phase we attempt to derive a refutation, via the inference engine decribed below, of a clause stating that the conjunction of the Non-M-literals is not contained in the extension. If a refutation of this clause can be derived then the Non-M-literals are contained in the extension. For each way in which a refutation of the clause can be derived a set of substitutions, S, is returned by the inference engine.

In the second phase we attempt to show for each set S in turn the negation of each M-literal is *not* contained in the extension.† If we succeed then a refutation of the denial has been derived, and S constitutes an answer to the denial.

To show that the negation of an M-literal is not contained in the extension we form a clause asserting that the M-literal is contained in the extension, and attempt to derive (via the inference engine) a refutation of this clause. If a refutation is derived then the extension contains the negation of the M-literal; conversely, if a refutation is not derived then the extension does not contain the negation of the M-literal.

Description of the inference engine

The inference engine is used to attempt to derive a *refutation of a clause*. It is a top-down theorem prover based upon a modified form of linear resolution [4]. A sequence of clauses

$$C_0, C_1, \ldots, C_n$$

constitutes a refutation of clause C_0 if

1. C_n is the empty clause;

† We assume that each M-literal, when modified by S, is ground. The reason for this restriction is essentially the same as that given by Clark in his description of the negation as failure inference rule [1].

2. For all i, $0 < n$, either

— C_i is a resolvent of C_{i-1} with either a derivation rule, a base fact, or a clause C_j where $j < i$; or

— C_i is a resolvent of C_{i-1} and a unit clause comprising the assumption literal of a default rule, and there is a refutation, via the proof procedure, of the denial comprising the right-hand side of that default rule.

This formulation differs from the standard formulation of linear resolution by the introduction of the alternative in 2.

Example 3. Consider again the GDDB of Example 1. To find a person who is not a capitalist the denial

(1) ← ~ Capitalist(X)

is passed to the proof procedure for evaluation. Because (1) contains no M-literals a refutation of (1) exists if a refutation of

(2) Capitalist(X)

can be derived via the inference engine. The resolvent of (2) and (R1) is

(3) ~ Socialist(X)

The resolvent of (3) and a clause comprising only the assumption literal of (D2) is the empty clause, and therefore a refutation of (3) exists if there is a refutation via the proof procedure of the denial

(4) ← Reads(X,pravda) & M Socialist(X)

There are two steps in the generation of a refuation of (4). The first step requires a refutation via the inference engine of the clause coresponding to the Non-M-literal of (4):

(5) ~ Reads(X,pravda)

which can be achieved with substitutions:

(6) { X / mikhail }

The second step requires us to show that the negation of the M-literal of (4) is not contained in the extension. To do so we form a clause asserting that the M-literal (modified by (6)) is contained in the extension and attempt to derive a refutation via the inference engine:

(7) Socialist(mikhail)

As the attempted refutation fails, the negation of the M-literal of (4) is not contained in the extension. Thus a refutation of (4) is derived, and hence also a refutation of (1). Consequently the substitutions created during the process (i.e. (6)) constitute an answer to the query 'who is not a capitalist?'

4.3 Update operations

The insertion of a deduction rule

When a deduction rule is inserted into the rule base, 'house-keeping' information detailing possible consequential changes to the extension resulting from the insertion is derived and recorded in the PD and PI lists for subsequent use in constraint checking (see section 4.4), and an identifier for the rule is returned to the user.

The deletion of a deduction rule

When a request is received to delete a deduction rule, information detailing the possible consequential changes to the extension resulting from the deletion is derived and recorded in the PD and PI lists before deleting the rule from the rule base.

The insertion and deletion of integrity constraints

When an integrity constraint is inserted into the constraint base it is marked as 'new' until the transaction is committed; an identifier for the constraint is then returned to the user. A request to delete a constraint simply results in the deletion of the constraint from the constraint base.

The insertion and deletion of base facts

After a base fact has either been inserted into or deleted from the fact base, the possible consequential changes to the extension are derived and recorded in the PD and PI lists for subsequent use in constraint checking.

4.4 Maintenance of the PD and PI lists

Introduction

During a transaction, two lists of unit clauses, called the 'possible deletions' (PD) and 'possible insertions' (PI), are constructed. These lists are used to optimize the constraint enforcement process when the transaction is committed (see section 4.5 below). The PD and PI list are defined as follows:

1. If L is a base fact deleted (inserted) by the transaction then L is an element of the PD (PI) list.
2. If

   $$L_0 \vee \ldots \vee L_n$$

   is a derivation rule deleted (inserted) by the transaction then L_0 to L_n are elements of the PD (PI) list.
3. If

   $$L_0 \leftarrow L_1 \,\&\, \ldots \,\&\, L_n \,\&\, \mathrm{M}L_0$$

   is a default rule deleted (inserted) by the transaction then L_0 is an element of the PD (PI) list.
4. If there is a clause L of the PD (PI) list, a set S of substitutions, and a derivation rule

$$L_0 \vee \ldots \vee \sim L_i \vee \ldots L_j$$

such that $\sim L_i^{(S)}$ is the negation of $L^{(S)}$, then $L_0^{(S)}$ to $L_{i-1}^{(S)}$ and $L_{i+1}^{(S)}$ to $L_j^{(S)}$ are also elements of the PD (PI) list.

5. If there is a clause L of the PD (PI) list, a set S of substitutions, and a default rule

$$L_0 \leftarrow L_1 \,\&\, \ldots \,\&\, L_n \,\&\, \mathrm{M}L_0$$

such that $L_i^{(S)}$ is identical to $L^{(S)}$, then $L_0^{(S)}$ is an element of the PD (PI) list.

6. If there is a clause L of the PI (PD) list, a set S of substitutions, and a default rule

$$\sim L_0 \leftarrow L_1 \,\&\, \ldots \,\&\, L_n \,\&\, \mathrm{M}\!\sim L_0$$

such that $\sim L_0^{(S)}$ is the negation of $L^{(S)}$, then $\sim L_0^{(s)}$ is an element of the PD (PI) list.

7. No other literals are elements of the PD (PI) list.

Example 4.
Consider the following GDDB.:

R1	Grandmother(X,Z) v ~ Mother(X,Y) v ~ Parent(Y,Z)
D1	~ Grandmother(V,W) ← M ~ Grandmother(V,W)

Consider also a transaction consisting solely of the insertion of

Parent(claudius,britannicus)

The PD and PI lists for this transaction are

PI	PD
Parent(claudius,britannicus)	~ Grandmother(X,britannicus)
~ Mother(X,claudius)	
Grandmother(X,britannicus)	

Example 5.
Consider the GDDB of Example 4, together with a transaction consisting solely of the insertion of the rule

Parent(A,B) v ~ Father(A,B)

The PD and PI lists for this transaction are

PI	PD
Parent(A,B)	~ Grandmother(V,W)
~ Father(A,B)	
~ Mother(X,Y)	
Grandmother(X,Z)	

Thus an element of the PD (PI) list may be interpreted as stating that the unit clause $L^{(S)}$ may have been deleted from (inserted into) the extension as a result of the transaction, for some set of substitutions, S. Clearly, in the presence of recursive derivation rules the PD and PI lists may contain an infinite number of clauses. However, we use the following 'stopping rule' to ensure that the PD and PI lists contain only finitely many clauses:

> 'If a clause C_1 is implied by a clause C_2 of the PD (PI) list, then C_1 is not added to the PD (PI) list.'

4.5 Integrity maintenance

When a request is received to commit a transaction, two actions are undertaken. First, the safety of the database is checked; then, if it is ascertained that the updated database is safe, the integrity constraints are checked with respect to the extension. If either the database is unsafe, or the extension is invalid, then the transaction is not committed: control is returned to the user, who may either

— roll back the transaction;
— delete the violated constraint; or
— insert and/or delete sufficient base facts and/or deduction rules to enable the transaction to be successfully committed.

If the updated database is safe and the extension does not violate an integrity constraint, then all constraints which are marked as 'new' are marked as 'old', the PD and PI lists are set to 'empty', and the transaction is committed.

Each integrity constraint is a denial constructed in such a way that if a refutation of the denial can be derived via the proof procedure, then the extension is invalid. The validation of the integrity constraints proceeds in two phases. In the first phase the constraints marked as 'new' are passed directly to the proof procedure for evaluation. In the second phase the elements of the PD and PI lists are used to select and optimize the constraints marked as 'old' in the following manner. At each step a clause is arbitrarily selected from either the PD or the PI list and is marked 'validated'. The literal of the selected clause is then used to select a number of integrity constraints which are then tested. The process terminates when either all clauses of the PD and PI lists are marked 'validated', or the database is found to violate a constraint. The constraints which are selected for validation depend upon whether the clause is selected from the PD or the PI list. Recall that an integrity constraint is (typically) a formula of the form

$$\leftarrow L_0 \ \& \ \ldots \ \& \ L_{n-1} \ \& \ \mathrm{M}L_n \ \& \ \ldots \ \& \ \mathrm{M}L_{n+m}$$

If the clause was chosen from the PI list then an attempt is made to unify the literal of the clause with each Non-M-literal of the same polarity of each constraint in turn. Conversely, if the clause was chosen from the PD list then an attempt is made to unify the literal of the clause with each M-literal of opposite polarity of each constraint in turn. Whenever such an attempt succeeds, the substitutions created by the unification process are carried out throughout the constraint, which is then passed to the proof procedure for evaluation.

Example 6. Consider the following constraint:
C1 ← Parent(X,Y) & M ~ Mother(X,Y) & M ~ Father(X,Y)

Assume that the following clause has been selected from the PI list.

Parent(claudius,britannicus)

The literal is of equal polarity to, and can be unified with, the Non-M-literal of C1. Therefore the substitutions are carried out throughout the constraint, resulting in the following constraint being passed to the proof procedure for evaluation;

C1′ ← Parent(claudius,britannicus) & M ~ Mother(claudius,britannicus) & M ~ Father(claudius, britannicus)

As a further example, C1′ would also have been passed to the proof procedure for evaluation had either of the following clauses been selected from the PD list:

Mother(claudius,britannicus)
Father(claudius,britannicus)

5. CONCLUSIONS

The Exegesis system enforces integrity constraints over a deductive database extended with default rules. In this respect we believe the system to be unique since previously described implementations of constraint enforcement systems for deductive databases enforce the constraints over a database 'completed' by use either of the negation as failure rule [5–8], or of the Closed World Assumption [9].

One area in which comparisons can be drawn between the Exegesis system and other constraint enforcement systems for deductive databases is in the method by which the constraints are selected for testing when the transaction is committed. Four classes of method can be distinguished in addition to that employed by Exegesis.

First, Kowalski [10,11] proposes that each constraint be tested in the form in which it was specified. Clearly, however, this method can lead to unacceptable inefficiency since it may redundantly check constraints which are unaffected by the transaction.

Kowalski *et al.* [8] and Decker [6] describe systems in which the *actual* consequential changes following from a database update are derived and used to select and partially instantiate constraints for testing. This approach may cause fewer constraints to be tested than the method employed by Exegesis, although derivation of the actual consequential changes is likely to be more costly than derivation of the possible consequential changes, since the fact base must be accessed in addition to the rule base.

Asirelli *et al.* [5] and Goebel *et al.* [7] describe systems in which data conflicting with the integrity constraints can be inserted into, but cannot to retrieved from, the database. Asirelli *et al.* propose the modification of the derivation rules to ensure that such data cannot be retrieved, whilst Goebel *et al.* describe a modification of the inference mechanism to achieve this objective.

Finally, both integrity constraints and derivation rules can be defined in Chang's Deduce-2 system: however, in Deduce-2 the integrity constraints are evaluated against only the fact base of the database. Thus integrity enforcement is likely to be efficient (since derived relations need not be computed), although some constraints (i.e. those involving recursively defined derived relations) cannot be defined over the fact base only.

Paradoxically, we believe Chang's approach, although the most primitive, to be the most promising, especially in the light of advances made over the past decade in query 'compilation' strategies for deductive databases [12,13]. Thus we are currently investigating methods of compiling integrity constraints into constraints which are evaluated against only the fact base of the database.

ACKNOWLEDGEMENTS

This work was mainly carried out in the context of the TriStarp project at Birkbeck College with the support of IBM (UK) Research Laboratories Ltd, the author being in receipt of an SERC (CASE) award. The final stages were financed under SERC (ALVEY) project number (GR/0/7306.5-IKBS/140. The help and advice of Mir Derakshan, Nigel Nicholson, and Alex Poulovassilis, and especially of Nigel Martin and Peter King, proved invaluable during the design and implementation of the Exegesis system.

REFERENCES

[1] Clark, K. L., Negation As Failure, in *Logic and Database*, Plenum Press, New York, 1978.

[2] King, P. J. H. and Small, C., Default Databases and Incomplete Information, Research Report KSG/CARDS/TR/C1, Knowledge Systems Group, University of Reading, 1987.

[3] Ullman, J. D., *Principles of Database Systems*, Pitman, London, 1982.

[4] Loveland, D. W., A Linear Format for Resolution, *Symp. on Automatic Demonstration*, Springer Lecture Notes in Mathematics, No. 125, pp. 147–162.

[5] Asirelli, P., de Santis, M., and Martelli, M., Integrity Constraints in Logic Databases, *J. Logic Programming*, **3** 221–232, 1985.

[6] Decker, H., Integrity Enforcement on Deductive Databases, *Proc. Int. Conf. on Expert Database Systems*, Charleston, South Carolina, 1986.

[7] Goebel, R., Furukawa, K., and Poole, D., Using Definite Clauses and

Integrity Constraints as the Basis for a Theory Formation Approach to Diagnostic Reasoning, *Third Int. Conf. on Logic Programming*, Springer Verlag, 211–222, 1986.

[8] Kowalski, R., Sadri, F., and Soper, P., Integrity Checking in Deductive Databases, *Proc. 13th Int. Conf. on Very Large Databases*, Brighton, England, Morgan Kaufmann, Los Altos, 1987.

[9] Chang, C. L., DEDUCE 2: Further Investigations of Deduction in Relational Databases, in *Logic and Databases*, Plenum Press, New York, 1978.

[10] Kowalski, R., Logic for Data Description, in *Logic and Databases*, Plenum Press, New York, 1978.

[11] Kowalski, R., *Logic for Problem-Solving*, North-Holland, Amsterdam, 1979.

[12] Bancilhon, F. and Ramakrishnan, R., *An Amateurs Introduction to Recursive Query Processing Strategies, proc. ACM SIGMOD*, Washington DC, 1986.

[13] Reiter, R., Deductive Question–Answering on Relational Databases, in *Logic and Databases*, Plenum Press, New York, 1978.

[14] Lloyd, J. and Topor, R., A basis for Deductive Database Systems, *J. Logic Programming*, **2**, 93–109, 1986.

10

Recursive query processing: fundamental algorithms and the DedGin System

Laurent Vieille
E.C.R.C†, Munich, Germany

ABSTRACT‡

This chapter first gives an informal presentation of theoretical techniques which provide, we argue, a sound and powerful framework for recursive query processing. Various combinations of these techniques enable us to account for and to generalize methods that have been proposed so far. Another combination produces a general-purpose procedure, called QoSaQ, which improves on existing methods. We then describe the DedGin query answering system, which is able to answer queries on large amounts of data actually stored in a relational database. DedGin implements the QSQR algorithm [26].

1. INTRODUCTION

Deductive database systems [12] enhance relational database management systems (DBMSs) in particular by allowing recursively defined queries (recursively defined views). In such a system, one may thus distinguish between *base* relations, which can store large amounts of facts, and *virtual* relations, which are defined by means of rules. Tuples for virtual relations are not explicitly stored in the database, but simply derived at query time. One may think, for example, of a financial database that will contain facts like *own*($firm_1$,*firm*) ($firm_1$ owns *firm*) and some derived relationships, e.g. *control,* defined by means of rules (written à la Prolog):

$$control(X,Y) \text{ :- } own(X,Y).$$
$$control(X,Y) \text{ :- } own(X,Z),\ control(Z,Y).$$

† The European Computer-Industry Research Centre is a joint Research Centre established by Bull, ICL and Siemens in January 1984.
‡ The material presented here derives from material published in [27,28].

A query answering procedure for queries on deductive databases must have several crucial properties, which we now list. *First,* it must return all the answers to a query (*completeness*) and then stop (*termination*) (we shall focus here in general on function-free rules for which termination can be ensured, and we shall mention some generalizations). *Second,* it must be *logically efficient,* i.e. it must be able to use a *Focus on Relevant Data (FRD) Strategy*. For instance, suppose our financial database stores two disjoint *control* trees, say of holdings *a* and *b*; our procedure should avoid considering the *non-relevant b*-firms (the films controlled by the holding *b*, but without any relationship to *a*) when retrieving the firms controlled by *a*. These two issues together already rule out the most classical bottom-up computations (or least-fixed-point computation [1]), which would compute the whole relation *control* before selecting the relevant tuples; they also rule out simple top-down computation, as performed for instance by Prolog interpreters, which would not terminate as soon as there is a cycle in the *own* relationship (this may happen!).

Besides the above two crucial properties, the chosen algorithm should be competitive on two further points. First, on the *complexity issue*: fixed-point operators are not able to focus on relevant data but their cost is always polynomial compared to the size of the whole database [14]. We must guarantee that focusing on relevant data does not lead in fact to more expensive procedures, for instance with an exponential cost. Second, it must be able to face the *physical issue.* By this, we mean that it must be able to adapt itself to the physical features of computers. Most important is of course the page-based input/output with secondary storage, or simply the page-based organization of central memory.

Our approach to this problem is called the Query/SubQuery (QSQ) approach. This approach was introduced in [26] where it led to two algorithms, QSQI and QSQR. The general interest of QSQR was recognized in the (now classical) overview by Bancilhon and Ramakrishnan [4]. The QSQR algorithm is at the core of the DedGin query answering system, which is fully connected to a relational system. The first (complete) version of DedGin was running in December 1985 and is still, to our knowledge, the only system offering such a range of facilities for handling recursive queries†. DedGin makes use of the Educe system [7,8], which is also discussed in Chapter 4 of this volume.

More recently, our work has first focused on providing a formal basis to the QSQ approach. This was achieved by the introduction of the SLD-AL resolution [29,30], which is general enough to handle all kinds of clause (rules) (i.e. also with function symbols). This work has yielded a new general-purpose procedure, called *QoSaQ* [31]. The main new feature of QoSaQ is to make general use of a so-called *global optimization* technique (QoSaQ=QSQ+glObAl), which permits the obtainment of a complete

† Query-by-Example — QBE — also provides recursive facilities, but they are, to our knowledge, limited to the transitive closure and to acyclic data (thus it should not be able to answer queries on *control*). The other systems we have heard of are limited to main-memory implementations.

answer to the top query *without* requiring this completeness to any (local) subquery (unlike earlier general-purpose methods). Accordingly, QoSaQ has several nice properties: (i) QoSaQ successfully faces all the issues discussed above; (ii) QoSaQ is competitive, in any case, with any other general-purpose procedure; (iii) in many cases, it performs as well as the best method known for this case; (iv) by varying some parameters in the basic QoSaQ procedure, one obtains other well-known procedures (up to slight differences), in particular the Magic set method [5,6,21] (similiar to the *Alexander* method [20]) and the counting-based methods [5,6,22].

In section 2, we informally introduce the various theoretical aspects that are at the basis of the QSQ approach; this material is developed in more detail in [29,30]. We then describe (section 3) the DedGin query answering component. As a conclusion, we discuss the orientations of our current work.

Example 1: *A final introductory example*
To complete this introduction, we give an example of a complex recursive definition. This definition is easy to understand and is provided mainly to show that the restricted classes of rules that are often considered in the literature (linear, . .) do not actually suffice in a deductive database environment. Let *parent, hu* (human-being) and *married* be base relations. The *same-generation* relation can be defined as: any *human-being X* is of the same generation as himself; *X* and *Y* are of the same generation if their respective parents *U* and *V* are *either* of the same generation, *or* are respectively of the same generation as *Z* and *W*, and *Z* and *W* are married. This yields the following set of rules:

sg(X,X) :- hu(X).
sg(X,Y) :- parent(X,U), sg(U,V), parent(Y,V).
sg(X,Y) :- parent(X,U), sg(U,Z), married(Z,W), sg(W,V), parent(Y,V).

2. AN INFORMAL PRESENTATION OF FORMAL ASPECTS

2.1 Completeness and logical efficiency: SLD resolution and the FRD strategy

The core of our approach is to develop techniques to enhance SLD resolution [15]. The aim is to obtain a resolution procedure which fulfills the various requirements listed in the introduction. The motivation is the (long recognized [12]) interest of resolution as a powerful framework for query answering. In particular, SLD resolution has, from our point of view, several nice features: (i) SLD trees are *complete* search spaces: any answer to a query is returned by at least one branch of the SLD tree; (ii) SLD trees allow *logical efficiency*: they are defined up to a so-called *selection function.*

Loosely speaking, SLD resolution consists of recursively resolving *goals* (i.e. sets of literals) with *clauses* (rules), starting from a top goal (or query) G_o. Given a current goal G, one first selects (using a *selection function*) *one* literal (or *subgoal*) SG out of G. SG is then unified with the head of a clause

Cl, and a new goal G' is derived from G by replacing SG by the body of *Cl,* while keeping the instantiations of the variables as provided by the unification. Example 2 provides two examples of trees obtained in such a way, for the query $r(X, c_o)$. Finally, observe that Prolog provides a particular implementation of SLD resolution and that it should not be confused with it: there are, as we shall see, other techniques to implement SLD resolution, in particular for a database environment.

In a *programming environment* (e.g. Prolog), the specification of the selection function is usually best left to the user, as it may affect termination. This is indirectly done by letting the system take the first literal to come and hence select the literals in the order given by the user (programmer). In *deductive* and relational *database* systems, choosing the/a good selection function will be the task of the *query optimizer*: two different selection functions can traditionally lead to evaluation costs differing by an order of magnitude. For instance, this optimizer may apply a *Focus on Relevant Data (FRD)* strategy, which corresponds to the heuristic 'make selections first', popular in database systems [4]. Informally, this consists of taking advantage of the constants appearing in the query to consider only the facts relevant to the query. In terms of SLD resolution, this corresponds to a selection function that *tries to choose a literal among the most instantiated ones* (whatever this precisely means).

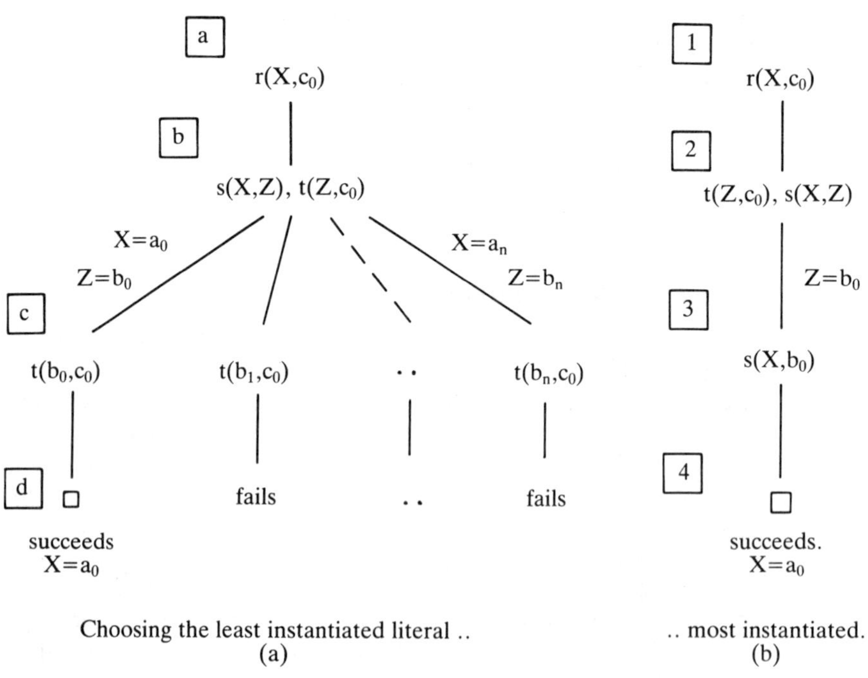

Fig. 1 — Illustration of the FRD Strategy.

Example 2
This example illustrates the utility of an FRD strategy in a database system. Figs 1(b) and 1(a) respectively display trees obtained by using and not using an FRD strategy. The respective size of the trees is a sufficient illustration of our point.

s	**t**
$s(a_0, b_0).$	$t(b_0, c_0).$
..	..
$s(a_q, b_q).$	$t(b_n, c_n).$

$r(X,Y)$:- $s(X,Z)$, $t(Z,Y)$.

▼

2.2 Subquery redundancy elimination and finite search spaces: SLD-AL resolution

A major drawback of SLD resolution is that it never avoids answering several (infinitely many) times the same subgoal. This leads to infinite SLD trees, even when the database is finite and function-free, i.e. in cases which seem rather simple. The SLD-AL resolution, as proposed in [29,30], can be seen as eliminating this *subquery redundancy* and rests on two simple principles. The *admissibility test* prevents similar subgoals to be indefinitely solved: a subgoal SG is non-admissible iff it is similar to a previous subgoal SG'. In the finite and function-free case, the admissibility test cuts off any infinite branch. The *resolution* of non-admissible subgoals with *previously derived lemmas* enables the production of further answers, by answering the remaining literals in the goal: SG is thus resolved exclusively against the answers/lemmas proved for SG'. called its *producers*. In what follows, we will call this two-fold mechanism the *AL-technique*.

The major properties of SLD-AL resolution† are: (i) SLD-AL trees *are always finite* for finite function-free databases; (ii) SLD-AL trees are *complete* search spaces: an SLD-AL tree returns all the answers to a goal; (iii) it allows *logical efficiency*: SLD-AL trees are defined up to a (local) selection function (an FRD strategy can thus be adopted).

Example 3. *An infinite SLD tree vs a finite SLD-AL tree*
We consider the transitive closure, *tc*, of the relation *p*.

$$p(a_1,a) \qquad p(a_2,a_1)$$

(1) $tc(X,Y)$:- $p(X,Y)$
(2) $tc(X,Y)$:- $tc(Z,Y)$, $p(X,Z)$

The SLD tree displayed in Fig. 2 for the goal $tc(Z_0,a)$ is infinite, as the same operation can be repeated infinitely many times on similar subgoals, namely the $tc(Z_i,a)$'s: the resolution of each $tc(Z_i,a)$ against the clause (2) introduces its successor $tc(Z_{i+1},a)$. Fig. 3 displays an SLD-AL tree corresponding

† SLD-AL resolution is defined for any type of clause, including that containing function symbols. Of course, in this case, SLD-AL trees are not necessarily finite.

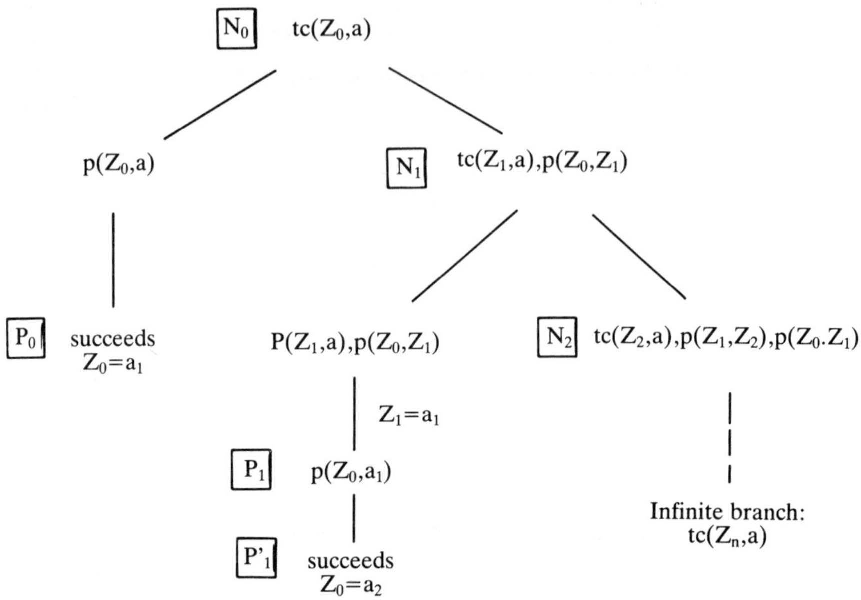

Fig. 2 — An infinite SLD tree for Example 3.

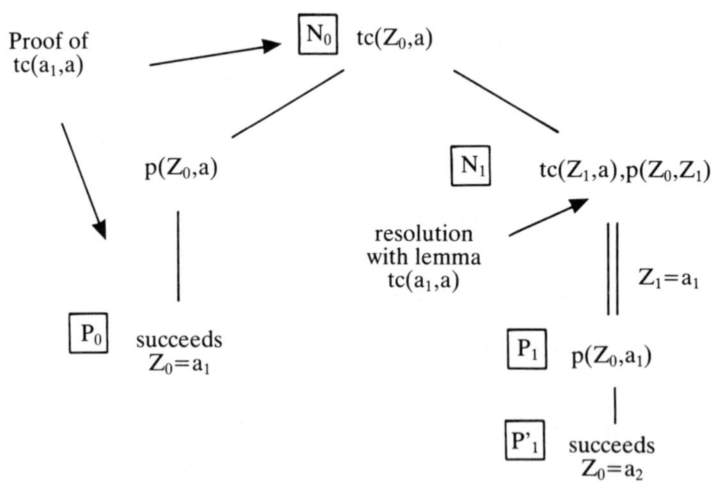

Fig. 3 — A finite SLD-AL tree for Example 3.

to Fig. 2. In our figures, we will always represent a lemma resolution by a double line, whereas resolution against clauses from the database is represented by a single line. The subgoal $tc(Z_1,a)$ is not admissible, as it is a variant of the root. Hence, it is resolved against a lemma $tc(a_1,a)$, which was previously provided at node P_0. This enables a further search of the tree to be made eventually producing the answer $tc(a_2,a)$.

2.3 Answer redundancy elimination

A second major drawback of SLD resolution (shared by SLD-AL resolution) is to return answers to subgoals in a potentially redundant manner, leading to further redundant processing. This is best illustrated through an example.

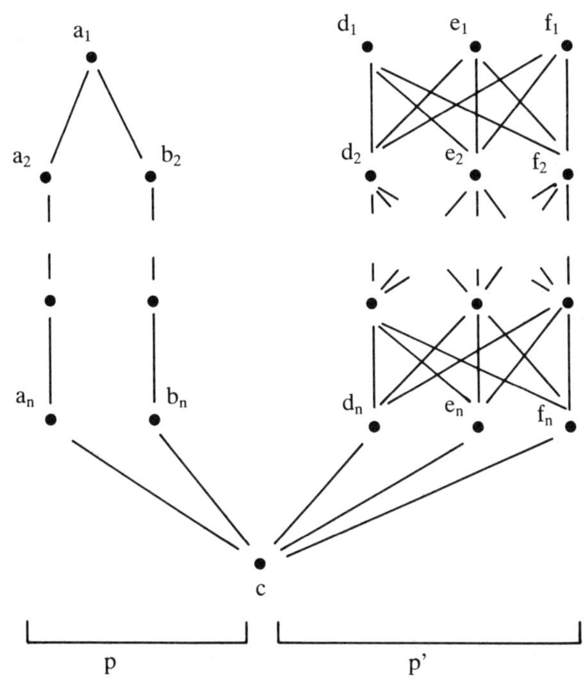

Fig. 4 — Data for Example 4.

Example 4

Consider for instance a simplified and modified form of the same-generation example, together with the data displayed on Fig. 4.

$p(a_1, a_2)$ $p(a_1, b_2)$

$p(a_i, a_{i+1})$ $p(b_i, b_{i+1})$ $1<i<n$

$p(a_n, c)$ $p(b_n, c)$

$p'(c, d_n)$ $p'(c, e_n)$ $p'(c,f_n)$
$p'(d_i, d_{i-1})$ $p'(e_i, d_{i-1})$ $p'(f_i, d_{i-1})$ resp. e_{i-1}, f_{i-1} $1<i<n+1$
$hu(c)$
$sg(X,X)$:- $hu(X)$.
$sg(X,Y)$:- $p(X,U)$, $sg(U,V)$, $p'(Y,V)$.

Starting from the query $sg(a_1, Y)$, a downwards search of the left-hand side of the data graph (the p part) leads to recursively setting the subqueries $sg(a_i, V_i)$ and $sg(b_i, V_i)$, and eventually $sg(c, V_{n+1})$. As illustrated by Fig. 4, both $sg(a_i, V_i)$ and $sg(b_i, V_i)$ accept the answers $V_i=d_i, e_i, f_i$. Further, one can derive *one* occurrence of $sg(a_i, d_i)$, $sg(a_i, e_i)$, $sg(a_i, f_i)$ from each occurrence of $sg(a_{i-1}, d_{i-1})$, $sg(a_{i-1}, e_{i-1})$, $sg(a_{i-1}, f_{i-1})$. It follows that, if no care is taken, $sg(a_n, d_n)$ can be derived *once;* $sg(a_{n-1}, d_{n-1})$ can be derived *three* times . . . $sg(a_{n-i}, d_{n-i})$ can be derived 3^i times.

Let us now see how the SLD/SLD-AL tree behaves in this case†. Going down the p part of the data graph, we generate the nodes $G(a_i)$ for the a individuals (we could do the same for the b individuals):

$$G(a_i): \qquad sg(a_i, V_i), p'(V_{i-1}, V_i), \ldots, p'(V_2, V_3), p'(Y, V_2)$$

Eventually two occurrences of the following goal, say G_a and G_b, are produced:

$$G_a, G_b: \qquad sg(c, V_{n+1}), p'(V_n, V_{n+1}), \ldots, p'(Y, V_2)$$

where G_a is derived from $G(a_n)$ and G_b is derived from $G(b_n)$.

Now, going up the datagraph along the p' part, further down the SLD/SLD-AL tree, we generate the goals for d_i (resp. for e_i and f_i):

$$Ans(a_i, d_i), Ans(b_i, d_i): \quad p'(V_{i-1}, d_i), p'(V_{i-2}, V_{i-1}), \ldots, p'(Y, V_2),$$

where $Ans(a_i, d_i)$ comes from G_a, and $Ans(b_i, d_i)$ comes from G_b.

Again, if no care is taken, from *each* node $Ans(a_i, d_i)$, $Ans(a_i, e_i)$, $Ans(a_i, f_i)$, we derive *one* occurrence of each $Ans(a_{i-1}, d_{i-1})$, $Ans(a_{i-1}, e_{i-1})$, $Ans(a_{i-1}, f_{i-1})$. It follows that, say, $Ans(a_{n-i}, d_{n-i})$ will be derived 3^i-times.

The sizes of both the SLD and the SLD-AL trees are exponential in n.

2.3.1 Local versus global optimization

Local optimization consists of eliminating redundant nodes while guaranteeing answer completeness to each (local) subquery. This means that for both $sg(a_i, V_i)$ *and* $sg(b_i, V_i)$, we will return *one* occurrence of the set of answers $V_i=d_i, e_i, f_i$. Following this strategy, we will consider that G_a and G_b are *not* redundant, as they will produce the *same* answers to *different local* subgoals.

When performing *global optimization,* we go one step further and guarantee completeness of the answer to the top goal without requiring this completeness for any local subquery. In particular, it appears that G_a and G_b will return exactly the same answers to the top query, but that they yield

† The SLD and SLD-AL trees are identical, except that one occurrence of $sg(c,V_{n+1})$ is not admissible and is directly resolved aginst the lemma $sg(c,c)$.

answers to different *local* subqueries. Global optimization will avoid processing one of them, say G_b, and will return answers only to the subgoals $sg(a_i, V_i)$, and not to the subgoals $sg(b_i, V_i)$.

2.3.2 A general treatment of redundancy elimination: db-subsumption

From the above examples, it should be clear to the reader, with a knowledge of theorem-proving, that the central notion for optimization should be the subsumption technique. This technique is traditionally used in theroem-proving to prune redundant parts of the search space (see [16] for further details). However, it is designed to preserve the *existence* of *one* solution in the search space, and it turns out that it does *not* preserve the *completeness* of the *set* of answers. In other words, suppose that a goal G_1 is subsumed by a goal G_2. Then, if an answer is found in the subtree rooted at G_1, one (potentially different) answer is also found in the subtree rooted at G_2. However, the *set* of *answers* for G_0 obtained in the subtree rooted at G_1 is *not necessarily* included in the set of answers for G_0 in the subtree rooted at G_2.

In [30], we introduce the enhanced *db-subsumption* test between *nodes.* Db-subsumption improves on subsumption essentially by taking into account the *output variables* of the nodes G_1, i.e. its variables that carry the values for the actual answers to G_0. Unlike simple subsumption db-subsumption preserves the completeness of the set of answers†.

2.4 Applications to deductive database systems: the QoSaQ procedure

Searching an (optimized) SLD-AL tree is not an easy task, first because of a coordination problem: a lemma *lem,* needed for the resolution of a non-admissible subgoal SG, may be proved only after SG is found. In order to resolve SG and *lem,* both must be available at the same time. A first solution consists of an *iterative deepening* depth-first search of the tree, where SG is resolved only with the lemmas present at the time SG is found. A repeated search of the tree ensures that SG is resolved with all the lemmas that are ever produced for it. A second solution consists of a *constructive,* breadth-first-like search of SLD-AL trees; accordingly, it requires storing non-admissible nodes until all the corresponding lemmas *lem* have been produced.

The second difficulty is a *storage* problem, which arises in particular when adopting a constructive search of SLD-AL trees: goals can be long sequences of literals, and efficient ways of representing and manipulating them must be provided. This can be solved by a decomposition of nodes into a sequence of tuples of constants, some of them being shared between several nodes. This representation has many advantages: (i) it provides a compact and manageable form for nodes; (ii) it is well suited for an implementation in a page-based environment; (iii) local and global optimi-

† Actually, the optmization must be based on a stronger form of (db-)subsumption, called *strong* (db-)subsumption, where the clause subsuming is required to be smaller than the clause subsumed. See [30].

zation can be implemented by the mere comparison of two tuples; (iv) similarly, in the case of SLD-AL resolution, the admissibility test is implemented as a simple comparison of tuples. For further details, the reader is referred to [30].

2.4.1 QoSaQ, QSQR and other methods for answering recursive queries

The various techniques we have introduced so far can be combined with each other in a number of different ways. Interestingly, it is possible to interpret the main methods that have been proposed in the literature as particular combinations of these techniques. They all suppose a tuple representation SLD/SLD-AL nodes.

QSQR [26]:

- Iterative deepening search of SLD-AL trees.
- Local optimization.

Magic sets[5,6,21] *(or Alexander* [20]*):*

- Constructive search of SLD-AL trees.
- Local optimization.

Counting methods [5,6] (these methods may not terminate — see also [13]):

- Search of SLD trees.
- Global optimization.

QoSaQ [31,30]:

- Constructive search of SLD-AL trees.
- Global optimization.

This clearly shows the interest of QoSaQ: (i) it is a general-purpose procedure which applies for all kinds of deductive database (including those containing negative literals in the body of clauses, in the stratified case [2]); (ii) it incorporates some kind of global optimization which, as shown in [4], may yield significant gains; (iii) it combines the advantages of earlier methods.

For completeness, we should mention that the incorporation of global optimization when searching SLD-AL trees introduces some serious technical difficulties, as the AL-technique requires that a complete answer is returned not only to the top query, but also to any *producer*. This technical difficulty can be solved along the various trade-offs discussed in [31,30]. The Magic-counting method [22] can be seen as a subcase of QoSaQ, as it applies only for linear queries.

2.4.2 An operational improvement on relational algebra: a semantics for duplicate elimination

The operational semantics of our procedures may appear to be tuple-based, since a (successful) resolution against a fact corresponds, in database terms, to retrieving a matching tuple in a relation. Hence, the interest of our approach might be questioned, as it has been recognized, when implementing relational systems [3], that set-oriented operators can be more efficiently implemented.

The first answer to the potential criticism consists in noting that, in our formalism, set-oriented operators can be described as particular search strategies. Optimized SLD and SLD-AL trees can be searched using any search strategy. In particular, one can use a search strategy which performs, in a sequence, all the resolutions of a subgoal with the matching tuples in a base relation, or interleaving, in a sort-merge manner, the scan of the subgoals and the retrieval of the tuples. This amounts to noticing that, after all, a so-called set-oriented operator is nothing more than an operation repeated on the tuples in the relations, in a particular and/or arbitrary order.

Further, we would like to argue that this is likely to provide a *better operational semantics than relational algebra.* A key point in the implementation of relational systems is the problem of duplicate elimination (see for instance [10]). Unfortunately, the duplicate elimination operation is not explicit in relational algebra, as its basic objects are *sets,* but this operation is *hidden* behind the set-theoretic notion of result and intermediate relation. In our formalism, duplicate elimination simply corresponds to redundancy elimination . . . .

2.4.3 An example

Example 5

$s(X,Y)$:- $p(X,Z)$, $q(Z,V)$, $r(V,Y)$.
?-$s(a,Y)$.

$p(a, b_1)$	$q(b_1, c)$	$r(c, d)$
..	..	..
$p(a, b_n)$	$q(b_n, c)$	$r(c, d)$

The SLD-(AL) tree of root $s(a,Y)$ displays n branches with the same shape (Fig. 5), first, a node labelled by $q(^*Z, V)$, $r(V,Y)$ (where $^*Z$ stands for one of the constants b_i), and then a node $r(c, Y)$. Clearly, by simply comparing the substitutions at all nodes $r(c,Y)$, we can conclude that $(n-1)$ of them are locally redundant. The representations by tuples used in QoSaQ (as in relational algebra) allows the representation of the constants b_i as a set $\langle ^*Z \rangle$. As the next step, this enables the processing of a 'join' operation with the relation q, yielding a set $\{c\ (c)\ .\ .\ .\ \}$, to be made. Set-theoretically, this set contains only one element, c. In SLD-AL resolution these $(n-1)$ redundant occurrences are identified as (locally) redundant, and are eliminated only if local optimization is 'turned on'. In relational algebra, this is left to the user/implementer as an 'implementation-dependent feature'.

2.5 Upper-bound for QoSaQ

The last result we would like to mention is an upper-bound to the number of intermediate tuples manipulated by QoSaQ when answering a (recursive)

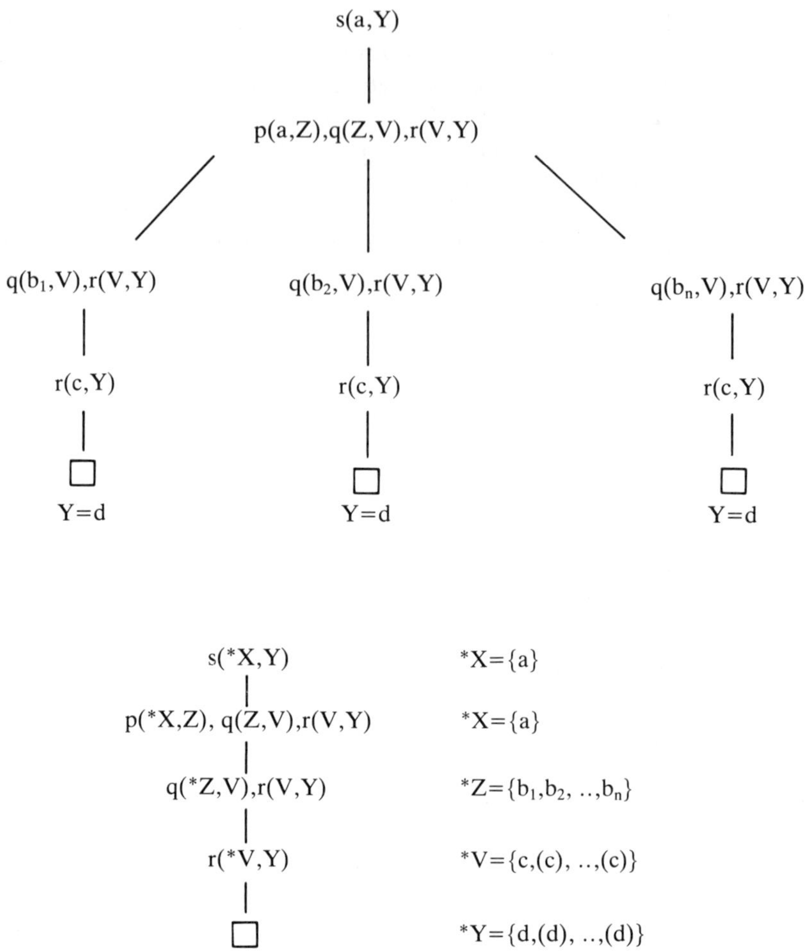

Fig. 5 — Translation of SLD trees into set-oriented operators.

query. This upper-bound† is $O(p^{a+k'})$, where p is the number of constants appearing in an intermediate tuple (the *relevant* constants), k' is a syntactic constant depending on the rules, and a is the maximal arity of a virtual predicate.

This upper-bound is of independent interest, as it validates, from the complexity point of view, the interest of a procedure 'able to focus on relevant data'. A previous upper-bound for the evaluation of recursive queries was provided by Chandra and Harel [9] and Immerman [14], who showed that the number of tuples manipulated by a least-fixed-point operator is $O(n^{2a+k})$, where n is the total number of individuals in the database, a is the arity of the recursive predicate and k is a syntactic constant

† Which depends on the selection function.

such that $a+k$ is greater than or equal to k'. In any case, our upper-bound is smaller than Immerman's. Further, in practical cases, p is usually much less than n, and our upper-bound is much smaller than Immerman's. This is a clear validation of the 'focus-on-relevant-data' approach.

2.6 Further relevant work

Tamaki and Sato introduced the OLDT resolution [24], which is similar to the *non-optimized SLD-AL* resolution. However, OLDT does not allow logical optimization, as rules are required to be preordered. Apparently, the first authors to introduce a notion similar to *db-subsumption* on SLD trees were Minker and Nicolas [17], but they did not investigate the same properties as those in our study. Apart from the work listed above, work in *deductive databases* includes Ullman's capture rules formalism [25]; however, the termination/completeness issue is not fully treated there. Our *cost metrics* (see also [30,31]) can be seen as a proper definition of the one used in [4].

3. THE DEDGIN QUERY ANSWERING SYSTEM

DedGin (**Ded**uctive Database En**Gin**e) is a deductive query answering database system developed as an extension to a relational DBMS. According to a more conventional database terminology, this system can be referred to as a 'view' (virtual relation) handling component which supports *recursive* 'view' definitions.

From the algorithmic point of view, DedGin implements the QSQR algorithm. From the implementation point of view, DedGin is organized in two parts: a view-definition (clause) precompiler which takes care of all query-independent treatment at compile time, and the effective query-evaluator which runs the generated code at query-time. Further, DedGin has been implemented in EDUCE [7,8], a logic programming system developed at ECRC, which offers, in an integrated way, both a loose coupling and a tight integration between (Mu-)Prolog [18] and the relational DBMS INGRES† [23].

The first (complete) version was available in December 1985, and the present version, although it does not incorporate all query optimization techniques that one may think of, already shows satisfactory performance (see section 3.3).

3.1 DedGin: the user viewpoint

As a (deductive) DBMS, DedGin offes two kinds of facilities: schema facilities, i.e. a set of primitives which permit the user to add, delete, modify derivation rules and/or to query upon (virtual) relations, and data manipulation facilities for database querying and updating. We will focus here on the

† INGRES is a trademark of Relational Technology.

facilities which are directly concerned with the virtual relations and the facts they support, the other facilities being provided by the underlying DBMS (INGRES/EDUCE).

3.1.1 The language for rule formulation

Using similar syntax as Prolog, a clause is written as

$$B \text{ :- } A_1, \ldots, A_n.$$

Where A_i can be a positive or a negative literal (preceded by *not*). As we do not have function symbols, a *term* or *argument* is either a variable (string of characters starting with an upper case letter) or a constant (an integer or a string of characters starting with a lower case letter).

Predicates in the body of DedGin clauses may be of three different types: they can correspond either to a *virtual relation* (appearing in the head of some rules), to a *base relation* (supported by the underlying DBMS) or to a *test* (evaluable predicate). Test predicates are either built-in ($<$, $>$, $=$, $\leqslant$, . . .) or (user) defined by means of Prolog (or C) programs. Note the absence of any control prediates such as the cut (!) or meta-predicates such as *var(X)* . . . .

Recursive predicates. A predicate *p directly depends on* the predicate *q* if *q* appears in the body of a clause defining *p*. Let the *dependence* relationship be the transitive (not reflexive) closure of the direct dependence relationship. *p* is said to be *recursive* if it depends on itself. *p* and *q* are *mutually recursive* if *p* depends on *q* and *q* depends on *p*.

We note that, unlike in most recursive query evaluation methods (e.g. see [4]), clauses in DedGin are not restricted to be Horn clauses since their bodies may contain negative literals. However, to ensure soundness, a negative literal is not allowed to be mutually recursive with the head of the clause (*stratified* database [2]).

Finally, clauses in DedGin have to obey a standard well-formedness condition, i.e. they have to be *range-restricted* [19]. This means that any variable occurring in the head, or in a test predicate, or in a negative literal of a clause must also occur in at least one positive literal of its body corresponding to a base or a virtual relation. Such a condition is required, broadly to guarantee the finiteness of the set of answers. For example, the following (non-range-restricted) definition would lead to an infinite number of solutions:

$$r(X,Y) \text{ :- } a(X,Y).$$
$$r(X,Y) \text{ :- } a(X,Z),\ Y=Y'+1,\ r(Z,Y').$$

3.1.2 Declaring and retracting user-defined test predicates

A test is a predicate called with *a priori*, all its arguments instantiated. Thus, a test does not return new instantiations and cannot be used as a generator of new values (see the range-restricted condition imposed on clauses in section 3.1.1). A test, as a boolean query, returns either *true* or *false*.

Built-in tests available in DedGin come from the implementation language (Mu_Prolog [18]): $<, \leqslant, \geqslant, >, ==$. DedGin allows the user to define his own tests by means of Prolog (or C) programs. Heads of these programs must be function-free. The user is responsible for storing and loading these programs.

DedGin will call a test only when, and as soon as, all its arguments are bound to constants. We note that the range-restrictedness condition imposed on clauses does imply that no test remain uninstantiated for ever. Thus, any test is eventually executed.

Tests must be declared (and retracted) to (from) DedGin by means of the following two primitives: *decl_test(Pred)* decrease *Pred* as a test; *retr_test(Pred)* retracts *Pred* as a test.

3.1.3 Schema manipulation facilities

We briefly describe various facilities which enable the user to manipulate database schema (meta)-information related to virtual relations.

In order to enter or modify the definition of a virtual relation, the user has just to call for the primitives *cons_dg* (or *recons_dg).* He is then prompted (*dg:* or *-dg:*) to enter derivation rules. Other primitives enable him to list all the rules present in the schema (*rules_dg*), or corresponding to a particular predicate *Pred* (*rule_dg(Pred)*) or to retract (*retract_dg(pred :- Body)*) rules defining *pred.*

Whenever the definition of a virtual relation, say *Pred*, is entered or modified, the corresponding derivation rules have to be (pre)compiled (*compile(Pred)*) to generate an efficient (in the FRD sense) and correct (termination and completeness) code for the query evaluator. This is done in such a way that rules corresponding to virtual relations related to *Pred* (i.e. mutually recursive with *Pred* or at a lower definition level) are (re)compiled if necessary.

Another set of primitives enables the user to ask whether a given relation is of a certain type, or to ask for the list of relations of a certain type: base relations (*base(rel)*), virtual relations (*virtual(rel)*), virtual non-recursive relations (*virt_nr(rel)*), and virtual recursive relation (*virt_rec(rel)*). Finally, the primitive *level(pred, List)* permits obtainment of the list of relations that are mutually recursive with *pred*, and *higher_lev(Pred1, Pred2)* enables querying whether *Pred1* depends on *Pred2*.

3.1.4 Database querying: the SQL and the Prolog interfaces

Queries on DedGin (base and virtual) relations can be expressed either in the SQL language or as a Prolog-like query to DedGin. These two interfaces are provided for different classes of user. The SQL query language is designed for *casual users*; accordingly, the answers are all printed on the screen. The Prolog interface is a *host language interface.* Several Prolog queries to DedGin can be included in a Prolog program. Answers to these goals are returned one-tuple-at-a-time, in accordance with Prolog backtracking behaviour.

For instance, given the base relations *director* and *own* and the virtual relation *control,* a query asking for the *executives* of the firm *holding1* (i.e. the directors of *holding1* or of a firm controlled by *holding1*) can be expressed in SQL by

```
        select direc from director
                where director.firm='holding1'
union
        select direc from control, director
                where control.firm=director.firm
                 and control.shareholder='holding1'
```

Note that the above query involves both virtual and base relations.

The same query can also be expressed by defining a virtual relation *executive* by the following two DedGin rules and then giving the goal *executive (X,holding1)* to the Prolog interface to DedGin.

executive(X,Y) :- director(X,Y).
executive(X,Y) :- director(X,Z), control(Z,Y).

The SQL interface essentially works by translating an SQL query into a Prolog program containing Prolog queries to DedGin. Hence, the same recursive query answering component is used. Hereafter, we focus on this query answering component.

3.2 DedGin: the implementation

The present version of DedGin has been implemented in (Mu)Prolog [18] on INGRES and relies on the Prolog/DBMS connection provided by the EDUCE system developed at ECRC [7,8]. EDUCE offers in an integrated way, two connections between the Mu-Prolog interpreter and INGRES: loose connection where the DBMS is accessed at the conceptual level (QUEL data manipulation language) and a tight integration where it is accessed at a lower level (access methods). If DedGin makes use of both routes, its query/answering component on which we essentially focus hereafter mainly relies on tight integration. There is a simple reason for this: efficiency for recursive query evaluation [7].

As discussed in section 2, the QSQR algorithm implemented in DedGin can be viewed as an enhancement of SLD resolution [29,30]. The current version of DedGin relies on Prolog to search the (modified) SLD tree as long as non-recursive (sub)goals are concerned. Recursive (sub-goals are handled by meta-level control† procedures. These procedures take a recursive (sub)goal as the argument, perform the admissibility test on this goal, and, according to the result of the test, perform a lemma resolution or pass the goal to Prolog for normal SLD resolution. Recursive predicates must thus be determined beforehand in order to introduce the correct calls to the control procedures. In DedGin, this is done by the clause (pre)compiler.

A big advantage of the design of the QSQR method is that it allows any ordering of (sub)goals (any local selection function). At the implementation

† Not to be confused with our relation *control* (shares) example.

level, one is thus free to choose the order: in particular it can be based on pure optimization criteria. The present version of DedGin makes use of a very simple criterion which turns out to be particularly efficient in the recursive case: choose a literal among the most instantiated ones. This strategy is contradictory with that of Prolog, since Prolog chooses the first literal to come. To resolve this contradiction, two approaches were envisaged: dynamically perform the reordering at query-time, or determine at compile-time, for each query pattern, a good evaluation order. The second solution was adopted in DedGin.

3.2.1 The clause (pre)compiler

Given the definition of a virtual relation, the compiler performs the following sequence of actions.

1. Seach the resolution tree of the predicate being compiled. Any node corresponding either to a predicate already compiled, to a test, or to a predicate appearing higher in this resolution tree (recursive cases) is not searched further. Any (virtual) predicate in this tree must be compiled, if not already done. (Mutual) recursions are detected.
2. For each predicate to be compiled, for each rule defining it, and for each posssible instantiation pattern for the head:
   (a) reorder the goals in the body according to the instantiation pattern (tests are inserted in such a way that they are evaluated when, and as soon as, all their arguments are bound to constants).
   (b) introduce the calls to the meta-level control predicates for each recursive predicate in the body of the (compiled) clauses.

Step 2(a) (reordering) corresponds to the optimization task of the (pre)compiler: the resulting code must evaluate the query efficiently. As this reordering is done at compile-time, the result is, for each rule, a set of compiled rules, each of them being used for goals with different instantiation patterns. The query evaluator will thus use only one of these sets of rules to answer a given query.

Step 2(b) (introduction of control) corresponds to the second task of the compiler: the production of a correct (complete and terminating) code.

As an example, consider the recursive rule defining the virtual relation *control*:

control(X,Y) :- own(X,Z,P), P>67, control(Z,Y).

Let us associate the mask *10* (resp. *01*) to the instantiation pattern of *control* where only the first (resp. the second) argument is instantiated. Then the rules produced by the compiler are very much like the following ones. The greater complexity of the real ones is due to the refinement of the optimization.

control10(X,Y) :- own(X,Z,P), P>67, rec_solve(control10(Z,Y)).
control01(X,Y) :- it_without_cont(control01(Z,Y)), own(X,Z,P), P>67.

Note that the order of literals in the rule corresponds to our criterion: first choose the most instantiated literal. The test (*P>67*) is called as soon as all its variables are instantiated. *it_without_cont* and *rec_solve* are calls to meta-level control procedures which are described in the next section.

3.2.2 The query evaluator

Admissibility test and lemma resolution

The query evaluator provides a set of meta-level control procedures. The two main tasks of these procedures are to perform the *admissibility test* and, if this test fails, to handle *lemma resolution.*

The *admissibility test* is described in [29]. It consists of comparing the current (recursive) subgoal with its predecessors in the resolution tree. If it is a variant of one of its predecessors, then the admissibility test fails; otherwise it succeeds. The solution adopted in DedGin to implement this test consists of storing subgoals in so-called *sets of instances* that are maintained using relational techniques (in temporary relations): the subgoals *control(holding1, Y), control(holding2, Y)* are stored as (unary) tuples ⟨*holding1*⟩ and ⟨*holding2*⟩ in a (unary) relation (called *control10*). Performing the admissibility test thus consists of searching in this set of instances a tuple matching the constants of the current subgoal.

The second main task of the query evaluator is to *handle lemmas*, corresponding to recursive predicates. It must first recognize when a lemma is provided, i.e. when the call to a recursive subgoal succeeds and returns the corresponding instantiation. A proved lemma is then stored in a temporary relation. Later, if a recursive subgoal corresponding to this predicate fails the admissibility test, it is simply resolved against the facts (lemmas) in this temporary relation (lemma resolution).

Concurrent goals: the notion of environment

A Prolog program can contain several calls to DedGin-defined predicates (in the case of DedGin being used by an application programmer). This implies that DedGin must be able to handle concurrent goals to the same predicate: as DedGin, in this context, computes and delivers answers one tuple at a time (à la Prolog), a second call to the same predicate (and even the same goal) can be given to DedGin before the answer to the first one is completed.

To handle concurrent goals on the same predicate, we have to differentiate the environment of two external calls to DedGin. In this way, subgoals and lemmas are privately owned by an *environment,* and shared use of the bookkeeping (lemmas and instances) between environments is not possible. Not doing so (i.e. allowing subgoals and lemmas to be shared between two different external calls) may lead to the incompleteness of the result. Consider, for instance, the following Prolog program:

$$p(X,Y) \text{ :- } R(X, Z), R(Z, Y), Y \neq a.$$
$$?\text{-}p(a,Y).$$

Suppose that *R* is a recursively defined virtual relation (supported by DedGin) and that there are only two facts derivable for *R* from the database,

R(a,a) and *R(a,b)*. Suppose further that, on the query *R(a,Z)*, the first answer is *R(a,a)* and the second one *R(a,b)*. On the query *?-p(a,Y)*, the first call to DedGin, i.e. *R(a,Z)* is issued; this call succeeds and returns *R(a,a)*. A second (concurrent) goal, i.e. *R(z,Y)*, is issued. As *R(a,Y)* is not a new subgoal (it is a variant of *R(a,Z)*), only lemma resolution will be performed on it. *R(a,a)*, being the only lemma proved for *R*, *Y=a*, is the only solution. But *Y=a* fails the last goal in the Prolog program (*Y≠a*). On backtracking, the first occurrence of *R* returns *Z=b*, but the second (concurrent) goal *R(b,Y)* fails. The Prolog goal *p(a,Y)* fails whereas *Y=b* was a correct answer.

The introduction of *environments* in DedGin solves this problem. A subgoal fails the test iff it is a variant of a subgoal belonging to the same environment. Lemma resolution is allowed only with lemmas of the same environment. However, DedGin knows when a goal is completely answered, and is able, in this case, to use previously completed work. Environments are kept in a stack parallel to the Prolog stack. Movements on this stack are performed when a call to DedGin starts, succeeds, fails, or backtracks.

Examples of meta-level control procedures

There are three main meta-level control procedures (Prolog predicates) and several secondary ones. We describe only the three main ones. The clause compiler determines which one to call. This choice is based on optimization critera, as soon as completeness/termination is preserved.

new_rec_lev(Goal) Called at the beginning of an environment. It creates the environment and handles moves on the environment stack on entrance, success, failure and backtrack. On success of *new_rec_lev*, the lemma that is proved for *Goal* is stored.

rec_solve(Goal) *Goal* is a recursive predicate but is called from inside an environment. *Rec_solve* performs the admissibility test and, when this test fails, a lemma resolution. On success of *rec_solve,* the lemma proved for *Goal* is stored.

it_without_cont(Goal) *It_without_cont* is called when one knows, for syntactical reasons, that *Goal* cannot be a new goal. The admissibility test is thus not performed, and lemma resolution is directly carried out. A good example is provided by the rule produced by the compiler for *control01* in section 3.2.1.

3.3 Performance

The performance of DedGin is both *satisfactory* and *encouraging*. Actually, we did not expect such performance, since the data manipulation techniques had not been our primary concern, in the present version of DedGin: response times are good for a prototype at this stage of development, and clearly show that the use of an FRD strategy (thus of an algorithm like QSQR) is needed to obtain reasonable answering times.

It is of course not possible to compare DedGin with any system providing the same kind of facilities, as, to our knowledge, no such systems have been implemented so far. However, we obtain some interesting figures by comparing, in very special cases, the performance of DedGin with two other systems. In the first case, we compare the Prolog evaluation strategy with that of DedGin by using the Prolog/DBMS connection provided by EDUCE. In the second case, we define a non-recursive query that, given to INGRES and run on identical data, returns the same answer as a recursive query given to DedGin. The figures given here are simply indicative; no systematic benchmarks have been carried out.

3.3.1 DedGin vs Prolog evaluation stategy

The definition of the *control* relation can be interpreted as a Prolog program. Moreover, if this definition is written as given below, and if the *own* relation is not cyclic, the corresponding Prolog program is able to answer any query upon *control* and to stop. It is thus possible, under these restrictions, to compare the Prolog evaluation strategy (in its integration with the DBMS provided by EDUCE) with that of DedGin (also using EDUCE).

control(X,Y) :- own(X,Y,P), P>67.
control(X,Y) :- own(X,Z,P), P>67, control(Z,Y).

An important difference between the evaluation strategy of Prolog and that of DedGin is that Prolog always chooses the first literal in the clause, whereas QSQR adopts an FRD strategy. It follows that the evaluation strategy of Prolog can be either bad or good, depending on the type of query. Consider for instance a query (type 10) like *control(X, holding1)* (what are the firms controlled by *holding1*). In this case, Prolog takes any firm *Z* in the database (by evaluation *own(X,Z)*) before checking whether *control(Z, holding1)* holds. This is a very bad strategy, as it amounts to computing the whole *control* relation. Consider now a query (type 10) like *control(holding1_aab,Y)* (what are the firms controlling *holding1_aab*). Then Prolog obtains the firms controlling directly *holding1_abb* by evaluating *own(holding1_aab,Z)* and then goes up the control tree by recursively calling *control(Z, Y)*: in this case, the Prolog strategy is similar to that of FRD.

We compared the answering times (to obtain all the answers) of DedGin and Prolog/EDUCE, for these two types of query (types 01 and 10). The *own* relation was stored on secondary storage (the *same* data are accessed in both cases). This relation was hashed on the second attribute and had an index on the first one. Measures were made for several sizes of the *own* relation. The figures were obtained on an empty VAX 11/785 (multi-user mode). Time is elapsed time. The query of type 01 had 31 answers, the recursive depth being up to 3 (thus this query involves three joins). The query of type 10 had 4 answers (up to a recursive depth of 4).

The resulting figures are in total accordance with our analysis. For queries of type 01, the answering time by Prolog is bad as soon as the relation is not small(~6.5 s for 100 tuples, ~330 s — i.e. > 5 min — for 1000 tuples, the 10 000 tuples query having to be stopped because of a main-memory overflow). DedGin performs much better: answering times remain around 3.7 s for both the 1000 and the 10 000 tuples queries. For queries of type 10, the control of the recursion in DedGin introduces an overhead that makes DedGin slower than Prolog, but do not forget that, as opposed to Prolog, DedGin guarantees termination and answer completeness. For data carefully chosen so that Prolog terminates, the Prolog answering time is around 0.45 s, whereas the DedGin answering time is 3 to 4 times slower. The DedGin answering time remains constant whenever a cycle is introduced in the data.

3.3.2 Comparison with INGRES

Knowing that a given firm *f1* controls other firms with up to three levels of indirection makes it possible to define a non-recursive query to retrieve the firms controlled by *f1*. This enables a comparison of DedGin and a relational DBMS to be made. Fig. 6 presents the QUEL 'translation' (under the above

```
range of e is own_by
range of f is own_by
range of g is own_by
retrieve (f.firm) where
(f.share_holder="Siemens_AG" and f.percent>67)
or (     (e.share_holder="Siemens_AG" and e.percent>67)
     and (      (f.share_holder=e.firm and f.percent>67)
          or (g. share_holder=e.firm and g.percent>67
             and f.share_holder=g.firm and f.percent>67)
          )
     )
```

Fig. 6.1 — The non-recursive QUEL query.

hypothesis) of the query *control(Var, const)* that was run on DedGin. This QUEL query was run on the public version of INGRES on the same (i.e. physically identical) database as for DedGin.

The performance of the public version of INGRES on this example was rather bad: the answering time for the 100 tuples query was *9 min* (under the same conditions as above) and the 10 000 tuples query had to be killed after several hours. These figures should not be taken too negatively for INGRES, as the version used here is known to be much less efficient than Commercial INGRES.

4. CONCLUSION

Future work on recursive query processing should focus on the design and implementation of a second generation query answering component. This system should improve on DedGin on several significant points: (i) from the algorithmic point of view (recursion handling), it should make use of the QoSaQ algorithm; (ii) it should investigate the use of the BANG file data structure [11] (see also Chapter 12 in this book); (iii) it should tend to optimize the page management, by using some kind of page(set)-oriented mechanism.

ACKNOWLEDGEMENTS

It is a pleasure to acknowledge the support and the advice of Jean-Marie Nicolas. Jorge Bocca designed and realized the EDUCE system. Alexandre Lefebvre realized the SQL interface. I would also like to thank Herve Gallaire and my colleagues in the KB group at ECRC for the nice and stimulating environment they provide.

REFERENCES

[1] Aho, A. and Ullman, J. D., Universality of Data Retrieval Languages, *Principles of Programming Languages,* 1979.

[2] Apt, K. R., Blair, H., and Walker, A., Towards a Theory of Declarative Knowledge, Preprints of the *Workshop on Foundations of Deductive Databases and Logic Programming*, Washington DC, USA, August 1986, 547–623.

[3] Astrahan *et al.* System R: Relational Approach to Database Management, *ACM-TODS* **1,** 2, June 1976, 97–137.

[4] Bancilhon, F. and Ramakrishnan, R., An Amateur's Introduction to Recursive Query Processing Strategies, *Proc. ACM—SIGMOD Conf.,* Washington DC, May 1986.

[5] Bancilhon, F., Maier, D., Sagiv, Y., and Ullman, J. D., Magic Sets and Other Strange Ways to Implement Logic Programs, *Proc. ACM Conf. on Princ. of Database Systems,* 1986.

[6] Beeri, C. and Ramakrishnan, R., On the Power of Magic, *Proc. 6th PODS Symp.,* San Diego, California, March 1987.

[7] Bocca, J., On the Evaluation Strategy of EDUCE, *Proc. ACM–SIGMOD Conf.,* Washington DC, May 1986.

[8] Bocca, J., EDUCE — A Marriage of Convenience: Prolog and a Relational DBMS, *Proc. 3rd Symp. on Logic Programming,* Salt Lake City, USA, Sept. 1986.

[9] Chandra, A. and Harel, D., Structure and Complexity of Relational Queries, *J. Computer and System Sci.,* **25,** 99–128, 1982.

[10] Dayal, U., Of Nests and Trees: A Unified Approach to Processing Queries that Contain Nested Subqueries, Aggregates, and Quantifiers, *Proc. 13th VLDB Conf.,* Brighton, England, September 1987, 197–208.

[11] Freeston, M., The BANG File: A New Kind of Grid File, *Proc. ACM–SIGMOD Conf.*, San Francisco, 27–29 May 1987, 260–269.

[12] Gallaire, H., Minker, J., and Nicolas, J. M., Logic and Databases: A Deductive Approach, *ACM Computing Surveys* **16,** 2, June 1984.

[13] Henschen, L. J. and Naqvi, S. A., On Compiling Queries in Recursive First Order Databases, *J. ACM,* **31,** 1, January 1984.

[14] Immerman, N., Relational Queries Computable in Polynomial Time, *Proc. 4th SIGACT Symp.,* ACM, May 1982.

[15] Lloyd, J. W., *Foundations of Logic Programming,* Springer-Verlag, New York, 1984.

[16] Loveland, D. W., *Automated Theorem Proving: A Logical Basis,* North-Holland, Amsterdam, 1978.

[17] Minker, J. and Nicolas, J. M., On Recursive Axioms in Deductive Databases, *Information Systems,* **8,** 1, 1983.

[18] Naish, L., *MU-PROLOG 3.0 Reference Manual,* Melbourne University, July 1983.

[19] Nicolas, J. M., Logic for Improving Integrity Checking in Relational Databases, *Acta Informatica,* **18,** 227–253, 1982.

[20] Rohmer, J., Lescoeur, R., and Kerisit, J. M., The Alexander Method: A Technique for the Processing of Recursive Axioms in Deductive Databases, *New Generation Computing,* **4,** 273–285, 1986.

[21] Sacca, D. and Zaniolo, C., Implementation of Recursive Queries for a Data Language Based on Pure Horn Logic, *Proc. 4th Int. Conf. on Logic Programming,* Melbourne, Australia, May 1987, 104–135.

[22] Sacca, D. and Zaniolo, C., Magic Counting Methods, *Proc. ACM–SIGMOD Conf.,* San Francisco, USA, May 1987, 49–59.

[23] Stonebracker, M., Wong, E. and Kreps, P., The Design and Implementation of INGRES, *ACM Trans. on Database Systems,* **1,** 3 (September 1976), 189–222.

[24] Tamaki, H. and Sato, T., OLD Resolution with Tabulation, *Proc. 3rd Int. Conf. on Logic Programming,* London, June 1986, 84–98.

[25] Ullman, J. D., Implementation of Logical Query Languages for Databases, *ACM Trans. on Database Systems,* **10,** 3 (September 1985), 289–321.

[26] Vieille, L., Recursive Axioms in Deductive Databases: The Query-SubQuery Approach, *Proc. 1st Int. Conf. on Expert Database Systems,* Charleston, USA, April 1986, 179–193.

[27] Vieille, L., Recursion in Deductive Databases: DedGin, a Recursive Query Evaluator, *Des Bases de donnees aux bases de connaissances,* Sophia-Antipolis, France, Sept. 1987. Also available as TR-KB-14, ECRC, Munich, Germany.

[28] Vieille, L., Recursive Query Processing: Theoretical and Practical Aspects. *Proc. 2nd French–Japan Symp. on Artificial Intelligence and Computer Science.,* INRIA, Sophia-Antipolis, France, November 1987.

[29] Vieille, L., Database-complete Proof Procedures Based on SLD-resolution, *Proc. 4th Int. Conf. on Logic Programming,* Melbourne, Australia, May 1987, 74–103.

[30] Vieille, L., Recursive Query Processing: The Power of Logic, Techni-

cal Report TR-KB-17, ECRC, Munich, Germany, October 1987. Submitted to *Theoretical Computer Sci.*

[31] Vieille, L., From QSQ Towards QoSaQ: Global Optimization of Recursive Queries, *Proc. 2nd Int. Conf. on Expert Database Systems,* Virginia, April 1987. To be published by Benjamin Cummings. Also as ECRC Technical Report TR-KB-18, 1987.

Part IV
New storage structures for databases

11

Benchmarking Prolog for database applications

M. H. Williams, P. A. Massey
Computer Science Department, Heriot-Watt University, Edinburgh
J. A. Crammond
Department of Computing, Imperial College, London.

ABSTRACT

With the growth in interest in declarative programming languages and knowledge-based systems, there has arisen a need to measure and compare the performance of different systems. In the case of the logic programming language Prolog, several sets of benchmark programs have been proposed for evaluating the performance of different implementations. However, one area which has been neglected is that of Prolog's suitability for handling large sets of facts and rules, an essential prerequisite for database and large knowledge-base applications This chapter puts forward a practical set of benchmarks for evaluating this aspect of Prolog.

1. INTRODUCTION

One of the consequences of the Japanese fifth generation computer programme has been to create an interest in evaluating the performance of logic programming systems. In the preparatory work, Furukawa *et al.* [1] introduced the term *Logical Inferences Per Second* (LIPS) as the basic unit of measurement, 1 LIPS being stated to be equivalent to approximately 100–1000 instructions per second on a conventional computer [2]. The objectives of the fifth generation programme include the design of high performance systems capable of up to 1 Giga-LIPS — a figure which has given rise to some controversy. However, whether or not these performance targets are achieved, they have focused attention on the need for measuring and improving the performance of such systems.

In the case of Prolog, various simple tests have been proposed as benchmarks for measuring the processing capability of Prolog systems. In particular, benchmark programs have been proposed by Moss [3], Wilk

[4,5] and Syre [6], and more recently a set of benchmarks has been proposed by Dickens and Bustany [7] as part of the Alvey research programme in the UK. However, while these benchmarks cover database indexing as one aspect which is exercised, they do not adequately test the effectiveness of systems in handling large sets of clauses.

One of the application areas for which logic programming languages offer considerable potential is that of databases. Their suitability for implementing database concepts was first recognized by Kowalski [8] and since then much work has been done on this [9,10]. Unfortunately, although they provide a very natural medium for expressing such concepts, they also suffer from the drawback that most current Prolog systems are very inefficient when handling large data sets. Thus there is growing interest in finding ways of combining database techniques with those of logic programming to produce systems which are both efficient and powerful.

In order to assess the success of such systems, yardsticks are required to measure and evaluate their performance in the context of database applications. This chapter explores a set of benchmarks which could be useful for this purpose.

2. TYPES OF BENCHMARK

Benchmarking is normally approached either from the bottom up — dealing first with single discrete operations and building up to complete application programs — or from the top downwards — starting with the application program and reducing it to its basic operations (attempting to identify those critical operations which have the most significant effects on the performance of the program). One further approach is to take existing programs, perform some sort of analysis on them and from this synthesize a **typical** or **dhrystone** program. The overall approach to benchmarking should, however, be one of iterative development. Benchmarks can generally be categorized into three levels. These are

Low — dealing with single operations (e.g. a single retrieval).
Medium — dealing with combinations of the low-level operations.
General — dealing with either real application programs whose performance characteristics are not necessarily understood, or a **dhrystone** benchmark program which is specifically written to behave as a **typical** program.

The benchmark tests described in this chapter are concerned essentially with the low and medium levels, while some programs which might be suitable for the general level are described in [11]. The approach to benchmarking which is taken in this chapter is that of bottom up. The reason for this is that there are currently very few large database application programs implemented in Prolog. Those known to us include Chat-80 [12], which comprises around 3000 clauses, a Molecular Biology Database [13] having approximately 40 000 clauses and a Real-Time Expert System called RESCU [11] (which is written in POPLOG). In view of this it is not really feasible to develop a **dhrystone** benchmark program at the present time.

3. BENCHMARK TESTS

In designing a set of benchmarks to assess the database handling capabilities of a Prolog system, it is useful first to consider what information is required. This can be achieved by using a set of questions, in this case directed at the database. Such questions might include [5,4]:

— What is the retrieval time for the first solution, the second solution, all solutions?
— What is the time to fail (time to retrieve the last solution and fail or time to find that no solution exists and fail)?
— What is the time taken to assert/retract a clause?
— What is the maximum number of clauses which can be inserted into the database?
— What is the time to consult a file? reconsult it?

Questions of this kind help to focus the attention on particular aspects of the system. The following sections describe the actual benchmark tests to be applied to the database.

3.1 Low level

As mentioned earlier, the tests in this section correspond to a single, simple Prolog instruction. They assess the time taken to perform the following operations.

(a) Search a set of clauses for a single solution.
(b) Search for a set of solutions.
(c) Search on:
    (1) all ground arguments
    (2) first argument
    (3) third argument
    (4) part of a structured argument value.
(d) Assert a clause.
(e) Retract a clause; retract all clauses with a given argument value.

3.2 Medium level

The tests in this section use combinations of these low-level operations. These are:

(a) combining the results of two relations in a **join** operation [14]. This is a common relational database operation;
(b) retrieving a list of solutions in a manner similar to findall, bagof, etc.;
(c) nested rule invocation.

3.3 Additional database benchmarks

This section covers additional features which should be tested.

(a) What is the maximum number of clauses which can be inserted into the database?
(b) What is the time to reconsult files of various sizes? Reconsult time can be tested without user intervention (as opposed to consult which cannot).
(c) Is there a facility to allow quick access to the clauses in compiled form, thus removing the need to consult the database clauses each time they are needed?

4. DATA GENERATION

In order to assess the variation in performance of the system with varying size of database, a variable-sized amount of data is needed. The data should be able to be produced by a single portable program or set of programs. The program should not require any outside information, except the size of data set to be produced and possibly the form of data needed. When testing the database handling capabilities of different systems, the form of the test data can have a significant effect on the results obtained.

A number of methods are available for artificially generating large amounts of data with a prescribed format. However, on close inspection the data generator programs are aimed at databases which are to be held in main memory and fail to be useful for assessing the capabilities of systems with respect to very large databases.

The benchmarks proposed recently as part of the Alvey programme by Dickens and Bustany [7] rely on the use of a generator program which generates unit clauses having the following format:

calendar(Day-of-week,Day-of-month,Month,Year).

Each clause is unique, but the number of different atoms generated is small. In [15] a data generator is given which generates data concerning a hypothetical conference. While the latter will generate a larger number of unique atoms, neither generator deals with the problem of structured terms. In addition to this limitation in the form of clauses, both data generators are limited in the number of clauses that they can reasonably generate. The following sections describe two data generators which can be used with the benchmark tests.

4.1 Space filling curve data set

One easy way of generating a very large set of facts is to set up a substantial two-dimensional grid of points and create a set of edges connecting them. Each point may be represented by a unit clause of form

vertex(Vertex_Name,X,Y).

and each edge by a clause of the form

edge(Edge_Name,Vertex_Name1,Vertex_Name2).

The Vertex_Name is created by concatenating the X and Y positions together, and the Edge_Name is created by joining two Vertex_Names together.

One simple and fast way of generating a large number of regularly distributed edges is to generate Peano, Hilbert or Murray polygons [16–18]. This data generation method guarantees uniqueness of each data item. Fig. 1 shows a Hilbert curve of level 4, which is described by a set of 256

Fig. 1 — A Hilbert curve of level 4.

vertex clauses and 255 edge clauses.

To generate a Hilbert curve, only two input values are needed — the screen size and the curve form. The program which, for reasons of efficiency, was written in C is given in Appendix 1. This program produces two data files, one containing the vertex clauses and one containing the edge clauses.

To create a large set of rules, a variation of this two-dimensional data set may be employed, which incorporates a form of incomplete information. Williams and Nicolson [19] have shown how incomplete information may be represented by means of Prolog rules. Suppose therefore one were to add a third dimension to the set of coordinates for the grid of points and then generate vertices in the form

```
vertex(Vertex_Name,X_Coord,Y_Coord,Z):-
    range(Z,Z_Upper,Z_Lower).
```

where Z is a variable and the other parameters are all constants. This reads *'vertex Vertex_Name has x- and y-coordinates X_Coord and Y_Coord and as z-coordinate a value (represented by Z) which is not known exactly but lies somewhere in the range Z_Upper >= Z >= Z_Lower*'. One can use the same method as before for generating the *x*- and *y*-coordinates of the grid of points while the limits on the ranges of the *z*-coordinate may be set up using a random number generator. The program to generate data of this form is the same as the one to generate simple vertices and is given in Appendix 1.

4.2 Pseudo-random data set

The Hilbert curve data generator described above is easy to use and will produce the data quickly. However, although the data generated contain many different atoms, they suffer from the second of the two previously outlined problems. They contain no structures. The data generator described below is one that has been developed to address this problem.

The data generator takes a *format list* which is used to describe the format of the data required. The actual data are produced using a pseudo-random number generator which has been integerized so that systems (e.g. Prolog-X) which do not have floating-point arithmetic will be able to use it. The use of integer-only arithmetic also avoids any rounding/truncating problems which might arise owing to differences in the various system implementations. The pseudo-random number generator will produce, depending on the range, a maximum of 131 072 unique numbers after which it will cycle. The generator is called as follows:

dg(Name,Format List,Uniqueness List,Clause).

A more complete description of the form of the arguments required by the data generator is given in Appendix 2. By repeated calling (on backtracking), files containing any number of clauses can be produced (depending on the limit of symbol table size). In generating the data set, a second file, called the **mark** file, is also generated containing information which can be used by the benchmark tests, currently the clause in the middle of database. Examples of possible output data are

(1) ?- dg(vertex,[int,int,int],[131072,360,360],Clause).
vertex(123637,327,255).
vertex(77570,352,34).
vertex(104739,319,321).

(2) ?- dg(net,[funct(const),[int,tail]],[10,900,90],Clause).
net(bb(cki),[64|_185]).
net(h(iqi),[8|_175]).
net(j(yqh),[80|_171]).

(3) ?- dg(names,[vlenlist(const,5,2,notail)],[9999],Clause).
names([rqie,pikf,tbqj,vijd]).
names([ljne,ffid,jhf,fljf,fdhb,llmd]).
names([omf,iiib,hmkb,ekoi,ljf]).

(4) ?- dg(names,[vlenfn(vlenlist(const,2,0.5,notail),4,2)],[99,999,10,10], Clause).
names(ke([uig,ljb,hhf],[moi,sic])).

```
names(oj([mcb,rnh,rmf],[lbb,lgf],[uke,ogc],[ngc,iff])).
names(jb([ndc],[nmd,hmd],[ig,blg])).
```

A listing of the program used to generate these data is given in Appendix 3.

5. MAIN TESTS

The benchmark test methodology used in gathering the following results is similar to that used by Wilk [5] and the Dickens and Bustany benchmarks [7]. A shell program is used to perform the actual test and to log any results. In some cases, however, the tests were terminated early because the hardware system itself could not cope and started to thrash.

For those tests which use the data generated by the pseudo-random data generator, the data have the following form:

```
cn(abba,96354,lls(lalla,allal),64646,[7474,43838,92921,86558]).
cn(dddd,8484,ala(lsls,slsl),4646,[4848,8282,131,43554,4361]).
```

This form was chosen so that it would contain structures of the two most common forms: lists and terms.

The following tests were all performed on a SUN-3 microcomputer system running BSD 4.2 UNIX.† The systems tested were NIP 1.5, Prolog-X and C-Prolog 1.5a. All the tests were performed using the same machine (with the files NFS mounted on a system which had the required disk space) and the same file system. In Tables 9, 10 and 11 the *number of clauses* refers to the number of vertex/3 clauses, while the same number (minus 1) of edge/3 clauses is also used in these tests.

5.1 Setting up the database

Once the datasets have been created by the data generation programs, the first set of results is obtained by determining the time taken to reconsult each dataset. Timings obtained for the three systems concerned are given in Table 1 for the pseudo-random datasets and Table 2 for the vertex datasets.

5.2 Low level

Each test in this category corresponds to a single discrete instruction. The first three tests were performed using the data set produced by the Hilbert curve program, while the remaining tests use the pseudo-random data set.

5.2.1 Retrievals

(1) The time to retrieve on all ground arguments. This attempts to find more than one solution. The search is for the clause *vertex('00',0,0)*. See Table 3.

(2) Time to retrieve on first argument (set of solutions). The search is for the clause *vertex('00',_,_)*. See Table 4.

† UNIX is a trademark of Bell Laboratories.

Table 1 — Time taken to reconsult the various-sized pseudo-random datasets†

Number of clauses	NIP	C-Prolog	Prolog-X
4	410	50	1650
16	1180	200	5133
64	4870	716	20800
256	19670	2951	85883
1024	78880	11734	335916
4096	322430	50416	1322483
16384	1363150	223316	5304384
30000	2564160	442215	9763000
40000	3455690	596033	12905267

† The results given in this and the following tables are all in milliseconds. All the tests excluding the two reconsult tests (Tables 1 and 2) were performed more than once and the figures given in the tables are the average times obtained. However, in the case of the two reconsults, because the timings involved were so large, each was performed only once.

Table 2 — Time taken to reconsult the vertex/3 datasets

Number of clauses	NIP	C-Prolog	Prolog-X
16	500	83	1784
64	1880	400	7284
256	7420	1450	29650
1024	30220	6166	120800
4096	125630	25950	517000
16384	594820	134183	1851533
65536	3284710	1728031	—

(3) Time to retrieve on third argument (set of solutions). The search is for the clause *vertex(_,_,0)*. See Table 5.

(4) Time to retrieve on tail of list argument (fifth argument, and again a set of solutions is retrieved), i.e. *cn(_,_,_,_,[_,T])*. See Table 6.

5.2.2 Updating the database

These tests use the pseudo-random data generator as a means of generating unique clauses to be asserted. It should be noted that in the case of systems which hold the clauses externally on secondary storage, both types of database updates should be performed in such a way as to use any of the available additional storage mechanisms (e.g. clauses held on disk).

Table 3 — Time to retrieve a single clause with all ground terms

Number of clauses	NIP	C-Prolog	Prolog-X
16	1	2	0
64	4	3	0
256	2	10	1
1024	5	35	12
4096	19	143	48
16384	70	585	201
65536	—	2475	—

Table 4 — Time to retrieve a set of solutions on 1st argument (using vertex datasets)

Number of clauses	NIP	C-Prolog	Prolog-X
16	2	1	0
64	2	1	0
250	3	9	4
1024	8	36	12
4096	20	141	48
16384	68	572	204
65536	—	2510	—

Table 5 — Time to retrieve on 3rd argument (a set of solutions), using the vertex datasets

Number of clauses	NIP	C-Prolog	Prolog-X
16	6	2	3
64	9	5	9
256	28	23	39
1024	89	86	153
4096	320	339	602
16384	1217	1342	2535
65536	—	5578	—

Table 6 — Time to retrieve on the tail of a list (5th argument using pseudo-random datasets)

Number of clauses	NIP	C-Prolog	Prolog-X
4	3	1	1
16	5	3	5
64	15	12	20
256	55	49	81
1024	230	206	334
4096	863	787	1300
16384	3540	3146	5431
30000	6251	6004	10023
40000	—	8119	13161

(1) The time taken to assert clauses into the database. See Table 7.
(2) The time taken to retract clauses from the database. See Table 8.

5.3 Medium level

The tests in this section require, in most cases, large amounts of backtracking over the sets of clauses.

5.3.1 Join operation

The following benchmarks use the Hilbert curve dataset, and each returns a set of solutions (via fail). See Tables 9 and 10.

(1) vertex(X,Middle_elem,_),edge(_,X,_).
(2) vertex(X,Middle_elem,_),edge(_,X,Y),vertex(Y,_,_).

5.3.2 Exhaustive searches

The following test uses the data generated by the Hilbert curve program.

(1) Search to find the horizontal edges along the middle row of the Hilbert curve. This test requires the X and Y Coordinates (Start_X,Middle_Y) of the start point, the maximum width of the Hilbert curve (Max_X) and an increment value (INC) which is the length of an edge. The results are shown in Table 11.

```
test(_,_,[Start_X,Middle_Y,Max_X,INC]):-
    solution(Edge_name,Start_X,Middle_Y,Max_X,INC).
solution(Edge_name,Start_X,Middle_Y,Max_X,INC):-
    x_inc(Start_X,X,Max_X,INC),          %Get X Co-Ord
    vertex(V1,X,Middle_Y),
    rest_test(V1,X,Middle_Y,Edge_name,INC).
rest_test(V1,X,Middle_Y,Edge_name,INC):-
    Next_X is X+INC,
```

Table 7 — Time taken to assert a single fact into the database

NIP	C-Prolog	Prolog-X
27.69	5.1	17.10

Table 8 — Time taken to retract a clause from the database

NIP	C-Prolog	Prolog-X
6.86	2.13	8.85

Table 9 — Time for a join operation between two clauses

Number of clauses	NIP	C-Prolog	Prolog-X
16	4	7	9
64	34	42	66
256	250	301	494
1024	1930	2325	3799
4096	15196	18277	29949
16384	121740	145056	246888

Table 10 — Time to perform a join operation between three clauses

Number of clauses	NIP	C-Prolog	Prolog-X
16	5	9	10
64	36	66	75
256	269	481	552
1024	2068	3750	4229
4096	16266	29635	32955
16384	133592	236329	286430

Table 11 — Time taken to find the edges which form a line across the middle of the Hilbert curve

Number of clauses	NIP	C-Prolog	Prolog-X
16	12	21	21
64	99	140	199
256	738	950	1490
1024	6188	7775	12468
4096	49130	61207	98909
16384	404931	494664	836266

```
        vertex(V2,Next_X,Middle_Y),
        rest_test2(V1,V2,Edge_name),!.
    rest_test2(V1,V2,Edge_name):-
        edge(Edge_name,V1,V2),!.
    rest_test2(V1,V2,Edge_name):-
        edge(Edge_name,V2,V1),!.
    x_inc(Start,Val,Max_val,INC):-        % return successive values
        Start=<Max_val,          %        on failure.
        (Start=Val;
        Val1 is Start+INC,
          x_inc(Val1,Val,Max_val,INC)).
```

The following two benchmarks give two possible ways of implementing a selective search over the whole database. The first approach is to select out the required clauses while the second tests each clause explicitly in the database against some condition (in the normal implementation manner of findall). Both use the data generated by the pseudo-random generator, and the results are given in Tables 12 and 13.

(1) find all those clauses whose fourth argument (integer) is a multiple of 500.

```
test(_,_,[Name,Arity]):-
    find(Name,Arity,130171,0,4,_),!.
find(Name,Arity,Range,Value,Arg_nos,[Clause|T]):-
    gen_mult(Value,Range,Val),
    functor(Clause,Name,Arity),
    arg(Arg_nos,Clause,Val),
    call(Clause),
    Val2 is Val+500,
    find(Name,Arity,Range,Val2,Arg_nos,T).
find(_,_,_,_,_,[]):-!.
gen_mult(Value,Range,Val):-
```

Table 12 — Time taken to find all the clauses in the database whose 4th argument is a multiple of 500

Number of clauses	NIP	C-Prolog	Prolog-X
4	630	720	459
16	976	1063	1180
64	2378	2396	4013
256	8166	7746	15386
1024	30930	29180	60463
4096	120600	114930	240176
16384	489390	442692	938543
30000	832562	817473	1733056
40000	—	1051926	I

I = Integer overflowed during test.

Table 13 — Time taken to find all the clauses in the database whose 1st argument is less than the sum of the list which is its 5th argument

Number of clauses	NIP	C-Prolog	Prolog-X
4	10	23	13
16	22	63	40
64	108	276	146
256	458	1183	599
1024	1816	4566	2343
4096	7136	17850	9190
16384	29516	71689	38743
30000	54820	133840	70603
40000	—	178723	92499

```
        Value>Range,!,fail.
    gen_mult(Value,Range,Value).
    gen_mult(Value,Range,V2):-
        Val is Value+500,
        gen_mult(Val,Range,V2).
```

(2) find all those clauses whose second argument is greater than the sum of the elements of the list which is its fifth argument.

```
test(_,_,[Name,Arity]):-
    find3(Name,Arity,_),
```

```
        % In a fully implemented findall an assert would be placed here.
        fail.
    test(_,_,_):-!.
    find3(Name,Arity,Clause):-
        functor(Clause,Name,Arity),
        call(Clause),
        arg(Arity,Clause,List),
        arg(2,Clause,Value),
        sum_list(List,Sum),
        Value>=Sum.
    sum_list([],0):-!.
    sum_list([H|T],Value):-
        sum_list(T,Val),
        Value is Val+H,!.
```

5.4 Rule invocation

The following tests are based on the use of the vertex/4 rule datasets. The tests are slightly modified versions of the simple retrieval operations, the only difference being that the Z co-ordinate is set to some particular value.

1. Search for a set of solutions to a query where the first three arguments are ground, i.e. vertex('00',0,0,-5). See Table 14.
2. Search for a set of solutions to a query where the first three arguments are unspecified and a solution exists, i.e. vertex(_,_,_,-5). See Table 15.
3. Search for a set of solutions to a query where the first three arguments are unspecified and no solution exists, i.e. vertex(_,_,_,-20). See Table 16. The only difference between this test and the previous test is that the goal call fails.

Table 14 — Time taken to search for a set of solutions to a query where first three arguments are ground, i.e. vertex('00',0,0,-5)

Number of clauses	NIP	C-Prolog	Prolog-X
16	2	2	0
64	4	3	1
256	2	8	4
1024	5	35	12
4096	20	144	48
16384	75	583	244
65536	—	2607	—

Table 15 — Time taken to search for a set of solutions to a query where the first three arguments are unspecified and a solution exists, i.e. vertex(_,_,_,-5)

Number of clauses	NIP	C-Prolog	Prolog-X
16	4	11	6
64	15	37	24
256	52	146	104
1024	204	579	415
4096	788	2322	1670
16384	3148	9292	7107
65536	—	39255	—

Table 16 — Time taken to search for a set of solutions to a query where the first three arguments are unspecified and no solution exists, i.e. vertex(_,_,_,-20)

Number of clauses	NIP	C-Prolog	Prolog-X
16	5	9	7
64	13	38	27
256	49	143	102
1024	197	578	417
4096	785	2326	1669
16384	3138	9290	7070
65536	—	39191	—

6. CONCLUSIONS AND FUTURE WORK

The benchmarks proposed in this chapter are aimed at assessing the database handling capabilities of a Prolog system for real applications. They focus primarily on the time taken to perform certain basic database operations, although the amount of space required does affect the results. The tests were performed on a SUN-3 microcomputer with 4 Mbytes of main memory using three different Prolog systems: NIP 1.5, Prolog-X and C-Prolog.

The sizes of the datasets for which measurements were taken in the case of reconsults and simple retrievals extend to around 65 000 clauses. The reason for this is that the different systems ran out of memory at some number between 30 000 and 70 000 clauses. This demonstrates clearly the limitations of current Prolog systems in dealing with database applications.

The times taken to reconsult large datasets were considerable and varied from about 10 min (for C-Prolog) to about 200 min (for Prolog-X) for a set of 40 000 clauses, as shown in Table 1. If this could be extrapolated to, say, 1 million clauses, this overhead would be unacceptable.

Many Prolog systems use indexing on the first argument to improve the efficiency of database accesses. This is the reason for structuring the tests in section 5.2.1 as they are. The first and second tests both have a constant in the first argument position, and systems which index on the first argument should perform well for these tests. The third and fourth tests seek to match on other argument positions. The difference in performance is reflected clearly in the results obtained in Tables 3 and 4 compared with Tables 5 and 6. Although, some of the results obtained show a drop in performance which is greater than would be expected, it is thought that this might be due to a possible interplay between the memory management techniques of the operating system and that of the Prolog systems.

The first test involving a join operation performs a join on a variable in the second argument position of the second predicate, thereby losing the advantage of indexing on the first argument. The second test includes this but in addition has a join on a variable in the first argument position of the second predicate. Since the latter should take advantage of indexing and is only a one–one join, one would not expect it to add much to the time for the first join operation, which has to be done by sequential search. This is borne out in Tables 9 and 10 for Nip and Prolog-X. In the case of C-Prolog there is a significant increase in the times observed between Tables 9 and 10, but this is consistent with the much higher time required by C-Prolog for retrieval on the first argument (Tables 3 and 4).

The tests involving rule invocation examine the handling of rules as opposed to facts. In systems where these are indexed on the first argument position too, the results given in Table 14 should not be very different from those in Table 3. This was indeed observed to be the case for the three systems under investigation. It should also be noted that the results given in Table 16 are very similar to those obtained in Table 15 since in both cases one has to enumerate all tuples. The results would have been different if large sets were constructed, e.g. with success on more than half the vertex clauses.

Various other conclusions can be drawn from the comparative results produced here, although it is not clear whether these would necessarily apply to other Prolog systems.

Since the development of benchmark programs is necessarily iterative, it is reasonable to consider the benchmarks proposed in this chapter as a first approximation to what a future set of tests would look like. The reasons for this are that there are as yet no very large Prolog database application programs around and until such applications are developed it is not possible to give anything other than an approach based on relational type database queries. Once a larger number of very large prolog application programs become available it will then also be possible to develop a **dhrystone** benchmark program. This will require both a static analysis [20] and a dynamic analysis of the programs.

7. THE BENCHMARK PROGRAMS

The full set of benchmark programs described in this chapter are available from the Computer Science Department at Heriot-Watt University.

ACKNOWLEDGEMENTS

The authors wish to acknowledge the financial support given by the Science and Engineering Research Council and by ICL under the Alvey initiative. We would also like to acknowledge the patience and advice given by the members of the Logic Database, Prolog Database Machine and Parlog Groups at Heriot-Watt University.

REFERENCES

[1] Furukawa, K., *et al.*, Problem Solving and Inference Mechanisms, *Proc. Int. Conf. on Fifth Generation Computer Systems*, Japan Information Processing Development Centre, October 1981.

[2] Treleaven, P., Japan's Fifth Generation Computer Systems Project, *Proc. Fifth Generation Conf.,* SPL International, London, 7–9 July 1982, 0–23.

[3] Moss, C., Prolog Benchmarks, Internal Report, Imperial College, London, 1986.

[4] Wilk, P. F., Prolog Benchmarking, Report AIAI-TR-14, AI Applications Institute, Edinburgh University, 1986.

[5] Wilk, P. F., The Production and Evaluation of a Set of Prolog Benchmarks, AIAI-TR-13, 1983.

[6] Syre, J. C., Benchmark Programs for Prolog Systems, Internal Report, European Computer-Industry Research Centre, Munich, 1986.

[7] Dickens, S. and Bustany, A., *Alvey Prolog Benchmarks*, Imperial Software Technology, Cambridge, 1986.

[8] Kowalski, R. A. Logic as a Database Language, Internal Report, Department of Computer Science, Imperial College, 1981.

[9] Neves, J. C., Anderson, S. O., and Williams, M. H., A Prolog Implementation of Query-by-Example, *Proc. 7th Int. Computing Symp.* B. G. Teubner, Stuttgart, 1983, 318–332.

[10] Williams, M. H., The Design of a Prolog Database Machine, *Proc. First SIGKME Workshop*, January 1987.

[11] Report on the Alvey Architecture Club's Collection of Benchmark Programs, *Proc. First SIGKME Workshop*, S. Lavington (ed.), IEE, January 1987.

[12] Wilk, P. F., Chat-80, Internal Report, Edinburgh University, 1980.

[13] Rawlings, C. J., Seifert, K., and Saldanha, J., A Large Knowledge Based System for Molecular Biology, *Proc. First SIGKME Workshop*, S. Lavington (ed.), IEE, January 1987.

[14] Thom, J. A., Ramamohanarao, K., and Naish, L., A Superjoin Algorithm for Deductive Databases, Technical Report 86/1, Depart-

ment of Computer Science, University of Melbourne, Australia, 1986.

[15] Overbeek, R. A. and Lusk, E. L., *Prolog Benchmark 1: Accessing Databases,* Argonne National Laboratory.

[16] Cole, A. J., A Note on Space Filling Curves, *Software — Practice and Experience,* **13**, 1151–1159, 1983.

[17] Witten, I. H. and Wyvill, B., On the Generation and Use of Space Filling Curves, *Software — Practice and Experience,* **6**, 519–525, 1983.

[18] Wirth, N. *Algorithms & Data Structures*, Prentice-Hall, Englewood Cliffs, NJ, 1986.

[19] Williams, M. H. and Nicolson, K. A., An Approach to Handling Incomplete Information in Databases, to appear in *The Computer J.*

[20] Matsumoto, H., A Static Analysis of Prolog Programs, Programming Systems Group, Note 24, AI Applications Institute, Edinburgh, 20 January 1985.

APPENDIX 1

```
/******************************************************/
/* This is a recursive C program to create a prolog data */
/*      file containing points visited in the production */
/*      of a "Hilberts Space Filling Curve".             */
/* The Algorithm is from N.Wirth "Algorithms & Data      */
/*     Structures".                                      */
/* ************************************************* */
/* This program produces data in two forms:              */
/*                                                       */
/*   form 1: vertex/4 rules as follows-                  */
/*           vertex(VName,X,Y,Z):-                       */
/*                      range(Z,Z_upper,Z_lower).        */
/*     and:                                              */
/*           edge(EName,VName1,VName2).                  */
/*                                                       */
/*           The middle clauses '00' has its range fudged*/
/*           to allow various tests to be performed.     */
/*                                                       */
/*   form 2: vertex/3 unit clauses as follows-           */
/*           vertex(VName,X,Y).                          */
/*     and:                                              */
/*           edge(EName,VName1,VName2).                  */
/*                                                       */
/*   It is called (once it has been compiled as "hilbert")*/
/*         hilbert <data-form> <curve-number>            */
/*   where:                                              */
/*         data-form    is 1 or 2 (for forms 1 or 2).    */
/*         curve-number is the maximum sized curve       */
/*                      number (2-10).                   */
/*                                                       */
/******************************************************/

#include <math.h>
#include <stdio.h>
#include <ctype.h>

#define  A  0                 /* Only for clarities sake */
#define  B  1
#define  C  2
#define  D  3

FILE  *data1,*data2;           /* output data files       */
int   X,Y;                     /* X + Y positions         */
int   Type;                    /* Type of Data required   */
int   ins[4][7] = {{D,2,A,3,A,0,B},
                   {C,1,B,0,B,3,A},
                   {B,0,C,1,C,2,D},
                   {A,3,D,2,D,1,C}};


/*****************************************************/
/* The Following procedure actually produces the curve */
/*     deciding where to go next.                      */
/*****************************************************/
```

```
proc(Instruction,I,U)
  int   Instruction,I,U;
{
 extern int ins[][7];
 int        i;
 if (I>0)
    {for(i=0;i<=5;i=i+2)
        {proc(ins[Instruction][i],I-1,U);
         move_xy(ins[Instruction][i+1],U);}
     proc(ins[Instruction][6],I-1,U);};
}

/***********************************************/
/* Move to the next point on the "screen" + output */
/*     the prolog clauses representing points that */
/*     have been visited                           */
/***********************************************/

move_xy(Rotation,U)
  int   Rotation, U;
{
 extern int  X,Y,Type;
 extern FILE *data1,*data2;
 int         Old_x,Old_y;
 int         Z_Upper,Z_Lower;

 Old_x=X;
 Old_y=Y;
 switch(Rotation) {
   case 0: X = Old_x + U;
           break;
   case 1: Y = Old_y + U;
           break;
   case 2: X = Old_x - U;
           break;
   case 3: Y = Old_y - U;
           break;};

 if (Type == 1)
   {/* vertex(X,Y,Z). - dataset */
    fprintf(data1,"vertex('%d%d',%d,%d).\n",X,Y,X,Y);
   }
 else
   {/* Generate Z co-ordinate information */
    /* Z_Upper always higher than Z_lower */
    if ((X==0) && (Y==0))
       {/* fudge values for test !!*/
        Z_Lower = -10;
        Z_Upper = 0;}
    else
       {Z_Lower=(rand() % 1000);
        Z_Upper=(rand() % 100000)+1000;};
    fprintf(data1,"vertex('%d%d',%d,%d,Z):-range(Z,%d,%d).\n",
                                          X,Y,X,Y,Z_Upper,Z_Lower);
  };
 fprintf(data2,"edge('%d%d%d%d','%d%d','%d%d').\n",
                                 Old_x,Old_y,X,Y,Old_x,Old_y,X,Y);
}
```

```
/***                          MAIN PROGRAM                          */

main(argc,argv)
  int argc;
  int *argv[];
{
 int          U,I,Width=20000,Max_Curve;
 extern FILE  *data1,*data2;
 extern int   X,Y,Type;
 char file1[8],file2[8];

 if (argc != 3)
    {printf("Incorrect number of arguments\n");
     exit(-1);};

 sscanf(argv[1],"%d",&Type);
 if (Type != 1 && Type != 2)
    {printf("\nUnknown Data Type number\n");
     exit(-1);};
 sscanf(argv[2],"%d",&Max_Curve);
 if (Max_Curve<2 || Max_Curve>10)
    {printf("\nCurve number out of range\n");
     exit(-1);};

 printf("\nProducing data...\n");

 for(I=2;I<=Max_Curve;I++)
    {/* Produce Data files */

     sprintf(file1,"%s%d","data1.",I);
     sprintf(file2,"%s%d","data2.",I);

     data1=fopen(file1,"a");        /* Open Output datafiles */
     data2=fopen(file2,"a");

     U= (int) ((float) Width/(float) (pow((double) 2,(double) I)-1));
     X= Y= (int) ((Width / U)*U);

     /* Output Start Point */

     if (Type == 1)
        fprintf(data1,"vertex('%d%d',%d,%d).\n",X,Y,X,Y);
     else
        fprintf(data1,"vertex('%d%d',%d,%d,Z):-range(Z,%d,%d).\n",
                           X,Y,X,Y,((rand() % 100000) + 1000),(rand() % 1000));

     proc(A,I,U);                   /*        Produce Curve        */

     fclose(data1);
     fclose(data2);
    };
  printf("\nCompleted\n\n");
 }
```

APPENDIX 2

The generator is called as follows:

dg(Name,Format List,Uniqueness List,Clause).

where the arguments are:

Name — this is the name/functor of clause to be generated.

Uniqueness List — this is a list of integers which gives the 'uniqueness' of the clauses arguments. This is effectively a range in which the pseudo-random number generator will guarantee to generate unique numbers (and from that unique arguments).

Clause — this is the return argument which will be unified with the clause generated.

Format List — this consists of an arbitrary length list which gives the *type* of the clause arguments, the various format types allowed by this data generator are:

- integers — this is defined by *int* appearing in the argument type list.
- constants — this is defined by *const* appearing in the argument type list.
- functors — this produced structures of the forn 'a(b)', 'a(b,c)' depending on the required format. The format is of the form
  funct(⟨type⟩,⟨type⟩,..,⟨type⟩)
- lists — this type is used to generate a list, the elements of which are of form ⟨type⟩. The format of this is
  [⟨type⟩,⟨type⟩,..,{⟨type⟩|tail}]
  If the last element type is 'tail' then an open list is generated. There is also a form of variable length list which can be generated. The defining format has the form
  vlenlist(⟨type⟩,⟨length⟩,⟨variation⟩, {tail|notail})
  The arguments have type ⟨type⟩. The mean arity is given by ⟨length⟩ and the variation on this arity is ⟨variation⟩. The fourth argument is *tail* for an open list and *notail* for a closed list.
- structures — this generates a structure with a variable number of arguments. The arguments are as for the variable length list format. The call format has the form
  vlenfn(⟨type⟩,⟨length⟩,⟨variation⟩)

APPENDIX 3

```
%%%%%%%%%%%%%%%%%%%%%%%%%%%%%%%%%%%%%%%%%%%%%%%%%%%%%%%%%%
%
%               PSEUDO-RANDOM DATA GENERATOR
%
%%%%%%%%%%%%%%%%%%%%%%%%%%%%%%%%%%%%%%%%%%%%%%%%%%%%%%%%%%
% Generate N files with M clauses in each upto a limit.

generate_dataset(System,Max_Clauses):-
  gen_nos(4,Nos_Clauses,Max_Clauses),
  reset_seed,
  generate_file(System,Nos_Clauses),
  Nos_Clauses > Max_Clauses.
generate_dataset(_,_).

%%%%%%%%%%%%%%%%%%%%%%%%%%%%%%%%%%%%%%%%%%%%%%%%%%%%%%%%%%
% Generate a Data and Marker file with "NOS_CLAUSES" clauses

generate_file(System,NOS_CLAUSES):-
  generate_filename(NOS_CLAUSES,'data.',FILENAME),
  generate_filename(NOS_CLAUSES,'mark.',FILENAME2),
  (from(1,NOS_CLAUSES,I),
    gen_data(System,NOS_CLAUSES,I,Data,FILENAME),
    marker(System,NOS_CLAUSES,I,Data,FILENAME2),
    fail;
  true),
  tell(FILENAME), told,
  tell(FILENAME2), told.

%%%%%%%%%%%%%%%%%%%%%%%%%%%%%%%%%%%%%%%%%%%%%%%%%%%%%%%%%%
% Generate a single clause.

gen_data(System,Nos_clause,I,Data,Filename):-
  dg(System,cn,[const,
          int,
           funct(const,const),
            int,
             vlenlist(int,5,3,notail)],
         [131072,
          131072,
           10,900,9999,
            131072,
             131072],empty,Data),
  tell(Filename),
  write(Data), write('.'), nl,
  tell(user), !.

%%%%%%%%%%%%%%%%%%%%%%%%%%%%%%%%%%%%%%%%%%%%%%%%%%%%%%%%%%
% Generates a marker point which will be held in the mark
% file ?

marker(System,Nos_clauses,I,Data,Filename):-
  i_div(System,Nos_clauses,2,HALF),    % Is it the middle clause?
  HALF=I,
  tell(Filename),
  write([Data,half]), write('.'), nl,
  tell(user).
```

```
marker(_,_,_,_).

%%%%%%%%%%%%%%%%%%%%%%%%%%%%%%%%%%%%%%%%%%%%%%%%%%%%
% Main Clause

dg(System,Name, ArgList, RangeList, ClauseType,Clause_out) :-
      do_args(System,ArgList, RangeList, Args),
      ClHead =.. [Name|Args],
      do_body(System,ClauseType, Name, Args, ClBody),
      (ClBody == [],
         Clause_out=ClHead;
       Clause_out=(ClHead:-ClBody)),!.

do_args(System,ArgList, RangeList, Args) :-
      do_args(System,ArgList, RangeList, _, Args).

do_args(System,[], R, R, []) :- !.

do_args(System,[var|Ts], Rs, Rs1, [_|Alist]) :-          % variables
      do_args(System,Ts, Rs, Rs1, Alist), !.

do_args(System,[int|Ts], [Range|Rs], Rs1, [I|Alist]) :-  % integers
      random(System,Range,I,_),
      do_args(System,Ts, Rs, Rs1, Alist), !.

do_args(System,[const|Ts], [Range|Rs], Rs1, [C|Alist]) :- % constants
      random(System,Range,I,_),
      int_to_const(System,I,C),
      do_args(System,Ts, Rs, Rs1, Alist), !.

do_args(System,[[HT|TT]|Ts], Rs, Rs1, [L|Alist]) :-      % lists
      do_args(System,[HT|TT], Rs, Rs2, L),
      do_args(System,Ts, Rs2, Rs1, Alist), !.

do_args(_,[tail], Rs, Rs, _).     % special end-of-list type

do_args(System,[Struct|Ts], Rs, Rs1, [S|Alist]) :-   % structures
      Struct =.. [funct|ArgTypes],
      do_args(System,[const|ArgTypes], Rs, Rs2, Slist),
      S =.. Slist,
      do_args(System,Ts, Rs2, Rs1, Alist), !.

                              % variable length lists
do_args(Sys,[vlenlist(Type,Avelen,Var,Withtail)|Ts],[Range|Rs],Rs1,[L|Alist]) :-
      random(Sys,_,R,N),
      Len is Avelen + ((Var * N)/10),
      mklist(Type, Len, AL),
      mklist(Range, Len, RangeList),
      ( Withtail == tail, append(AL, [tail], ArgList) ;  ArgList = AL ),
      do_args(Sys,ArgList, RangeList, L),
      do_args(Sys,Ts, Rs, Rs1, Alist), !.

                              % var length structures
do_args(System,[vlenfn(Type,Avelen,Var)|Ts],[FRange,ARange|Rs],Rs1,[S|Alist]):-
      random(System,_,R,N),
      Len is Avelen + ((Var * N)/10),
      mklist(Type, Len, ArgList),
      mklist(ARange, Len, RangeList),
```

```
    do_args(System,[const|ArgList], [FRange|RangeList], Slist),
    S =.. Slist,
    do_args(System,Ts, Rs, Rs1, Alist), !.

do_body(_,empty, _, _, []) :- !.
do_body(_,literal(X), _, _, X) :- !.
do_body(_,recursive, Name, Args, ClBody) :-
    ClBody =.. [Name|Args], !.

do_body(_,_, _, _, []) :- !.

mklist(_, N, []) :-
    N =< 0.
mklist(Elt, N, [Elt|L]) :-
    N1 is N - 1, mklist(Elt, N1, L).

%%%%%%%%%%%%%%%%%%%%%%%%%%%%%%%%%%%%%%%%%%%%%%%%%%%%%%
% from(Lower,Upper,Value) Count from Lower to Upper on failure -
%                    following Wilk's paper.

from(I,I,I):-!.

from(L,N,I):-
  N1 is (L+N)//2,           % C-Prolog
% N1 is (L+N) div 2,          % Nip 1.5
  from(L,N1,I).

from(L,N,I):-
  L1 is (L+N)//2+1,          % C-Prolog
% L1 is (L+N) div 2+1,         % Nip 1.5
  from(L1,N,I).

%%%%%%%%%%%%%%%%%%%%%%%%%%%%%%%%%%%%%%%%%%%%%%%%%%%%%%
% Random Number Generator:        Uses Integer Arithmetic Only

random(System,Range,Num,_):-         % Generate Number in Range
    nonvar(Range),
    new_seed(Tmp),
    i_div(System,Tmp,16384,T1),
    T2 is Tmp mod 16384,
    i_div(System,(Range*T1),32,Num1),
    i_div(System,(Range*T2),524288,Num2),
    Num3 is Num1 + Num2,
    i_abs(Num3,Num),!.         % So that a Positive number always rtn.

random(System,Range,Num,Deviation):-  % Generate Number+Deviation*10
    var(Range),
    new_seed(Tmp),
    i_div(System,Tmp,16384,T1),
    T2 is Tmp mod 16384,
    i_div(System,(10000*T1),32,Num1),
    i_div(System,(10000*T2),524288,Num2),
    Num3 is Num1 + Num2,
    i_abs(Num3,Num),          % So that a Positive number always rtn.
    ntable(Deviation,Area),
    Area >= Num,!.

% Set Seed Value
```

```
reset_seed:-
      retract(seed(_)),
      retract(cycle_start(_)),
      asserta(seed(12345)),
      asserta(cycle_start(12345)),!.

% Generate a new seed value

seed(12345).
cycle_start(12345).              % Start of Cycle Value

new_seed(New_val) :-
      old_seed(X),
      New_val is (125 * X) mod 524288,
      assert(seed(New_val)),!.

old_seed(Seed):-
      seed(Old_seed),
      retract(cycle_start(Old_seed)),
      retract(seed(Old_seed)),
      Seed is Old_seed + 13,
      assert(cycle_start(Seed)),!.
old_seed(Seed):-
      retract(seed(Seed)),!.

% a normal distribution table.

ntable(-40,  0).
ntable(-35,  4).
ntable(-30,  13).
ntable(-25,  62).
ntable(-20,  228).
ntable(-15,  668).
ntable(-10, 1587).
ntable(-5 , 3085).
ntable( 0 , 5000).
ntable( 5 , 6915).
ntable( 10, 8413).
ntable( 15, 9332).
ntable( 20, 9772).
ntable( 25, 9938).
ntable( 30, 9987).
ntable( 35, 9996).
ntable( 40, 9999).

%%%%%%%%%%%%%%%%%%%%%%%%%%%%%%%%%%%%%%%%%%%%%%%%%%%%%%%
% Simple type conversions

int_to_const(System,I,C) :-
      I1 is I+1,
      int_to_letters(System,I1,L),
      name(C,L), !.

int_to_letters(System,0, []).
int_to_letters(System,N, [N2|L]) :-
      i_div(System,N,10,N1),
      N2 is (N mod 10) + (N1 mod 16) + 97,  % 97 == 'a'
      int_to_letters(System,N1, L).
```

```
%%%%%%%%%%%%%%%%%%%%%%%%%%%%%%%%%%%%%%%%%%%%%%%%%%%%%%%%%%%%%%%%
% i_div: perform integer division.

i_div(_,V1,V2,0):-
  V1 = 0;V2 = 0,!.
i_div(nip,V1,V2,OV):-
  OV is trunc(float(V1)/float(V2)),!.
i_div(c-prolog,V1,V2,OV):-
  OV is floor(V1/V2),!.

%%%%%%%%%%%%%%%%%%%%%%%%%%%%%%%%%%%%%%%%%%%%%%%%%%%%%%%%%%%%%%%%
% i_abs(X,Y): Unifies Y with the absolute value of X

i_abs(X,Y):-
  X < 0,
  Y is -1 * X,!.
i_abs(X,X):- !.

%%%%%%%%%%%%%%%%%%%%%%%%%%%%%%%%%%%%%%%%%%%%%%%%%%%%%%%%%%%%%%%%
% Append Two Lists

append([],L,L):-      !.
append([H|T],L,[H|T1]):- append(T,L,T1).

%%%%%%%%%%%%%%%%%%%%%%%%%%%%%%%%%%%%%%%%%%%%%%%%%%%%%%%%%%%%%%%%
% Generate Filename Given A Nos and a Template (ie. "TemplateNos")

generate_filename(Nos_clause,Template,Filename):-
  name(Nos_clause,NCL),
  name(Template,DL),
  append(DL,NCL,FL),
  name(Filename,FL),!.

%%%%%%%%%%%%%%%%%%%%%%%%%%%%%%%%%%%%%%%%%%%%%%%%%%%%%%%%%%%%%%%%
% Generate succesive powers of 4 upto a limit (ie. 4, 16, 64, etc..)

gen_nos(Start,_,Max_nos):-
  Start > Max_nos,!,
  fail.

gen_nos(Start,Start,Max_nos):-
  Start =< Max_nos.

gen_nos(16384,30000,_). % Include here any additional data sizes
gen_nos(16384,40000,_).

gen_nos(Start,Nos,Max_nos):-
  New_start is Start * 4,!,
  gen_nos(New_start,Nos,Max_nos).
```

12

Grid files for efficient Prolog clause access

Michael Freeston
European Computer-Industry Research Centre, Arabellstr. 17, 8000 Munchen 81. West Germany

ABSTRACT

A common feature of the expressive power of fourth-generation database query languages and of Prolog is the lack of predictability in the form of queries. This calls for a very flexible indexing scheme in both contexts. The problems encountered in developing such a scheme for Prolog reflect the fact that there has so far been relatively little effort to develop similarly flexible file indexing mechanisms for classical database systems. If, however, such a mechanism could be devised, it could also help to solve the more general problem of efficient Prolog clause indexing. This chapter describes research which has led to the development of a new multi-dimensional file structure, called the BANG file.

1. INTRODUCTION

Indexing in Prolog poses particular difficulties. Classical database hashing techniques provide an adequate solution while the database remains entirely resident in main memory, but new and acute problems arise when attempts are made to perform unification directly with clauses stored on disk.† Perhaps this is why efforts in this direction have tended to focus on 'sledgehammer' hardware solutions, rather than looking for new software approaches.

A two-stage approach to unification has recently gained favour, in which the first (pre-unification) stage filters out as many mis-matches as possible, using a relatively crude matching technique based on a hashed index of clause heads. The second stage then attempts full unification on the

† Why bother, when main memory will soon be big enough to store everything? The reason is that memory will still be paged, and the same fundamental data access problems will remain. Many of the data structures developed for disk-based storage will therefore be applied to persistent main memory with little adaptation.

remaining candidate clauses. The particular attraction of such a scheme is that the first stage filtering mechanism can be implemented in special hardware and can thus be very fast. It is then only a short step to move both the procedure index and the corresponding clauses (source or compiled) to disk. The Prolog database is then no longer limited by main memory capacity, and only clauses which pass the pre-unification filter reach main memory.

But if Prolog procedures can be accessed individually on disk, what now is the difference between a Prolog database and a relational database? In terms of extensional data, the answer is that there is no fundamental difference. The difference, of course, is in the intentional data — the rules — of Prolog, which have no relational database equivalent. So, viewed from the backing storage, the system has become a relational database, somehow incorporating rules, with a Prolog front-end.

Why, then, are currently available relational database file access techniques not adequate for Prolog? There are two main reasons. First, relational databases are founded on the principle that the structure of every tuple in a relation is the same, fixed and defined in the database schema. In contrast, the structure of Prolog rules is not fixed. Unless this difference can be resolved, Prolog rules cannot be accommodated within a relational environment. Second, and more surprising, current relational file access mechanisms do not perform well enough on facts, according to the criteria of the Prolog programmer.

A query on a Prolog procedure containing only facts is exactly equivalent to a relational partial match query, but the indexing facilities offered by the two systems are, at least in principle, very different. The traditional database philosophy is that the indexes are chosen to match the pattern of queries on the relation. This is a perfectly reasonable approach when the user interface is menu-driven — as is still the case in the great majority of commercial database applications — because the form of the queries is entirely predictable — indeed, enforceable.

But it makes little sense when the menu is replaced by a fourth-generation query language, in which the user is free to pose practically any query. The innocent expectation of such users is that the speed of response to a query will depend on the amount of information specified (e.g. the *number* of attributes with specified values in a partial match query) and not on the particular *combination* of attribute values supplied.

In this context, the Prolog philosophy seems much more appropriate. Indexing in Prolog is, by database standards, a very crude affair. The user is not supposed to know anything about the indexing mechanism, only that the presence of an index will somehow speed up access generally. However, this does not strike the Prolog programmer as restrictive, because he realizes that, in a non-deterministic program, a whole series of queries on a procedure may be generated, in which any combination of its arguments may or may not be instantiated.

But the indexing methods used by Prolog have serious deficiencies, when considered both from a Prolog and a relational point of view. Direct hashing schemes cannot support range queries on dynamically varying data distributions. This doesn't matter in Prolog, in that it is not possible to execute a range query directly, but it is an unacceptable limitation in a relational database. Bit filtering methods in Prolog, such as superimposed coding, not only sacrifice order information, but also lose all clustering information. For example, each clause in the set which matches a query on a large procedure will very probably be located in a different disk page.

Perhaps, if Prolog and relational databases had continued to develop along separate paths, these problems and incompatibilities would not have been the cause of any great concern, or particular interest. But once serious attempts are made to unify the two, then the problems must be fully understood, and answers found. This explains how the research described below arose. The particular problems of indexing Prolog clauses have emphasized the increasing inadequacy of classical database indexing methods in the face of new patterns of usage. So they have provided an additional impetus to the search for a well-behaved, multi-dimensional file structure for classical relational databases.

If this problem could be solved, then although it might prove of little additional value in the Prolog context, it would greatly add to the flexibility of conventional databases. Even if it could only accommodate facts and not rules, a multi-dimensional file would at least be much more in the spirit of Prolog, and might be able to support a class of set-oriented operators in a unified Prolog–relational system. If, however, it could be extended to include rule indexing, so much the better.

The objective of the study which led to the development of the BANG file was the development of a general data/knowledge-base file structure in which the *average* response time to a query could be minimized, in an environment in which no particular form of query is considered to be more probable than another. The attraction of a multi-dimensional file structure is that the overall search space can always be reduced, whatever the combination of attribute values, or ranges of values, specified in a query†, without the update overheads of secondary indexes or inverted files.

Previous research in this direction has followed three distinct lines:

1. Tree structures: a generalization to *n* dimensions [1–6].
2. Multi-dimensional extendible hashing [7–9].
3. Grid files: an explicitly geometric approach, representing *n*-tuples as points in a partitioned *n*-dimensional hyperspace [10–13].

A detailed review of recent work in these areas [14] was encouraging, to the extent that a number of novel approaches have been demonstrated to be effective for certain classes of application. But all appeared to have some serious drawback as a general database support structure. Of the various possibilities, the grid file approach seemed to have more potential than the others for further innovation and improvement.

This conclusion led to a further study, in the course of which a new design

† . . . unless of course the query covers every tuple in the file!

emerged [15]. It has been christened the BANG file: A Balanced And Nested Grid file. It combines features of previous grid file designs with a tree-structured directory which has much in common with a prefix B-tree. Most importantly the directory maintains the self-balancing property of a B-tree, and always expands at the same rate as the data, whatever the data distribution. As a structure for representing spatial objects, it has a partitioning strategy which accurately reflects the clustering of points in the data space, while maintaining a high density of data storage.

In fact, one of the contributions which the development of grid files has made to file design is that it has emphasized the advantages of describing file structures explicitly in geometric terms — even when the structure is not of a grid file type, or its application is not graphical. It is much easier to understand the form of a structure, and the effect of operations on it, if the representation is directly visual.

2. PRINCIPLES AND DEFINITIONS

We assume that the physical file is composed of randomly accessible fixed-size disk blocks to which we may assign unique identification numbers. We will also assume that the data to be stored in this file are in the form of tuples (records), each composed of the same fixed linear structure of attributes (fields). That is, the data are in relational form. This does not necessarily mean that the tuples are of fixed length.

The tuples of an n-ary relation can be represented as points in an n-dimensional hyperspace, the dimensions of which are the domains of the n attributes. The problem is simply how to allocate the tuples in this hyperspace to the set of disk blocks in the file. An optimal solution to the problem is not so simple.

In geometric terms the obvious thing to do is to divide up the data space into a set of hyperrectangles or block regions, each of which corresponds to a disk block. Note, however, that there is no reason in principle why these block regions should be rectangular. But common sense (which we should remind ourselves is not always to be relied on) suggests that the block regions should be bounded by planar surfaces, each of which is orthogonal to the axis of a domain. This still does not mean that the block regions must be rectangular. They could contain concavities. Nor does it follow that any of the planes in the division must bisect the entire data space (Fig. 1(a). Nevertheless, let us begin with the conceptually simpler assumption that the data space is to be divided into hyperrectangles by partitioning each dimension as shown in Fig. 1(b). The immediate questions which arise are: how many partitions should be set up, and where should they be placed? If each block region corresponds to one disk block, then clearly partitions must be so arranged that no block region contains more tuples than can be contained in one disk block. And if the search for a tuple is not to favour one key attribute over another, then the number of disk blocks to be searched should be the same, whichever dimension the key lies in. This implies that the number of partitions in each dimension should be the same, if possible.

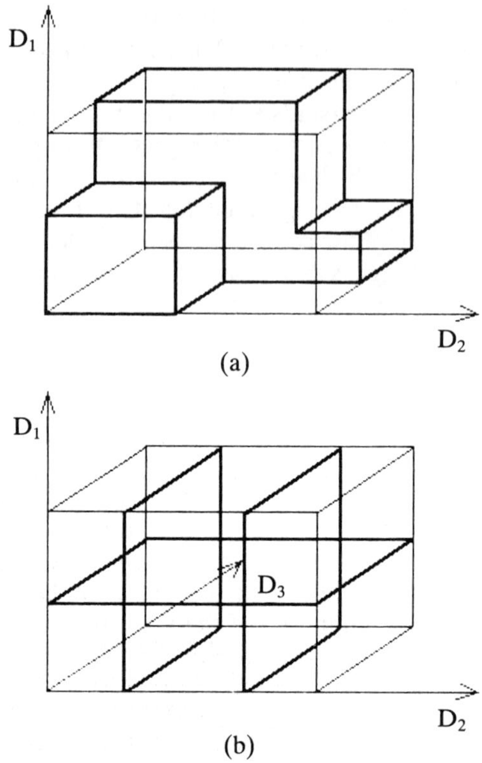

Fig. 1.

When the addition of a tuple would cause a disk block to overflow, then either the block region corresponding to it must be divided, by adding an additional partition, or the previously defined partition boundaries must be moved, or both.

In the BANG file, the data space is partitioned by a sequence of binary divisions, and the dimension selected for the next division is chosen according to a pre-defined order of cycling through all the dimensions. The same partitioning sequence is applied throughout the data space, but the partitioning *operation* is applied selectively to individual block regions. It is important to note that a block region may be recursively partitioned many times before a new region is created: *any* size of region may be created within another, provided that the enclosed region is a member of the set of all block regions which could be created by the chosen partitioning (see Fig. 2).

The recursive partitioning is terminated when the best (nearest) possible balance is obtained between the two split regions. In the special case when the two split regions are of equal size, they are referred to as 'buddies'.

The number of partitions (i.e. the length of the partitioning sequence)

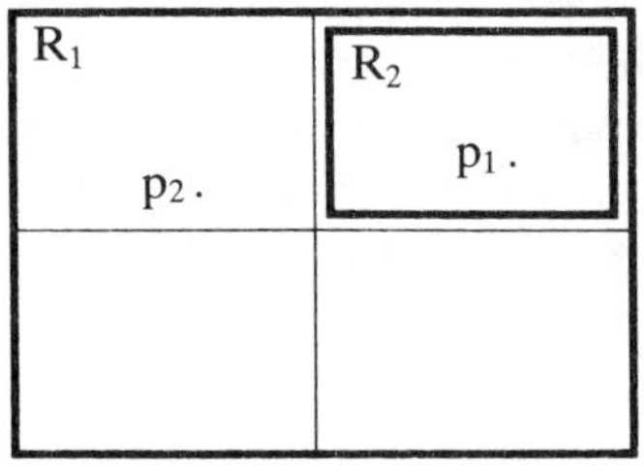

Fig. 2.

required to create a particular block region is a measure of its *granularity*, and is termed the *level number* or simple *level* of the block region. (For example, if Fig. 2 represents the entire data space, then block region R_1 is at level 0, and block region R_2 is at level 2). The level corresponding to the smallest block region so far created is called the *grid level*, and block regions of this size are termed *grid regions*. (In Fig. 2, the grid level is 2, and region R_2 is a grid region.)

A *block region identifier*, composed of a number pair (*level number, block region number*), is assigned to every block region, and uniquely identifies it in the set of all possible block regions at every level. The block region number is generated as a string of bits representing the partitioning sequence required to create the region. For example, suppose that the region R_1 shown in Fig. 2 represents the entire data space. Then its block region identifier is [0,0]. If it now splits about the vertical partition shown, then the left-hand split region is [1,0] and the right-hand split region is [1,1]. If both these regions now split about the horizontal partition, the lower-left region is [2,0] and the upper-left is [2,1]. The lower right-hand region is [2,2] (i.e. block region number is binary 10) while the upper right-hand region is [2,3] (block region number is binary 11). The numbering scheme therefore depends on the order in which the dimensions of the data space are partitioned.

This mapping has the important property that the block region number of *any* block region enclosing the same point in the data space can be generated from the mapping by which a tuple is itself mapped to that point. The value of each attribute of the tuple is transformed — whatever the domain type — into a variable-length bit string, in such a way that the original ordering on the domain of the attribute is preserved, if the bit string is interpreted as an unsigned integer. (Character strings can generally be used directly, but the transformation of integers and reals is machine dependent.) But for an unsigned integer, expressed in binary form, the sequence of its bit values, from the most to the least significant, determines a sequence of binary partitions on the domain of the integer. And whatever the level of the partition, the integer always lies within it.

Conversely, for every sequence of binary partitions which defines some region of the data space, there is a corresponding sequence of bits selected from among the set of attribute values of the tuples located within that region. If all the bits from all the attributes are used, the bit string formed is the mapping from the tuple value to its position in the data space, or rather, to the block region number of the smallest possible grid region enclosing the tuple (An example is given in Fig. 3). As the least significant bit of this

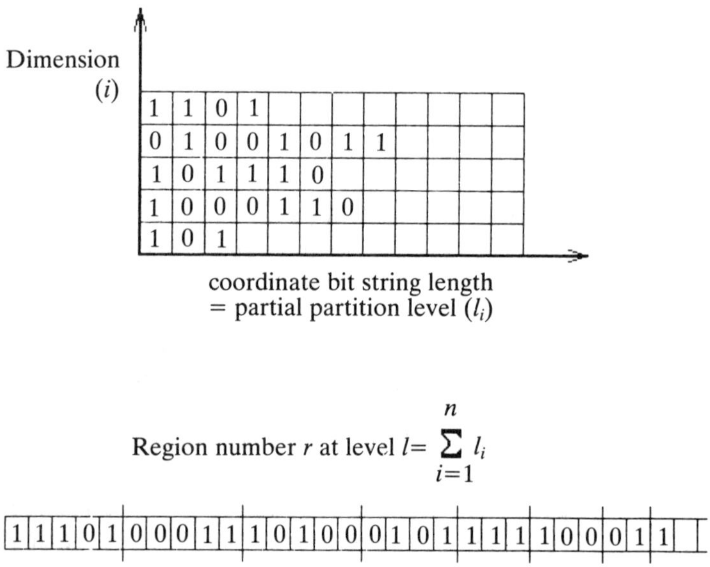

Fig. 3.

number corresponds to the most recent partition, it follows that, each time the least significant bit is stripped from the block region number, the number of the next larger block region which *could* enclose the tuples is generated.

Since one block region can enclose another, and each block region corresponds to a disk block, there is clearly a potential for ambiguity in the placement of tuples in disk blocks. This ambiguity is resolved by introducing a further concept, the *logical region*. A logical region is a block region *minus* the block regions which it encloses. Thus, although every block region maps to a physical disk block, the data subspace represented by the disk block is that of the corresponding logical region.

For example, Fig. 2 shows a BANG file representation of a data space partitioned into two block regions R_1 and R_2. R_1 encloses the entire data space, and R_2 is enclosed or *nested* within R_1. These two block regions define two logical regions L_1 and L_2: L_2 is the space enclosed by the boundaries of R_2; L_1 is the space enclosed by R_1 *minus* R_2. Therefore R_2 alone defines L_2, but *both* R_1 and R_2 are necessary to define L_1.

In general, every logical region of the BANG file is defined by a *set* of block regions. One member of this set represents a rectangular space which encloses all the other members of the set. These enclosed block regions represent subtractions from the enclosing block region.

The logical regions into which the data space of the BANG file is partitioned are therefore defined by block regions, but are not necessarily block regions themselves. In other words, *the logical regions do not have to be hyperrectangles*. They can contain concavities, and have internal as well as external boundaries. It is even possible for a local region to be disjoint, i.e. to be composed of subspaces which do not intersect and which have no common boundary. Most importantly, *a logical region always spans the space which it encloses*. This is not in general true for a block region.

However, the logical regions and the sets representing them are — as the name implies — purely logical constructs. Only block regions are represented explicitly. But each data page holds the tuples mapping to a logical region, not to a block region. Likewise the partitioning algorithm attempts to balance the distribution of tuples between logical regions.

3. ORGANIZATION OF THE DIRECTORY

The BANG file has a tree-structured directory with the self-balancing property of a B-tree. The entries in the leaf nodes of the tree point to the data pages, each of which directly represents a logical region of the data space, and contains the set of (source) tuples located in that logical region. There is no defined ordering on the tuples within a data page. Each level of the directory tree, from the leaves to the root, represents a recursive repartitioning of the data space into regions enclosing regions.

Each directory page contains a header which holds a few bytes of control information, a set of variable-length entries, and a page entry table containing pointers to the start of each entry. The structure and storage order of the entries is the key to the BANG file representation of the data space. Each entry is a triplet representing a block region. In principle, the triplet has the form

[disk page number, level number, block region number]

However, it is not generally necessary to store the complete block region number in a directory entry, because the directory page itself represents a block region, which encloses all the block regions represented within it. Therefore all entries within the same directory page must share the same partition sequence — and hence the same bit string in the block region number — down to the directory page level. Hence it is only necessary to store the *relative level number*, i.e. the level relative to that of the enclosing directory page, and the *block region prefix*, which is the bit string for the relative entry level. A directory entry thus takes the form

[disk page number, relative level number, block region number prefix]

In the current implementation, there is a compromise between these two representations, for efficiency reasons. In order to be able to make comparisons by byte rather than by bit during directory search and update operations, remainder bits from one directory level† are carried down to the next. Provided that the *absolute partition level* is accumulated during the descent of the directory tree, the position of the start bit of the next prefix can be easily computed. (Note that entries are of variable length, which accounts for the need for a page entry table. The length of an entry prefix can be computed from the absolute level of the directory page, and the relative level number.)

4. INSERTION AND RETRIEVAL

In principle, the search key is generated from the source tuple as described above, but in practice it is generated dynamically during traversal of the directory tree. When the search descends to a page at the next level, a comparison is made between the absolute level of the smallest block region in the page and the current length of the search key bit string. If the search key is shorter, it is extended.

The insertion (and retrieval) of a tuple in the correct logical region is achieved by an ordering of entries within the directory page which reflects the definition of a logical region. The entries are ordered by block region number within level, and the page is searched from highest level number to lowest, i.e. from smallest to largest block region. The upper and lower limits to the range of entries of highest level number are established by binary search. A second binary search is then made within this range for an entry which matches the search key (i.e. if the leading bits of the search key match the block region number). If no match is found, the search is repeated within the range of the next higher level (smaller level number) in the page, and so on.

It is important to note that, if the search key matches an entry which represents some block region R, then it will also match any other entry representing a block region which encloses R. However, there is no ambiguity in locating a tuple in R, because the order of search means that the innermost enclosed region will always be found first.

For example, let R_1 and R_2 in Fig. 2 now be *logical* regions. Then R_2 is represented by the block region identifier [2,3], and R_1 is represented by the set of identifiers {[0,0], [2,3]}. But the (root) directory page only contains the two entries [d_1,0,0] [d_2,2,3], where d_1 and d_2 are the identifiers of the data pages representing logical regions R_1 and R_2 respectively.

Suppose that a tuple which maps to point p_1 in logical region R_1 of the data space is to be inserted. The search key is generated from the tuple, and the directory page is searched for the lowest level entry which matches the key. The smallest block region which would match the key is [2,2], which is not recorded in the directory. So the search through the directory continues

† Beware of confusing *directory level* with *partition level*. A directory page at one level of the directory tree may contain entries for block regions at many partition levels.

until, in this very simple example, a match is found at the next entry [d_1,0,0], and the tuple is inserted into page d_1.

If the tuple to be inserted maps to point p_2 in logical region R_2, a match is found at the first entry [d_2,2,3] in the search order, and the tuple is stored in page d_2. However, note that in this case the second entry in the directory would also match the key, but is not reached.

This example demonstrates that, although the directory does not contain any explicit information about logical regions (as opposed to block regions), there is no confusion in the placement of tuples in the correct logical region, because of the order of searching in the directory. Exactly the same algorithm is applied when retrieving a tuple except that, once the target data page has been found, a linear search must be made within the page because the tuples are not ordered within it.

5. THE PARTITIONING ALGORITHM

The partitioning algorithm is invoked whenever the insertion of a tuple causes a data bucket to overflow. The algorithm partitions the logical region corresponding to the overflowing bucket into two logical regions, one enclosing the other. The procedure is recursive: first the region is partitioned as shown in Fig. 4(b); then the region containing more tuples than the other

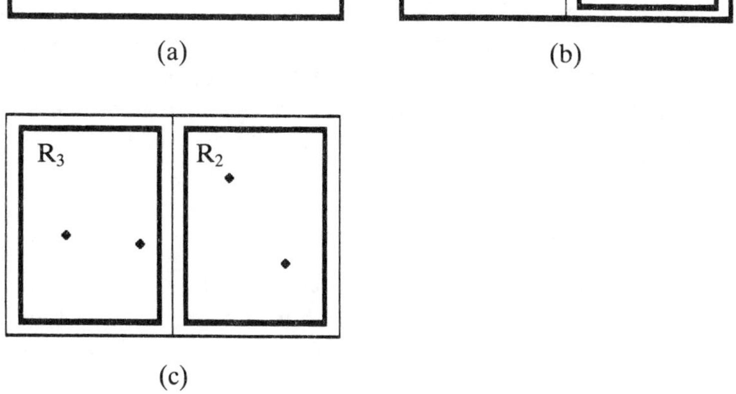

Fig. 4.

is progressively halved until the balance is reversed. The best balance is then chosen. If balance is achieved at the first level of division, then Buddy regions are created (Fig. 4(c)). If not, then the external boundary of the original logical region remains the same, but a new logical region is created within it (Fig. 4.(b)).

Fig. 5 shows the creation of a sequence of partitions as tuples are added.

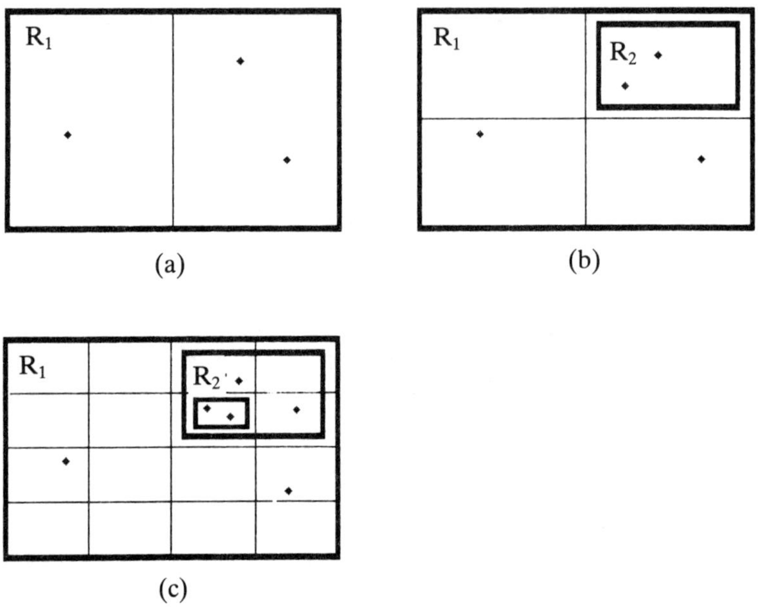

Fig. 5.

Note that the partition configuration shown is not unique: in general there are many possibilities. Which one actually occurs depends on the *order* in which the tuples are added. Fig. 6 illustrates a refinement on the algorithm applied in Fig. 5. In Fig. 6 the splitting of an enclosed region is always treated as a continuation of a higher level split. This sometimes allows a redistribution with the enclosing region, so that no new data bucket is created.

6. UPDATING THE DIRECTORY

When a new logical region is created by splitting a data bucket, an entry for it must be inserted into the leaf directory page which contained the original region entry. If the regions resulting from the split are buddies, then the original entry must also be modified.

If the insertion causes the directory page to overflow, then it is itself split, which may in turn cause overflow at the next higher directory level and so

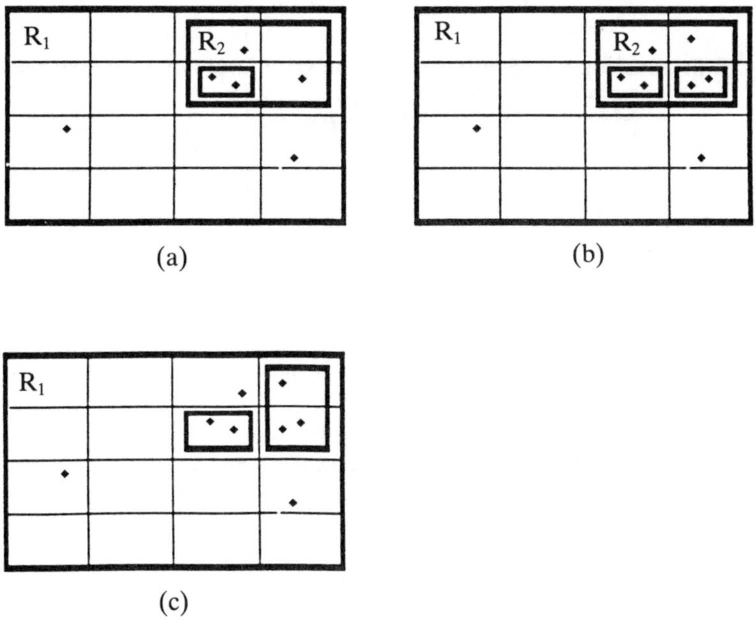

Fig. 6.

on, in the same way as a B-tree. (Note, however, that the B-tree always divides an overflowing region precisely in half, while the BANG file only achieves a best balance.) Directory pages are split on exactly the same binary partitioning principle as data pages. The effect, however, is different in a number of important respects because, although a directory page itself represents a logical region, it contains the set of logical sub-regions — not data points — into which the page has been further partitioned. Essentially, it is the property of *enclosure* which makes the partitioning of regions different from the partitioning of points. The nature of this difference, and the means of accommodating it, is best explained by an example.

Suppose that a two-dimensional data space is partitioned as shown in Fig. 7, and that the corresponding BANG directory consists of only one page. If we try to locate a tuple which maps to point P in the data space, then, according to the BANG directory search algorithm, the directory page is scanned from the largest level number to the smallest until a block region prefix is found which matches the search key. In this particular example only region **d** encloses point P. (Note that this is actually the *last* directory entry scanned, because it is the largest region.) Since there is only directory page, the matching entry points directly to the data page which contains the tuple at P.

Now suppose that additional tuples are inserted, until data page **d** splits into pages **d** and **g**. Suppose also that the directory page is very small, so

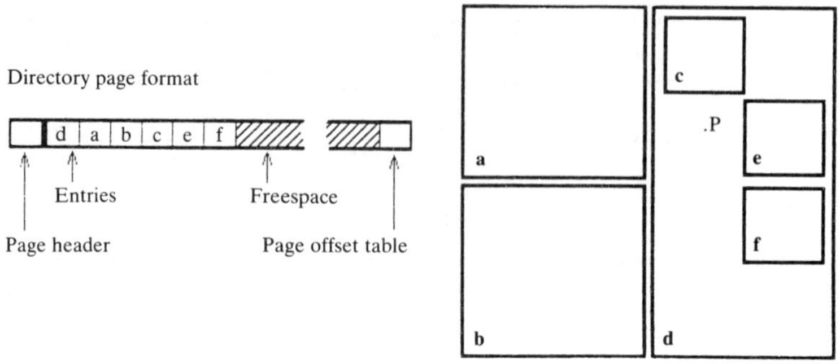

Fig. 7.

that it too splits when the new directory entry for page **g** is added. This in turn generates a new root directory page, so that there are now two directory levels, and a configuration of regions as shown in Fig. 8.

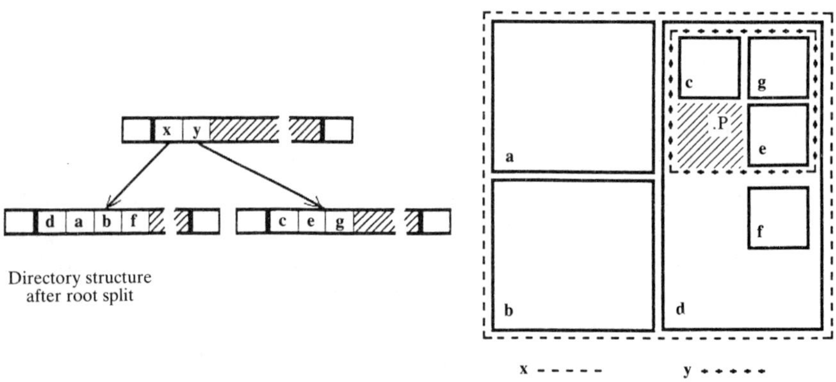

Fig. 8.

The problem should now be clear. Logical region **y** at the upper directory level no longer spans the space which it encloses. The shaded area—the part of the space not spanned by region **y**—is still part of logical region **d** which now lies in the other page at the upper directory level. Therefore, if we search again for a tuple which maps to point P, the first match found at the upper (root) directory level directs the search down to page **y** at the lower directory level, but there is no match at all for the search key in this page. The tuple at P is lost.

The solution in this example is to *force* logical region **d** to split (i.e. to split before it overflows naturally) into regions **d** and **h** (Fig. 9(a)), and to

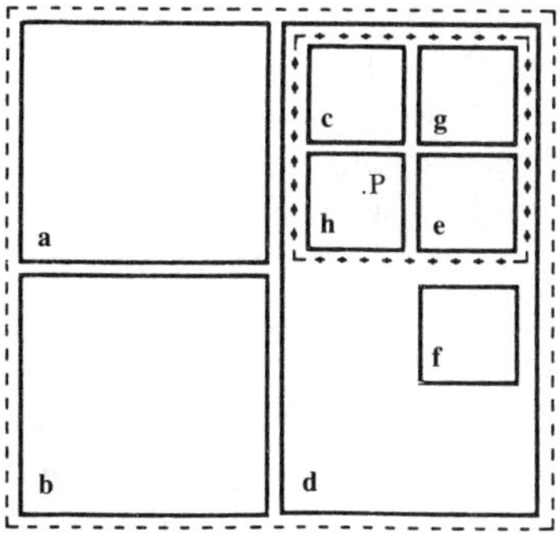

Fig. 9(a).

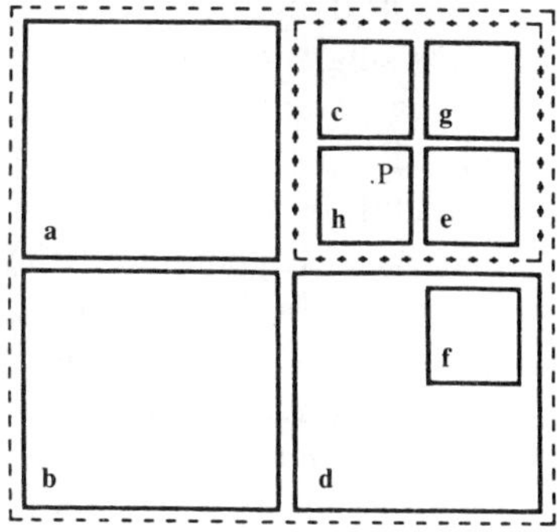

Fig. 9(b).

assign the entry for page **h** to the directory page representing region **y**. Logical region **y** now spans, and logical region **x** is block region **x** minus block region **y**. In this particular example, block region **d** can be reduced in size, as shown in Fig. 9(b)), but this is not always the case.

Note that forced splitting of a region means that it is forced to split before it overflows naturally, and that the new partition is not chosen by the criterion of best balance in this case. There will therefore be a reduction in the average occupancy of such regions. But since only a very few regions are affected in this way, the effect on the average occupancy of the whole file is very small. (It measures less than 1% in files of 1 Kbyte pages).

Unfortunately, however, this may not be the end of the spanning problem because, if logical region **d** is itself a directory page, then the newly created logical region **h** may not be spanned by the union of the regions which it encloses. The general solution to the spanning problem is therefore recursive. The recursion terminates when the enclosed region, created by forced splitting, spans — which may be at the level of the original overflowing directory page, or at a lower level. Since data pages directly represent subspaces of the data space, the recursion will always terminate at the data page level.

Details of the general 'span check' algorithm to be applied on splitting a directory page representing a logical region R into two logical regions R_1 and R_2 are given in [16]. The algorithm includes a check that the directory regions resulting from a split are of minimal size. If they are not, they are made so. The minimality condition is important for two reasons: first, it avoids a complication which otherwise has to be introduced to prevent the possibility of the creation of empty directory pages — which would never again be referenced, but would slowly degrade file performance; and second, it is important to the efficiency of range and partial match queries that their area of search is as small as possible.

Recombination of logical regions is more straightforward. In principle, a depleted region can recombine with any of the regions which it directly encloses, or with its Buddy (if it exists), or with its immediately enclosing region (if one exists), or with any region which is not separated from it by an enclosing region. It is this flexibility which allows the BANG file to adapt to changing data distributions without degradation of file performance. In practice, however, it is neither necessary nor desirable to implement all the possibilities — it is more a question of what is the minimum functionality necessary to maintain good file performance under any kind of changes of data distribution and file size. This question is still being studied, but the preliminary conclusion is that it is sufficient to allow the depleted region to merge with its buddy or, when there is no buddy, to merge with its enclosing region . If no buddy or enclosing region exists, then it merges with that region such that the resulting region is the smallest possible. The same sequence of tests for merger candidates is followed when the candidate exists, but the occupancy of the merged region would exceed a pre-defined maximum.

7. PERFORMANCE MEASUREMENTS

Some performance figures are included to demonstrate a number of important properties of the BANG file. Fig. 10 shows the behaviour of a two-dimensional BANG file, in which both attributes are composed of a (different) randomly generated character string, 48 bytes long. The page size is 1 kbyte. The first graph shows the average percentage occupancy of data pages as the file grows. The vertical lines indicate the points at which the directory expands to an additional level — in this example, to a maximum of three levels. The second graph shows the same information for directory pages, and the third shows the ratio of directory to total file occupancy.

It will be seen that, after the insertion of about 1000 tuples, the data occupancy shows little variation from about 67%, which is typical of a B-tree, or any other structure which expands by splitting pages into two. The steep oscillations in the occupancy of the directory are also typical, and are due to the fact that, for uniform data distributions, all the pages at the same directory level tend to overflow at the *same* overall file size. However, the *average* directory page occupancy is again about 67%.

Although the first two graphs in Fig. 10 show that the same page occupancy level is achieved for both data and directory pages, this alone does not guarantee that the *ratio* of directory to data remains constant. This ratio is shown in the third graph of Fig. 10. It will be seen that the ratio rapidly tends to a value of around 2%. The actual value of this ratio depends on the average number of entries per directory page, i.e. the 'fan-out ratio', which depends on the average directory entry length and the page size. The directory is so small because it is a *prefix* tree structure, and hence very compact.

In order to gain a clearer understanding of exactly how the BANG file partitions the data space for a non-uniform data distribution, pictures of the block regions were generated from the directory information. The first such

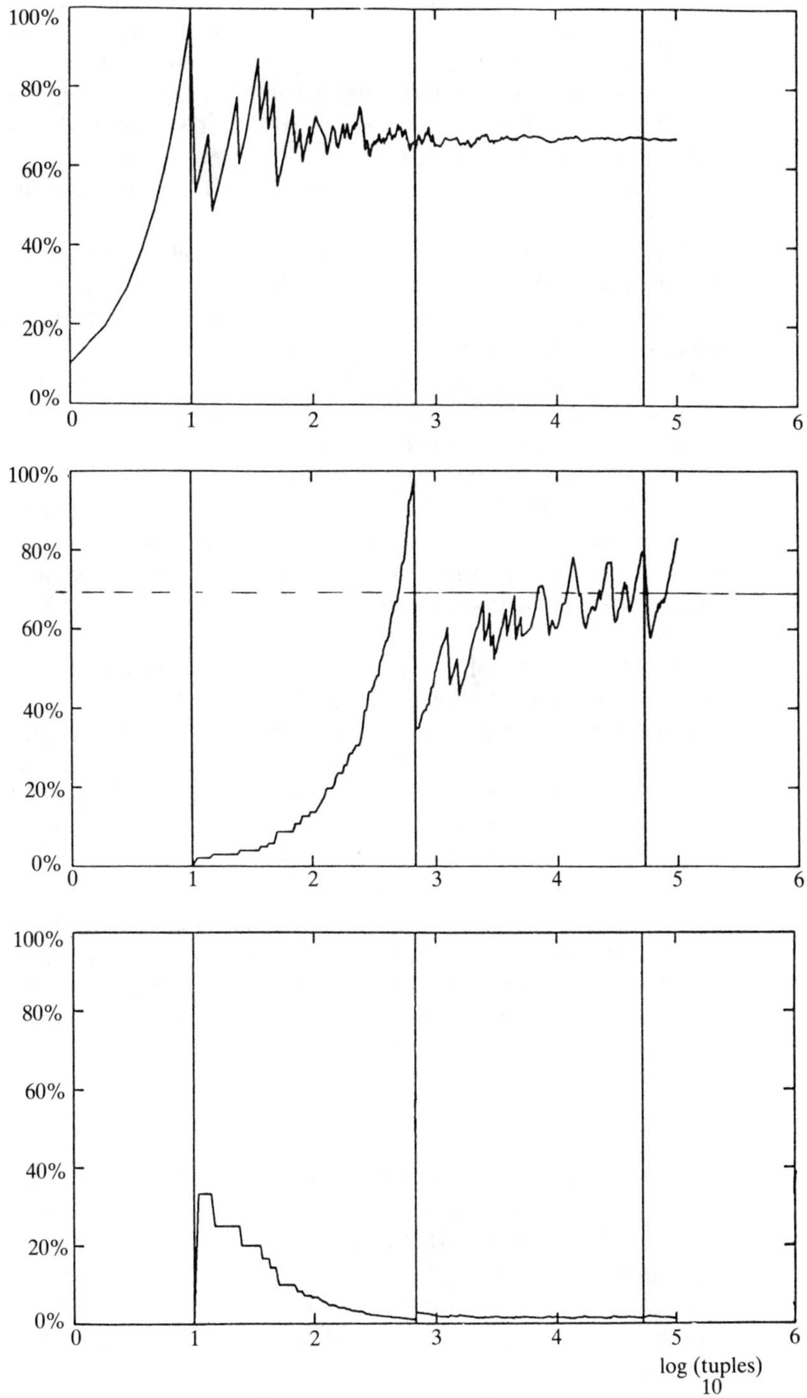

Fig. 10.

attempt resulted in something of a shock (Fig. 11). It was then realized that, merely to avoid producing control characters, the random character-string generator had been restricted to lower case alphabetic characters. The tuples generated therefore were not actually uniformly distributed at all, but uniformly distributed within 26 highly restricted subspaces! The upper inset of Fig. 11 shows a magnification of the circled region. This demonstrates very clearly, however, how economically the BANG partitioning algorithm divides the data space.

The rest of the figures are restricted to the safer domain of integers for the attribute values. Fig. 12 shows the appearance of a truly uniform distribution, and that the observed performance is in fact no different from the character-string case. The remaining figures 13–16 show the results of tests on a variety of other data distributions — data clusters, an inverse linear correlation, a non-linear correlation (about a sine curve) and a non-linear function (again a sine curve). It will be seen that in no case is the data or directory occupancy less than that for a linear function case. (The directory/total file size ratio is around 17% in these examples, because a page size of only 200 bytes was used in order to test performance with a 4-level directory.) Similar tests have been carried out for files of up to 8 dimensions. No significant variation in these performance figures has been observed.

As a further test of the potential value of multi-dimensional file structures, a comparison was made between a BANG file used as a one-dimensional file structure (equivalent in performance to a prefix B-tree), and alternatively as a three-dimensional structure, on a relation with three attributes. One of the attributes was chosen as the key for the one-dimensional file; all three were of course used for the three-dimensional file. Queries were then posed, using every possible combination of instantiated attributes — from an exact match query with all three attribute values specified, to a partial match query with any one of the three attributes specified. With equal numbers of each of such queries, and a file of 10 000 tuples, the *average* number of data pages searched was more than six times less for the three-dimensional file. As the file size increases, this difference also increases.

8. CONCLUSION

Multi-dimensional file structures are not a miracle. In the test described above, when only the single key attribute of the one-dimensional file was instantiated in a query to the three-dimensional file, it took 40 times longer. You never get something for nothing. But multi-dimensional files do offer more flexibility: they can still be used as one-dimensional files when all file accesses are certain to use a single key. When the form of the query is unpredictable, then a multi-dimensional configuration will give a much smoother performance and, on average, a much better performance, without the overheads of secondary indexing.

So what about Prolog? The hope is that, in the construction of an

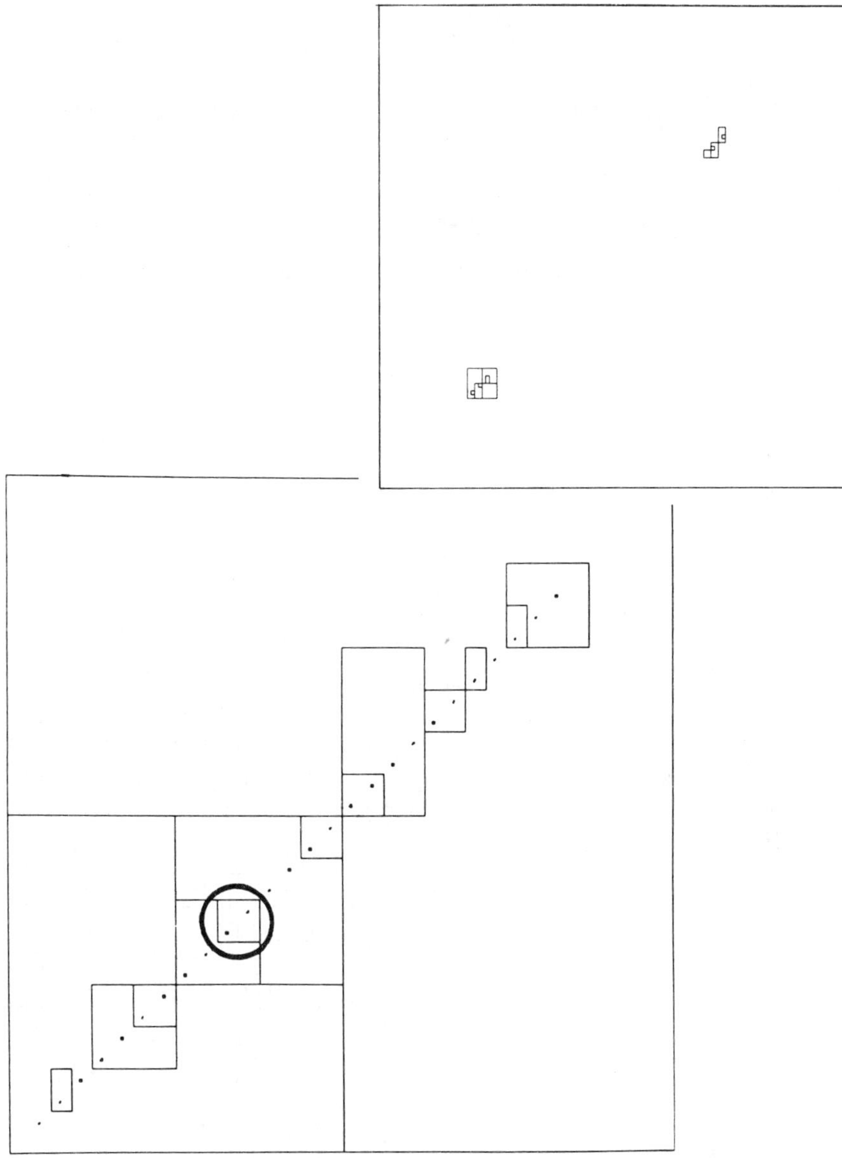

Fig. 11.

integrated knowledge base containing Prolog rules as well as facts, the BANG file will prove to be a powerful weapon, responding efficiently to unpredictable search patterns. But that's another long struggle away.

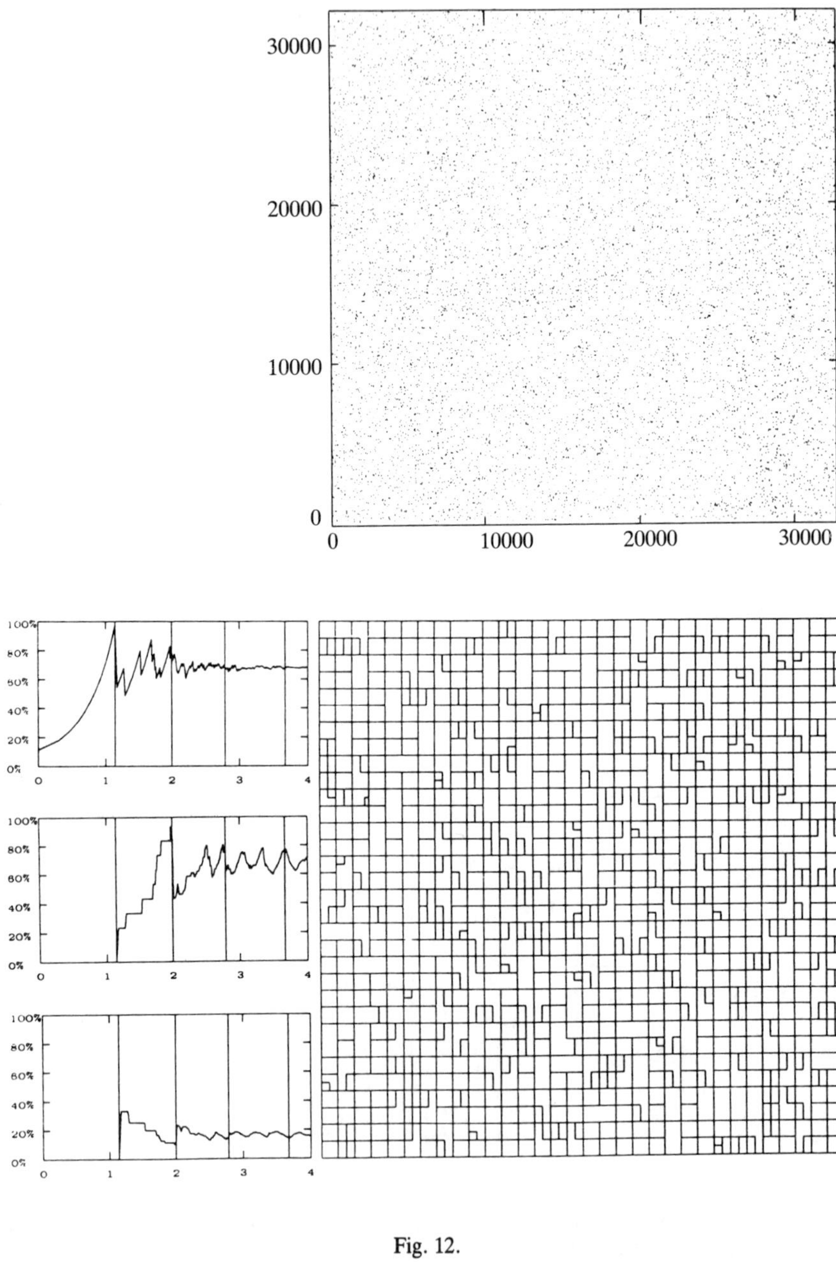

Fig. 12.

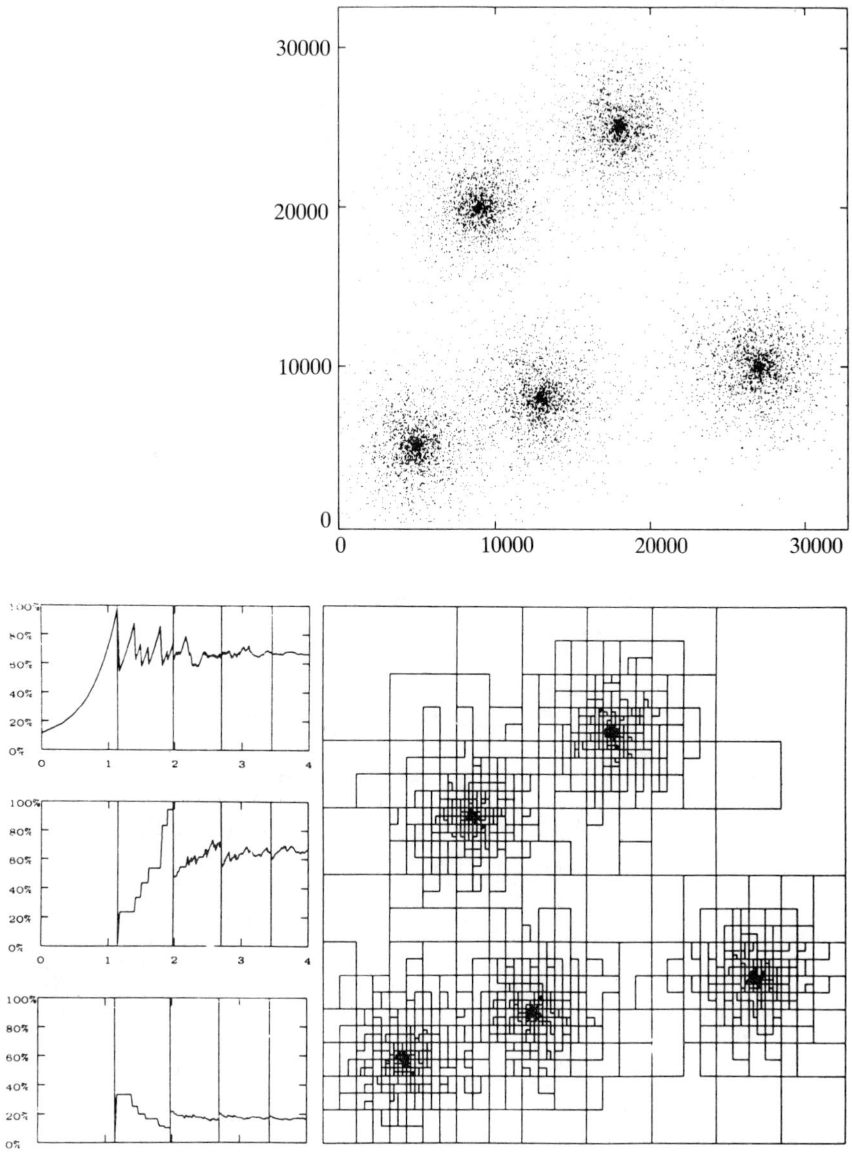

Fig. 13.

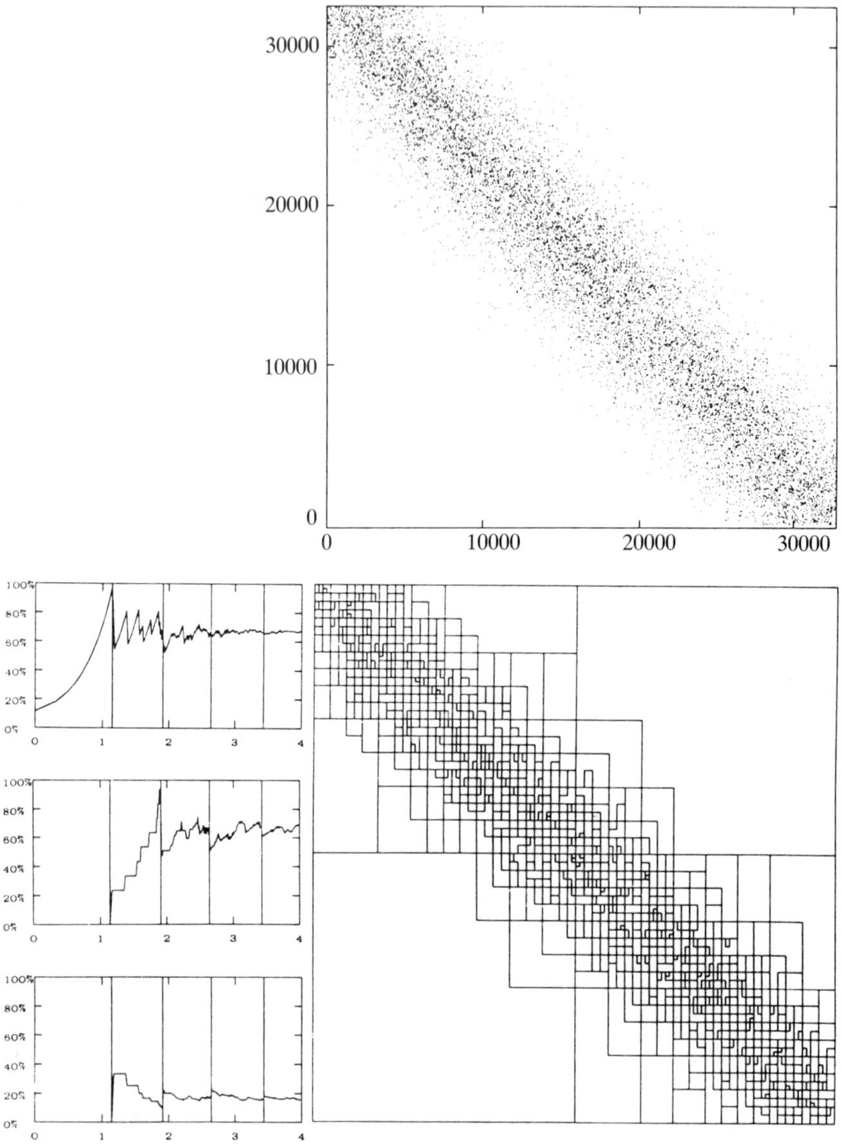

Fig. 14.

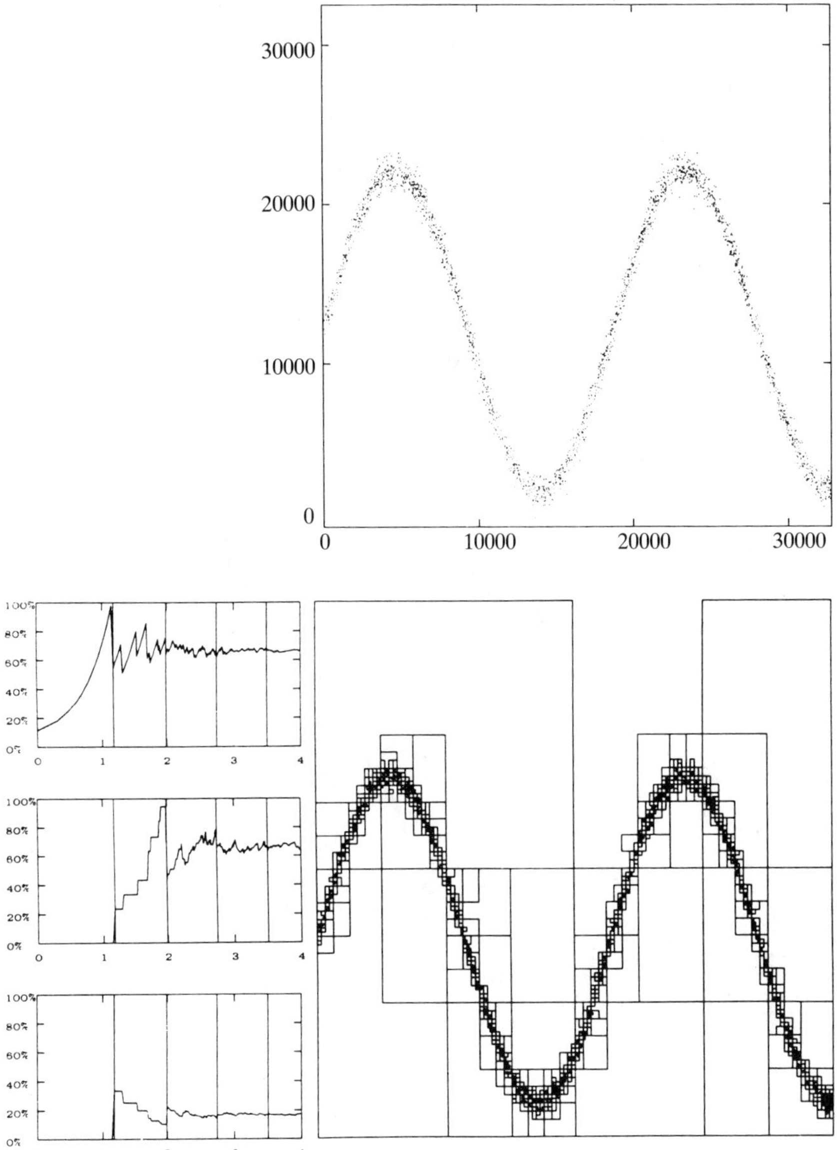

Fig. 15.

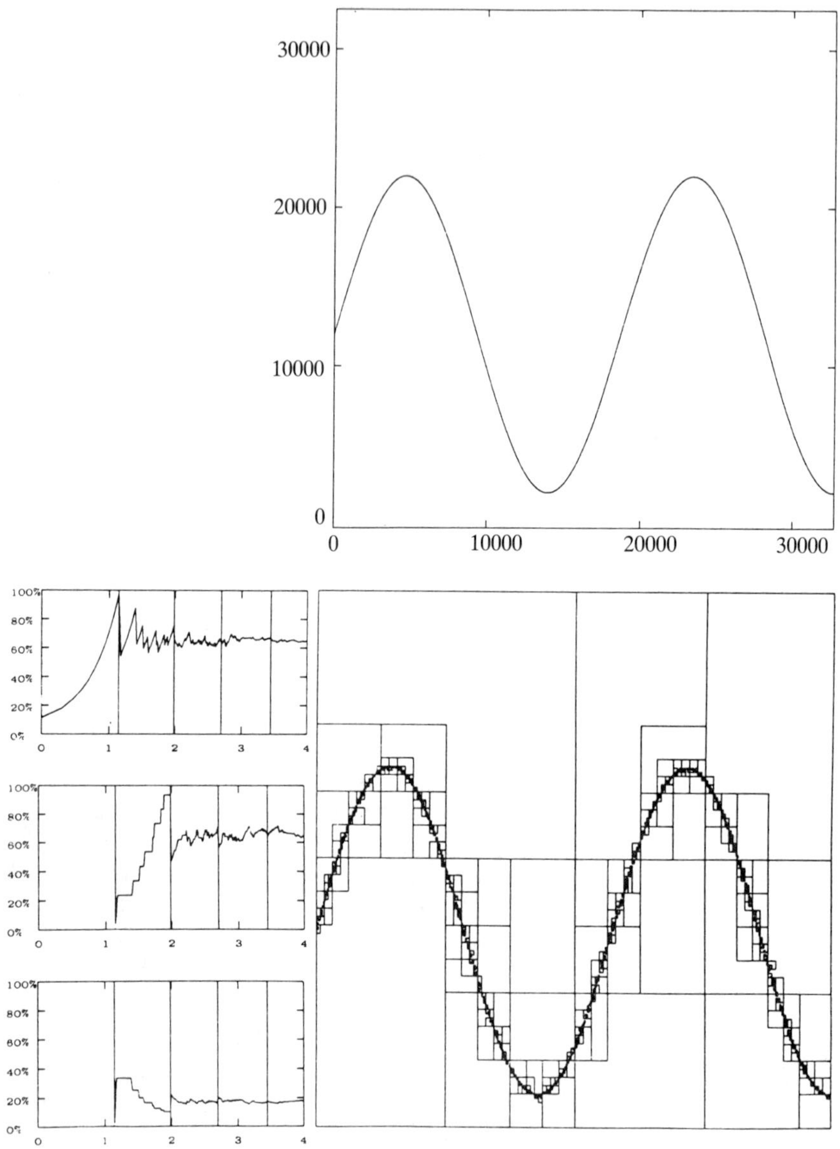

Fig. 16.

REFERENCES

[1] Bentley, J. L., Multidimensional Binary Search Trees in Database Applications, *IEEE Trans. on Soft. Eng.*, **SE-5**, No. 4, 333–340, July 1979.

[2] Bentley, J. L. and Friedman, J. H., Data Structures for Range Searching, *ACM Computing Surveys,* **11**, No. 4, December 1979.

[3] Robinson, J. T., The K-D-B-Tree: A Search Structure for Large Multidimensional Dynamic Indexes, *Proc. ACM–SIGMOD Conf.,* 1981.

[4] Gardarin, G., Valduriez, P., and Viemont, Y., Les Arbres de Predicats, INRIA, Rapports de Recherche, No. 230, April 1983.

[5] Ohsawa, Y. and Sakauchi, M., The BD-tree — A New *n*-Dimensional Data Structure with Highly Efficient Dynamic Characteristics, *Proc. IFIP 9th World Computer Cong*. Paris, September 1983.

[6] Orenstein, J. A., Spatial Query Processing in an Object-oriented Database System, *Proc. ACM–SIGMOD Conf.*, Washington DC, June 1986.

[7] Fagin, J., Nievergelt, J., Pippenger, N., and Strong, H. R., Extendible Hashing: A Fast Access Method for Dynamic Files, *ACM–TODS,* **4**, No. 3, September 1979.

[8] Ouksel, M. and Scheuermann, P., Storage Mapping for Multidimensional Linear Dynamic Hashing, *Proc. 2nd Symp. on Principles of Database Systems*, Atlanta, 1983.

[9] Otoo, E. J., A Multidimensional Digital Hashing Scheme for Files with Composite Keys, ACM, 1985.

[10] Nievergelt, J., Hintenberger, H., and Sevcik, K. C., The Grid File: An Adaptable, Symmetric Multikey File Structure, Internal Report No. 46, Institut fuer Informatik, ETH Zurich, December 1981.

[11] Burkhard, W. A., Interpolation-based Index Maintenance, *Proc. ACM–SIGMOD–SIGACT Symp.*, 1983.

[12] Hinrichs, K. H., The Grid File System: Implementation and Case Studies of Applications, Doctoral Thesis Nr. 7734, ETH Zurich, 1985.

[13] Ozkarahan, E. A. and Ouksel, M., Dynamic and Order Preserving Data Partitioning for Database Machines, *Proc. 11th Int. Conf. on Very Large Data Bases*, Stockholm, August, 1985.

[14] Freeston, M. W., Data Structures for Knowledge Bases: Multi-dimensional File Organisations, ECRC, Technical Report TR-KB-13, 1986.

[15] Freeston, M. W., The BANG file: A New Kind of Grid File, *Proc. ACM–SIGMOD Conf.*, San Francisco, 1987.

[16] Freeston, M. W., The BANG File, ECRC Technical Report TR-KB-13, 1987.

13

The NU-Prolog deductive database system

Kotagiri Ramamohanarao, John Shepherd, Isaac Balbin, Graeme Port, Lee Naish, James Thom, Justin Zobel, Philip Dart
Department of Computer Science, University of Melbourne, Parkville, Victoria 3052, Australia

ABSTRACT

We describe the current state of the design and implementetion of the NU-Prolog Deductive Database system. The ultimate aim of the NU-Prolog project is to produce a unified logic/database system, where programs may be expressed declaratively, in a form close to first-order logic, and at the same time efficiently access very large knowledge bases. The system addresses the problem of integrating a logic engine with a database system at a number of levels: query languages, indexing schemes to efficiently access large quantities of data, efficient join facilities, novel computational methods for answering queries, and transaction processing for concurrent updates.

1. INTRODUCTION

At an abstract level, mathematical logic provides a uniform framework for the expression and manipulation of information. One of its greatest strengths, from the point of view of computer science, is that the manipulation of information can be given a semantics which is declarative. That is, the semantics can be expressed without reference to a sequence of operations. Research in the field of logic programming is concerned with developing logic-based programming systems which manipulate data efficiently. Prolog is a logic programming language which has been successfully used as a general programming language.

Techniques have been developed for traditional database query systems to manipulate large amounts of information very efficiently. The way information is handled in these systems can be expressed within a subset of logic. These systems typically allow the information to be transformed using a fixed set of operations, but fall short of providing a general computational mechanism for transforming data; for example, it is not possible to express the transitive closure of a relational in a traditional database system. *Deductive databases* [19] extend the expressive power of database systems by adding recursion. At a semantic level they are equivalent to logic programs; operationally, however, a query can be processed using either a top-down or a bottom-up computation method. These two methods are the extremes of the range of computation methods that might be employed by a deductive database system.

This chapter reports the developments so far in integrating a database facility with the Nu-Prolog system [51]. The investigation has proceeded at several levels: from low-level database indexing schemes; through mixed computation methods for programs containing recursion and negation; to high-level query optimization by program transformation. At the user-interface level, NU-Prolog provides a query language based on the syntax of first-order logic. The ultimate aim of the NU-Prolog project is to develop a unified logic/database system which retains the logic programming style, and can efficiently access predicates consisting of very large numbers of facts. The system presents a uniform interface and provides efficient access to all predicates in the system, whether they are stored in main memory as part of the logic engine, or whether they reside on secondary storage in the database system.

Our philosophy is to exploit existing techniques wherever possible. At the lower levels of the system, techniques such as tuple indexing and join processing developed for relational databases have been adapted for use in the NU-Prolog system. At higher levels, there are a number of possible computational methods and it is still an active area of research to determine which method is the most effective in a given situation. In all of these methods we can make use of standard query optimization techniques such as unfolding, common subexpression elimination and reordering of goals.

In this chapter we review the methods used by the NU-Prolog deductive database system to solve several important problems. An overview of the user interface of the system (the NU-Prolog query language) is given in section 2. Section 3 describes our clause indexing scheme for providing efficient access to large databases. The interface between the database system and the logic engine is examined in section 4. Section 5 describes an efficient join operation which exploits our clause indexing scheme. Section 6 examines bottom-up computational methods which we have developed for recursive query processing on deductive databases. A technique for handling concurrent updates to deductive databases based on transaction processing is detailed in section 7.

We are presently extending the system in a number of directions: developing methods for evaluating queries to recursive database programs containing negation; designing a uniform intermediate language to compile the database into, which is more amenable to direct execution by the lower levels of the system; and investigating issues pertaining to the choice and definition of sideways information passing strategies.

1.1 Terminology

Deductive databases have their origins in two traditionally distinct fields of computer science: logic programming and databases. These fields have developed their own terminologies, but deal with similar concepts. This has led to a situation where there is a confusing mixture of notations in use, and so we devote the remainder of this section to defining the notation used in this chapter. (The reader who is interested in further tracing the development and terminology of the deductive database field will find a comprehensive set of references in [4].)

The basic components of logic programs, as defined in [27], are *variables*, *constants*, *function symbols*, and *predicate symbols*. We adopt the Prolog convention of denoting variables by strings of characters beginning with an upper case letter; constants, function symbols and predicate symbols (*relation names*) are denoted by strings of characters starting with a lower case letter.

A *term* is a variable, a constant, or a function symbol applied to other terms as in **f(t,t2,...,tn)**. An *atom* is of the form **p(t1,t2,...,tn)**, where **p** is a predicate symbol and **t1,t2,...,tn** are terms. A *literal* is either an atom, or an atom preceded by ~, the negation sign. A *rule* (*clause*) is a statement of one of the forms

p :- q1,q2,...,qn. or **p.**

p is atom and **q1,...,qn** are literals. **p** is called the *head*, the conjunction **q1,q2,...,qn** is called the *body*, and each **qi** is a *body literal.* A rule of the form **p.** is also known as a *unit clause.* Without loss of generality, a *query* **a**, where **a** is an atom, is a statement of the form **?-a.** A *goal* is a conjunction of literals, where each literal is called a *sub-goal.*

An atom, **p(t1,t2,...,tn)**, is *ground* when all of its terms, **t1,t2,...,tn**, are ground (that is, contain no variables); where **p is a predicate (relation) symbol, ⟨t1,t2,...,tn⟩** is known as a *tuple* of **p**. A *fact* is a ground unit clause. A *predicate* (also called a *relation*) is a set of clauses, all of which have the same predicate symbol and same number of arguments in the head. A *base predicate* is a predicate defined solely by facts. A *derived predicate* is a predicate which is not defined solely by facts. A *database* is an (unordered) set of rules. We use the terms database and program interchangeably.

2. THE NU-PROLOG QUERY LANGUAGE

A major aim in the design of the NU-Prolog language is to allow programs to be written more logically than is possible with other versions of Prolog; NU-Prolog is a step towards purely declarative logic programming. The body of a NU-Prolog rule and goal can take the form of an arbitrary first-order formula. In addition, NU-Prolog provides aggregate functions, and a declarative **if-then-else** construct. The NU-Prolog user interface make the NU-Prolog language available as a query language with facilities for the multikey sorting of answers, and the concise specification of insertions, deletions and updates.

Lloyd and Topor [26] have shown how a program containing arbitrary first-order formulae in the bodies of its rules can be transformed to a program with clause bodies consisting of a conjunction of literals. NU-Prolog provides both existential and universal quantification using the binary prefix operators **some** and **all** in the form **Quantifier Variables Formula,** to quantify the variables in the term **Variables** over the scope **Formula**. Conjunction, disjunction, implication are provided by the five infix operators ',', ';', =>, <=> and <= used in the form **Formula Operator Formula**. Negation is provided in the form **not Formula**. Five aggregate functions are currently provided: **solutions**, **count**, **max**, **min** and **sum**; other can be easily added.

NU-Prolog supports queries of the form **Head : Body** where **Head** is a term and **Body** is a NU-prolog formula. Different forms for the head of a query are recognized. If the head of a query is empty, the query is answered by printing either **Yes** or **No**. If the head of a query is of the form **Term sorted** or **Term sorted Keylist**, then answers to the query will be sorted or multikey sorted, with duplicates removed. Sort keys can be specified with one of the prefix operators + or − to indicate ascending or descending order. Answers to queries are printed in the form of **Term** (or **Head** if **sorted** is not specified) with the bindings generated by running the body of the query. For example, a query could be run as follows:

?- A/B sorted +A, −B : member(A/B, [2/3, 4/5, 2/6]).

2/6
2/3
4/5

Insertions can be performed with a statement of the form **insert Termlist where Body**. For each of the bindings generated by running the body of the insertion, each of the terms in **Termlist** will be asserted. For example, the following insertion will create a unary relation of the suppliers who supply only red parts.

?- insert redSupplier(S) where supplier(S),
all P supplies (S,P) => part(P,red).

Deletions can be performed with a statement of the form **delete Termlist where Body**. For each of the bindings generated by running the body of the deletion, in conjunction with the terms of **Termlist**, each of the terms in **Termlist** will be removed from the database. For example, the following deletion will delete the suppliers who don't supply any red parts.

?- delete supplier(S) where not (some P (supplies(S,P), part(P,red))).

Updates can be performed with a statement of the form **update Updatelist in Atomlist where Body**, where **Updatelist** consists of terms of the form **Var to Atom**. For each of the bindings generated by running the body of the update, in conjunction with the terms of **Atomlist**, each of the terms in **Atomlist** will be retracted, and asserted with **Var** replaced by **Atom**. For example, the following update will change the colour of any yellow part to red.

?- update C to yellow in part(P,C) where C = red.

The **where Body** component of an insertion, deletion or update may be omitted; this is equivalent to using **where true.**

These facilities, in combination with the history mechanism and command editing facilities of the NU-Prolog user interface, combine to provide a powerful, yet concise database query interface.

3. INDEXING SCHEMES FOR EFFICIENT RECORD ACCESS

As logic programming is applied to more and more diverse areas, there will be an increasing need for logic programming systems to manipulate and reason about very large knowledge bases. Databases used in 'real-world' applications may contain base predicates consisting of millions of facts (for example, a census which records information about each individual in a country). Similarly, it is not difficult to imagine a large expert system which reasons in a complex problem domain (such as medicine) requiring tens of thousands of rules in a single derived predicate to capture some of the relationships associated with the domain. When dealing with such large amounts of data, indexing schemes are essential to efficiently locate the subset of rules/facts in a predicate which are 'relevant' to answering a query on that predicate.

A query which has values specified for a subset of its arguments is known as a *partial-match query*. The execution of a partial-match query on a predicate selects the subset of tuples in the predicate that have the specified values for the ground arguments.

For example, the query **employee(_,secretary,_,_)** would match facts such as

employee(john,secretary,admin,22000)
employee(jane,secretary,research,24000)
employee(judy,secretary,sales,25000)

or any fact in the **employee** predicate with **secretary** as the second argument.

One well-known class of indexing schemes for answering partial-match queries employs superimposed codewords [46,50]. The NU-Prolog deductive database system uses a generalization of these schemes [44] which allows indexing on general Prolog terms containing variables and function symbols, as well as ground facts.

3.1 Superimposed codeword indexing schemes

In a superimposed codeword (*simc*) indexing scheme, each fact in the database has an associated *descriptor* — a bit-string formed by superimposing (bitwise OR-ing) the *codewords* for the individual arguments of the fact. A codeword is a bit-string which represents the hash value of a ground argument. One possible method of codeword generation is to use the ground argument as a seed for a random number generator which indicates the bit positions to be set to one.

In order to determine which facts satisfy a partial-match query, the descriptor for the query (formed by OR-ing the codewords for the non-variable arguments) is AND-ed with the descriptor for each fact in the database. For any matching fact, the bits in the fact descriptor are a superset of the bits in the query descriptor. The AND operation results in a bit-string which is identical to the query descriptor for these facts.

Unfortunately, because of the way descriptors are constructed, it is also possible for facts which do *not* match the query to have descriptors whose bits are a superset of the query descriptor bits. This leads to facts which match the query at the descriptor level but which do not actually match the query; these are termed *false matches.* A search of the fact descriptors, as described above, will indicate a number of these non-matching facts as potential matches in addition to all of the correctly matching facts. By choosing a large codeword size one can make the probability of false matches occurring very close to zero.

3.1.1 An example

Consider a database of employee records, where each fact has four attributes:

employee(Name,Position,Dept,Salary)

We generate a 15-bit codeword for each attribute by setting two bits, determined by hashing the key value into a seed number and generating two random numbers in the range 0 to 14 from this seed. Using this scheme we generate codewords for some sample key values as shown in Fig. 1.

Key value:	Codeword:	Key value:	Codeword:
john	00010 00000 10000	**admin**	00010 00100 00000
jack	00100 00001 00000	**research**	00000 00010 00001
jane	10000 00000 00001	**sales**	00100 00000 10000
clerk	01001 00000 00000	**20000**	00000 00000 00110
secretary	00000 00110 00000	**22000**	00000 00010 00001
manager	00000 01000 01000	**24000**	01000 00000 01000

Fig. 1 — Example codewords.

To generate a descriptor for a fact such as **employee(john,clerk, admin,22000)**, we OR together the codewords for the attributes:

john	00010	00000	10000
clerk	01001	00000	00000
admin	00010	00100	00000
22000	00000	00010	00001
OR	——	——	——
Descriptor	01011	00110	10001

A query such as **employee(_,clerk,admin,_)** would have the following descriptor, generated by OR-ing the two specified attributes:

clerk	01001	00000	00000
admin	00010	00100	00000
OR	——	——	——
Descriptor	01011	00100	00000

The complete database comprises the facts and their associated descriptors shown in Fig. 2.

Rec#	Record	Descriptor:
0	employee(john,clerk,admin,22000)	01011 00110 10001
1	employee(jane,secretary,admin,24000)	11010 00110 01001
2	employee(jack,clerk,research,20000)	01101 00011 00111
3	employee(john,manager,admin,24000)	01010 01100 11000
4	employee(jack,secretary,sales,20000)	00100 00111 10110

Fig. 2 — Sample database.

Consider the following query and its associated query descriptor:

employee(_,_,admin,24000) 01010 00100 01000

In order to answer this query on the example database we AND the query descriptor with each fact descriptor in turn to determine whether the corresponding fact is a 'match'. This indicates facts #1 and #3 as potential matches.

Note that for the purpose of our example, we have chosen a small codeword size (15 bits), and have set only a small number of bits in the codeword for each attribute. These are two of the paramaters available to the database designer; choosing optimal values for these parameters is an important problem. If the codeword is too small, then we cannot represent relations with many attributes without incurring an increase in the false match probability. Similarly, if we set more than a small fraction of the bits in the codeword, then the superimposing leads to a potential increase in false matches. However, if we set insufficient bits in the codeword, we cannot 'discriminate' as well between different attributable values. Methods for deriving optimal parameters are discussed in [44].

3.2 Performance optimizations

Superimposed codeword indexing schemes efficiently determine which facts have a high probability of matching the query. However, the performance of *simc* database systems can be considerably enhanced by using traditional database system optimization techniques. The NU-Prolog deductive database system uses knowledge of the distribution of query types, clustering of data, efficient data structures in the codeword file, and effective buffering schemes to improve its retrieval performance.

In answering a query in a *simc* indexing scheme, the query descriptor must be compared (AND-ed) with every fact descriptor, and so the whole descriptor file must be read from secondary storage. However, in general, only a small fraction of bits are set in the query descriptor and so only a few bits of each fact descriptor need to be examined. Therefore, following [46,50], we arrange the fact descriptors in bit-sliced fashion. Instead of viewing the descriptor file as **N** bit-strings, each containing **b** bits, we view it as **b** bit-strings (*slices*) each containing **N bits. The ith** slice is a list of the **ith** bits of all descriptors (the length of a *slice* is equal to the number of facts in the database). When the **kth** bit in the **ith** slice is set, this indicates that the **kth** fact has the **ith** bit set in its descriptor. The result of AND-ing the slices specified by the query decriptor is a slice which represents a list of all potentially matching facts; that is, the **jth** fact is a potential match if the **jth** bit in the resultant slice is set.

The amount of descriptor data which must be read can be even further reduced by using a two-level descriptor scheme [50]. In such a scheme, the database is divided into segments (pages), corresponding to pages on the physical device. Each fact is allocated to a segment at insertion time and a descriptor is maintained for each segment, derived from the decriptors of the facts in the segment. Answering a query in a two-level scheme is a two-stage process: we first examine the segment descriptors to determine *matching segments* (those which might contain matching facts), and then examine the fact descriptors only in the matching segments.

Even though *simc* indexing schemes can efficiently determine the potential matches in a database, retrieval performance can still be poor if the matching records are scattered over a number of segments. Clearly, it is desirable to allocate facts to segments in such as way that, on average, matching records come from only a few segments, thus minimizing the number of disk accesses. This is achieved in the NU-Prolog deductive database system by employing a *clustering* scheme based on the distribution of query types [40–43].

A *query type* **Q** is a subset of the attributes of a relation which indicates which attributes are specified in a query of that type. Let p_Q be the probability of specifying a query of type **Q**. Facts are allocated to pages (segments) within the database file by means of a hashing scheme (*multi-key hashing*) which allocates zero or more bits to each attribute of the tuple. Consider a file consisting of 2^d pages, where $d \geq 0$. The pages are numbered from **0** to 2^{d-1}. Each attribute A_i (from **k** attributes) has a hashing function h_i which maps from the key space of A_i to a bit string. From this string, $\mathbf{d_i}$ bits are selected, such that $\mathbf{d_1}+\cdots+\mathbf{d_k}=\mathbf{d}$. We wish to give more weight (larger $\mathbf{d_i}$) to attributes which are more often specified. The more bits we allocate for a particular attribute, that is, the larger its $\mathbf{d_i}$ value, the less bits are available in the rest of the address which are determined by the other attributes and hence fewer segment addresses are available for records having the same value for this attribute. By choosing appropriate $\mathbf{d_i}$ values we can ensure that, for the most common query types, we retrieve as few segments as possible. The problem of minimizing the average query cost (finding the best clustering) is then reduced to a matter of choosing optimal values for the $\mathbf{d_i}$ under the given query type distribution. The $\mathbf{d_i}$ values can be calculated using the schemes described in [2,41].

Further performance improvements can be obtained from sensible memory-management schemes. Segment buffers are large (generally the size of one disk page), and reading them more often than necessary leads to significant amounts of input/output. In our implementation, we retain segment buffers in memory until we reach some limit on memory and then reclaim buffers via a least recently used strategy. However, one needs to be cautious in choosing the total buffer storage space, or, in a virtual memory system, one might end up trading database disk accesses for page faults.

3.3 Extending *simc* indexing for Prolog

Standard *simc* indexing schemes assume that all the unit clauses in the external database are facts, that is, contain no variables. In addition, they treat arguments, such as **g(1)**, as strings of characters without considering their internal structure. Since we want to allow indexing on arbitrary unit clauses in the external database, our indexing scheme must be able to support variables and function terms.

3.3.1 Representing variables

In order to represent variables in unit clauses (ignoring terms with function symbols for the moment), we append *mask bits* to the end of each descriptor to denote which arguments are ground. Each bit in this *mask* is associated with a particular argument in the unit clause. A mask bit is set to zero when the corresponding argument is ground. When the mask bit is set to one, the corresponding argument is a variable (and consequently contributes no bits to the descriptor), and any non-matches on this argument are ignored. The matching process now becomes somewhat more complicated: for each argument, if the associated mask bit in either the query descriptor or the fact descriptor is set to one, we treat that argument as a match, regardless of codewords. If both mask bits are zero, we compare the codewords of the argument in the query and the fact to determine whether there is a match on that argument. If all arguments successfully match, then we have found a potentially matching fact.

The process of determining matches now becomes slightly more complicated. The query now constitutes a set of query codewords, one for each of the specified attributes. A potential match occurs with a fact when each of these codewords satisfies a matching property with respect to the fact descriptor. A query codeword has this matching property when either its bit-string is a subset of the fact descriptor bit-string or the corresponding mask bit is set in the fact descriptor. We AND the bit-slices related to a particular attribute value and, as well, we OR the bit-slice for the mask corresponding to that attribute. This process is repeated for each attribute value and the results are AND-ed together to give us the potential facts which match the query.

3.3.2 Representing terms

In representing the structure of a function term, we consider the term first as a single argument to determine the total number of bits which it provides in the descriptor. A user-defined weighting scheme is then used to determine how many bits are derived from each component of the term. Codewords are generated for each component of the term according to this scheme, and the codeword for the entire term is then formed by superimposing the codewords for the components.

To handle variables within a term, we require the database designer to specify the maximum *indexing complexity* of the term (that is, the maximum number of components in the term which will be used for indexing purposes) and allocate one mask bit for each component. If a term is less complex than the specification indicates, we simply ignore the mask bits which were allocated for the 'unused' components. If the term is more complex than the specification, we prune it; that is, we ignore any components 'outside' the specification. Note that the entire term is always stored in the external database; parts of the term are 'ignored' only for indexing purposes.

For example, a maximum structure specification such as **X(Y(Z))** implies that terms such as **f(g(c))**, **f(h(a))** and **f(b)** can be fully indexed. A term such as **f(g(h(d)))** is pruned to **f(g(h))** in the indexing representation, while **f(a,b)** is truncated to **f(a)**. Owing to this pruning, neither **d** nor **b** contributes codewords to the descriptor generation. Note that while terms such as **f(a,b)** and **f(a)** might appear to be identical after the truncation of **b**, the indexing scheme uses the arity as well as the functor in generating the codeword and therefore generates distinct codewords.

3.3.3 Example

We wish to obtain descriptors for the following facts:

p(f(a,X),d)   **p(X,d)**   **p(f(a,b),X)**   **p(g(c,b),X)**

Let us assume that the codewords for the individual attributes are as shown in Fig. 3. The complete database with descriptors (including mask bits) and bit-slices is shown in Fig. 4. The asterisks indicate that the values of the corresponding mask bits are ignored in the matching process. This is because we never allow the functor component of a structure to be unspecified.

For a query **p(f(a,X),Y)** we have the query codewords

Key value:	Codeword:	Key value:	Codeword:
f	00010 00000 10000	**a**	01001 00000 00000
b	00000 01010 00000	**c**	10000 00000 00010
d	00010 00100 00000	**g**	00000 00001 00001

Fig. 3 — Further example codewords.

Rec#	Record:	Descriptor:
0	**p(f(a,X),d)**	01011 00100 10000 0010
1	**p(X,d)**	00010 00100 00000 1**0
2	**p(f(a,b),X)**	01011 01010 10000 0001
3	**p(g(c,b),X)**	10000 01011 00011 0001

Rec#	Descriptor:																		
0	0	1	0	1	1	0	0	1	0	0	1	0	0	0	0	0	0	1	0
1	0	0	0	1	0	0	0	1	0	0	0	0	0	0	0	1	*	*	0
2	0	1	0	1	1	0	1	0	1	0	1	0	0	0	0	0	0	0	1
3	1	0	0	0	0	0	1	0	1	1	0	0	0	1	1	0	0	0	1
Slice#	0	1	2	3	4	5	6	7	8	9	10	11	12	13	14	m0	m1	m2	m3

Fig. 4 — Sample bit-sliced database.

f 00010 00000 10000
a 01001 00000 00000

To determine the potential matching facts for this example, slices #3 and #10 are AND-ed for the attribute value **f** and then OR-ed with its mask (slice #m0), yielding a result which we will denote $\mathbf{R_1}$. Similarly, slices #1 and #4 are AND-ed for the attribute value **a** and then OR-ed with its mask slice (slice #m1), resulting in $\mathbf{R_2}$. $\mathbf{R_1}$ and $\mathbf{R_2}$ are then AND-ed to give the set of all potential record matches, **R**.

R = **(((1** AND **4)** OR **m1)** AND **(3** AND **10))** OR **m0**

Fig. 5 shows the complete process.

3.3.4 Representing Prolog rules

To store rules in the external database, a rule such as **p(X,Y):-q(X,Z),r(Z,Y)** may be represented as a unit clause **:-(p(X,Y),(q(X,Z),r(Z,Y)))**. The indexing scheme would use only the first argument, since we only match with the head of the rule. However, this representation stores all rules in one predicate (the :- predicate) and NU-Prolog programs typically contain large numbers of rules with considerable variation in the arity and complexity of arguments in the head. It is thus necessary either to define a very general structure for the head, most of which will usually be wasted, or to lose indexing information due to pruning when searching on rules with large heads. For better performance, all rules defining a derived predicate could be stored in a format such as **p(X,Y,(q(X,Z),r(Z,Y)))**, which would be transformed into the standard rule-form after retrieval from the database.

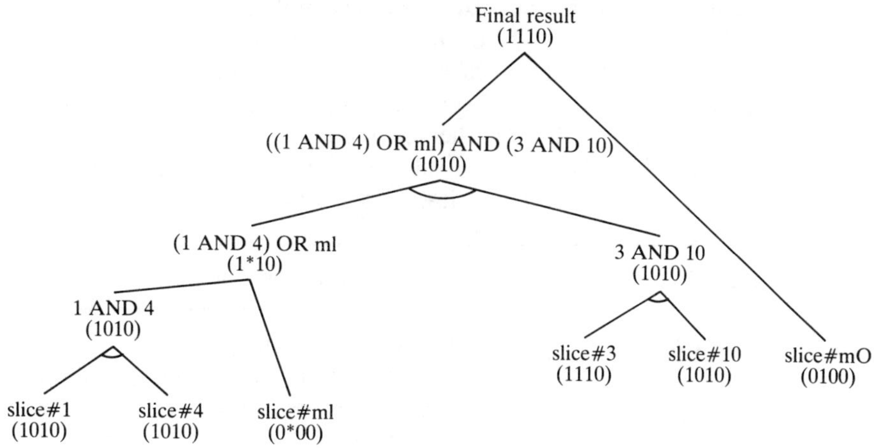

Fig. 5 — Matching computation with masks.

3.4 *simc* indexing schemes for dynamic files

In some applications, the number of facts in a relation may grow or shrink by orders of magnitude over the lifetime of the relation. We call such relations *dynamic*, to contrast them with *static* relations where the number of facts changes very little. The NU-Prolog deductive database system has two *simc* indexing schemes available, one to deal with (relatively) static relations, and one for dynamic relations of ground facts. Because the *simc* indexing schemes for static relations described above uses a bit-sliced organization for storing decriptors, the user must specify an upper bound on the number of facts which are stored in a relation.† Several techniques have been proposed for indexing dynamic databases [25,42]. All are based on clustering and, in particular, on multi-key hashing where each argument contributes a portion of the index (segment address) bits. The index bits are interlaced to form the final index, but, unlike clustering in the static case, the number of bits allocated to each argument can grow and shrink as the number of facts in the database changes. In our dynamic *simc* indexing scheme (*dsimc*), the superimposed codeword descriptor serves the dual roles of a hash value and a segment address. Because of this, it is not possible to use mask bits to describe variables and only facts may be stored by dynamic *simc* databases.

3.5 Performance of an example database

To evaluate the performance of these schemes, we built a database containing 500 000 records which described paths between machines in the UUCP network:

† In fact, the database *can* be expanded, but only at the cost of massive reorganization of the index and data files.

path(Source,Destination,Cost,[Node,Node,...,])

We used a 'false match' rate of 1 in one million at segment level and of 1 in 2000 at record level. The **Source** field contributed most of the indexing bits. The **Node**-list attribute was not used at all for indexing, since we assumed that it would always be unspecified (the primary use for the database being to *discover* paths through the network).

Using the *dsimc* indexing scheme employed by the NU-Prolog deductive system, we obtained the following performance figures:†

Insertion rate:	17 records per CPU second
Retrieval rate:	(query dependent) 260 records per CPU second (maximum) 220 records per CPU second (average)

In the above table, the retrieval rates were measured over 100 queries of the form **path(source,_,_,_)**, each of which has approximately 1500 answers.

For 100 random queries of the form **path(source,dest,_,_)**, each of which was known to have a unique answer, we obtained the following matching rates:

Average segment matches:	2.0
Average record matches:	1.1

4. NU-PROLOG/DATABASE INTERFACE

As far as the Prolog Programmer, is concerned, external database predicates should appear as much as possible like predicates in the internal database. This has been achieved to a large extent in the NU-Prolog deductive database system, but at some level the system needs to be told which predicates are to be implemented as external predicates and the parameters which should be used for their implementation. This section briefly decribes the interface to the database system which is presented to the Prolog programmer and examines the implementation of the connection between the logic engine and database system.

4.1 External database predicates

There are three main predicates for manipulating external databases: **dbCreate**, **dbDefine** and **dbCons**. The predicate **dbCreate** creates a

† The figures are taken from an implementation in C on a Sun 3/140 with 12 Mb of memory and a 141 Mb SCSI-interface Micropolis disk drive.

database, which is simply a directory in the UNIX file system containing a number of auxiliary files used by the NU-Prolog system and one subdirectory for each predicate. The predicate **dbCons** is used to gain access to the predicates in an external database. The call **dbCons(db)** consults an external database called **db** making all predicates in the database available to the Prolog process. The external database predicates may then be used in precisely the same way as internal database predicates. The only difference, as far as the Prolog programmer is concerned, is that the changes made to external database predicates are permanent.

The **dbDefine** predicate creates new external database predicates, and allows the user to specify some of the properties of the predicate so that the indexing scheme can be configured to give the most efficient access. **dbDefine** takes four arguments as follows:

dbDefine(Db, Functor, Arity, [Param$_1$=value$_1$, . . .])

where **Db** is the name of the database, **Functor** is the predicate symbol, and **Arity** indicates how many arguments the predicate has. The fourth argument allows the programmer to configure the indexing scheme by modifying various parameters such as

avrec	average length of records (in bytes)
nrec	maximum number of records
segsize	size of segments (in bytes)
template	description of weights and choice vectors for all attributes in the relation

4.1.1 Example

Consider a database describing a network of computers such as the UUCP network. A model of this network will describe entities such as nodes and connections. Let is say that we use two relations, **node** and **conn**, to model the network.

The **node** relation contains the (unique) network name of computer, and a brief description of the location of the machine. This can be implemented as a Prolog predicate **node/2**, containing facts such as

```
node(mulga, "Computer Science, Melbourne University, Australia")
node(munnari, "Computer Science, Melbourne University, Australia").
node(seismo, "Centre for Seismic Studies, Virginia, USA").
```

The **conn** relation decribes network connections by giving the names of the **node**s at either end, and a cost. This can be implemented as a Prolog predicate **conn/3**, containing facts such as

```
conn(munnari, seismo, 150).
conn(munnari, mulga, 10).
```

Before we can assign parameters to a relation, we must determine various properties of the relation. It is useful to know the average size of a record, that is, how many characters will be required to store the textual representations of the values of the fields. If records are very large, then we might wish to increase the segment size to allow a reasonable number of records per segment (at least 50). It is also useful to know approximately how many facts there are likely to be in the relation. We need to know the types of queries which are going to be asked on the relation. In the example, it is highly likely that we will be asking for a list of all sites which are connected to a given site and so we will often have the first field specified in a query on the **conn** relation. It is far less likely that we will ask for all sites which have a given cost, and so we would expect the cost field of the **conn** relation to be infrequently specified in queries.

Let us suppose that the average site name is 7 characters long, and the average site description is 40 characters long. Then the average **node** record will require 50 characters to store (7 for the site name, 40 for the description, plus a comma to separate the fields and two quotes around the description). If the average cost is a four-digit number, then **conn** records will require 20 characters (14 for two site names, 4 for the cost value, and 2 commas to separate the fields). Assuming that there are around 10 000 sites (therefore 10 000 **node** records), and that each site is connected to 10 others, then there will be around 100 000 **conn** records.

The following calls to **dbDefine** will create the **node** and **conn** predicates with optimal parameters derived from the above considerations:

```
dbDefine(net_db, node, 2,
  [scheme=simc,
   avrec=50,
   nrec=10000,
   template="g:0:0(g:1:7fffffff,g:0:0)"])
dbDefine(net_db, conn, 3,
  [scheme=simc,
   avrec=20,
   nrec=100000,
   template="g:0:0(g:8:29228922,g:4:12892289,g:1:44545454)"]).
```

The template parameters require a little explanation; syntactically, they have the same structure as a fact in the corresponding relation except that the predicate functor and the arguments are replaced by three-tuples which give weight and clustering information for each argument. The first element of the tuple indicates whether variables are used for the argument; the second indicates (relatively) how likely the argument is to be used in a query; and the third gives the cluster mask, which indicates how many bits the argument will contribute to the multi-key hash.

In the **node** example, the template is set up to indicate that we will never use the second field for indexing; note that in this case all of the clustering is also performed on the first field. We have designed the template for the **conn** relation on the basis that we are very likely to ask queries using the first field (weight:8), occasionally using the second field (weight:4), and very rarely using the cost field (weight:1). The **g** values in the template fields indicate that the corresponding fields are always ground.

4.2 Logic engine/database interface

The top-down computation method is well suited to answering queries on predicates of the internal database (which is usually implemented as part of the logic engine). The mechanisms required in the engine to do this are: create a stack frame when a query is first issued, advance a marker when backtracking and delete the stack frame when all answers have been obtined. Answering queries to the external database using the method can be achieved by having the backtracking information on the call stack refer to files on secondary storage in the same way that it normally refers to internal lists of rules.

An important aspect of the interface is the mechanism by which tuples are transferred from secondary storage into the working memory of the NU-Prolog engine. In our implementation, facts are retrieved from the database in textual form and 'read' into working memory by the NU-Prolog reader. In addition, queries are sent to the database system using the NU-Prolog printing predicates. In the initial implementation of the NU-Prolog deductive database system, it was discovered that, in answering a query which returned a large number of answers, up to 80% of the computation time was spent inside the NU-Prolog reader, parsing the facts retrieved by the database system. The interface now employs its own parser to reduce this bottleneck by an order of magnitude.

In the future, we plan to investigate implementations where the database system uses the same internal representation of terms as the NU-Prolog engine. One way of achieving this is to map the database directly into the working memory of the Prolog system. Uniform virtual memory [18] ensures that the database part of memory is shareable so that multiple processes can access and update the database concurrently. However, for large databases there are problems with loading and resolving references to the very large numbers of symbols used in large base predicates. This can be handled by using dynamic linking methods involving indirect/multiple symbol tables.

An advantage of textually based interfaces is that they permit relatively simple integration of the logic engine with *existing* database systems. All that is required are routines to map between the printable representation of records as tuples and their representation as Prolog terms. We have followed this approach in connecting NU-Prolog to Unify's† SQL interface [61] so that the system can access existing Unify databases.

5. THE SUPERJOIN ALGORITHM

A conjunction of Prolog goals which depends on only base predicates can be naturally viewed as a join operation. For example, the query **?-p(X,Y),**

† Unify is a trademark of the UNIFY Corporation.

q(Y,Z), joins **p** with **q**, on the second attribute of **p** and the first attribute of **q** (the *join variable* **Y**). Although partial-match indexing significantly improves the efficiency of the join operation, it is still inefficient in the sense that data pages may be retrieved several times. In this section, we describe the join algorithm incorporated into the NU-Prolog deductive database system, the *superjoin* algorithm [52], which attacks the problem of repeated page retrieval for top-down computations.

When answering the query **?-p(X,Y),q(Y,Z)**, the naive top-down approach finds a solution for **p(X,Y)** and then, using the binding generated for **Y**, finds solutions for **q(Y,Z)**. This process, which is repeated for all solutions of **p(X,Y)**, requires multiple re-scannings of the **q** relation and the possible re-reading of the data pages where the **q** facts are stored.

The *superjoin* algorithm organizes access to the facts so as to minimize repeated retrieval of data pages. Unlike other join algorithms, this algorithm does not require a separate partitioning phase. Instead, it makes use of the clustering properties of the multi-key hashing used in the *dsimc* indexing scheme. Conceptually, each sub-goal **q** in the conjunction is evaluated as a number of sub-queries, where each sub-query **q($\bar{t}$)** accesses a disjoint region of the external database containing the **q** facts. There is one such region for each hash value of the join variable, where we consider only that part of the hash value which is used in the index of both relations. Since these regions are much smaller than the total database, they can usually be buffered entirely in memory, so that no data page is read more than once during the processing of the join.

The *superjoin* algorithm is suitable for large relational databases accessed from computers with large main memories. The algorithm maintains excellent performance from very small relations to very large relations. In addition, it supports queries containing arbitrary constraints, disjunctions, negations, and existing quantifiers, which makes it useful as an intermediate-level optimization technique for deductive database systems. A complete deductive database system would include a higher level which would handle rules and recursion transforming each query into possibly several sub-queries to be processed efficiently by the *superjoin*, which in turn would access a low-level interface to the external database.

The *superjoin* algorithm fits naturally into Prolog's top-down computation rule, but it can also be used effectively with other computational methods such as bottom-up query evaluation. In the context of a top-down computation, one disadvantage of *superjoin* is that it may require large amounts of buffer space when processing recursive rules. An implementation of the *superjoin* algorithm has been incorporated into the external database facilities of NU-Prolog [51]. Initial experiments with the current implementation have shown significant improvement (more than 50% in some cases) over the naive Prolog partial-match join.

5.1 Example for join operations

We assume that facts are allocated to pages by means of a multi-key hashing scheme (see section 3.2). The requires the use of a *choice vector*, which defines a mapping between the strings of $\mathbf{d_i}$ bits and the page number. The choice vector was introduced for handling dynamic files in [25,41]. A choice vector specifies a permutation of the $\mathbf{K d_i}$ bits selected from the hash values of the attributes.

Suppose the hash functions $\mathbf{h_i}$ map "**y0**" to the string of bits "**...000**" and "**y1**" to "**...001**" and "**y2**" to "**...010**" and similarly for "**z0**", "**z1**", "**z2**". etc. For each attribute, we choose the last $\mathbf{d_i}$ bits to construct the choice vector.

Consider a predicate **q(Y,Z)**, the hash functions $\mathbf{h_i}$ and $\mathbf{h_2}$ would map the value **Y** to a string "$\mathbf{...Y_3Y_2Y_1}$" and the value **Z** to a string "$\mathbf{...Z_3Z_2Z_1}$" respectively, where $\mathbf{Y_i}$ and $\mathbf{Z_i}$ can take values **0** or **1**. We loosely refer to these strings of subscripted variables as bit strings. If **q(Y,Z)** is stored in $\mathbf{2^3}$ pages, then we might set $\mathbf{d_i = 2}$ and $\mathbf{d_2 = 1}$. Thus the bits $\mathbf{Y_2}$, $\mathbf{Y_1}$, and $\mathbf{Z_1}$ would be selected from the bit strings generated by the hash functions.

The choice vector could be any one permutation of these bit-strings, such as $\mathbf{Y_1Z_1Y_2}$. Thus tuples would be stored in the file as shown in the **q** predicate in Fig. 6.

p

page	tuples
X_1Y_1	p(X,Y)
0 0	p("x0", "y0") p("x2", "y2")
0 1	p("x0", "y1") p("x2", "y1")
1 0	p("x1", "y0")
1 1	p("x1", "y1")

q

page	tuples
$Y_1Z_1Y_2$	q(Y,Z)
0 0 0	q("y4", "z0") q("y4", "z2")
0 0 1	q("y2", "z2")
0 1 0	q("y4", "z1")
0 1 1	q("y2", "z1")
1 0 0	q("y1", "z2")
1 0 1	q("y3", "z2")
1 1 0	q("y1", "z1")
1 1 1	q("y3", "z1") q("y7", "z1")

Fig. 6 — **p** and **q** predicates.

For a query containing variables, only some of the bits will be specified. Thus several pages will need to be searched. Answering the query **?-q("y3",Z)** requires the following steps:

(1) Hash "**y3**" to the bit string "**...011**" from which we select just the last two bits since $\mathbf{d_1 = 2}$, namely $\mathbf{Y_2Y1 = 11}$.
(2) Since the second attribute is a variable, the bit $\mathbf{Z_1 = *}$, where * represents an unknown bit.

(3) Search the pages where $Y_1Z_1Y_2 = 1*1$ (namely pages **101** and **111**) for tuples which match the query; this would retrieve the tuples

q("y3","z2")
q("y3","z1")

5.2 Partial match joins

It is possible to apply these partial match schemes directly, for instance, in a Prolog system which finds answers a tuple at a time [33,44]. In answering the query

?-p(X,Y),q(Y,Z) (Q1)

a straighforward implementation in Prolog would begin by reaching the first page of **p** (page **00**). Prolog would get the first solution from this page, namely the tuple

p("x0","y0")

and try to find tuples from the second predicate which match. Since **"y0"** hashes to **"...00"**, only pages **000** and **010** from **q** would need to be read. However, as there are no matching tuples, Prolog would proceed with the second solution from the page of **p** in a similar fashion. Thus, the second solution

p("x2","y2")

would join with the tuples

q("y2","z2")
q("y2","z1")

This would require reading pages **001** and **011** from **q** since **"y2"** hashes to **"...10"**. After exhausting all the tuples in the first page of **p**, Prolog would proceed in a similar fashion with subsequent pages of **p**.

This scheme for implementing joins fits in naturally with other relational operators such as selection. For example, the query **?-p("x0",Y),q(Y,Z)** performs a selection on **p** while performing the join, reducing the number of pages which need to be considered.

Using partial-match retrieval to implement joins creates a workable system. However, there is one important inefficiency; for most queries this approach requires that many pages need to be read more than once. In query (Q1), for example, each tuple in **p** causes a separate partial-match query on **q** which results in two pages being read. All four pages of **p** are read and, since there are six tuples in **p** twelve page reads from **q** will occur (including some repeat reads) in the following sequence: **000, 010, 001, 011, 100, 110, 100, 110, 000, 010, 100, 110**.

5.3 The superjoin algorithm

Multiple reading from pages of disk in the naive tuple at a time algorithm can be eliminated by keeping pages in main memory buffers. In query (Q1) above, if we allocate twelve buffers (four for the **p** predicate and eight for the **q** predicate) then no page needs to be read from disk more than once. If buffers are allocated on demand then only ten are needed because no **Y** values in **p** hash to "**...11**", so two pages of **q** are never read (**101** and **111**). This simple method, of buffering all pages which are read, is not feasible with large predicates. Available main memory is limited and, in large database systems, is usually much less than the total size of the predicates. Hence it is desirable to substantially reduce the number of buffers required in main memory.

If we use multi-key hashing and the join attributes have the same hash function, then it is possible to partition the join into several *sub-joins*. Each sub-join accesses only some of the tuples required for the full join. The result of the full join is simply the union of the results of all the sub-joins. The *superjoin* algorithm partitions a join and orders the execution of the sub-joins so as to minimize the number of buffers required, while still only reading the pages of each predicate from disk at most once. [30] also considers partitioning joins, partitioning the predicates such that a join on the predicates can be broken into sub-joins of disjoint sets of tuples. We consider a finer partitioning which does not have disjoint sets of tuples in each partition but which allows us to further reduce the number of buffers required.

5.4 Partitioning into sub-joins

A simple partitioning of query (Q1) results in four sub-joins, each being the join of a different page of **p** with the relevant four pages of **q**. Each sub-join only considers tuples with a particular hash value for $\mathbf{Y_1}$ and $\mathbf{X_1}$. If we read the pages of **p** sequentially, nine buffers are sufficient (one for the **p** predicate and eight for the **q** predicate). Only seven buffers are needed if they are allocated on demand.

By changing the order in which we access the pages of the **p** predicate we can reduce the number of buffers needed. Suppose, instead of accessing tuples from **p** in the order the pages are stored (**00**, **01**, **10**, **11**), we read the pages in the order **00**, **10**, **01**, **11**. That is, we read all the pages in **p** such that $\mathbf{Y_1}$ is **0** before reading the pages in **p** in which $\mathbf{Y_1}$ is **1**. While we are joining tuples from the pages **00** and **10** in **p** the tuples will all hash to $\mathbf{Y_1}=\mathbf{0}$, thus matching tuples will only appear in the pages **000**, **001**, **010**, **011** from **q**. Later when we join tuples from the pages **01** and **11** in **p** the tuples will all hash to $\mathbf{Y_1}=\mathbf{1}$ and matching tuples will only appear in the pages **100**, **101**, **110**, **111** from **q**. When this is done, the number of buffers required is reduced to only five (one for the **p** predicate and four for the **q** predicate, whether or not buffers are allocated on demand.

It is possible to further reduce the number of buffers required by a more complex partitioning. In the optimal partitioning, each partition consists of tuples with particular hash values for $\mathbf{Y_1}$, $\mathbf{Y_2}$ and $\mathbf{Z_1}$. This partitions the join into eight sub-joins. Each sub-join consists of all tuples in one page of the **q** predicate and, on average, half the tuples in two pages of the **p** predicate. For example, the sub-join, where $\mathbf{Y_1Z_1Y_2}=\mathbf{001}$, consists of all tuples in page

001 of **q** and the tuples in pages **00** and **10** of **p** with hash value such that $Y_2 = 1$. If the sub-joins are done in increasing values of $Y_1Z_1Y_2$ then the number of buffers required is three (two for **p** and one for **q**. The same is true with increasing values of $Y_1Y_2Z_1$. However, with any other permutation of Y_1, Y_2 and Z_1 more than three buffers are required if no page is to be read from disk more than once (see the sub-section on *superjoin* execution).

5.5 Sfb-vector

Our base of bit-strings, such as $Y_1Z_1Y_2$, in the previous section can be formalized by defining an *sfb-vector* (slow–fast bits vector). An sfb-vector is a string of elements of the form V_j, where **V** is the name of variable in the query and **j** is an integer specifying a bit position in the hash value of **V**. Given an sfb-vector of length **f**, an *sfb-value* is a string of **0**s and **1**s of length **f**. The elements in the sfb-vector will define the partitioning of the join, and each sfb-value corresponds to a single partition. A partition consists of the sets of tuples from each predicate which *match* the sfb-value. A tuple matches an sfb-value when the hash bit values from the tuple which correspond to the elements of the sfb-vector are the same as the corresponding bits of the sfb-value. For example, given the sfb-vector for query (Q1) is $Y_1Y_2Z_1$ then the partition for the sfb-value of **001** is the sets {**p("x0","y0"),p("x1","y0")**} and {**q("y4","z1")**}. Sfb-values are generated in increasing order, so the order of the elements of the sfb-vector defines the order in which the sub-joins are done.

Given an sfb-vector, an sfb-value and a choice vector for a file, a set of pages in that file is identified. For example, the sfb-vector for query (Q1) is $Y_1Y_2Z_1$ and the choice vector for **p** is X_1Y_1; in this case, the sfb-value **001** would identify the pages ***0** in **p** (that is **00** and **10**). The matching tuples of **p** for the partition **001** are a subset of the tuples in these pages.

The *superjoin* generates a sequence of sfb-values from 0 to 2^{f-1} and performs a sub-join for each value. The sfb-vector and choice vectors are used to access the corresponding pages of the files. Only tuples which match with the sfb-value are considered. A set of tuples, one from each predicate in the query, with common values for the join variable(s) must appear in the same sub-join. Thus the union of the sub-joins is the same as the whole join.

5.6 Superjoin execution

We now describe the execution mechanism in more detail, including the management of buffers. Associated with each predicate call is a pool of buffers. Consider a predicate **P**; let **e** be the maximum value such that the most significant **e** bits of the sfb-vector are also in the choice vector for **P** (that is, are used for indexing **P**). These are called the *slow bits* for this predicate.

Each sub-join is executed like a partial-match join. However, in answering the partial-match queries, we only consider tuples which match both the query and the sfb-value. If pages on disk need to be accessed, new buffers are allocated on demand. The pages remain buffered and may be accessed several more times until the current values of the slow bits change.

However, when these bits change, the pages are never accessed again, since the sub-joins are done in order of increasing sfb-value. Therefore, the whole buffer pool for that call can be deallocated.

During execution of the *superjoin*, the addresses of the pages in the buffers always match the current value of the slow bits. Thus there is a maximum of $\mathbf{2^{c-e}}$ buffers in the buffer pool of the relation at any one time, where **c** is the length of the choice vector. The number of buffer pages for an *n*-way join is the sum of those needed for each relation:

$$\mathbf{nbufs} = \sum_{i=1}^{n} 2^{c_i - e_i}$$

$\mathbf{c_i}$ is the choice vector length of the **ith** predicate and
$\mathbf{e_i}$ is the number of slow bits for the **ith** predicate.

The sfb-vectors should be constructed so that this cost function is minimized.

5.7 Query optimization

Query optimization takes place at several levels. We briefly outline how the *superjoin* can be used with various higher level query optimization techniques, such as described in [20,22,55]. Given an expression consisting of calls to database predicates, other Prolog predicates and logical connectives, the following optimizations can be performed: removing redundant computations, common subexpression elimination [21], distribution of union over join, insertion of existential quantifiers (equivalent to decomposition [59] and isolating independent sub-queries [57]) and reordering of goals [35,57]. Once the optimizations have been performed, the *superjoin* can be applied to the resulting expression(s).

Databases containing rules can use the *superjoin* in the following way. When there is no recursion involving database access, unfolding can be used to obtain a single expression which is equivalent to the query. This can be processed as outlined above. For recursive databases, unfolding is no longer possible in general, and we must use more elaborate program transformations with bottom-up computation ([6,10,11,13,31,47,49]) or use methods similar to Earley deduction ([39,56]). Bottom-up methods are iterative and the *superjoin* can be used in each iteration to evaluate relational expressions. In Earley deduction methods the *superjoin* can be used in the reduction step, which is similar to an iteration on a single relational expression in the bottom-up methods.

Further work needs to be done to integrate the *superjoin* with other optimizations including the task of determining when to apply the *superjoin* (possibly using the methods of [60]) and integrating the *superjoin* with a recursive query evaluation scheme. Two other areas requiring further research are choice vector determination [41] and predicate reordering. We are currently investigating other algorithms for constructing sfb-vectors. Other methods for defining partitions and orderings are also being considered.

6. RECURSIVE QUERY OPTIMIZATION

Bottom-up computation deals with many tuples at a time and can naturally employ the existing optimization techniques developed for relational databases. As a consequence, bottom-up computation is the focus of much research into deductive databases. We are developing a mechanism whereby the answers to nominated databases queries can be computed bottom-up within the NU-Prolog system.

Bottom-up methods for answering a query to a database are essentially refinements of the following scheme. A set of ground atoms **S**, initialized with the database facts, is constructed by repeatedly *applying* the rules to **S** until no new atoms are generated. A rule is applied to **S** by adding the head of a ground instance of the rule to **S** whenever all body literals of this instance are in **S**. The answers to the query are those instances of the query in the final set **S**. The scheme is guaranteed to terminate in the absence of function symbols because the number of ground atoms that can be constructed is finite. In [5], the construction of the solution set is expressed in terms of the iterative solution of a system of equations, where the equations are assignment statements which define how the tuples generated in one iteration are used to generate tuples in later iterations.

We write iterative equations using a set on the left, and a set or union of sets on the right. Consider the familiar ancestor predicate where **anc(X,Y)** is true if **Y** is an ancestor of **X**, and where **parent(X,Y)**, a base predicate, is true if **Y** is a parent of **X**. We omit base predicate facts for brevity.

6.1 Example

```
anc(X,Y) :- parent(X,Y).
anc(X,Y) :- anc(X,Z), anc(Z,Y).
```

Since the first rule depends on the base predicate **parent**, it only needs to be applied once. The iterative equations specifying the operation of a bottom-up computation for this database are

$$\mathbf{anc_0(X,Y)} = \mathbf{parent(X,Y)}$$

$$\mathbf{anc_{j+1}(X,Y)} = \mathbf{anc_j(X,Y)} \cup [\mathbf{anc_j(X,Z), anc_j(Z,Y)}] \quad \text{for} \quad \mathbf{j} \geq \mathbf{0}$$

More formally, the sets of tuples are denoted by the following two forms, where $\bar{\mathbf{t}}$ is a vector of terms.

(1) $\mathbf{p_j(\bar{t})}$ denotes the set of $\langle \bar{\mathbf{t}} \rangle$ tuples of the **p** relation which have been evaluated at the **jth** iteration. If a set denoted by this form appears on the left of an equation, the tuples of the set are constructed by evaluating the

expession on the right. If the set appears on the right, it is used to generate new tuples.

(2) $[\mathbf{p1}(\bar{t}_1),\mathbf{p2}(\bar{t}_2),\cdots,\mathbf{pn}(\bar{t}_n)]\langle\bar{t}\rangle$ denotes the set of $\langle\bar{t}\rangle$ tuples that can be generated by applying appropriate relational operators to $\mathbf{p1}(\bar{t}_1),\mathbf{p2}(\bar{t}_2),\ldots,\mathbf{pn}(\bar{t}_n)$. Sets denoted in this form may only appear on the right-hand side of an equation. Since it is clear from the context of the equation which terms are to be generated, we omit the $\langle\bar{t}\rangle$ subscript.

The major drawback of naive bottom-up computation is the number of tuples which may be unnecessarily generated. Broadly speaking, there are two types of tuples which are generated unnecessarily — *redundant* tuples and *irrelevant* tuples.

6.2 Redundant tuples

Many tuples are *redundant*, that is, generated more than once. The differential approach suggested in [5,9,12] is one refinement to limit the number of such tuples. Using this approach, each tuple generated during an iteration is constructed in terms of at least one tuple generated during the previous iteration. Therefore, a set of tuples will not be used to repeatedly generate the same tuples at each iteration. In [7], the differential method is generalized for non-linear recursive databases. Returning to the ancestor relation, the iterative equations corresponding to the improved differential computation are

$$\delta\mathbf{anc_0(X,Y)} = \mathbf{parent(X,Y)}$$

$$\mathbf{anc_0(X,Y)} = \varnothing$$

$$\mathbf{anc_{j+1}(X,Y)} = \mathbf{anc_j(X,Y)} \cup \delta\mathbf{anc_j(X,Y)}$$

$$\delta\mathbf{anc_j(X,Y)} = \mathbf{[[}\delta\mathbf{anc_{j-1}(X,Z),anc_j(Z,Y)]} \cup \mathbf{[anc_{j-1}(X,Z),} \delta\mathbf{anc_{j-1}(X,Z)]]} - \mathbf{anc_j(Z,Y)} \quad \text{for } \mathbf{j} \geqslant \mathbf{0}$$

6.3 Irrelevant tuples

Many tuples are *irrrelevant*, that is, play no part in answering the query. We do not need to generate these tuples even once, and so we start by considering only relvant rules. *Relevant rules* are those whose head predicate is the query predicate, and predicates called by the query predicate, directly or indirectly. However, not all tuples generated by the relevant rules help us to answer a given query. Bottom-up evaluation of an untransformed database generates irrelevant tuples because it does not make use of ground terms in the query or variable bindings in the derived literals in the same goal-driven way that a top-down computation does.

There are two basic approaches toward limiting the generation of these irrelvant tuples. The first approach seeks to modify the standard bottom-up computation and achieve a run-time oriented solution [23,56]. The second approach seeks to a perform a compile-time transformation of the original database into an equivalent form which enables a standard bottom-up computation to focus on relevant tuples. Two examples of this approach are magic sets [11,13] and counting sets [11,48]. Our research [6,8] has investigated the use of *magic set* transformations on function-free databases that include negation in the body of rules. In addition, we are currently investigating the magic set based integration of evaluable predicates such as $>$ or $+$ into the bottom-up computation [45].

6.4 Stratification and allowedness

There are two properties that databases should have in order to answer queries both soundly and efficiently. The class of *stratifed* databases [14] was defined to make the model theory manageable when negation body literals are included in the database, by disallowing certain combinations of recursion and negation such as **p :- ~p**. For this class, there is a natural way of selecting a particular minimal model [3] as the intended one. Since a computable semantics has been defined for this class of databases, we require that the database be stratified. *Allowedness* [15,29] is a syntactic characterization of *domain independence* [53]; domain independence ensures that the semantics of a database (given by its set of positive logical consequences) does not change when new constants are added to the language [27]. Our magic set algorithm preserves both stratification and allowedness. We have defined an extended notion of allowedness [6] and shown that by using *allowed sideways information passing strategies*, an allowed database remains so after the magic transformation. Consider the following database:

```
query(Y) :- – b(Y).
```

If we ask the query **?-query(1)** then it is quite clear that we can evaluate the query without floundering despite the fact that the definitions of allowedness in [15,29] disallow this database. We define a new definition of allowedness which takes full account of the effect of a particular query on the bindings generated at run-time by using the adorned database of Ullman [54].

An adorned rule is *allowed* if every variable appearing in either a free argument position of the head or negative body literal also appears in a positive body literal or a bound argument position of the head. In the above example, **Y** is adorned as a bound variable by the query and so the database is allowed.

As an illustration of how we compute magic sets for stratified databases, consider the following labelled but untransformed database and sips which is unstratified after performing the usual magic set transformation to the negative literal.

```
p(X,Y) :- b(X,Y).
p(X,Y) :- ~n_q(X,Z),a(Z),p(Z,Y).      {p(X,Y)}→x~n_q(X,Z)
                                      {p(X,Y),~n_q(X,Z),a(Z)}→zp(Z,Y)
```

```
n_q(X,Y) :- c(X,Y).
n_q(X,Y) :- c(X,Z),n_q(Z,Y).      {n_q(X,Y),c(X,Z)}→z n_q(Z,Y)
?-p(2,Y)
```

The computation of **p** tuples using the second rule cannot proceed until the tuples satisfying ~**n_q** have been inferred. The first arc of the sip associated with the second rule dictates that **X** is bound before an attempt is made to infer ~**n_q** tuples. Therefore, only those ~**n_q** tuples with the same binding as **X** are *relevant*. In answering ~**n_q(X,Y)**, top-down inference methods ask the query **n_q(X,Y)** and then use the information to infer the set of tuples satisfying ~**n_q**.

Two points about this process bear highlighting: (1) the positive query asked by the inference mechanism in order to answer a negative literal is separated from other queries that are asked: (2) in order to answer an (partially) instantiated negative literal, the positive query that is asked can have the same (partial) instantiation. Point (2) depicts the essential difference in efficiency of the model building process performed by a top-down computation as compared to the bottom-up computation of an untransformed database. A bottom-up interpreter must build the *entire* model corresponding to the **q** facts. On the other hand, the top-down approach, only builds the *relevant* subset of that model.

Our modification of the standard bottom-up methods is again expressed in terms of a system of iterative equations. In the first step of magic set algorithms, arguments bound by the user's query are used to initialize the magic set of the query predicate with a tuple. Similarly, following point (1) above, when answering the negative literal ~**n_q**, we require that the bottom-up method commences a separate bottom-up computation to answer **q**. That is the set of tuples associated with each predicate is initialized to the facts of the predicate, and only rules relevant to the computation of **n_q** are considered. The magic set of **n_q** is initialized in keeping with the context of ~**n_q**, after which the relevant tuples satisfying **n_q** are found.

Equations corresponding to the magic rules for positive literals and the modified rules are generated in the standard way after applying labelling. Equations corresponding to the magic rules for negative literals are constructed in a special way in order to achieve an equivalent initialization operation as used by a top-down computation. The relevant iterative equations are

$$\mathrm{p}_0(X,Y)=\emptyset$$

$$\mathrm{p}_{j+1}=(X,Y)\mathrm{p}_j(X,Y) \cup [\mathrm{magic\_p}_j(X),\mathrm{b}(X,Y)] \cup [\mathrm{magic\_p}_j(X),\sim\mathrm{n\_q}^j(X,Z),\mathrm{a}(Z),\mathrm{p}_j(Z,Y)]$$

$$\mathrm{magic\_p}_0(Z)=\{\langle 2\rangle\}$$

$$\mathrm{magic\_p}_{j+1}(Z)=\mathrm{magic\_p}_j(Z) \cup [\mathrm{magic\_p}_j(X),\mathrm{a}(Z),\sim\mathrm{n\_q}^j(X,Z)]$$

$$\mathrm{n\_q}_0(X,Y)=\emptyset$$

$$\mathbf{n\_q_{j+1}(X,Y)=n\_q_j(X,Y) \cup [magic\_n\_q_j(X),c(X,Y)] \cup [magic\_n\_q_j(X),c(X,Z),n\_q_j(Z,Y)]}$$

$$\mathbf{magic\_n\_q^j_0(X)=magic\_p_j(X)}$$

$$\mathbf{magic\_n\_q_{j+1}(Z)=magic\_n\_q_j(Z) \cup [magic\_n\_q_j(X),c(X,Z)]}$$

The bottom-up computation iterates for each value of **j** until no new tuples for any of the relations are produced. Let us examine what occurs when the tuples for **p** at iteration **j+1**, that is, $\mathbf{p_{j+1}(X,Y)}$, are evaluated. The set $\mathbf{p_j(X,Y)}$ and the conjunction $\mathbf{[magic\_p_j(X),b(X,Y)]}$ are dealt with in the standard way. The conjunction $\mathbf{[magic\_p_j(X),\sim n\_q^j(X,Z),a(Z),p_j(Z,Y)]}$ is different. The variable **j** which normally denotes the iteration number is used in the superscript of $\mathbf{n\_q^j}$ to symbolically indicate a *separate* computation. Observe that $\sim\mathbf{n\_q^j}(X,Z)$ does not have a subscript because the tuples in $\mathbf{n\_q^j(X,Z)}$ are determined to completion, using a separate bottom-up computation. This set of tuples is used to eliminate matching tuples satisfying $\mathbf{magic\_p^j(X),a(Z),p_j(Z,Y)}$ in accordance with the usual bottom-up method. Finally, the tuples in $\mathbf{p_{j+1}}$ are evaluated using suitable projection and union operations.

Each time we initiate a separate $\mathbf{n\_q^j(X,Z)}$ query, a new initial set of **magic_n_q** tuples is constructed. These are the tuples of $\mathbf{magic\_n\_q_0}$, where the superscript symbolically highlights the fact that each initialization is separate.

In summary, the process of answering a query **q** on a database **D** and sips **S** is performed according to the following sequence of steps.

(1) Check that **D** is stratified by looking for negative cycles in the dependency graph.
(2) Obtain the adorned database $\mathbf{D^A}$ by applying the adornment algorithm.
(3) Check that every adorned rule in $\mathbf{D^A}$ is allowed and that every sip in **S** is allowed.
(4) Obtain $\mathbf{D^L}$ and S^L by applying the labelling algorithm to $\mathbf{D^A}$ and **S**.
(5) Apply the magic set algorithm to $\mathbf{D^L}$ and $\mathbf{S^L}$.
(6) Using the iterative equations, execute the bottom-up process described above.

6.5 Improvements

By using a *generic* query where the adornment of the query is given without specific bindings, steps (1)–(5) need only be performed once. For example, a database may be compiled expecting the following adornments for the **ancestor** predicate — **bf**, **fb**, and **bb**. The equations for computing the **ancestor** relation corresponding to these adornments are stored in a library. When a query of the form $\mathbf{?\text{-}ancestor^{bf}(\bar{t})}$ is asked, the corresponding system of equations is loaded, $\mathbf{magic\_ancestor^{bf}}$ is initialized with the bound arguments of $\bar{\mathbf{t}}$, and step (6) is performed. The choice of which generic queries to compile and store in a library can be set by compile-time options or by a database system administrator.

The purpose of labelling was to label positive literals so that they are syntactically independent of one another. This means that common tuples may be computed twice for predicates **p_**α and **p_**β, where α and β are in the range **1** to the *counter* associated with **p**. This source of inefficiency can be removed by making the following modifications to the bottom-up method.

(1) When tuples for a predicate **p_**α (or **n_p**) are being computed, the set of initial **p_**α (or **n_p**) tuples is assigned the set of **p** tuples rather than $\emptyset$.
(2) When the computation of tuples for a predicate **p_**α (**n_p**) is complete, these tuples are added to the set of **p** tuples.

7. TRANSACTION PROCESSING

For deductive database systems to be of practical use, their facilities for updating the database must ensure consistency in a multi-user environment. The basic update primitives of Prolog, **assert** and **retract**, have been widely criticised, even for general programming, and do not lend themselves to implementation in a multi-user environment. A simple modification to Prolog would be to call **assert** and **retract** between primitives which specify the start and end of a transaction. Concurrency control and integrity constraint checking could also be incorporated into this system. However, there are problems with this approach such as the undefined semantics of **assert** and **retract** [58] and inefficient integrity constraint checking.

We first describe **assert** and **retract** and review several problems associated with them in the context of database systems. An alternative which overcomes many of the problems is then proposed: a **transaction** primitive [37] for updating database relations consisting of ground facts without duplicates. This primitive has a well-defined semantics and ensures that sets of insertions and deletions are performed atomically. Updates of rules are necessary for general programming and likely to be important in future database systems. Our approach may be useful for this, but more research is needed, especially in the area of the semantics of updating rules.

7.1 Problems with assert and retract

The basic primitive for inserting clauses into the database in Prolog is **assert**. It inserts its argument, which is a single clause (either a fact or a rule). If it contains variables at the time of the call, a clause with variables is inserted into the database. **Assert** always succeeds initially and fails when the computation backtracks. There are two minor variants of **assert** — **asserta** and **assertz**. These insert the clause at the start or the end, respectively, of the predicate definition.

Clauses are deleted from the database in Prolog by calling **retract**. Initially, **retract** deletes the first clause in the database which unifies with the argument of **retract**. On backtracking, the next matching clause is removed (with most versions of **retract**, at least). Retract fails when there are no remaining matching clauses. Retract can be used to remove just some of the matching clauses by using cut. Prolog also has a **retractall** primitive which always retracts all clauses with matching heads.

The exact result of combining **call**s, **retracts** and **assert**s to a single predicate varies between different Prolog systems ([32] lists nine inconsistent implementations) and even different versions of the same system (including MU-prolog, C-Prolog and Quintus Prolog). Usually it is not specified exactly what should happen. The problems with the semantics of **assert** and **retract** are further discussed in [58].

Asserta and **assertz** are not appropriate for most database applications. The user does not normally specify *where* individual facts are inserted. Rather, the position is determined by the storage structure of the predicate, for example sorted or hashed. This is decided by the user (or database administrator) when the predicate is created, to allow efficient retrieval.

To implement **assert** and **retract** in Prolog it is necessary to read (by **call** and **retract**) and write (by **assert** and **retract**) predicates concurrently. Consider the goal **?-p(X),assert(p(b))** where **p** has at least one fact. The call to **p(X)** does not complete before **assert(p(b))** is called. Thus the data structures associated with **p** must allow concurrent reading and writing.

Even with a simple implementation in main memory with little or no indexing this is quite difficult, especially if memory is to be reclaimed when clauses are retracted. In an external database system, the problems with **assert** and **retract** become much more severe. Even in the single-user case, concurrent access is required to data structures on disk which may be quite complex. Multi-user access creates even more difficulties (see below). The normal solution to the problems of concurrent reading and writing is to only allow one writer or several readers but not both readers and writers at any time. Naive Prolog database implementations (such as [33]) will deadlock if given queries such as the example above.

A database system based on logic should provide good support for integrity checking. A major question which arises when adding integrity constraints to a Prolog database system is when the constraints should be checked. Checking after each **assert** or **retract** is not adequate. Many simple updates require retracting a fact then asserting a similar fact. Integrity cannot be enforced between these two operations. Some way of grouping asserts and retracts into atomic updates is needed. We must also consider what happens when the integrity constraints fail. There must be some way of rolling back the changes which have been made, which generally requires a copy of what changes have been made. Some method of storing the updates between each integrity check should therefore be provided. This can lead to an improvement in efficiency because many integrity constraints can be checked by analysing just the updates, rather than the entire database [38]. A simplification procedure for integrity constraint checking which uses a notion of transaction similar to ours is given in [28].

Many applications of databases systems involve several users processing transactions concurrently. Some form of database consistency (independent of integrity constraints) must be maintained with multi-user access. Many operations must be treated as atomic: for example, reading an item from the database, incrementing it, and then writing it. Some way of specifying concurrency control is therefore needed. The way these problems are normally solved is with the concept of a *transaction* (a collection of updates which must be done atomically). Unfortunately, conventional Prolog systems do not provide a transaction facility and the use of **assert** and **retract** for database updates in a multi-user situation can leave the database inconsistent. To achieve consistent database updates we need to provide a transaction primitive for Prolog which can use one of the many schemes for maintaining database consistency (see below).

Database systems also need to maintain database consistency in the event of a hardware or software system failure. This is usually done by maintaining: backup copies of the database; a log of changes to the database; a record of which transactions are completed. This allows recovery of completed transactions and rolling back of partially completed transactions when the system restarts after a failure [16,55]. Although **assert** and **retract** can easily be altered to generate a log of updates, it is not possible to decide which updates should be rolled back without some additional language feature.

7.2 A Prolog transaction primitive

At the highest level we view a database as having a sequence of states, where each state transition is caused by the execution of a transaction. The semantics at this level depends on the individual programs operating on the database and how they interact. Our work does not specifically address this problem, although the complexity of the semantics is reduced by defining transactions. The issues of concurrency and atomicity of certain operations are addressed and the number of database states may be greatly reduced, since many small changes can be packed into a single transaction.

We concentrate on the design of the programming language primitive for the individual transactions. Our main criteria are that the primitive is sufficiently expressive, practical to implement with current techniques, has well-defined and simple semantics (for individual transactions) and fits in well with logic programming (specifically NU-Prolog [51]). The aim is to use this primitive in application programs, instead of **assert** and **retract**. Higher level query languages which support updates could also be translated into this primitive.

In our system, a *transacation* is a function which maps an old database state, plus some input, to a new database state. A simple way to specify this is with a definition of the new database state in logic. For example, suppose there is a single predicate **p**; for each fact in the database, we want to increment its argument, if greater than 20, by some input **Inc**. The following formula defines **p′** in the new database state in terms of **p** in the old database state and the input.

∀A,B p′(A) ↔ p(B), if B > 20 then A is B+Inc else A = B.

This style of update has very attractive semantics and is something we could aim for in deductive database systems. However, for the current generation of implementations a lower level primitive is necessary for efficiency. Database state transitions are implemented by inserting and deleting facts into/from the database. The translation of a formula specifying the new database state into a formula specifying an efficient way of making the changes is not straightforward. Current logic programming systems give the programmer fine control over how a computation is done, and this should also be the case for computing updates.

This leads back to the idea of the programmer specifying what facts should be inserted and deleted. A very simple modification to Prolog would be to call **assert** and **retract** between primitives which specify the start and end of a transaction. Some kind of concurrency control (such as [1]) and integrity constraint checking could be incorporated. Problems with this approach include unclear semantics and inefficient integrity constraint checking.

A transaction can also be specified by defining two sets: the facts to be deleted (**DEL**) and the facts to be inserted (**INS**). We can define the new database state (the set of facts **New_db**) in terms of the old state (**Old_db**), **DEL** and **INS**:

$$\textbf{New\_db} = (\textbf{Old\_db} - \textbf{DEL}) \cup \textbf{INS}$$

This definition corresponds to performing deletions before insertions. It has several advantages over performing insertions first (the two methods are equally powerful). First, it results in smaller intermediate databases. Second, it results in a simpler specification for transactions in the common case of 'modifying' (as opposed to inserting or deleting) several facts. Consider the previous example. We want all the incremented values in the new database, even if they were in the old database. If insertions are done first, we must be careful to avoid newly inserted values being deleted immediately. Third, work on integrity constraint checking assumes a transaction is made up of a set of deletions followed by a set of insertions.

Like the new database state, the insert and delete sets could be defined separately in logic. The previous example could be expressed:

$$\forall \textbf{A}\ \textbf{p(A)} \in \textbf{DEL} \leftrightarrow \textbf{p(A), A>20.}$$

$$\forall \textbf{A,B}\ \textbf{p(A)} \in \textbf{INS} \leftrightarrow \textbf{p(B), B>20, A is B+1.}$$

A major advantage this has over **assert** and **retract** is that there is a well-defined *declarative* semantics for the overall change to the database. However, the naive implementation would access the entire **p** predicate twice, and as before, optimizing such computations is not trivial. We propose to have a single formula which allows the programmer complete control over the execution but defines both **INS** and **DEL**. We retain well-defined declarative semantics, although they can be more difficult to extract. There is an obvious tradeoff between simple semantics and control or expressibility. Our proposal gives full expressibility and progammer control but sacrifices a little simplicity of the semantics.

The syntax of our transaction primitive is as follows:

all Local_vars transaction Goal

Local_vars is a term containing variables local to **Goal** (the same as other universally quantified variables in NU-Prolog [36,51]). If there are no local variables, **all Local_vars** may be omitted. **Goal** is any Prolog goal and may also contain calls to the procedures **db_insert** and **db_delete**. As an example, the previous specification of a transaction can be trivially transformed into our primitive as follows:

```
all A.B transaction
    ( p(A), A > 20, db_delete(p(A))
    ;
     p(B), B > 20, A is B+1, db_insert(p(A))
    )
```

A more efficient version, which results in **p** only being called once, is

```
all A.B transaction
    (P(A), A > 20, B is A+1, db_delete(p(A)), db_insert(p(B)))
```

Any goal may be used, except that **db_insert** and **db_delete** may not appear inside negative subgoals such as **not** and the condition of **if** or additional quantifiers. Also, **db_insert** and **db_delete** may only appear inside that goal of a transaction. Predicates which could be updated may only be called inside a transaction. For example, **p(X), transaction db_insert(p(a))** would not be allowed. **Transaction** is only called when all the global variables (**Inc** in the examples) are ground. This could be implemented by delaying the execution or by aborting with an error message.

When **transaction** is called, all solutions to the goal are found. Each solution may cause several insertions and deletions. However, they are saved rather than performed immediately. After all solutions have been found, the transaction attempts to *commit*. If this is successful, the updates are made — first all the deletions then all the insertions. An attempt to delete a non-exisisting fact could generate a warning or error.

For the purposes of finding solutions to the goal, **db_insert** and **db_delete** are equivalent to true. Each solution corresponds to a sequence of successful calls (the selected literals in an SLD refutation for the goal). Each call to **db_insert** or **db_delete** in these sequences results in an update. The update is the call to **db_insert** or **db_delete** with the final variable bindings for the solution (the answer substitution), and must be ground. Calls which do not lead to solutions do not result in updates.

7.3 Solving the problems

7.3.1 Semantics

Transaction has much in common with an all solutions predicate. The design of such a predicate with well-defined declarative semantics is discussed in [34]. It is important that local and global variables are distinguished. If the global variables are ground at the time of the call, then finding the set of solutions to the goal is deterministic. Many all solutions predicates are non-deterministic — returning different lists of solutions for different instantiations of the global variables. Non-determinism may be useful in other contexts but we do not consider it desirable within update primitives.

Because **db_delete** and **db_insert** always succeed and only change the database at the end of the transaction, the declarative semantics for the solutions to the goal is straightforward. Both primitives can be considered equivalent to true.

Since **db_insert** and **db_delete** only appear in the top-level goal of the transaction, we can derive a declarative definition of what facts are inserted and deleted as follows. The goal is logically transformed into a disjunction, such that each **db_insert** and **db_delete** appears at the top level of one of these disjuncts. For each solution to each disjunct, the **db_insert**s and **db_delete**s in that disjunct will be performed. More formally, suppose the disjunctive form of the goal is ($G_1; G_2; \cdots; G_n$); then

$$\mathbf{DEL} = \{ X\theta | \mathbf{db\_delete(X)} \text{ appears in some } \mathbf{G_i} \wedge \mathbf{G_i}\theta \textbf{ is true} \}$$

$$\mathbf{INS} = \{ X\theta | \mathbf{db\_insert(X)} \text{ appears in some } \mathbf{G_i} \wedge \mathbf{G_i}\theta \textbf{ is true} \}$$

where θ is some answer substitution.

Consider a further extension to the increment sample. Suppose that if the new value is greater than 100, we want to insert the fact into predicate **q** instead of **p**.

```
all A.B transaction
    ( p(A), A > 20, B is A+1,
        ( db_delete(p(A))
         ;
          B =< 100, db_insert(p(B))
         ;
          B > 100, db_insert(q(B))
        )
    )
```

The disjunctive form of the goal contains three disjuncts:

```
( p(A), A > 20, B is A+1, db_delete(P(A))
 ;
  p(A), A > 20, B is A+1, B =< 100, db_insert(p(B))
 ;
  p(A), A > 20, B is A+1, B > 100, db_insert(q(B))
)
```

This gives declarative definitions of what facts are deleted from and inserted into **p** and **q**:

∀ A,B p(A) ∈ DEL ↔ p(A), A > 20, B is A+1.
∀ A,B p(A) ∈ INS ↔ p(B), B > 20, A is B+1, A =< 100.
∀ A,B q(A) ∈ DEL ↔ p(B), B > 20, A is B+1, A > 100.

Since updates depend on answer substitutions, and calls which result in failure do not cause updates, any two goals which can be logically transformed into the same disjunctive form will result in the same sets **DEL** and **INS**. Since all deletions are done before all insertions, we have a precise logical characterization of the overall change to the database.

7.3.2 Implementation

An obvious implementation of **transaction** would involve **db_insert** and **db_delete** saving their arguments when called (without renaming variables) and undoing this on backtracking. These saved updates need to be added to **INS** and **DEL** whenever a solution is found. After finding all solutions, the transaction must attempt to commit (see section 7.2). If this succeeds, the actual changes to the database are made, using **DEL** then **INS**.

An alternative way to calculate **INS** and **DEL** is to transform the goal. Each occurrence of **db_insert(X)** or **db_delete(X)** in the goal is replaced by **V_i = insert(X)** or **V_i = delete(X)**, respectively, where **V_i** is a newly introduced variable. At the end of the goal a list containing all the new variables can be passed to the predicate **save_updates** which accumulates **INS** and **DEL**. The goal in the first transaction example is transformed as follows:

```
( p(A), A > 20, V1 = delete(p(A))
;
 p(B), B > 20, A is B+1, V2 = insert(p(A))
),
save_updates([V1, V2])
```

Save_updates checks whether each variable is instantiated (to see if the corresponding equality was called) and, if so, saves the update.

In this system, the problems of concurrent reading and writing from one invocation of Prolog disappear, because access to database predicates is restricted to within transactions, and updates are only done at the end of transactions. In addition, the packaging of a set of updates together may reduce disk accesses. However, if the set of updates for one transaction is very large then large temporary predicates may need to be created. This is unavoidable in many cases, since *in situ* updates are not always possible (if key fields are altered), integrity and consistency need to be maintained, and crash recovery must be possible.

7.3.3 Integrity constraints

Integrity constraints should be checked at the end of each transaction. It is best to do so after the **INS** and **DEL** sets have been constructed but before the database is actually updated. At this stage there is enough information available to check the constraints efficiently. As **transaction** produces a set of deletions and a set of insertions, we can use the simplification procedure [28] for consistency checking.

This method compiles the integrity constraints into a set of goals which may access **INS**, **DEL** and the database. If the initial database satisfies constraints and the goals succeed, the modified database must also satisfy the integrity constraints. If any of the goals fail, then the modified database would violate the integrity constraints, so the transaction should generate an error or fail. However, no roll back is needed, since the database has not been changed.

7.3.4 Concurrency

Database consistency is formalized by the notion of serializability [17]. A concurrent execution of a set of transactions is said to be serializable if it has the same result as some serial ordering of the transactions. **Transaction** can be used as a basis for concurrency control by adopting a concurrency control scheme that guarantees serializability. However, the schemes proposed in the literature (two-phase locking [17], optimistic concurrency control [24], and a hybrid scheme all have problems in the context of deductive databases. We briefly outline how a form of optimistic concurrency control could be implemented which avoids these problems.

A global data structure is kept which contains information about what parts of the database each currently executing transaction has read. The granularity of this information is not vital. Recording what pages or what predicates have been read is probably best in most systems. Finer granularity results in more potential concurrency but greater overheads.

Before a transaction modifies the database it must attempt to commit. This is an atomic operation which only one transaction can do at one time. If it is able to commit, it kills all other transactions which may have read data it is about to modify. The changes to the database are then all made.

When a transaction is killed, it must roll back and restart. Rolling back is simple, since the only charges have been to the local **INS** and **DEL** sets. Transaction killing is best implemented with signals, to avoid extra work accessing the database, However, any mechanism would do, as long as the transaction rolls back and restarts eventually, instead of committing.

8. CONCLUSION

The techniques used in the NU-Prolog deductive database system may be effectively applied to a wide range of databases. Superimposed codeword indexing schemes provide efficient access to large databases of Prolog terms. Many useful systems can be implemented using the simple top-down computational method in combination with the superjoin algorithm. For large databases containing recursion, bottom-up methods are preferable, especially when their efficiency has been enhanced by the differential approach and magic sets. To make the system useful in multi-user environments, we employ a clean, concurrent update facility based on transactions.

ACKNOWLEDGEMENTS

This work was supported by the Australian Commonwealth Department of Science, Pyramid Technology (Australia), the Australian Research Grants Commission, and the Commonwealth Scientific and Industrial Research Organisation.

REFERENCES

[1] Acharya, S. and Buckley, G., Transaction Restarts in Prolog Database Systems, *Proc. ACM–SIGMOD*, S. Navathe (ed.), 1985, 364–373.

[2] Aho, A. V. and Ullman, J. D., Optimal Partial-match Retrieval when Fields are Independently Specified, *ACM Trans. on Database Systems* **4**, June 1979, 168–179.

[3] Apt, K. R., Blair, H. A., and Walker, A., Towards a Theory of Declarative Knowledge, *Preprints of Workshop on Foundations of Deductive Databases and Logic Programming*, Washington, DC, August 1986, 546–628.

[4] Balbin, I. and Lecot, K., *Logic Programming: a Classified Bibliography*, Wildgrass Books, Melbourne, Australia, 1985.

[5] Balbin, I. and Ramamohanarao, K., A Differential Approach to Query Optimisation in Recursive Deductive Databases, Technical Report 86/7, Department of Computer Science, University of Melbourne, Australia, 1986.

[6] Balbin, I., Port, G. S., and Ramamohanarao, K., Magic Set Computation for Stratified Databases, Technical Report 87/3, Department of Computer Science,University of Melbourne, Australia, 1987. Submitted for Publication.

[7] Balbin, I. and Ramamohanarao, K., A Generalisation of the Differential Approach to Recursive Query Evaluation, *J. Logic Programming*, To Appear (1987).

[8] Balbin, I., Meenakshi, K., and Ramamohanarao, K., An Efficient Labelling Algorithm for Magic Set Computation on Stratified Databases, Technical Report 88/1, Department of Computer Science. University of Melbourne, Australia, 1988. Submitted for Publication.

[9] Bancilhon, F., Naive Evaluation of Recursively Defined Relations, *Proc. Islamadora Conf. on Database and AI*, 1985. *On Knowledge Base Management Systems,* Brodie, M. L. and Mylopoulos, J. (eds.), Springer-Verlag, 1986.

[10] Bancilhon, F. and Ramakrishnan, R., Performance Evaluation of Data Intensive Logic Programs, *Preprints of Workshop on Foundations of Deductive Databases and Logic Programming*, Washington, DC, August 1986, 284–314.

[11] Bancilhon, F., Maier, D., Sagiv, Y., and Ullman, J. D., Magic Sets and Other Strange Ways to Implement Logic Programs, *Proc. 5th ACM–SIGMOD–SIGACT News Symp. on Principles of Database Systems*, Washington, DC, 1986.

[12] Bayer, R., Query Evaluation and Recursion in Deductive Database Systems, Technical Report, Technische Universität München–18503, Instut für Informatik, Technische Universität München, February 1985.

[13] Beeri, C. and Ramakrishnan, R., On the Power of Magic, *Proc. 6 ACM–SIGMOD–SIGACT News Symp. on Principles of Database Syst.*, San Diego, California, March 1987, 269–283.

[14] Chandra, A. K. and Harel, D., Horn Clause Queries and Generalisation, *J. Logic Programming*, **2**, 1–15, 1985.

[15] Clark, K. L., Negation as Failure, in *Logic and Data Bases*, H. Gallaire and J. Minker (eds.), Plenum Press, New York, 1978, 293–322.

[16] Date, C. J., *An Introduction to Database Systems*, 4th edn, Addison-Wesley, Reading, Mass. 1985.

[17] Eswaran, K. P., Gray, J. N., Lorie, R. A., and I. L. Traiger, The Notions of Consistency and Predicate Locks in a Database System, *Comm. ACM*, **19**, 624–633, 1976.

[18] Fabry, R. S., Capability-based Addressing, *Comm. ACM* **17**, 403–412, 1974.

[19] Gallaire, H., Minker, J., and Nicolas, J., Logic and Databases: a Deductive Approach, *ACM Computing Surveys*, **16**, 153–185, 1984.

[20] Grant, J. and Minker, J., Optimization in Deductive and Conventional Relational Database Systems, in *Advances in Data Base Theory*, Vol. 1, H. Gallaire, J. Minker and J. Nicolas (eds.), Plenum Press, New York, 1981, 195–234.

[21] Hall, P. A. V., Optimization of Single Expressions in a Relational Data Base System, *IBM J. Research and Development*, **20**, 244–257, 1976.

[22] Jarke, M. and Koch, J., Query Optimization in Database Systems, *ACM Computing Surveys*, **16**, 111–152, 1984.

[23] Kifer, M. and Lozinskii, E. L., Filtering Data Flow in Deductive Databases, *Proc. Int. Conf. on Database Theory*, Rome, Italy, September 1986, 186–202. Published as *Lecture Notes in Computer Science 243* by Springer-Verlag.

[24] Kung, H. T. and Robinson, J. T., On Optimistic Methods for Concurrency Control, *ACM Tran. on Database Systems*, **6**, 213–226, 1981.

[25] Lloyd, J. W. and Ramamohanarao, K., Partial-match Retrieval for Dynamic Files, *BIT*, **22**, 150–168, 1982.

[26] Lloyd, J. W. and Topor, R. W., Making Prolog More Expressive, *J. Logic Programming*, **1**, 225–240, 1984.

[27] Lloyd, J. W., *Foundations of Logic Programming*, Springer-Verlag, New York, 1984.

[28] Lloyd, J. W., Sonenberg, E. A., and Topor, R. W., Integrity Constraint Checking in Stratified Databases, Technical Report 86/5, Department of Computer Science, University of Melbourne, Melbourne, Australia, 1986.

[29] Lloyd, J. W. and Topor, R. W., A Basis for Deductive Database Systems II, *J. Logic Programming*, **3**, 55–67, 1986.

[30] Marek, W. and Rauszer, C., Query Optimization in Databases Distributed by Means of Product Equivalence Relations, *Preprints of Workshop on Foundations of Deductive Databases and Logic Programming*, Washington, DC, August 1986, 315–337.

[31] McKay, D. P. and Shapiro, S. C., Using Active Connection Graphs for Reasoning with Recursive Rules, *Proc. Seventh IJCAI*, 1981, 368–374.

[32] Moss, C., Cut and Paste — Defining the Impure Primitives of Prolog, *Proc. Third Int. Conf. on Logic Programming*, London, July 1986, 686–694. Published as *Lecture Notes in Computer Science 225* by Springer-Verlag.

[33] Naish, L. and Thom, J. A., The MU-Prolog Deductive Database, Technical Report 83/10, Department of Computer Science, University of Melbourne, Melbourne, Australia, November 1983.

[34] Naish, L., All Solutions Predicates in Prolog, *Prog. 1985 Symp. on Logic Programming*, Boston, Mass. 1985, 73–77.

[35] Naish, L., *Negation and Control in Prolog*, Springer-Verlag, New York, 1986.

[36] Naish, L., Negation and Quantifiers in NU-Prolog, *Proc. Third Int. Conf. on Logic Programming*, London, 1986, 624–634. Published as *Lecture Notes in Computer Science 225* by Springer-Verlag.

[37] Naish, L., Thom, J. A., and Ramamohanarao, K., Concurrent Database Updates in Prolog, *Proc. Fourth Int. Conf. in Logic Programming*, Melbourne, Australia, May 1987.

[38] Nicolas, J. M. and Yazdanian, K., Integrity Checking in Deductive Databases, in *Logic and Data Bases*, H. Gallaire and J. Minker, (eds.), Plenum Press, New York, 1978, 325–346.

[39] Porter, H. H., III, Earley Deduction, Technical Report CS/E-86-002, Oregon Graduate Center, Beaverton, Oregon, March, 1986.

[40] Ramamohanarao, K. and Lloyd, J. W., Dynamic Hashing Schemes, *Computer J.*, **25**, 478–485, 1982.

[41] Ramamohanarao, K., Lloyd, J. W. and Thom, J. A., Partial-match Retrieval Using Hashing and Descriptors, *ACM Trans. on Database Systems*, **8**, 552–576, 1983.

[42] Ramamohanarao, K. and Sacks-Davis, R., Recursive Linear Hashing, *ACM Trans. on Database Systems*, **9**, 369–391, 1984.

[43] Ramamohanarao, K., and Sacks-Davis, R., Partial-match Retrieval Using Recursive Linear Hashing, *BIT*, **25**, 477–484, 1985.

[44] Ramamohanarao, K. and Shepherd, J., A Superimposed Codeword Indexing Scheme for Very Large Prolog Databases, *Proc. Third Int. Conf. on Logic Programming*, London, August 1986, 569–576.

[45] Ramamohanarao, K., Meenakshi, K., and Balbin, I., Constraint Propagation Using Magic Sets, in preparation, Department of Computer Science, University of Melbourne, Melbourne, Australia, 1988.

[46] Roberts, C. S., Partial Match Retrieval via the Method of Superimposed Codes. *Proc. IEEE*, **67**, 522–528, 1979.

[47] Rohmer, J., Lascoeur, R., and Kerisit, J. M., The Alexander Method

— A Technique for the processing of Recursive Axioms in Deductive Database Queries, *New Generation Computing*, **4**, 273–285, 1986.

[48] Sacca, D. and Zaniolo, C., The Generalized Counting Method for Recursive Logic Queries, *Proc. Int. Conf. on Database Theory*, Rome, Italy, September 1986, 31–53. Published as *Lecture Notes in Computer Science 243* by Springer-Verlag.

[49] Sacca, D. and Zaniolo, C., Implementation of Recursive Queries for a Data Language Based on Pure Horn Logic, *Proc. 4th Int. Conf. on Logic Programming*, University of Melbourne, May 1987.

[50] Sacks-Davis, R. and Ramamohanarao, K., A Two Level Superimposed Coding Scheme for Partial Match Retrieval, *Information Systems*, **8**, 273–280, 1983.

[51] Thom, J. A. and Zobel, J., (eds), NU-Prolog Reference Manual, Version 1.1, Technical Report 86/10, Department of Computer Science, University of Melbourne, 1986 (Revised April 1987).

[52] Thom, J. A., Naish, L., and Ramamohanarao, K., A Superjoin Algorithm for Deductive Databases, *Preprints of Workshop on Foundations of Deductive Databases and Logic Programming*, Washington, DC, August 1986, 118–135.

[53] Topor, R. W., Domain Independent Formulas and Databases, Technical Report 86/11, Department of Computer Science, University of Melbourne, Melbourne, Australia, 1986.

[54] Ullman, J. D., Implementation of Logical Query Languages for Databases, *ACM Trans. on Database Systems*, **10**, 289–321, 1985.

[55] Ullman, J. D., *Principles of Database Systems*, 2nd edn, Pitman, London, 1985.

[56] Vieille, L., Recursive Axioms in Deductive Databases: the Query/Subquery, Approach, *Proc. First Int. Conf. on Expert Database Systems*, Charleston, L. Kerschberg (ed.), 179–194, 1986 and Chapter 10 of this book.

[57] Warren, D. H. D., Efficient Processing of Interactive Relational Database Queries Expressed in Logic, *Proc. Seventh Int. Conf. on Very Large Databases*, Cannes, France, 1981, 272–281.

[58] Warren, D. S., Databases, Updates, in Pure Prolog, *Proc. 1984 Int. Conf. on Fifth Generation Computer Systems*, Tokyo, Japan, November 1984, 244–253.

[59] Wong, E. and Youssefi, K., Decomposition — a Strategy for Query Processing, *ACM Trans. on Database Systems*, **1**, 223–241, 1976.

[60] Zaniolo, C. and Krishnamurthy, R., Safety and Optimization of Horn Clause Queries, *Preprints of Workshop on Foundations of Deductive Databases and Logic Programming*, Washington, DC August 1986, 518–543.

[61] Zobel, J. and Ramamohanarao, K., Accessing Existing Databases from Prolog, Technical Report 86/17, Department of Computer Science, University of Melbourne, Australia, 1986.

14

An object-oriented database for storage and analysis of protein structure data

Norman W. Paton and Peter M. D. Gray,
Department of Computing Science, University of Aberdeen, King's College, Aberdeen, Scotland

ABSTRACT

In recent years, a number of new applications for database technology have emerged, such as CAD/CAM and software design. These new applications have led to the development of a number of domain dependent database systems, many of which are based on the object-oriented paradigm.

Protein structure data presents a number of challenges for the database designer, such as how best to represent ordered sequences and how to permit the incorporation of new insights into an existing database.

A Prolog interface to an object-oriented database has been developed with a view to the storage of protein structure data. Prolog modules provide an Abstract Data Type mechanism which is used to support objects and the methods over them, and data are held as linked structures in persistent storage. The schema used is an extension of the Functional Data Model.

In this chapter we discuss the characteristics a database for use with protein structure data should exhibit, describe our system based upon Prolog and the Functional Data Model, and illustrate its use with protein structure data.

1. INTRODUCTION

In the 1970s, the main thrust of database research was directed at the *relational data model* [1] which resulted in significant progress being made in several fields, including data modelling and the use of non-procedural languages. As the decade progressed, dissatisfaction was felt at the lack of expressiveness of the relational model for certain applications. This led to proposals for modifications to the basic model such as the *entity-relationship model* [2] and *RM/T* [3], and to proposals for completely new data models.

In the late 1970s a number of proposals were put forward for *functional data models* [4,5] which represent real-world objects as *entities*, and relationships between entities as *functions*. These and other *object-oriented* data models have brought a new range of application areas such as CAD/CAM [6] and software design [7] within the scope of database technology.

Running in parallel with, but largely separate from, the increasing interest in object-oriented data models was research into the relationship between logic and databases [8,9]. Much of the current interest in *expert database systems* [10] or *knowledge-based management systems* [11] in which artificial intelligence and database technologies are integrated centres upon implementations of logic and databases.

In this chapter we describe a system in which Prolog is used as the front-end to an object-oriented database, looking in particular at its suitability for use with protein structure data.

2. DATABASES FOR PROTEIN STRUCTURE ANALYSIS

2.1 Requirements

Before different categories of system can be compared it is necessary to have a set of criteria by which they can be judged. There follows a list of requirements which we feel are especially relevant for protein structure data.

1. The data model should include mechanisms which permit the schema to describe the semantics of the database. Adequate semantic expressiveness results in less complex schemas and queries [12].
2. The query language should be at a high level, powerful and easy to use. For biochemical applications, mathematical functions should be available and queries should be able to recognize an ordering in the data. Methods for computing derived data should be closely integrated with the data and easily extended.
3. It should be possible to integrate the database system with existing software for graphics and sequence analysis, and with artificial intelligence tools which are becoming available.
4. The schema should be extensible to permit the inclusion of new observations in an existing database.
5. It should be possible to view the data in the database from different levels of abstraction, so that a user who is interested in, for example, secondary structure topology need not wade through a sea of coordinate data when searching for strands which are antiparallel.

2.2 Relational databases

Relational databases have been, and are being, used for the storage of data on molecular structures [13,14]. Relational databases use proven technology, are easily understood and have high-level non-procedural query languages. We now consider relational databases in the light of the five requirements given in section 2.1.

1. As mentioned in the introduction, the relational model has been found to be lacking in semantic expressiveness for some applications. It is necessary to create *relationship relations* for modelling many-to-many relationships and there is no subtype–supertype hierarchy. The need to invent relations to model relationships results in large numbers of relations which often have to be *joined* by queries. The join operation in relational algebra is expensive in computing time, so complex queries may be prohibitively slow.
2. Relational query languages [15] are at a high level and are non-procedural (although they are often embedded in a conventional high-level language). However, they are often unsuitable for numerical computation and they regard relations as unordered sets. This last point means that given one residue in the sequence of a protein, there is no direct way of finding the *previous* or *next* residues.
3. The straightforward structure of relations is conducive to the sharing of data between software systems. Relational database systems have been coupled to graphics systems [13], but do not generally have data types rich enough to permit convenient tight coupling. Relational databases have been used as components in expert database systems [16], but object-oriented databases are more closely related to frame structures used in artificial intelligence.
4. Some recompilation is required when the schema of the database is modified. The ease with which this recompilation can take place is implementation dependent.
5. All relational database systems have some form of view mechanism.

2.3 Object-oriented databases

In object-oriented databases an attempt is made to map *real-world* objects and relationships directly into the representation scheme of the data model. In earlier data models it was often necessary to break up complex real-world objects to facilitate their storage using the more restrictive structures of the database [17]. There is also the concept of an *object-identifier* which is an internal reference to an object. The properties of an object are normally clustered together along with the object, in contrast to the domain or property centred clustering of relational databases.

In object-oriented programming systems, *methods* are pieces of code associated with a particular class of object. These methods are invoked when a *message* is *sent* to the object, and the approach used to obtain the result is hidden from the originator of the message. In the Prolog/FDM system as with most object-oriented programming systems, methods are stored along with the object descriptor, but the function invocation mechanism of DAPLEX replaces the message-sending scheme of the object-oriented programming paradigm.

There are many proposals for object-oriented databases. We shall concentrate here on our Prolog interface to an extension of the functional data model (FDM) [5] which is described in section 3.

1. Object-oriented databases are more semantically expressive than relational databases and have 'pre-computed' joins represented by relationship functions.
2. Prolog is more powerful than conventional relational query languages, as recursive relationships can be defined. Prolog has often been interfaced to relational database systems, but it can also be used as a *navigational* query language, guiding a search through a network of objects [18,19]. Prolog is not suitable for large numerical calculations, but calls can be made to PS-algol [20] from Prolog for computationally expensive tasks.
3. Relational views of the object-oriented database can be generated for use by other systems. Our Prolog system is interfaced to a *persistent heap* [21] in which data of any type can be stored. This facility could be used for the direct storage of graphical objects. As expert systems can be written in Prolog, a Prolog interface to a data base is a suitable starting point for building Expert Database System applications [22].
4. Our object-oriented database system is extensible in that new entity classes and functions can be added piecemeal.
5. Views of the database can easily be generated using Prolog clauses [23].

3. PROLOG/FDM OVERVIEW

3.1 Functional Data Model

The Functional Data Model has entities and functions as its basic notions. An *entity* or *object* is a token representing a real-world object. The properties of an entity are defined by single or multi-valued functions over the entity which can return scalars or entities. These multi-valued functions permit direct modelling of one:many and many:many relationships. Entity classes can be arranged in a generalization hierarchy such that the properties of a supertype are inherited by all its subtypes.

In the Prolog/FDM system (PFDM), functions over entity classes are represented by *methods* written in Prolog, and the result of the function can either be stored in the database or be derived at run-time.

In PFDM, functions can be declared which take scalar parameters and return entities. This facility permits direct representation of ordered sequences as required for protein data.

A possible representation of student *Bill Smith* who has *computing* as his *major_subject* was born in *1967* and takes courses *Computing* and *Mathematics* is given in Fig. 1. Note that the result of the *age* function is derived at run-time from *year_of_birth* rather than directly stored. In the diagram, each entity instance is given in capitals which denote its class (e.g. STUDENT).

3.2 System architecture

The PFDM system has three main components:

1. A core written in the database system language PS-algol. PS-algol data structures are used to hold the network of entities and relationships on

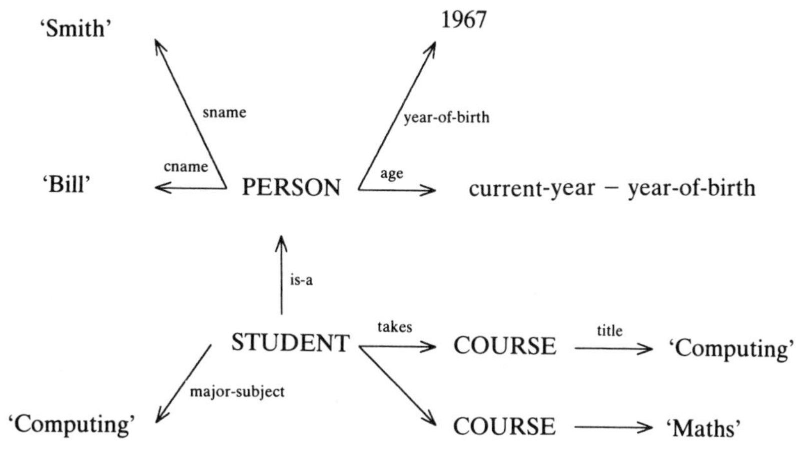

Fig. 1 — Semantic network of part of university database.

disk. This network is accessed by PS-algol routines called from Prolog and is completely transparent to the user.
2. Methods written in Prolog which are made available to the application programmer and which control Prolog's access to the network on disk.
3. Utilities such as parsers and routines for the bulk loading of data. These are written in Prolog and run as applications, rather than forming part of a large database kernel.

The architecture of the system is described in Figs. 2 and 3. Methods are available which permit:

1. Entity classes and the functions over them to be added and removed.
2. Entity instances and function values to be retrieved, modified and deleted, and entities to be accessed directly or sequentially.
3. The subtype of an entity instance to be obtained from its supertype.

3.3 Use of modules

In Persistent Prolog (Perlog) [24], local terms are used to provide an Abstract Data Type (ADT) mechanism by ensuring that all the methods for an ADT are in the one module and that all occurrences of the ADT are within the head of a method wrapped in local terms. This approach restricts the operations which can be applied to the ADT to the methods declared in its module, In the PFDM system, each entity class is viewed as an ADT to which the appropriate methods can be applied.

When a database module is created by parsing a schema such as that in Fig. 5, a set of default methods which perform the operations listed in section 3.2 are read into the module. Because the representation of the data is known only to the methods which are hidden from the application program, the form of representation can be changed without having to modify the application.

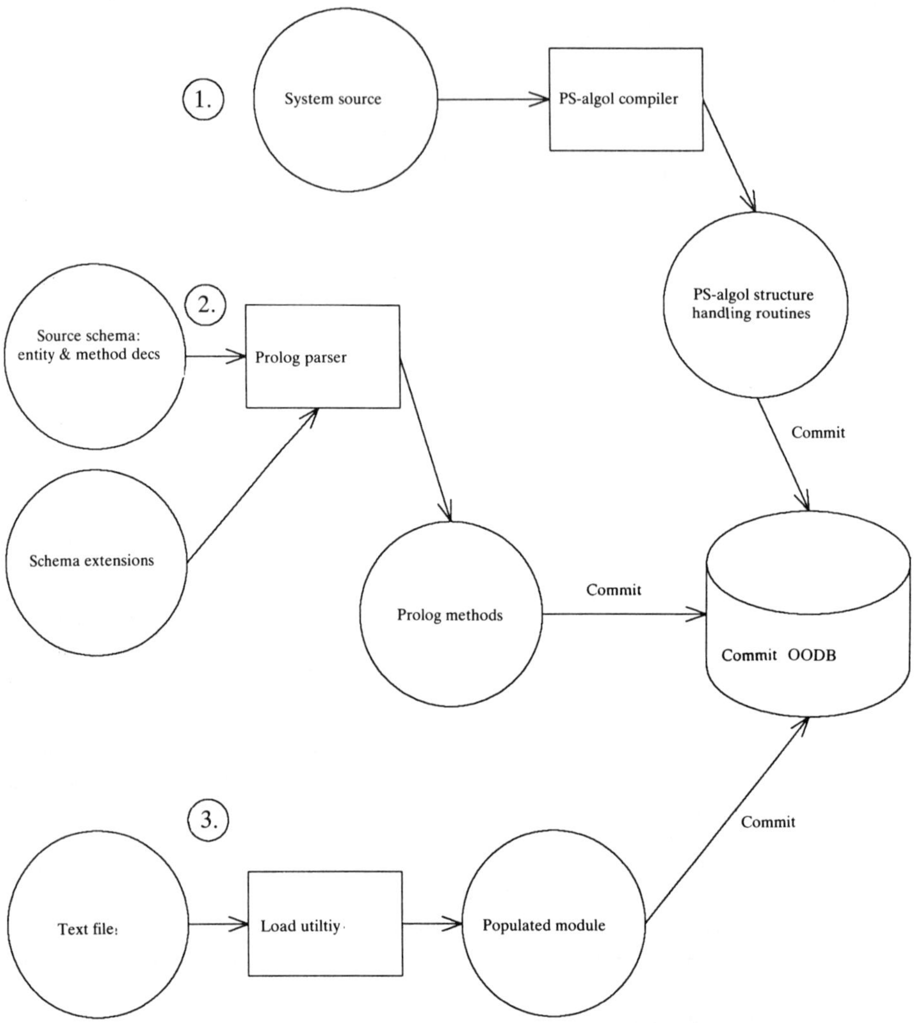

Fig. 2 — Database architecture: stages in the construction of a database. 1. System manager compiles PS-algol structure-handling code which is committed into a global database from which it can be called by Prolog. 2. The user enters Prolog and restores the FDM system. The parser is invoked on a schema file which contains module descriptions and declarations of entity classes. Modules created or updated by the parser are committed to separate databases. 3. The database is populated from data in load tables by a load utility written in Prolog which calls the methods defined in 2.

When a PFDM module is committed [25], the PS-algol data structures associated with the entity classes in the module are written to disk along with the Prolog methods. Thus PFDM is both structurally and behaviourally object-oriented in the sense used by Dittrich [17]. A database can be stored in several modules which may be restored independently or together, and links between modules can be created.

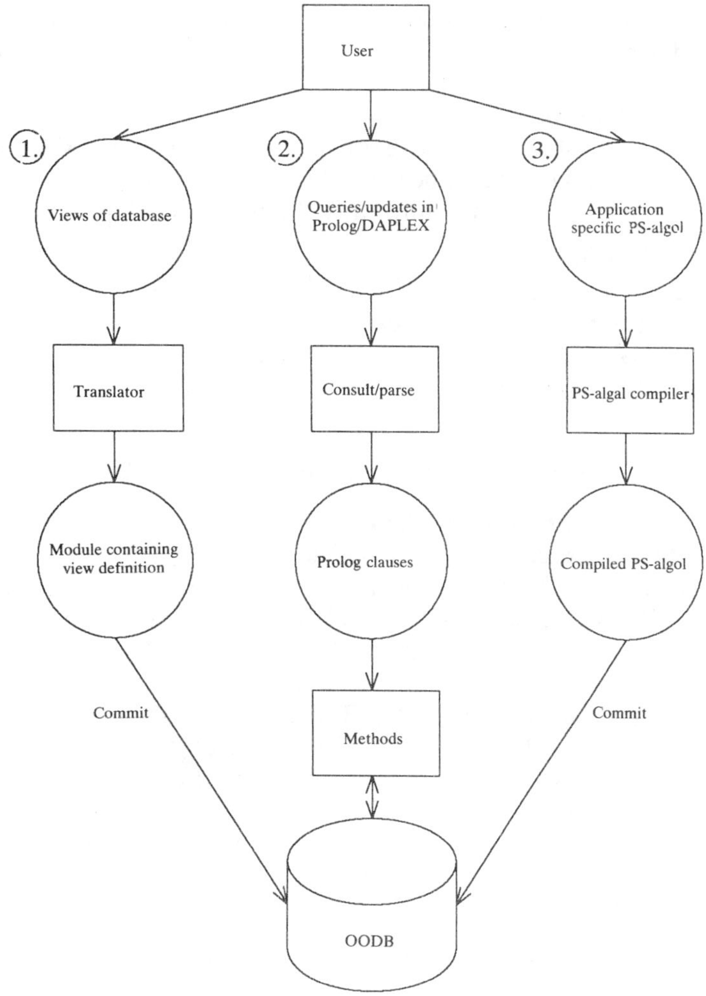

Fig. 3 — Using the database: 1. View definitions expressed in Prolog or DAPLEX are processed to produce Prolog modules describing a subset of the methods in one or more databases. 2. Queries or updates expressed in Prolog or DAPLEX access the database via the methods. 3. Application-specific PS-algol routines for computation or database access are compiled and committed into a global database.

3.4 Use of methods

In PFDM, methods expressed in Prolog are stored in modules along with the entity descriptors and instances of the classes to which they relate. User-defined methods are called using the same top-level predicates as the default methods which manipulate stored FDM data (e.g. getfunctionval, update-funtionval, getentity) and thus the two are indistinguishable to the application program. Methods can be arbitrarily complex and may call out to

PS-algol for calculations or to use non-standard storage techniques. A method for hydrogen-bond calculation on the protein structure database is described later.

3.5 User interface

One advantage of database systems based upon Prolog is that different views of the data can easily be defined and different front-ends produced. In our system there are presently three different ways of querying the database:

1. Directly in Prolog.
2. In a version of DAPLEX [5] which is parsed by a Prolog parser to generate a query in Prolog.
3. Using an interactive *database browser* running on a micro interfaced to the mini running the database.

4. A PROTEIN STRUCTURE DATABASE

4.1 Description of database

We are experimenting with a number of Proteins from the Brookhaven Databank [26] which contains data on protein structures obtained from X-Ray Crystallography. Brookhaven Databank files are first converted to Prolog clauses by an extended version of *CONVRT*, a Fortran program developed at ICRF to produce clauses suitable for the study of secondary topology using Prolog [27]. These data are then converted by a Prolog program to a form suitable for use by the load utility of the PFDM.

The Bachmann diagram for the FDM schema for this database is in Fig. 4, and the schema is in Fig. 5. In the schema, a double-headed arrow '->>' declares a multi valued relationship and a single headed arrow '->' declares a single-valued relationship.

Example 1

```
declare overlaps(structure) ->> structure
```

declares a multi-valued relationship between structures — one structure can overlap one or more other structures.

Example 2

```
declare protein_name(protein) -> string
```

declares a single-valued function on a protein returning a string. A protein can have at most one name.

Example 3

```
declare strand ->> structure
```

declares a new entity type strand which is a subtype of the entity type structure.

Example 4

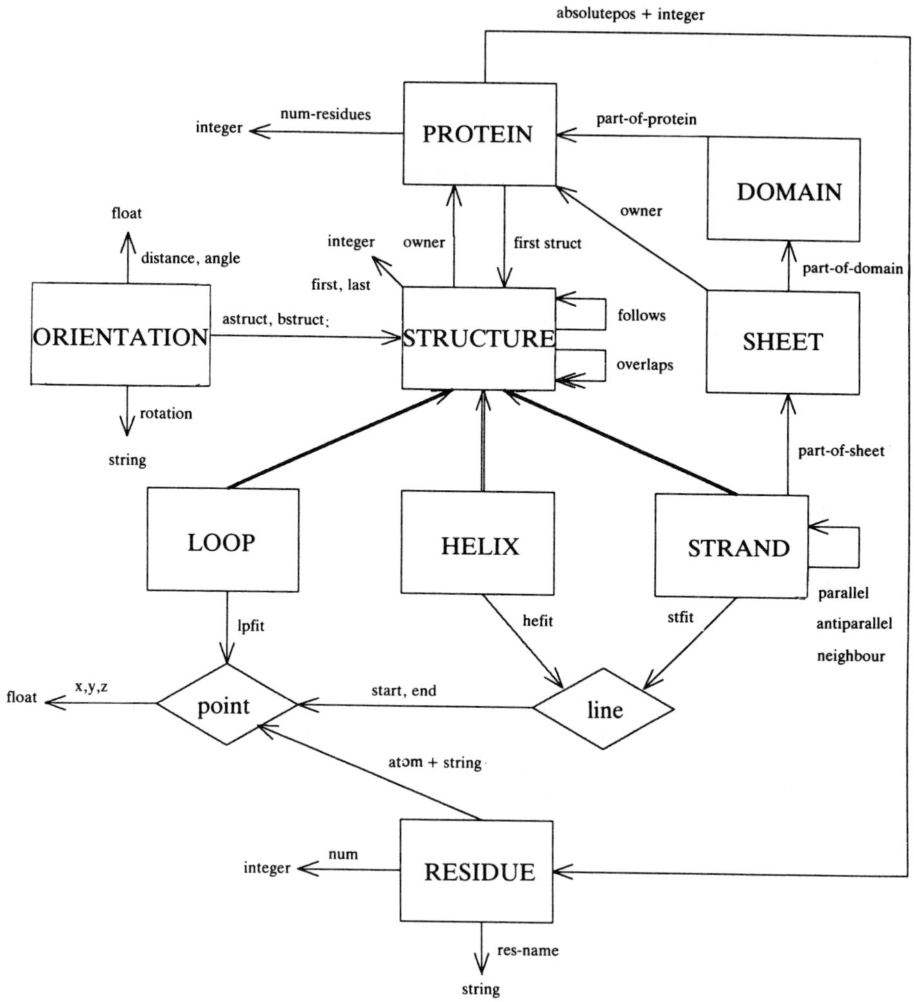

Fig. 4 — Bachmann diagram of schema.

declare absolutepos(protein,integer) -> residue

facilitates direct access to the residues in a Protein given an integer for the ordinal number of the residue.

Example 5
Keys can be compound and are defined in the schema using *key_of*. The statement

key_of domain is key_of(part_of_protein),domain_name

can be read as 'the key of an entity in class *domain* is obtained by

```
create module proteinb1 in proteindb1
    declare protein ->> entity
    declare domain ->> entity
    declare sheet ->> entity
    declare structure ->> entity
    declare orientation ->> entity

    declare strand ->> structure
    declare loop ->> structure
    declare helix ->> structure

    declare point ->> value_entity
    declare x(point) -> float
    declare y(point) -> float
    declare z(point) -> float

    declare line ->> value_entity
    declare start(line) -> point
    declare end(line) -> point

    declare first_struct(protein) -> structure

    declare astruct(orientation) -> structure
    declare bstruct(orientation) -> structure
    declare distance(orientation) -> float
    declare angle(orientation) -> float
    declare rotation(orientation) -> string

    declare owner(structure) -> protein
    declare first(structure) -> integer
    declare last(structure) -> integer
    declare follows(structure) -> structure
    declare overlaps(structure) ->> structure

    declare stfit(strand) -> line
    declare hefit(helix) -> line
    declare lpfit(loop) -> point

    declare protein_name(protein) -> string
    declare num_residues(protein) -> integer

    declare domain_name(domain) -> string
    declare sheet_name(sheet) -> string
    declare structure_name(structure) -> string

    declare parallel(strand) -> strand
    declare antiparallel(strand) -> strand
    declare neighbour(strand) -> strand

    declare part_of_sheet(strand) -> sheet
    declare part_of_domain(sheet) -> domain
    declare part_of_protein(domain) -> protein

    key_of protein is protein_name
    key_of domain is key_of(part_of_protein), domain_name
    key_of sheet is key_of(part_of_domain), sheet_name
    key_of structure is key_of(owner), structure_name
    key_of orientation is key_of(astruct), key_of(bstruct)
end_module
```

Fig. 5 — Schema of protein database (continued next page).

```
create module proteindb2 in proteindb2
    declare residue ->> entity
    declare part_of(residue) -> string
    declare num(residue) -> integer
    declare res_name(residue) -> string
    declare atom(residue,string) -> point
    key_of residue is part_of, num
end_module
extend module proteindb1
    declare absolutepos(protein,integer) -> residue
end_module
extend module proteindb1
    define point_to_coords(point) -> plog
    define distance(point,point) -> float
    consult methods file "dist"
end_module
extend module proteindb2
    define hydrogen_bonded(residue) -> plog
    consult methods file "hb"
end_module
```

Fig. 5 (continued from previous page) — Schema of protein database.

concatenating the key of the entity which is returned by *part_of_protein (domain)* onto the scalar value returned by *domain_name(domain)*'.

The database is stored in separate modules as an aid to updating. Entity classes and functions are associated with particular modules by the *create module* statement in the schema. The schema of an existing database can be extended with new entity classes and functions using *extend module* as in Fig. 5.

In the Bachmann diagram given in Fig. 4, entities are shown in rectangles and *value-entities* in rhombi. Value-entities are keyless entities used to represent compound scalars. Single-line arrows with single heads represent single-valued functions and single-line arrows with double heads represent multi-valued functions. Double-line arrows point from a subtype to its supertype. All single-argument functions between entities are invertible.

Prolog queries can trace their way along any single-line arrow in the diagram using the *getfunctionval* method and can start at any entity using *getentity*.

A method has been written which uses a heuristic search technique to find hydrogen bonding between backbone residues in proteins stored using the schema given in Fig. 4. Given a residue, the algorithm steps outward along the sequence in both directions looking for backbone atoms which are close enough in space to form hydrogen bonds with atoms planar to the α-carbon of the given residue. A prolog term is returned which indicates which remote residue is bonded to which local atom. It is assumed that the coordinates of hydrogen atoms are not stored in the database. The size of step along the sequence is calculated using the simple rule

step size = (distance from start)/(max distance between residues)

The schema which is parsed to declare the methods used is in Fig. 5, and the top-level Prolog code of the method is in Fig. 6.

5. APPLICATIONS OF THE PROTEIN DATABASE

5.1 Previous work with Prolog

Prolog has already been used by protein chemists for studying sequence data [28] and for representing and reasoning about protein structures [27,29]. We are primarily concerned with storing and analysing data relating to the proteins whose structures are known (about 200) rather than with pattern-based scans of the much larger sequence databanks. The work of Rawlings and co-workers shows that Prolog clauses can conveniently be used to hold data from the Brookhaven Databank and illustrates the suitability of Prolog for analysing secondary-structure topology. Our work is complementary to this in that we also use Prolog as a query language, but represent data using the object-oriented paradigm, rather than as Prolog unit clauses in a more relational style.

Traditionally, protein chemists have examined protein structures using complex graphics systems designed for molecular modelling. These systems are ideal for viewing and modelling single proteins, but are not well suited to answering questions over many structures. We envisage that the protein chemist will work with the database and graphics systems concurrently, studying a structure on the screen then asking the database if it can find something related to his particular interest. Data retreived from the database can be sent for displaying via a UNIX† socket to the graphics system.

For instance, when modelling the structure of a new protein from the structure of a homologous protein, insertions are particularly difficult to handle [30]. The database will permit the protein chemist to search for lengths of sequence, the structure of which is retrieved and displayed.

† UNIX is a trademark of Bell Laboratories.

```
hydrogen_bonded(residue,get,Residue,Result) :-
  check_type(Residue,residue,Residue),
  getfunctionval(part_of,Residue,PName),
  getentity(protein,PName,Prot),
  getfunctionval(num_residues,Prot,NumResidues),
  % assert start of queue of candidates
  retractall(hb_queue(_,_,_,_)),
  getfunctionval(num,Residue,Num),
  (Num \== 1 ->
        % look at earlier Residues
        Previous is Num-1,
        getfunctionval(absolutepos,Prot,Previous,Res1),
        assert(hb_queue(Previous,-1,3,Res1))
  ;
        true
  ),
  (Num \== NumResidues ->
        % look at subsequent Residues
        Next is Num+1,
        getfunctionval(absolutepos,Prot,Next,Res2),
        assert(hb_queue(Next,1,3,Res2))
  ;
        true
  ),
  planar_backbone_coords(Prot,Residue,Num,NCoords,CCoords, OCoords),
  hbond_pos(CCoords,OCoords,NCoords,HCoords),
  find_hydrogen_bonds(CCoords,NCoords,OCoords,HCoords,Prot, Result).

  % Given the coordinates of the planar backbone atoms associated with
  % a residue, and the name of the Prot, look for Hydrogen bonds on
  % both the C=0 and N-H atoms

  find_hydrogen_bonds(CCoords,NCoords,OCoords,HCoords,Prot, Result) :-
    retract(hb_queue(RNum,Direction,Distance,CurrResidue)),
    (Distance<7, % have a closer look
      planar_backbone_coords(Prot,CurrResidue,RNum,CurrN, CurrC,CurrO),
      hbond_pos(CurrC,CurrO,CurrN,CurrH),
      % check closeness of residues
      (distance(CurrH,OCoords,D1), D1<1.0, Result=hbond(CurrResidue,o);
        distance(HCoords,CurrO,D2), D2<1.0, Result=hbond(CurrResidue,h);
        % move on to next one
        NextPos is RNum+Direction,
        getfunctionval(absolutepos,Prot,NextPos,NextResidue),
        getfunctionval(atom,NextResidue,c,NextC),
        getfunctionval(point_to_coords,NextC,NextCC),
        distance(NextCC,CCoords,NextDist),
        assertz(hb_queue(NextPos,Direction,NextDist,NextResidue)),
        find_hydrogen_bonds(CCoords,NCoords,OCoords,HCoords, Prot,Result));
  % no bond, move along suitable amount
  PlacesToMove is Distance/3.0, integer(PlacesToMove,IPlacesToMove),
  NewPlace is RNum+IPlacesToMove*Direction,
  getfunctionval(absolutepos,Prot,NewPlace,NextResidue),
  getfunctionval(atom,NextResidue,c,NextC),
  getfunctionval(point_to_coords,NextC,NextCC),
  distance(NextCC,CCoords,NextDist),
  assertz(nb_queue(NewPlace,Direction,NextDist,NextResidue)),
  find_hydrogen_bonds(CCoords,NCoords,OCoords,HCoords, Prot,Result)).
```

Fig. 6 — Hydrogen-bonded method.

5.2 Future directions

In recent years, interest has grown in knowledge-based methods for protein structure prediction [31], and artificial intelligence (AI) techniques are being applied to the structure prediction problem [32]. We believe that an information system can be built in which the protein chemist is given a consistent view of data from a range of sources. Traditionally, protein structure data have only been accessible to protein chemists with expensive graphics systems, but the advent of databases of protein structures will extend the number of users and the type of use made of Brookhaven Databank data.

The increased availability of Brookhaven Databank data should increase the level of understanding of protein structures and help in the formulation and verification of rules for molecular modelling along the lines of those for loops [14].

ACKNOWLEDGEMENTS

This work is partly supported by grant GR/D/32765 from the UK Science and Engineering Research Council.

The authors are grateful to Dave Moffat for his contributions to the design of the database, to Chris Rawlings and ICRF for supplying the protein structure data and to John Fothergill for increasing our understanding of protein chemistry.

REFERENCES

[1] Codd, E. F., A Relational Model of Data for Large Shared Data Banks, *Comm. ACM*, **13**, 377–387.

[2] Chen, P. S., The Entity-relationship Model — Towards a Unified View of Data, *ACM–TODS,* **1**, 9–36, 1976.

[3] Codd, E. F., Extending the Database Relational Model to Include More Meaning, *ACM–TODS,* **4**, 397–434, 1979.

[4] Buneman, P. and Frankel, R. E., FQL — A Functional Query Language, *Proc. SIGMOD 79*, 52–59, 1979

[5] Shipman, D., The Functional Data Model and the Data Language DAPLEX, *ACM–TODS,* **6**, 140–173, 1981.

[6] Ketabchi, M. A. and Berzins, V., Modelling and Managing CAD Databases, *IEEE Computer*, 93–102, February 1987.

[7] Mylopoulos, J., Bernstein, P. A., and Wong, H. K. T., A Language Facility for Designing Database Intensive Applications, *ACM–TODS,* **5**, 185–207, 1980.

[8] Warren, D. H. D., Efficient Processing of Interactive Relational Queries Expressed in Logic, *Proc. 7th VLDB*, Cannes, 272–281, 1981.

[9] Gallaire, H., Minker, J. and Nicolas, J.-M., Logic and Databases: A Deductive Approach, *ACM Computing Surveys,* **16**, no. 2, 153–185, 1984.

[10] Kerschberg, L. (ed.), *Proc. First Int. Workshop on Expert Systems*, 1984.

[11] Brodie, M. L. and Mylopoulos, J., On Knowledge Base Management Systems, Springer-Verlag, 1986.
[12] Atkinson, M. P. and Kulkarni, K. G., Experimenting with the Functional Data Model, in *Databases — Role and Structure*, Stocker, Gray and Atkinson (eds.), 311–338, Cambridge University Press, 311–338, 1984.
[13] Todd, S., Morffew, A., and Burridge, J., Application of Relational Database and Graphics to the Molecular Sciences, *Proc. 3rd British Nat. Conf. on Databases*, Longstaff (ed.), 1–13, 1984.
[14] Blundell, T. L., Barlow, B. L., Sibanda, J. M., Thornton, J. M., Taylor, W., Tickle, I. J., Sternberg, M. J. E., Pitts, J. E., Haneef, I. and Hemmings, A. M., Three-dimensional Structural Aspects of the Design of New Protein Molecules, *Phil. Trans. Roy. Soc.,* **317**, 333–344, 1986.
[15] Date, C. J., *Introduction to Database Systems*, Vol. 1, 4th edn. Addison-Wesley, Reading, MA, 1986.
[16] Sciore, E. and Warren, D. S., Towards an Integrated Database–Prolog System, *First Int. Workshop on Expert Database Systems*, Kerschberg (ed.), 1984.
[17] Dittrich, K. R., Object-oriented Database Systems: the Notion and the Issues, *Proc. Int. Workshop on Object-oriented Database Systems*, Dittrich and Dayal (eds.), 2–4, 1986.
[18] Zaniolo, C., Prolog: A Database Query Language for All Seasons, *Proc. First Int. Workshop on Expert Database Systems*, Kerschberg (ed.), 1984.
[19] Gray, P. M. D., Efficient Prolog Access to Codasyl and FDM Databases, *Proc. ACM–SIGMOD*, Navathe (ed.), 437–443, 1985.
[20] Atkinson, M. P., Bailey, P., Cockshott, W. P., Chisholm, K. J., and Morrison, R., Progress with Persistent Programming, in *Databases — Role and Structure*, Stocker, Gray and Atkinson (eds.), Cambridge University Press, 245–310, 1984.
[21] Moffat, D. S. and Gray, P. M. D., Interfacing Prolog to a Persistent Data Store, *3rd Int. Conf. on Logic Programming*, London, E. Shapiro (ed.), 577–584, Springer-Verlag, 1986.
[22] Gray, P. M. D., Integration of Databases and Expert Systems through Prolog, presented at AI Conference, San Sabastian (Sept. '87).
[23] Gray, P. M. D., *Logic, Algebra and Databases*, Ellis Horwood, Chichester, 1984.
[24] Moffat, D. S. and Gray, P. M. D., Perlog: A Prolog with Persistence and Modules, *Computer J.,* **31**, 110–115, 1988.
[25] Moffat, D. S., Modular Commitment in Persistent Prolog, see Chapter 15 of this book.
[26] Bernstein, F. C., *et al.*, Protein Data Bank: A Computer-based Archival File for Macromolecular Structures, *J. Mol. Biol.* **112**, 535–542, 1977.
[27] Rawlings, C. J., Taylor, W. R., Nyakairu, J., Fox, J., and Sternberg, M. J. E., Using Prolog to Represent and Reason about Protein Structure, *Proc. 3rd Int. Conf. on Logic Programming*, Shapiro (ed.), 536–543, 1986.

[28] Lyall, A., Hammond, P., Brough, D., and Glover, D., BIOLOG — a DNA Sequence Analysis System in Prolog, *Nucleic Acids Research,* **12**, no. 1, 633–642, 1984.

[29] Morffew, A. J. and Todd, S. J. P., The Use of Prolog as a Protein Querying Language, *Computers and Chemistry,* **10**, no. 1, 9–14, 1986.

[30] Feldmann, R. J., Bing, D. H., Potter, M., Mainhart, C., Furie, B., Furie, B. C. and Caporale, L. H., On the Construction of Computer Models of Proteins by the Extension of Crystallographic Structures, *Annals, N.Y. Acad. Sci.,* **439**, 12–43, 1985.

[31] Blundell, T. L., Sibanda, B. L., Sternberg, M. J. E., and Thornton, J. M., Knowledge-based Prediction of Protein Structures and Design of Novel Molecules, *Nature,* **326**, 347–352, 1987.

[32] Hayes-Roth, B., Buchanan, B., Lichtarge, O., Hewett, M., Altman, R., Brinkley, J., Cornelius, C., Duncan, B., and Jardetzky, O., Protean: Deriving Protein Structures from Constraints, *Proc. AAAI-86*, 904–909, 1986.

15

Modular commitment in persistent Prolog

David S. Moffat
Systems Designers Ltd.† Pembroke House, Camberley, Surrey

ABSTRACT

Commitment in a Persistent Language is the atomic operation which copies new and updated objects to disk. In early implementations, persistence commitment had a global scope in that *all* touched objects were copied to disk but when the system supports interactive updates where users may make many exploratory changes, as is the case in Prolog, a selective commit is required. The obvious solution is to specify the database roots from which the transitive commit algorithm must start. However, users of the new commit must be more aware of exactly what objects are reachable from the database roots since unnoticed references may result in committing objects unintentionally. In Perlog [1], a Prolog with persistence, modules serve both as program name spaces and as the unit of commitment. Committing a module has the effect of copying all the clauses from the named area of the clause base to a persistent database. Thus having modules as the unit of commitment allows us to project the run-time name space onto the persistent store. This chapter discusses Perlog's modules and their role in commitment.

1. INTRODUCTION

Relational databases (RDBs) are easily modelled in Prolog by having unit clauses as tuples and by using Prolog queries as a domain-oriented relational calculus and consequently much work has been done to investigate interfacing RDBs to Prolog from both a database and a logic programming perspective. Gallaire [2] and Jarke [3] are good summary papers in this area. However, there are many types of object that do not fit easily into the relational model, e.g. lists, nested terms structures, semantic networks, bitmaps and vectors, and so we have investigated the utility of a generalized object store for Prolog.

† Formerly at the Department of Computing Science, University of Aberdeen.

PS-algol [4] is a procedural-based programming language that makes persistence an orthogonal property of all objects in the language. Underlying PS-algol is a Persistent Objective Management System (POMS) [5] that manages the transfer of heap objects to and from disk. The POMS can recover from aborted transactions, supports concurrency and only retrieves objects incrementally as and when their disk pointers are dereferenced. The intention is that a programming language that provides persistence for all its data types will ease the building of database applications. It has already been used to implement the Extended Functional Data Model [6].

In the Perlog project [1,7,8] we have made persistence a property of all Prolog objects and have also interfaced Prolog to PS-algol. Its architecture is illustrated in Fig. 1. The POMS has been separated out from the PS-algol

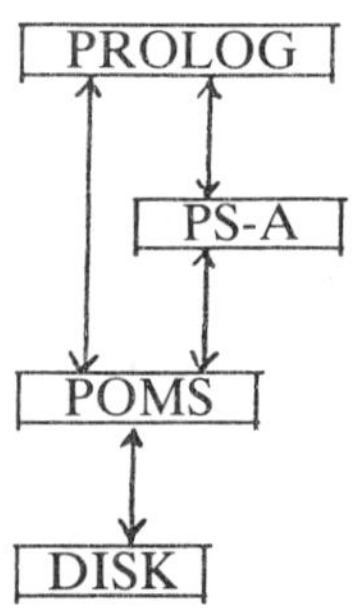

Fig. 1.

interpreter and direct links forged between it and the Prolog interpreter [9]. The data structures used by Prolog were modified to include self-describing information to be acceptable to the POMS. Several Prologs already had a *save* predicate that made complete core dumps of the interpreter's internal state, and the Prolog: POMS interface can be seen as a sophisticated version of these. It works at the level of a module rather than the entire clause base, restores incrementally, supports concurrent access, and has a recovery mechanism.

The interface between Prolog and PS-algol is a tightly coupled one, communication being at the level of object rather than text, and alternative solutions can be passed back to Prolog in the backtracking manner — Moffat [7] explains this in more detail. We have used the PS-algol component for coding tasks more suited to a procedural programming language, e.g. special hashing algorithms.

This chapter looks more closely at commitment across the Prolog:POMS interface and how this relates to modules. The next section presents a model of modules in Perlog. Section 3 gives an example of the utility of modules — specifically how they can be used to support Abstract Data Types (ADTs).

Section 4 gives details of updates to modules. Section 5 describes the issues of commitment. Section 6 describes details of Perlog's implementation. A conclusion is given in section 7.

2. MODULES IN PERLOG

Prolog started out as a flat language where all procedures resided in the same name space, but with large applications, some kind of modularity is required. There have already been many implementations of modules in Prolog that have aimed at partitioning the name space: Perlog has this goal too but is also concerned with making modules an abstraction of the persistent partitions on secondary store.

There are many Prolog systems with modules, but disregarding their superficial differences they fall into two camps. There are Predicate Based (PB) systems [10,11] where predicates are all associated with particular module spaces, while terms and atoms belong to the one global space. This means that terms used as data have the same representation in all modules, but when they are used as arguments to meta-predicates they have to be assigned a module context. This coercion of terms in modularized predicates complicates meta-call and turns out to be quite dangerous, as it can be used to call predicates that were not even exported and to assert clauses into any module. The alternative is to have an Atom Based (AB) system [1,13] where all data and procedural structures with the same name in the same module share the same atom symbol in their representation. This ensures that they have the same scope and gives meta-call a simpler semantics. The AB system is more general than the PB one in that it makes name hiding available to data as well as to procedures. In the next section it is shown how this can be used as a foundation for an ADT facility.

In Perlog, individual modules can be committed and later restored into different module configurations, so it is important that they can be easily decoupled from each other and easily linked back. To achieve this, an extra level of indirection is maintained, whereby all objects in a module are represented by *immediate* symbols that are independent of other modules. In order that modules are not totally isolated, symbols that have been designated as *global* have references to shared symbols in a public module and symbols for imported names have references into the modules that actually make the exports. Unification has been extended to check the equality of the shared symbols when immediate symbols are unequal and *call* does an extra indirection when it handles imported predicates. In order that the origin of an object may be found, all symbols have a reference back to their own symbol table.

A desire for independent module commits has resulted in modules having their own symbol tables. With separate symbols, objects from different modules can always be told apart and so this also provides a good basis for implementing an AB system.

3. LOCAL TERMS AS ADTs

ADTs are used as a means of ensuring a modular approach to programming. The data types' representations are hidden within a module and only one set of predicates, called the ADT methods, are supplied which can manipulate objects of the type. All access to the ADT has to go via these method predicates.

Since local terms will not unify with templates from other modules they can be used as structures in which to hide type representations. Consider the following example where a module *m* has a type representation for some object and provides two methods for accessing it.

```
module m.

export newobj, method1, method2.
local t.

newobj(X, t(Y)) :- mk_obj(X, Y).
method1(t(X), A, B) :- .....
method2(t(X), t(Y)) :- .....

endmod.
```

The *export* declaration makes its arguments available for importing into other modules. *Newobj* will be called from outside with its first argument bound and it returns some object *Y* hidden inside *t/1*. This local term can be passed about in the caller's environment but its internal details cannot be dicovered by unification. If the local term is used as an argument to either *method1* or *method2* then the object contents become accessible again. Data hiding has been achieved by ensuring that the objects concerned do not pass out of the module without the protection of a local term.

This is not a formal ADT mechanism but can be seen as a primitive for implementing one. Furukawa *et al.* [14] discuss a Prolog with compulsory ADTs that could be built upon local terms. In Gray *et al.* [8] the concept of ADTs is taken much further as a programming technique in the domain of the Functional Data Model.

4. UPDATING MODULES

Updates are achieved by use of the built-in predicates, assert and retract. They complicate the semantics of Prolog and rarely have identical behaviour in different implementations but none the less are essential for many applications. They are used for saving values over backtracking, as in the case of setof; for simulating global variables, e.g. tracing and debugging toggles; for making direct edits to the program and most importantly for assimilating new knowledge. Examples of adding knowledge occur in learning programs, user modelling and experimenting with possible worlds.

In an AB system the destination module of an assert is determined by the modularity of its argument. An assert of an imported term adds a clause to the exporting module, and an assert of a local term adds a clause to the module whence it came. In Perlog the level of indirection between imported and exported predicates means that external asserts into a module can be distinguished from its own internal ones and it is possible to declare a module to be write-protected from either external or internal updates. When local terms occur as arguments to export predicates, as in the method example above, they can get passed out to other modules where they are termed *foreign locals*. If they are data objects they act as impenetrable structures, and if they are procedures they act as absolute references to the local procedures. Foreign locals can be included as arguments to dynamically asserted local clauses, as they could quite legitimately be representing some ADT defined in another module. A module that contains a new foreign local can only be committed to disk if the home module of the foreign local is also being committed, otherwise the two modules would become inconsistent.

5. COMMITMENT

The POMS maintains a heap that is central to the mechanics of persistence. When the POMS is asked to make a *commit*, it copies to disk all new and updated objects that are reachable from the root of its heap. The languages that sit atop the POMS build up their data structures from its heap objects if they want them to have the opportunity to persist. All the structures used to represent code in Perlog are POMS heap objects, but the control stacks are not because they could not be efficiently represented and more importantly because they have a global scope across modules.

There is a *table* data structure in PS-algol that can store values under scalar keys and it is convenient for building simple database applications. When the contents of a table are relatively flat it is quite easy for a programmer to comprehend exactly what is being committed, but if a complex network of objects has been constructed then the extent may not be clear.

A failing with the current commit algorithm [5] is that it is global across the whole heap and either none or all updated objects are copied to disk. This denies the possibility of saving some valid updates made to one database while ignoring erroneous or trial ones made to another. In principle there is nothing to prevent the commit procedure accepting a list of database names from which to start the transitive closure and hence have selective commits, but still programmers have to be aware of the full extent of a possibly complex heap. The problem is that new objects are allocated Persistent Identifiers (PIDs), or disk pointers, from the same database as the last visited object during the computation of the closure, and if new objects can be reached from different database origins one has little control over where they are finally placed on persistent store. As an extreme example, if a new database is created and populated and before it is committed another database is given a reference into it, then at commit time it is possible that the contents of the new database will be 'sucked' over into the other one. In order that cross-database references can easily be followed, each database records the other databases that it can reach and when the POMS is asked to open a particular database it will also open every other reachable database. Since databases are the write-lockable units of concurrency, establishing the correct inter-dependencies is very important. The problem with PS-algol is that databases have a real significance with respect to data sharing but there is no way of explicitly associating objects with particular databases.

In Prolog the only concept of store is the clause base into which clauses are asserted. Since all objects are represented by immediate symbols that have references back to their module symbol table, it is always clear to which module a clause belongs and therefore the module is the obvious unit for establishing object:database relationships. Also, modules have low cohesion between themselves and are easily separated. There is a built-in predicate *persistas(Module)* that associates a new module with a PS-algol database. Modules and databases are usually 1 to 1 although groups of modules can be packaged up in the same database but they are then subject to having the same read and write access modes. There are the predicates *create_mod(ModName)* and *create_db(DbName, Pass)* which create new modules and databases respectively. Modules that have been connected to a database by persistas can be committed either by being in the argument list of *commit/1* or by *commit_all/0*. The *restore* predicate is used for opening modules that have been previously committed and making them available to Prolog.

6. IMPLEMENTATION

Figure 2 illustrates a selection of the data structures used by the interpreter to represent a module and its clauses. From the symbol table hangs two *term blocks*. Each term block has a *module* pointer back to its symbol table and a *chars* pointer to the characters that make up its name. If a term occurs as the head of a clause its term block has a *clause* pointer that points to a *head:body* pair and thence a representation of the head's arguments and the components of the body. If there is no definition for a body component within the same module, its term block has an *import* pointer into another module's symbol table. *Arg2* is an example of a foreign local that is represented in some other module's table. So the diagram represents something of the form A:−B,C, where A has two arguments, the second of which is a foreign local, and B is imported.

When a module is committed, the symbol table is taken as the root for transitive closure. The network of heap objects seems far reaching but really it is very self-contained since the only external pointers are those for imports and foreign locals. The POMS commit algorithm has been extended to cope with these external pointers. Imports get written to disk if they were nil (uninstantiated) pointers so that restored modules are independent of previous bindings. Foreign locals must be preserved on disk and they lead the commit algorithm to term blocks in other symbol tables. If such a foreign term block is a new object or an updated old one, it has to be written to disk

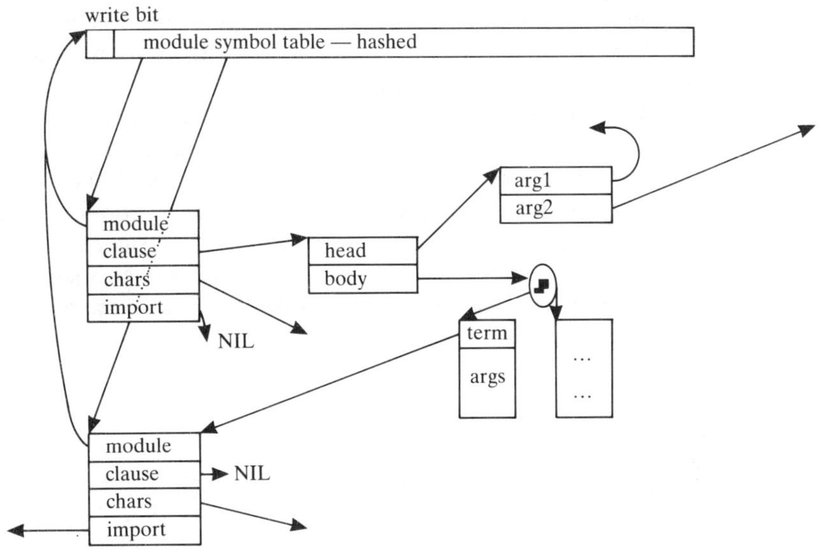

Fig. 2. — Data structures of Perlog.

and it is an error if its module is not on the commit list. If the foreign local is new then it must be allocated a PID and instead of making it go into the same database as the current module its own *module* pointer is used to find out where it should go.

The crux of the implementation is that the units of commitment are relatively disjoint but those objects that are shared between modules have references back to their home module so that they can be placed in the correct database.

In order to get an idea of the performance of modular commitment it is compared with CProlog's save command which creates core images, although these core images cannot be shared and do not have the same range of types as found in persistent databases. The POMS does its I/O in object-sized amounts and so is much slower than save for the initialization of a persistent state, but for subsequent access it out performs save if the hit rate is less than 10%.

7. CONCLUSION

In Prolog where a program is actually a database of clauses, modules serve both as program and as database units. To enable modules to be flexibly recombined most external references are severed when they are committed and have to be relinked by name when they are restored. Our version of ADTs where type representations are hidden inside local terms can produce foreign local references when ADTs occur as arguments to facts asserted dynamically. These foreign locals cannot be severed and could give problems if the internal representation of Prolog objects did not carry self-references to their own modules which are used by a modified commit algorithm to ensure that shared objects are allocated to the correct database. The allocation of new clauses to modules is well defined and gives users control of the placement of objects in persistent store. Before PS-algol could be used to implement a persistent system with interactive updates and modular commitment similar to Perlog it would need an *associate(object, database)* primitive that ensures an object is assigned to a particular database were a commitment to be made. In Perlog the association is made when the code is consulted in the context of a module or when new objects are read into specific modules.

ACKNOWLEDGEMENTS

I am grateful to Peter Gray for guidance throughout the Perlog Project, to Norman Paton for exercising the system and to Colin Campbell and Steve Messick for commenting on a draft of this chapter. This work was supported by a grant from the U.K. Science and Engineering Research Council.

REFERENCES

[1] Moffat, D., S. and Gray, P. M. D., Perlog: A Prolog with Persistence and Modules, to be published, *Computer J.*, special issue on Databases, 1987.

[2] Gallaire, H., Logic Data Bases vs Deductive Data Bases, *Proc. Logic Programming Workshop 1983*, Algarve, ed. L. M. Pereira, 1983.

[3] Jarke, M. and Vassiliou, Y., Coupling Expert Systems and Database Management Systems, in *Artificial Intelligence Applications for Business*, ed. W. Reitman, Ablex, Norwood, NJ, 1984.

[4] Atkinson, M. P., Bailey, P., Cockshott, W. P., Chisholm, K. J., and Morrison, R., Progress with Persistent Programming, in *Databases — Role and Structure*, Stocker, Gray and Atkinson (eds.), Cambridge University Press, 1984.

[5] Brown, A. L., CPOMS — A Revised Version of Persistent Object Management in C, PPR-13-85, Dept. of Computing Science, University of Glasgow, 1985.

[6] Kulkarni, K. G., Extended Functional Data Model — User Manual, PPR-7-83, Dept. of Computing Science, University of Glasgow, 1983.

[7] Moffat, D. S. and Gray, P. M. D., Interfacing Prolog to a Persistent Data Store, *3rd Int. Conf. on Logic Programming*, London, 1986.

[8] Gray, P. M. D., Moffat, D. S., and Paton, N., A Prolog Interface to a Functional Data Model Database, *Proc. EDBT*, Springer-Verlag, 1988.

[9] *C-Prolog User's Manual*, Pereira, F. C. N., *et al.*, EdCADD, Dept. of Architecture, University of Edinburgh, 1983.

[10] *SD-Prolog Reference Manual*, Systems Designers plc, Camberley, 1986.

[11] *Quintus Prolog 2.0 Release Notes for Beta-test*, Quintus Computer Systems, 1986.

[12] Atom Based Systems are More Secure, Working Paper, Alvey Logic Programming Environment Project, Systems Designers, 1987.

[13] Szeredi, P., Module Concepts for Prolog, SZKI, 1251 Budapest P.O.B. 19, 1983.

[14] Furukawa, N. and Yonezawa, Modularization and Abstraction in Logic Programming, ICOT Report TR-022, Tokyo, 1983.

Part V
Applications

16

A data-driven execution mechanism for transaction-oriented information systems

Raf Venken and **Daniel Donner**
BIM Research & Development, Kwikstraat 4, B-3078 Everberg, Belgium

ABSTRACT

This chapter briefly outlines the principal objectives and intermediate results of the ESPRIT Project, Rubric, which investigates how business rules can be captured, formalized and exploited in a software engineering environment for building transaction-oriented information systems. It then concentrates on the design level of this software engineering environment which is the basis for generating a rapid prototype of the information system. Further details are provided in describing the prototype architecture and its underlying data-driven execution mechanism.

1. INTRODUCTION

User demand for reliable computer systems, together with the realization that most failures are due to poor specifications and design, has resulted in the emergence of a number of information system methodologies and development environments. Despite their use, users continue to report long lead times, inadequate estimates and imperfect performance. The major shortcoming of these contemporary methods is said to be that the modelling of the real world, in which the application has to operate, is achieved only in information systems terms, i.e. in terms of processes and data rather than in appropriate real-world-oriented terms.

The Rubric project investigates an alternative approach to information system development based on the explicit capture and representation of business rules. This rule base should allow for a more effective system evolution, offering its direct exploitation in the running information system. This new paradigm finds its justification in the fact that a continuously maintained organization's knowledge base should support the development of the information system. In particular, business policies should be explicitly maintained and kept separate from the procedures and elementary operations which implement the policies.

At higher levels of the information system development environment, the Rubric project wants to build further on existing modelling techniques as adopted in information engineering and tries to combine them with novel techniques into an object-oriented framework. The modelling and analysis tools will be implemented using a Prolog-based frame system.

At the lower level, the prototype mechanisms and application generation of Rubric are based on two principles: a data-driven execution mechanism and object-oriented programming techniques. The interface between the prototype and the MMI is based on the same data-driven techniques underlying conventional spreadsheets. No explicit control information is specified; the execution is driven by declarative rules which describe the relationships between the fields on the screen and the internal data of the application. The interface with the database tries to extend the conventional database facilities with object-oriented facilities such as triggers, inheritance and object-oriented structuring.

This chapter describes the intermediate results of the ESPRIT Project, Rubric, as a whole focusing on how business rules can be captured, formalized and exploited in a software engineering environment for building transaction-oriented information systems. It then concentrates on the design level of this software engineering environment which is the basis for generating a rapid prototype of the information system. Further details are provided in describing the prototype architecture and its underlying data-driven execution mechanism.

2. THE RUBRIC PHILOSOPHY

The Rubric philosophy can be summarized in the following two statements.

1. Information system constructs must be defined in declarative terms.
2. The development must follow an object-oriented approach.

The first statement is an attempt to use a declarative approach for describing the static part (information structure, integrity constraints) as well as the dynamic part of the information systems (the behaviour of the system).

The second statement refers to the framework that needs to be followed by the developer when using the Rubric tools. The concept of an object, rather than functional analysis, drives an object-oriented development.

Five basic activities have been identified which constitute the Rubric paradigm:

(a) object definition and relationships between objects;
(b) definition of integrity constraints on these objects;
(c) definition of the objects' behaviour expressed in rules;
(d) definition of the objects' operational parameters;
(e) definition of the interaction between the rules.

We will not go into further detail concerning these five activities, but rather concentrate on one single aspect: how to capture the behavioural aspect of an information system and how this information can be exploited in a running system.

3. THE DYNAMICS OF AN INFORMATION SYSTEM

The whole Rubric project is centred around the concept of an object. So instead of partitioning a complex system following a functional decomposition approach, partitioning is effected on the object level. The behaviour of an object class is divided into smaller Object Behavioural Units (OBUs). Each OBU models part of the dynamic behaviour of the object class, while the total number of OBUs model the complete behaviour.

Each OBU contains so-called dynamic rules. They express how the OBU will react to signals arriving from the environment or from other OBUs: change the internal state of the information system by issuing signals to other OBUs or by invoking a transaction.

A dynamic rule has the following format:

WHEN signal IF preconditions THEN action_part

Because of the potential high volume of rules and the complexity of their inter-dependency, there is need for a higher level of abstraction. The proposed model to verify the inter-dependencies of dynamic rules is the augmented petri-net model. This model is based on sound mathematical foundations and is also suited for animation purposes. The augmented petri-net model has graphical facilities to represent the WHEN-and IF-part of the dynamic rules and the time-ordering of the rules.

This petri-net tool together with more conventional modelling tools such as E-R-diagrams will enable the analyst to define an application in a very declarative way. These graphical tools are implemented using a Prolog-based frame system. The information and knowledge entered by the analyst are stored in frames capturing the essential features of the system to be developed.

4. THE RUBRIC FRAMES AT DESIGN LEVEL

We give a few examples of the main frame types the Rubric system is able to capture and to represent at the design level of the application development:

```
Entity-frame : entity
   *relationship : entity
   constraint : expression
   derivation : expression
   subclass_of : entity

Relationship_frame : relationship
   from : entity
   to : entity
```

inverse_of : relationship
cardinality : expression

Integrity_frame : integrity
about : entity
constraint : expression

Context_frame : context
about : entity
dynamics : behavioural_units

Behavioural_unit_frame : behavioural_unit
context : context
dynamics : transaction rules

Transaction_rule_frame : transaction_rule
defined_in : behavioural_unit
when : trigger
if : precondition
then : transaction, signal

Trigger_frame : trigger
type : signal or clock
carries : entity

Transaction_frame : transaction
user_input : MMI_screen
data_view : data_view_expression
*access_right : database_entity
local : entity
constraint : expression
derivation : expression

Application_frame : application
combines : transaction_rule

These frames enable us to define OBUs that combine transaction rules (or dynamic rules). These rules describe the reaction of the information system to external triggers. These rules can be grouped into one or more applications. A transaction finally describes the behaviour of a system in terms of derivations on basic entities, fields on the screen and database tuples (Fig. 1).

The application controller handles user requests to start a transaction (Fig. 2). It finds the definition of the transactions in the Rubric frame system. The appropriate frame is handed over to the transaction interpreter, which is linked with the man–machine interface and the database.

5. THE TRANSACTION INTERPRETER

A transaction frame contains the following information:

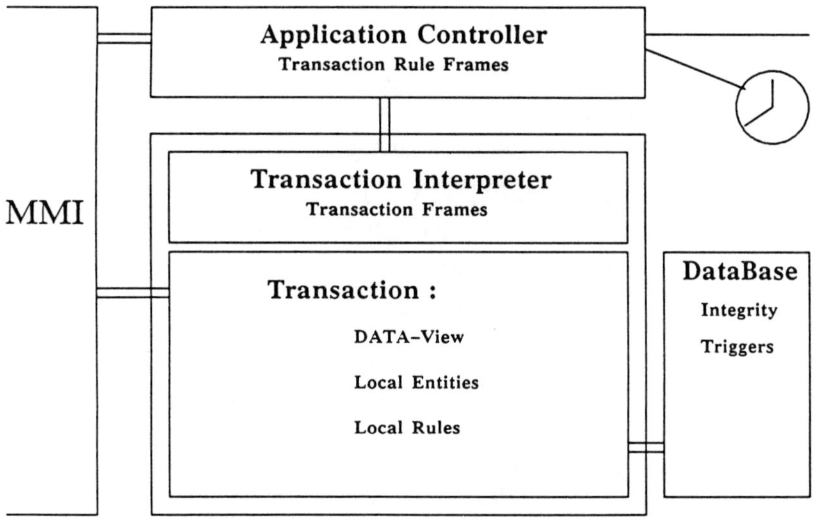

Fig. 1 — Rubric application architecture.

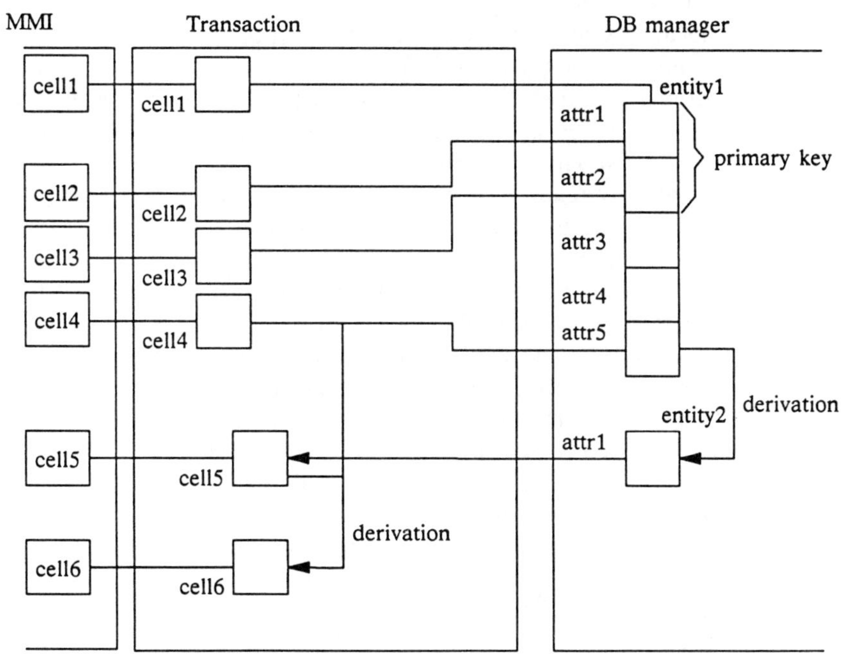

Fig. 2 — A graphical representation of a transaction.

TRANSACTION transaction_name TRIGGERED BY trigger

DATA VIEW:
{ cell_name: class_name, property_name }...

[ACCESS:
{ class_name: access_mode }...]

[LOCAL ENTITY:
{ cell_name: class_name, property_name }...]

[CONDITIONS:
{ logical expression }...]

[DERIVATIONS:
{ general derivation expression }...]

The Data View slot defines the cells appearing on the MMI-screen, which are linked with an attribute of an entity class in the database.

The Access slot defines the way an entity class in the database can be accessed: access_mode may be R (read), W (write) or RW (read and write).

The Local Entity slot defines local cells having no direct link with the database but used to hold temporary values which are not to be stored in the database.

The Conditions slot contains additional integrity constraints to be verified (e.g. involving the local entities), while the Derivations slot allows for local derivations to be expressed about the accessible cells.

The execution mechanism underlying the transaction interpreter is inspired by the execution mechanism of conventional spreadsheets. In these spreadsheets the user is able to define two types of cells: value-cells and derived cells. The user can input a value in the first type and the system automatically generates the values for the second type, using the derivations entered by the user in terms of mathematical expressions involving both types of cell.

The same execution mechanism applies to the Transaction Interpreter, except that possibly not all relevant cells are displayed on the screen, e.g. the local entities, some attributes of the database entities. There are also different types of rules expressed between the different cells: data-views, very general derivation rules, integrity constraints. These are invoked whenever values become available in the different cells, e.g. the user supplies values in the MMI-fields, a value is derived from others, or the database comes back with the answers to queries.

The data-views describe the relationship between the fields on the screen and the data in the underlying database.

Some cells are linked with an attribute of an entity in the database (cell2 to cell4). Others (such as cell5) are linked with an entity which is derived from other entities in the database. The last type are local cells (cell6) which are derivable from other cells (in this case from cell4 and cell5).

A special type of cell is the control cell (cell1) which allows the user to specify which action he wants to undertake (read, write, modify, delete).

Finally there is a commit/abort button, such that the final user can validate or cancel the transaction currently being executed.

Executing a transaction is completely data driven: the actions are performed on the basis of derivations, links or integrity constraints which are expressed in terms of dependencies on internal or external cells.

This means that the derivations, the links with the database and the integrity constraints are executed as soon as the input values become available, leading to new values in other cells, an abort of the transaction or a database query, modify or delete to be executed, which leads also to possible new values in other cells.

6. A MORE DETAILED DESCRIPTION

Note that the interaction with the MMI from the transaction interpreter is restricted to asking values from the user. The MMI must respond with the name of the cell and the value. This allows for a wide range of MMIs to be used: full-screen, menu-driven or advanced graphics and multi-window interfaces (Fig. 3).

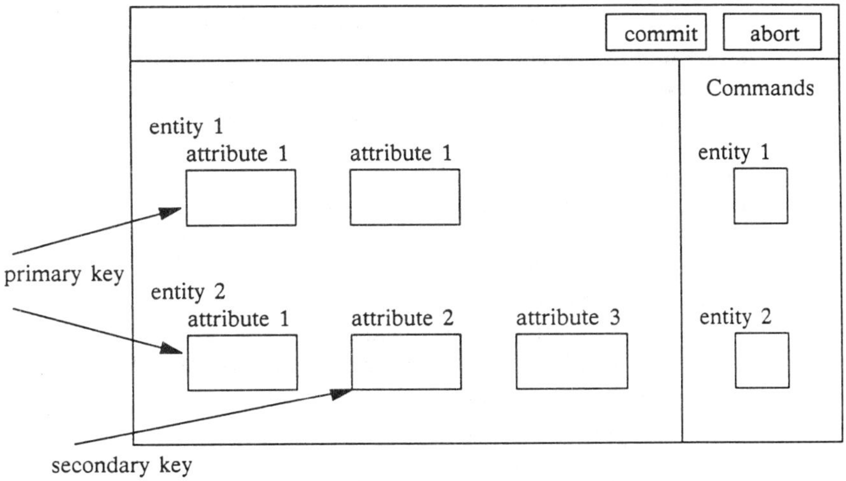

Fig. 3 — A possible MMI screen.

The interaction with the user is restricted to the following sequence:

command:	to create, modify, delete, query a database entity
fill in cells:	repeatedly give a value to a cell

leave: commit or abort the transaction

The effect of providing values depends on the command given:

query: when a key is filled in, the query is executed
modify: when the primary key is filled in, a query is executed, the user may continue by changing the values of the other fields; the modify operation will be executed upon the final commit
delete: when the primary key is filled in, a query is done; the delete operation is executed upon the final commit
create: the user fills in the fields, the creation is executed as soon as the primary key is supplied.

The transaction frame must also contain more detailed information about which attributes constitute the primary or secondary keys of the database entities. This allows the interpreter to issue the correct queries as soon as the appropriate cells have been filled with values by the final user. In general the database manager responds with additional information (in the case of a query, for example, or with derived information) that must be transmitted to the MMI or kept in local entities.

This requires a database system that is able to handle the normal relational database operations such as query, modify, delete and create, but the concept of transaction should be available as well. This allows for a very straightforward integration between the transaction interpreter and the database. The operations requested by the interpreter are executed immediately by the database, although the internal mechanisms of the database system allow the complete transaction to be rollbacked on request of the user.

A possible program skeleton for the transaction interpreter follows:

```
main program:-
initialize internal datastructures for transaction
do until commit
        request value from MMI
        if commit
          forward commit to database
          display possible derived information or error messages
        else if command
          validate command
        else if value cell
          derive the successor cells
          verify the integrity constraints
          forward values to the DB manager
              (if current command is a query and if primary key, e.g. also
              forward command)
          display the DB derived information
          derive successor cells of the DB derived information

forward command with values :-
```

```
if command is Modify or Query or Delete
and key for the entity completely filled in
        query DB manager
   else if command is Create
        send values
```

This skeleton is implemented in BIM_Prolog using an in-core database handler. It will be further developed and integrated with an existing relational database system.

7. SOME FURTHER EXTENSIONS

It is intended to further extend this scheme with facilities to describe batch transactions, the main difference being that it must be possible to specify iterations and not just simple user interactions.

A second extension is at the database side. In the complete Rubric design discipline we make a distinction between transaction and subtransaction. Transactions are triggered by an explicit user request or a clock condition, while subtransactions are triggered by internal transitions. These are expressed in terms of very general conditions on non-volatile data of the information system, called state conditions. Subtransactions are to be executed whenever these state conditions change value, e.g. when stock-level becomes low then reorder. These subtransaction rules can be integrated in the general petri-net mechanism introduced above.

The invocation of these subtransactions is analogous to the invocation of the transactions; however, this invocation mechanism should be integrated with the database system or built on top of an existing one. Recent developments of commercial databases go in the same direction. They generalize the concept of integrity constraint into general dynamic rules. It is possible to specify the reaction of the database system when a condition is violated (i.e. a state condition). This concept would nicely fit the Rubric approach to prototyping.

ACKNOWLEDGEMENTS

This chapter reflects results from the ESPRIT Project, RUBRIC, funded by the European Commission. The partners who contributed to this project are: James Martin Associates, Holland; UMIST, United Kingdom; and Microfocus, United Kingdom.

REFERENCES

[1] Venken, R. and Bruynooghe, M.,. Prolog as a Language for Prototyping of Information Systems, in: R. Budde, K. Kuhlenkamp, L. Mathiassen, H. Zuellighoven (eds.), *Approaches to Prototyping*, Springer-Verlag, New York, 1984.

[2] Venken, R. *et al.*, The Rubric Project: A New Paradigm for Infor-

mation Systems Development, in *Proc. Conf., on Automating Systems Development*, Leicester Polytechnic, April 1987.

[3] Macdonald, I. G., Automating Information Engineering, in *Proc. Conf. on Automating Systems Development*, Leicester Polytechnic, April 1987.

[4] Jarke, M. and Venken, R., Database Software Development as Knowledge Base Evolution, in *ESPRIT '87 Achievements and Impact*, Commission of the European Communities, North-Holland, Amsterdam, 1987, p. 892.

17

On transaction processing knowledge-based systems and databases

Toshio Nomura and **Stephen Lunn**
Telecomputing plc, 244 Barns Road, Oxford OX4 3RW, UK

ABSTRACT

This chapter is concerned with the implementation of knowledge-based systems within the on-line transaction processing environments of business computing, and with the concomitant requirements to interface knowledge-based modules with external programming languages and conventional data stores. In order to illustrate the need for knowledge-based systems tools and techniques in dealing with complex, volatile and ill-defined problem areas in business and to identify key characteristics of the underlying technology, three application systems with distinct features are described.†

1. INTRODUCTION

This chapter is concerned with the implementation of knowledge-based systems within on-line transaction processing environments, and with the concomitant requirements to interface knowledge-based modules with external programming languages and conventional data stores.

We begin with a brief survey of the most salient characteristics of transaction processing environments, of the motivation behind using IKBS (intelligent knowledge-based systems) techniques in such environments, and of the implications of the foregoing for the IKBS tools and techniques that are used (section 2).

We go on to look at the relevant features of the TOP-ONE product developed and used at Telecomputing plc, and in particular at multi-user aspects of access mode, consultation, concurrency and recovery in section 3, and at the calling interface from external languages to knowledge-based modules, the method of invoking external language modules within a

† A preliminary version of this chapter was presented at the 1987 SEAS anniversary meeting, Edinburgh, 1987; see [11].

knowledge-based component, the general technique employed for handling conventionally stored data, and a communication method between pc/ workstation-based Prolog systems in section 4.

Finally, in section 5, we look at three case studies, illustrating how the approaches and techniques outlined above are employed in practice. Each case is representative of a different type of knowledge-based system, namely (1) an expert system embedded within conventional COBOL applications, (2) an intelligent front-end/back-end to a large corporate database, and (3) a distributed problem-solving system with processing distributed between workstations and mainframe.

2. TRANSACTION PROCESSING SYSTEMS

The earliest transaction processing (tp) systems to be automated were airline reservation systems. These are the order processing and stock recording systems of the airline industry; it did not take long for other industries to apply tp techniques to those applications in their own areas. Now tp systems are ubiquitous in business computing, with a leading role even in such computation-intensive applications as manufacturing requirements planning systems.

A transaction is a unit of work involving a change of state that has the properties of

1. atomicity: the transaction is a 'success unit': either it happens completely, or it does not happen at all.
2. durability: once done, it cannot be undone except by a compensating (or 'anti-') transaction.
3. consistency: the transaction must obey legal protocols, e.g. in double-entry bookkeeping, debits and credits must balance at the start and at the end of a transaction, although they will be temporarily out of balance during the transaction, as the various ledger accounts are posted serially.

Conventionally, systems designers think of a transaction as a 'message pair', i.e. input message from terminal, processing, output message to terminal. To the user, however, several message pairs tend to be needed to effect a unit of work such as booking a prospective client into a seat on an aircraft. 'Nested' transactions also occur: a transaction to book a holiday may contain within it transactions to book a flight, hire a car, book a hotel, etc. The reader is referred to Gray [6] who provides a comprehensive explanation of transaction concepts.

Transaction processing systems typically serve many users; in some cases several thousand terminals may be on-line simultaneously. Usually the number of transaction types is far less than the number of users; thus there will be many users doing similar things at the same time, often to the same data, e.g. several travel agents or booking desks reserving seats on the same flight at the same time. Transaction volumes can run into tens or, in extreme cases, many hundreds of thousands of transactions per hour. Thus transaction processing systems are typically

1. high performance — in particular, overheads incurred per transaction are minimized.
2. secure — against accidental or deliberate misuse.
3. resilient in the event of failure of any component, i.e. they should be
   - fail-safe: only transactions currently being processed should be affected by any failure
   - fail-soft: failure of part of the system should not take the whole system off the air
   - fail-fast: failure should be detected as it happens, before its effects are compounded.
4. recoverable — in particular, it should always be possible to reconstitute a database to a state consistent with the completion of the last successful transaction.

Also, since many transactions can be processed simultaneously, there is a need to control concurrent access to shared resources, e.g. database entries, and to avoid deadlocks.

Systems software packages, called tp monitors, provide these general facilities, often in conjunction with complementary facilities embedded in database management systems. Typical tp monitors are CICS and IMS/DC on IBM mainframes running DOS/VSE or MVS operating systems, TPS and TPMS on ICL mainframes running VME.

A wide variety of data management regimes is employed within tp systems; not infrequently some variety is present within a single system. The main classes of data management system are direct access files such as IBM's VSAM, inverted file or linked file systems, such as the TPS Directory System and TOTAL hierarchical systems such as IMS/DB, network systems such as IDMS, and relational systems such as DB/2 and IDMS/R.

The programming language most commonly used for tp work is COBOL, or PL/1. Proprietary 4GLs (fourth generation languages) have made some headway, though far less then predicted, owing in part to the complexity of typical tp systems, and their need for very high performance.

Terminal networks are highly populated with dumb, 'green-screen' terminals, with dumb colour terminals, application-specific workstations such as bank tellers' machines, pos (point of sales) terminals or weighing machines, and local area networks of pcs.

The detailed motivation for using IKBS in this sort of environment varies as much as the companies that are doing it. In broad terms, though, there are consistent drives to increase automation, and to use systems as strategic means for competitive advantage, particularly among those companies where use of IT is under control.

These drives lead to attempts to implement applications that are more complex, more volatile and less structured than hitherto. Using conventional business computing tools and methods, only applications that are fairly simple, very stable in terms of requirement and easily structured can be tackled.

The foregoing has a number of consequences for the IKBS tools that are used to deliver these complex systems into the business computing environment. These include the following:

1. Embedded expert system or knowledge-based modules must be 'callable' from COBOL, PL/1, and some 4GLs with a standard calling interface similar to that used to access a database.
2. Knowledge-based modules frequently need access to conventionally stored data, often for update as well as retrieval: such access must be shared with other users of the data, hence concurrency control considerations apply.
3. Knowledge-based modules need to call external language procedures.
4. The systems must run on the machines that are in use (e.g. IBM mainframes and compatibles), under the software regimes that are in use (e.g. CICS under MVS/XA), being accessed over the terminal networks that are in use. (i.e. mostly populated by dumb screens, or LANs, i.e. local area networks of pcs and workstations).
5. Since real business applications have very divergent requirements for knowledge representation, inference, explanation, user interface and help/user support facilities, an open-ended language system (e.g. a Prolog system) is preferred to form the base software.

These considerations actually constituted the greater part of the design brief for the IKBS features of Telecomputing's TOP-ONE product, which is described in the next two sections.

3. TOP-ONE FEATURES

TOP-ONE is a comprehensive applications implementation and delivery environment for business computer systems, which contains a multi-user, mainframe implementation of the logic programming language Prolog, specially designed and developed for the business data processing environment by Telecomputing plc.†

It runs on IBM DOS/VSE and MVS machines and compatibles under the CICS transaction processing system, and on ICL VME machines under TPS or TPMS transaction processing systems. It fully supports tp-oriented features such as concurrency control, resilience, recovery and security.

The basic syntax of TOP-ONE Prolog is based on the standard Edinburgh Prolog [4] with numerous business-oriented built-in functions and data-handling extensions.

It allows on-line access to conventional files and databases, for retrieval and update, which are fully shareable with other TOP-ONE applications or tp applications. It also provides a comprehensive external language interface with conventional languages such as COBOL and fourth generation languages.

The following subsections describe features unique to TOP-ONE which

† Research and Development work leading to improvements to TOP-ONE is partially funded under the UK Alvey Project IKBS/058, 'Business Applications of Expert Systems.

are not present in other Prolog implementations, because they arise from the multi-user capability. The reader should refer to [12] for a detailed summary of TOP-ONE's background and functionality.

3.1 Update scope, consultation and access mode

3.1.1 Update scope

TOP-ONE supports various types of change to knowledge bases. The user/programmer is able to specify whether the update action, i.e. 'assert', 'retract', 'update' and 'acquire', to the knowledge base is temporary or permanent, and backtrackable or non-backtrackable.

Temporary changes are visible only to the consultation making them. Permanent changes are invisible to other consultations until and unless the consultation making them ends with success.

3.1.2 Consultation

A consultation is an atomic unit of interaction between the user and a knowledge base. If a consultation does not terminate with success, the state of the knowledge base will return to the original state before the consultation started, and all temporary and permanent changes to the knowledge base will be rolled back. On the other hand, if the consultation successfully ends, then all permanent changes made to the knowledge base during the consultation are committed.

3.1.3 Access mode

Like databases and conventional files, knowledge bases contain information that may be of interest to a number of different users for various purposes. TOP-ONE supports three types of access mode. The access mode to be used during a consultation is determined by setting parameters in the calling environment.

(1) LOCAL ACCESS — This is roughly equivalent to read-only access. Only temporary changes may be made to the knowledge base, which are invisible to other consultations, and which are cancelled automatically when the consultation ends.
(2) SHARED ACCESS — This is roughly equivalent to write access. Both temporary and permanent changes may be made to the knowledge base; however, the permanent changes remain invisible to other consultations until and unless the consultation ends with success. Any number of local and shared consultations can concurrently access a knowledge base.
(3) EXCLUSIVE ACCESS — This is a special type of write access, which prevents any other consultation from accessing the knowledge base at the same time. It would normally be used for system activities such as changing operator definitions, defining new argument indexes, etc.

3.2 Recovery and concurrency

TOP-ONE is multi-user in that it is a fully re-entrant, multi-threading program, allowing and processing multiple, concurrent consultations on the same knowledge base, with full capability for each consultation to update in a clear, safe and controlled way.

In an on-line tp environment, the system is both resilient and fully recoverable; in the event of complete system failure or a failure of a single thread, all affected consultations are wound back to start of consultation or end of last successful message pair, whichever is more recent, by the warm restart or message-abort processing.

4. TOP-ONE INTERFACES

In order to achieve full success in applying knowledge-based technology to the commercial environment, it is essential that the base software be tightly integrated with existing systems and conventional data stores [1,7].

In this section, we will outline basic implementation principles and mechanisms of TOP-ONE interfaces to/from existing languages, to data files, and also to/from other Prolog systems running on a pc or a workstation.

Subsection 4.1 is concerned with the COBOL interface to TOP-ONE, as a typical calling interface from external languages. This mechanism is used in the later application, credit control, in 5.1 to realize an embedded expert system within ordinary tp-transactions, where procedural COBOL and rule-based Prolog coexist, complementing each other in order to extend the scope of automation.

Subsection 4.2 is concerned with the TOP-ONE interface to conventional languages and data files. TOP-ONE can read or write records residing in conventional files by means of a facility which enables the user to handle conventional data as native data in a knowledge base and operate on them within the backtracking mechanism. Write access includes insert, delete and update actions on conventionally stored records, with concurrency control common to TOP-ONE and the surrounding tp environment. (Note that, though TOP-ONE interfaces to proprietary DBMs such as DB2 is an important topic, it is beyond the scope of this chapter.)

Subsection 4.3 outlines the communication mechanism between TOP-ONE and other Prolog systems by means of passing Prolog structures as the communication protocol. According to this method, a task can be shared between two Prolog systems, one running on a pc or on a workstation, catering for single-user aspects of the task such as presentation and dialogue management of user interface, and the other running on a mainframe, taking advantage of true multi-user operations, on-line access to existing data and tight integration with conventional systems. The software configuration of the Bid Estimation Support Application discussed in 5.3 is based on this technology.

4.1 COBOL interface to TOP-ONE Prolog

Typical of other calling interfaces from external languages to TOP-ONE Prolog, the TOP-ONE/COBOL interface allows the use of the Prolog mechanism from a COBOL application program running in tp or batch mode and provides the user with the following facilities:

— Starting a consultation
— Continuing a consultation
— Forcing the end of a consultation
— Abandoning a consultation

The interface allows COBOL applications to access and update the available knowledge bases. Hence, applications can make use of Prolog for rule-based system components, leaving COBOL to handle the procedural processing activities. Prolog rules and facts in TOP-ONE knowledge bases may be changed on-line without having to update the COBOL applications.

For example, 'TPSCPSC' (COBOL to Prolog Start Consultation) is used to start a standard consultation by calling

```
CALL TPSCPSC USING CONTROL-AREA
                   KNOWLEDGE-BASE-DATA
                   STATUS-INDICATORS
                   INPUT-BUFFER
                   OUTPUT-BUFFER
```

where

CONTROL-AREA is an area containing the consultation name, diagnostics requirements and exception monitoring level.

KNOWLEDGE-BASE-DATA is an area in which the required knowledge base is named and the access mode defined.

STATUS-INDICATORS is an area containing TOP-ONE system reply information on consultation and buffer status, and exception conditions.

INPUT-BUFFER is an area supplied to all start and continue calls containing the data to be passed to the inference engine. On a start call the first term in the buffer will be the initial goal for the consultation.

OUTPUT-BUFFER is an area used in start and continue calls to receive any output data.

(See TOP-ONE/COBOL Interface Guide [15] for details.)

4.2 Interface to conventional languages and data files

In the previous section, we have seen a common kind of interaction between TOP-ONE's inference engine and conventional systems by making calls (Prolog goals submitted) to the inference engine from an application written in COBOL or some other conventional language. This section deals with the facilities available for other types of communication with conventional languages and data files. These are briefly:

(1) Facilities for calling tried and tested routines written in other languages such as COBOL, FORTRAN, BCPL and Assembler, and for supplying them with the data they need to work on.
(2) Facilities for retrieving data from existing conventional files, returning the data to the inference engine for use in further processing.

The following subsections explain first an overview of the general-purpose invoke mechanism that underlies the specific facilities available, and then explanations of the above types of facilities.

4.2.1 Invoke mechanism

The invoke mechanism makes use of a single buffer for communication between the inference engine and the conventional language routine. This single buffer is used to pass parameters to the routine and to retrieve the results it generates.

There are three stages in the process of invoking a conventional language routine from the inference engine, as follows.

1. Writing the values of parameters for the routine to the buffer. These parameters will normally be TOP-ONE variables, either instantiated to specific values to be used by the routine, or uninstantiated to await results generated by the routine.
2. Making the external call to the routine.
3. Reading back the results generated by the routine. These usually take the form of values that can be used to instantiate the uninstantiated variables passed as parameters to the external routine at step 1.

The invoke mechanism is used to provide a simple interface to these phases, standardizing the process and cutting down the amount of programming that needs to be done.

For system software, this mechanism is implemented by a general-purpose BIF called 'invoke'.

At the application level, there are a number of BIFs with names such as 'bcpl', 'cobol' and 'fortran'. To invoke a routine in a given language, simply use a BIF with the name of that language; the arguments passed and the operation of the BIF are essentially the same regardless of what language is used. The most important argument passed to all of these BIFs is the name of the external routine to be called.

The 'spec' BIF is used to determine formats for input as well as output. It thus combines read and write format specifications, allowing one statement to be used instead of two if the format is to be used for the input and output of a given value. If the external call has not yet been made, a 'spec' is equivalent to a write; if it has already been made, the inference engine treats it as a read.

'spec' has the general form, spec(Term, Picture), where Term identifies a variable and Picture specifies the format that values for that variable will have. The following is an example:

```
Order_record( Order_No, Date, Part_No, Quantity) :-
              spec( Order_No,    "9999"),
              spec( Date,        string(8)),
              spec( Part_No,     "9999"),
              spec( Quantity,    integer(4)).
```

In many ways, 'spec' is approximately equivalent to a COBOL PIC clause. It defines how logical objects should be mapped on to the buffer to ensure that values input and output are interpreted correctly. Note that if a data dictionary or metadata system is in use then the series of 'spec' calls associated with a particular record type can be generated automatically.

4.2.2 Interface to conventional language

Routines written in conventional languages can be called by the general-purpose BIF 'invoke' for system software, or by means of the correspondingly named BIFs 'bcpl', 'cobol', 'fortran', etc., for applications. Each of these BIFs has three variants, as follows:

arity1: For example, bcpl(Prog), where Prog identifies both the external routine to be called and the corresponding functor in the knowledge base.

arity 2: For example, cobol(Prog,Name), where Prog identifies the external routine to be called and Name identifies the corresponding functor in the knowledge base.

arity 3: For example, fortran(Prog,Before,After), where Prog identifies the external routine to be called, Before identifies a corresponding functor from which initial instantiations are to be taken for use as parameter values, and After identifies a corresponding functor whose arguments will be instantiated by means of the results returned.

For both the arity 1 and the arity 2 variants, it is normal for the input/out requirements to be defined by one set of 'spec' BIFs: those associated with the functor in the knowledge base. The input format is therefore the same as the output format.

For the arity 3 variant, there are two different sets of 'spec' BIFs: those associated with the Before functor, which define what is to be written out to the external routine, and those associated with the After functor, which define what is to be read back from the external routine. This variant therefore allows input and output formats to differ, in their mapping of the same part of the communication buffer.

4.2.3 Interface to conventional data store

Facilities for handling conventional data are provided by the inference engine's conventional data handler BIF, iecdh/8. This permits access to files with any conventional file structure, allowing the inference engine to retrieve, add, delete, and update records in a variety of ways.

The BIF, bcpl/1, which is used to invoke external modules is used in accessing conventional data files. An external module IECDH (i.e. Inference Engine Conventional Data Handler) is provided to make the request through the supporting tp system, and there is also a functor called iecdh/8 which sets up request parameters in a communication buffer. When it is called after the file access, it determines the success or failure of the call, whether the call is resatisfiable or not, and calls a user-written functor to unpack any record values returned.

The form of invocation is

iecdh(Request,LFName,Lock,P_Key,Keylen,Keyspec,Recntrl,Recspec)

where

Request:	A string indicating the type of operation required, i.e. read, readnearest, readafter, readnext, insert, update, writenext, or delete.
LFName:	The logical file name of the file to be accessed.
Lock:	A number to indicate that the record accessed is to be locked.
P_Key:	Physical key value specifying the actual position of a record in the specified file.
Keylen:	The length of the logical key in bytes.
Keyspec:	Specification of logical key to be used in retrieving records. Take the form of a functor, each of whose arguments corresponds to a component part of the key.
Recntrl:	A functor used to skip over field values at the start of the record area that are not normally used
Recspec:	Specification of the format of the record to be retrieved, updated, inserted or deleted.

When iecdh/8 is called, it succeeds or fails in the same way as any other goal, though it has built-in side-effects. Generally,. iecdh/8 read operations are potentially resatisfiable and write operations are not.

The BIF iecdh/8 has three metacalls to user-supplied functors referred to as Keyspec, Recntrl and Recspec. These functors are for key details, record header and record details.

Keyspec should comprise calls to the spec/3 BIF, one for each part of the key. The first parameter of spec/3 is the value to be stored as the key part. This may be a string or a number, an instantiated variable or an uninstantiated variable. The second parameter is the picture of the key part. If the first parameter is uninstantiated, then either zeros or spaces will be set depending on the picture type (number or character). The third parameter should always be set to 'notrail', indicating that the key is presented on the first call through the file access, but will not be remembered on backtracking. The key used in backtracking is maintained by the external module IECDH in association with the functor iecdh/8.

4.2.4 Examples of conventional data access

Let us consider a simple record, 'ORDERFILE', with record map:

Order No	Order Date	Part No	Quantity

0 4 12 16 20

where 'Order No' field has picture '9999', i.e. a 4-digit number, which is the key field of the record, 'Order Date' field has picture 'X(8)', i.e. 8-character string, 'Part No' field has picture '9999', and 'Quantity' field has picture '9(4)', i.e. 4-digit number.

Then the Prolog subgoal order/4 which retrieves the order record from 'ORDERFILE', given 'Order No', can look like

```
order( Order_No, Date, Part_No, Quantity) :-
   bcpl( iecdh( "read                ", "ORDERFILE", 0, 0, 4,
              order_key( Order_No), _,
              order_rec( Order_No, Date, Part_No, Quantity))).
```

where order_key/1 and order_rec/4 are Keyspec and Recspec defined according to

```
order_key ( Order_No) :-
              spec( Order_No,      "9999",      notrail).

order_rec( Order_No, Date, Part_No, Quantity) :-
              spec( Reply,          string(4)),
              spec( P_key,          string(8)),
              spec( Filler,         integer(20)),
              spec( Order_No,       "9999"),
              spec( Date,           string(8)),
              spec( Part_No,        "9999"),
              spec( Quantity,       integer(4)).
```

Similarly, the Prolog subgoal update_order/4 which updates Date, Part_No and Quantity fields of the order record with given Order_No to new values, New_Date, New_Part and New_Qty, can look like

```
update_order( Order_No, New_Date, New_Part, New_Qty) :-
   bcpl( iecdh( "update              ", "ORDERFILE", 0, 0, _,

              _, _,
              order_rec( Order_No, New_Date, New_Part, New_Qty))).
```

4.3 Communicating between TOP-ONE and other Prolog systems

The established communication method between TOP-ONE Prolog on a mainframe and other Prolog systems running on pc/workstations is by means of passing the high level communication protocol of Prolog structures.

In this way, a single task, i.e. resolution of a series of Prolog subgoals, can be shared and distributed between workstations and mainframe, taking the maximum advantage of both single- and multi-user features of Prolog systems.

The following subsection 4.3.1 briefly describes a facility, called COMPASS transactions, part of the TOP-ONE product, by which it becomes possible to define a TOP-ONE Prolog program as a transaction in its own right. This makes it unnecessary to have the program called from an application, and supports direct interaction with the mainframe inference engine.

Subsection 4.3.2 will explain how TOP-ONE Prolog and a workstation-based Prolog fit together via the COMPASS transaction facility. Roughly, from the viewpoint of the mainframe, workstations are virtual terminals from which appropriately specified COMPASS transactions on the mainframe receive input messages and to which the transactions write output messages both in terms of Prolog structures.

4.3.1 COMPASS transaction

The definition of a COMPASS transaction is made by means of the COMPASS Application Definition subsystem. The logic of the program is written as an ordinary Prolog program, but the Application Development subsystem enables the requirements for interaction and overall control to be defined quickly and easily.

The interaction between COMPASS and the transaction in Prolog is controlled by the Conversation Control subsystem and the standard Prolog handler. The sequence of events is as follows.

1. When the standard Prolog handler receives a message that tells it that a consultation is to begin, it uses the message identifier and the logical terminal number to generate a consultation identifier.
2. The standard Prolog handler supplies to the inference engine a buffer containing the initial goal **mmm( ).**, **data**, where **mmm** is the message identifier translated to lower case, for use as a goal in the form of a zero-arity functor, and **data** is the set of related values to be used in its resolution, derived from the input message.
3. Values for use in resolution are acquired by the Prolog program by means of read BIFS in the normal way.
4. Results are built up in the output buffer in the usual way, by means of the write and cursor control BIFs.
5. The contents of the output buffer are displayed by means of special TIFs (transaction implementation functions), which are library functions written in Prolog. The TIF normally used is tpspdisplay/4 (which defines the layout of text output and control characters). This is followed by the end of the consultation or an interrupt forced by either the force_output/0 BIF or the force_io/0 BIF.
6. The transaction is ended. If resolution has been successful, this is done by means of the full-stop sequence ., or by end/0. If an error has occurred, this can be notified via the tpspenr/2 TIF.

Output from the COMPASS transaction is formatted by means of the TIF:

```
tpspdisplay(Tdisp,Cdisp,Sequence,Reentry)
```

where Tdisp gives the position in the output buffer where text output can be found and Cdisp gives the position where control output can be found. Text and Control output must already be formatted for the appropriate logical terminal interface routine. Sequence is set to 'X' if the message is to be ended, 'A' if it is to be aborted, and 'O' if it is to be continued.

Take, for example, the following output specification:

```
tababs(101),write("0000"),writenumber(Custno,"9999"),
write(Custname),tababs(201),write("CENQ111"),
tpspdisplay(101,201,"X",0).,
```

This formats text output beginning at position 101 and control character output beginning at position 201. The formatted output is actually forced out by the '.,' that ends the consultation.

4.3.2 Prolog structure passing

We will illustrate how TOP-ONE Prolog and a pc-based Prolog fit together via the COMPASS transaction facility by the following two examples. We assume that a pc/workstation-based Prolog can communicate with the mainframe through a standard micro/mainframe link software equipped with API (application program interface) and the Prolog's external code module via a communication network.

The first example uses a Prolog subgoal solve_single(Goal), on a pc which tries to resolve subgoal Goal in the pc's Prolog environment; failing that, the pc passes Goal to TOP-ONE Prolog on the mainframe via the COMPASS transaction facility, together with message identifier sgl (for single).

A mainframe-based Prolog goal, sgl/0, is defined so that it reads Prolog term, Goal, from the input buffer, evaluates Goal by call/1, and writes the more instantiated Goal to the output buffer. The consultation of subgoal, sgl/0, ends after finding the first result; however, it writes 'none' if the read Goal does not succeed at all.

On the other hand, the second example describes solve_multiple(Goal) on a pc where the consultation on mainframe, mpl/0 (for multiple), is suspended after the first result of Goal has been written, and upon backtracking on solve_multiple(Goal) on the pc, the TOP-ONE's consultation is resumed and the next result will be returned to the output buffer until the workstation sends 'no more' to TOP-ONE or if Goal does not succeed any more; in this case, 'none' will be sent to the pc.

CASE 1:

```
    (on workstation)

    solve_single(Goal) :- call(Goal).
    solve_single(Goal) :- solve_single_on_mainframe(Goal).

% solve_single_on_mainframe(Goal)sends sgl( ).,Goal., to COMPASS
% which in turn calls goal sgl( ).

(on mainframe)
   sgl( ) :- reading_request_single(Input), call(Input),
             writing_reply_single(Input).,
   sgl( ) :- writing_reply_single(none).,

   reading_request_single(Input) :-
                preprocess_control_msg_single,
```

```
                read(Input).,

    writing_reply_single(Reply) :-
                writing_control_msg_single,
                writeq(Reply),write(".")
                space_fill_buffer,
                tpspdisplay(125,61,'X',0), end.,
```

CASE 2:
(on workstation)

```
    solve_multiple(Goal) :- call(Goal).
    solve_multiple(Goal) :- solve_multiple_on_mainframe(Goal).

% solve_multi_on_mainframe(Goal sends mpl( ).,Goal., to COMPASS
% which in turn calls goal mpl( ).
```

(on mainframe)

```
    mpl( ) :- reading_request_multiple(Input),
             call(Input),
                    writing_reply_multiple(Input),
                    reading_request_multiple(Next),
                    ( Next=no_more,
                      writing_reply_multiple( none)
                    ;
                        fail)
             ;
             writing_reply_single(none).,

    reading_request_multiple(Input) :-
             preprocess_control_msg_multiple,
             read(Input).,

    writing_reply_multiple(none) :-
             writing_control_msg,
             writeq(none), write("."),
             space_fill_buffer,
             tpspdisplay(125,61,'X',O),
             end.,

     writing_reply_multiple(Reply) :-
             writing_control_msg,
             writeq(Reply), write("."),
             space_fill_buffer,
             tpspdisplay(125,61,'X',O),
             force_io.,
                % force_io/o forces a return to the calling
                % program, giving back the output buffer and
                % requesting new input data.
```

Notes:

(1) It is possible to incorporate error messages to reply messages from mainframe to workstations.

(2) In general, a program which generates Output as a reply, given Input as a request, may be any Prolog program. What we have considered is simply call/1.

4.4 Other interfaces

TOP-ONE can be used as a free-standing Prolog environment, or integrated with conventional batch or tp programs. It can also be integrated with various 4GL products with their native screen painting, application and data definition, and transaction generation facilities. Thus the environmental aspects of an intelligent on-line tp system can be interactively declared through an appropriate 4GL, and complex processing logic associated with them in TOP-ONE.

5. APPLICATIONS

5.1 Credit control

The first application which we examine is concerned with expert systems embedded within ordinary transactions. This system has the particular features of true multi-user operation, on-line access to existing data, and simple integration with conventional procedural components.

An industrial sales order processing system handles the supply of components to a wide range of domestic and export customers. Some products are made to order; others are supplied direct from stock. The system, written in COBOL, is currently being augmented by a number of intelligent modules, in order to reduce manual involvement and paperwork, cut turnaround times, reduce inventories, improve credit control, and optimize distribution.

In this section, we concentrate on the credit control function for domestic customers.

5.1.1 Conventional order processing system

Fig. 1 shows the work-flow for 'direct from stock' orders ('make' orders are excluded for reasons of clarity) before the intelligent components were added to the system.

Enquiries and orders are received by phone, telex or on paper — usually the customer's purchase order stationery. Interpretation consists of identifying the specific customer, including invoice address and delivery point, the product and quantity required.

Interpreted orders are then priced: this is simple for small-quantity orders from low-turnover customers, and gets more complex the bigger the order and the more important the customer.

A variety of general and customer-specific discount schemes apply, sometimes additive and sometimes exclusive: the customer must be given the best price, and shown how the price was arrived at.

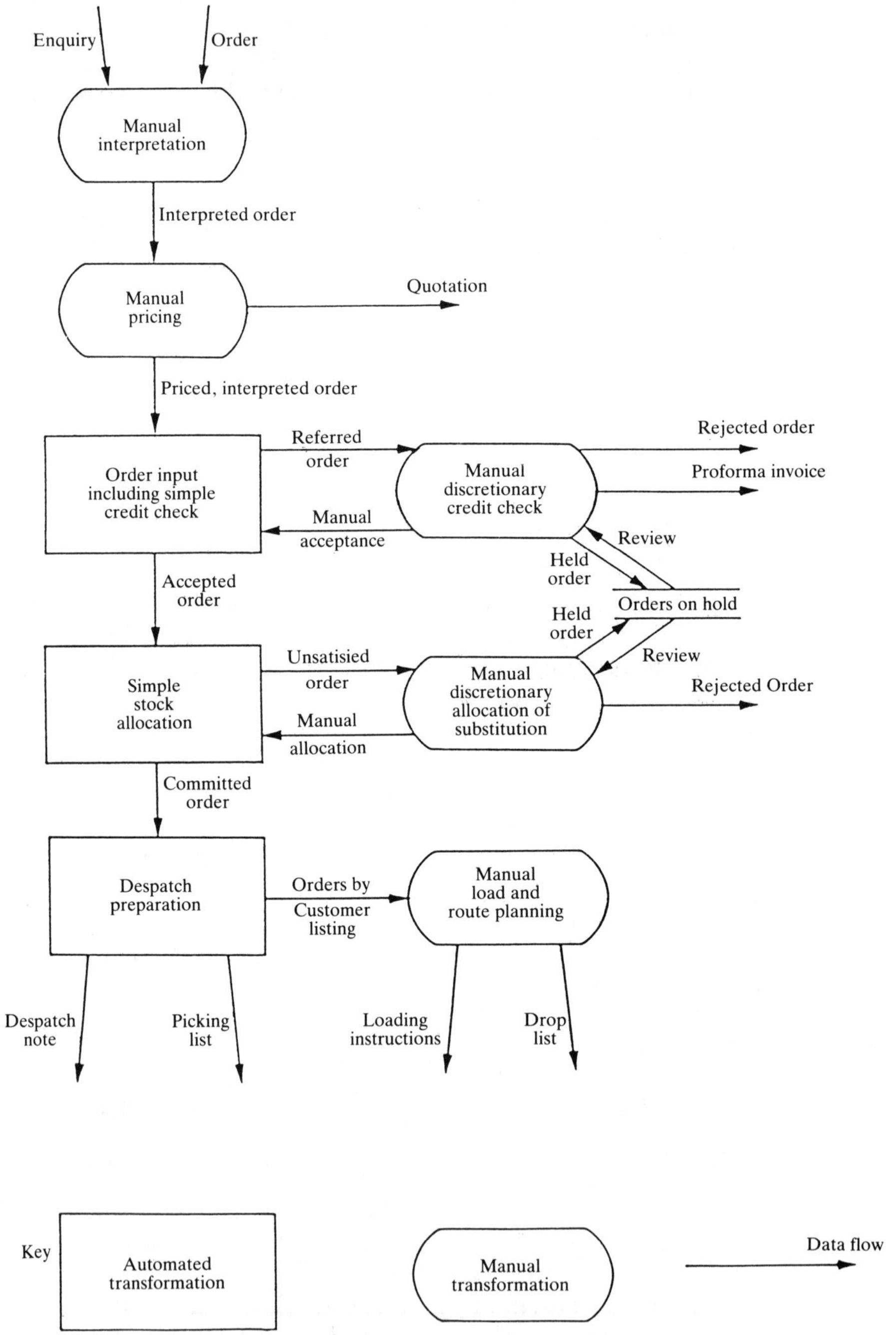

Fig. 1 — Sales order processing work-flow with conventional COBOL system.

Orders are then input through an on-line system written in COBOL, which performs a simple credit check, as described below:

1. Each customer is allocated a credit category from
   - A: unlimited credit
   - B: limited credit
   - C: no automatic credit
   - X: no credit allowed

   A specific credit limit is set for each category B customer.
2. The COBOL rules for credit checking are

```
if CATEGORY=A
  then ACCEPT ORDER
if CATEGORY=B
  then
      if (CURRENT DEBT+VALUE OF OUTSTANDING
              ORDERS +VALUE OF ORDER(=<CREDIT LIMIT
        THEN ACCEPT ORDER
      else REFER ORDER TO CREDIT CONTROL
if CATEGORY=C
   then REFER ORDER TO CREDIT CONTROL
if CATEGORY=X
   then REJECT ORDER
```

The net effect of these rules is that some orders from category B customers and all orders from category C customers are referred to credit control. Category B and C customers place approximately 70% of orders (by volume, not value).

Accepted 'direct from stock' orders then go through stock allocation and distribution procedures.

5.1.2 Credit control component

The credit control module runs on-line; its overall architecture is illustrated in Fig. 2.

The inferencing procedure is straightforward backward chaining, initiated from COBOL by passing a buffer to PROLOG containing a goal of the form

```
extend_credit_for( CUSTOMER, ORDER, REPLY),
```

where CUSTOMER is instantiated to the customer number and ORDER to the order number. Prolog predicate extend_credit_for/3 is typically defined according to

```
extend_credit_for( CUSTOMER, ORDER, yes) :-
     total_exposure_to( CUSTOMER, low),
     risk_index_of( CUSTOMER, acceptable),
     informed( credit_controller, accepted
                                        ( CUSTOMER, ORDER)).
extend_credit_for( CUSTOMER, ORDER, no).
```

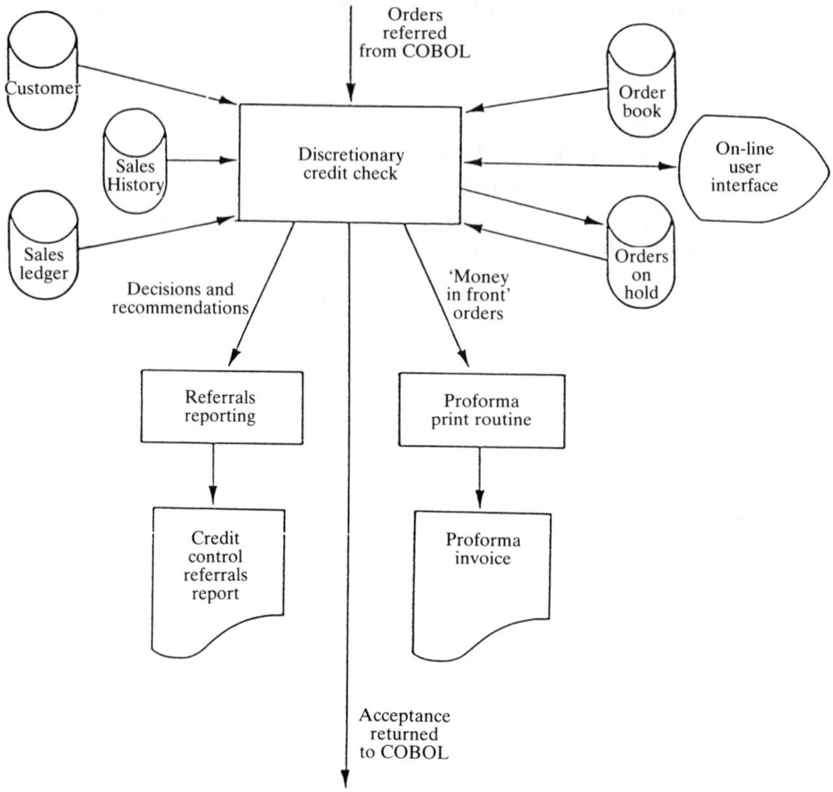

Fig. 2 — Architecture of credit control component.

and subgoals total_exposure_to/2, risk_index_of/2 and informed/2 are also defined appropriately, accessing facts in the knowledge base and conventional files.

Visibility of the system within the Credit Control department should be limited to the facilities of the on-line user interface, and the referrals report. The on-line interface allows credit controllers to review orders that the system has placed 'on hold', to ask for explanations of decisions or recommendations given on the referrals report, to short-cut the printing of the referrals report, and, given appropriate access rights, to maintain the rules in source form.

The benefits of the credit control module are expected to be

1. quicker turnaround of orders: the automatic check is faster than the manual check; it is done immediately at order input; and orders will no longer stack up in the Credit Control 'in tray'.

2. the more routine workload will be removed from the Credit Control department, thus freeing their time for more difficult problems.
3. credit control decisions should become more consistent: it is expected that the proportion of orders accepted may increase slightly.

5.2 Underwriting information system

The second case is concerned with an intelligent front-end and intelligent back-end to a large insurance company database for an Underwriting Information System.

A major problem in dealing with a large, complex database is that relatively laborious data preparation, query definition and results interpretation have to be exercised by the user who may know little about how the underlying database is structured.

The use of IKBS techniques to build an intelligent front-end to large databases allows the user to specify his information requirements in more familiar terms by holding the domain's conceptual schema [2,10,14].

The role of the intelligent back-end in this case is to post-process the results of queries and analyses by interpreting the results, discarding uninteresting information, highlighting interesting effects of anomalies, and possibly preparing the way for refinement of the analyses.

5.2.1 Portfolio performance analysis

A motor insurance company has a large database of insurance policies and claims. Major underwriting tasks include analysis of this database to set rates, monitor underwriting performance, assess the need for policy changes or endorsements, and identify potentially profitable business opportunities.

In order to make a profit in the underwriting, the 'estimated claims' to 'earned premium' ratio is required to be less than a certain value, depending on business sector characteristics such as business volume, distribution of claim sizes, etc.; a higher ratio indicates that the rates should be increased to achieve a profit. A nominal value of the ratio is around 75%.

What the underwriter wants is a system which scans through the large databases of claims and policies by aggregating the results in terms of various factors of interest, interprets the results by discarding uninteresting cases and then presents him anomalous case descriptions which contribute to bad portfolio performance. It would be desirable as well if the system recommends ways of breaking down anomalous cases for further analysis.

5.2.2 Base data

The first thing the underwriter is required to do is to specify the base data which will be the sample space (i.e. universe) in the rest of the performance analysis following, and which often has much fewer records, e.g. 1% or less, due to aggregation, compared to the original POLICY and CLAIM databases. In order to do this, he may specify a selection condition and a set of attributes, called category attributes [3,8].

A selection condition is a collection of

<attribute name><operator><value>,

joined by logical 'and', where <attribute name> is an attribute name of some predicate used in metadata 'structure', <operator> is=, \=, <, <=, > or >=, and <value> is a string or a number.

Let us assume that the underwriter is concerned with last year's performance figures of car maker, FORD, which have comprehensive cover. Other factors he wants to take into account are car model and type, CC, car's age, driver's age and rating area where the rating area is greater than or equal to 3.

In this case, the selection condition is

car_maker = "Ford"
and cover_type = comp
and claim_year = 1986
and rating_area >= 3,

and the category attributes are car_model, car_type, 'CC', car_age, driver_age and rating_area, where car_age is calculated by a rule using this_year and registration_year.

The system automatically establishes the definition of two structures, 'base_data' and 'aggregate_data', and calculates the actual data which form the sample space of all subsequent analyses.

Note that in generating 'base_data', the system classifies each claim into one of the three grades according to

low if claim_cost / premium <= 0.75
medium if claim_cost <= 50,000
high if claim_cost > 50,000

5.2.3 Intelligent front-end

In the same manner as defining 'base_data' in the previous section, the underwriter specifies a selection condition and category attributes in order to undertake a performance analysis.

By adding more constraint(s) to a selection condition, the underwriter can focus on a smaller subset of 'base_data'; on the other hand, if more category attributes are specified, it means that he is analysing 'base_data' by partitioning it into much finer subgroups.

If the underwriter wants to see a wider division of 'base_data', he can do this by loosening either some selection condition or some category attributes(s).

For example, let us assume that he wants to analyse the performance by breaking down by 'car_model'; in this case, there is no selection condition (in addition to the original ones), and the only category attribute is 'car_model'. The result of analysis is stored under predicates 'analysed_base_data' and 'analysed_aggregate_data', and may look like Table 1.

Table 1 — Portfolio performance analysis

car_model	low_tally med_tally high_tally	low_cost med_cost high_cost		
	total_tally	total_cost	total_premium	performance
FIESTA	1205 17 2	£350 000 £ 12 000 £120 000		
	1224	£482 000	£620 00	78%
ESCORT	. . .			

grand_tally	grand_cost	grand_premium	grand_performance
10 340	£5170 000	£6475 000	80%

5.2.4 Intelligent back-end

Given 'analysed_base_data' and 'analysed_aggregate_data' as a large number of facts resulting from a performance analysis, the task of the intelligent back-end system is to interpret each fact of 'analysed_base_data', one by one, determining whether it presents some anomaly by using 'interpret' rules: if it does, it is classified as bad; otherwise it is good.

The underwriter usually ignores bad portfolio performance if it is caused by one or two incidents with very large claims; but he is certainly concerned with bad performance if it is created by persistent occurrences of relatively large claims. Rules in 'interpret' are a collection of such heuristics. Examples are:

```
interpret
    if      performance<=0.75
    then    class=good.
    /* if performance is less than 75% */
interpret
    if      high_tally <=2
    and     (total_cost-high_cost) / total_premium<=0.75
    then    class=good.
    /* if very high costs were claimed at most twice, and if the performance
    becomes less than 75% without those */
interpret
    if      low_tally<=total_tally * 0.5
    then    class=bad.
    /* if the majority of claims become medium or high */
```

5.3 Bid estimation

The third case, the Bid Estimation Support System being developed under the UK Alvey Project IKBS/058, entitled 'Business Applications of Expert Systems', gives intelligent support to the estimators in an aerospace company responsible for costing the manufacture of complex mechanically engineered components at the 'bid' or 'tendering' stage of the project.

The menu-driven, window-based user interface running on pcs communicates with the main expert system on TOP-ONE on the mainframe, by passing requests and results in Prolog structures. The expert system accesses the existing database for materials, manufacturing and purchase order data, and also maintains a history of previous estimates.

5.3.1 Alvey project

The primary objective of the project is to demonstrate how TOP-ONE can be used to build a live, industrial-scale expert system, fully integrated with the on-line tp systems and databases of a user site; and how such an application can tackle crucial areas of the business for which conventional methods alone can do little.

The project was instigated and led by Telecomputing, who are also responsible for most of the knowledge engineering and expert system implementation aspects.

The industrial demonstrator site is a leading UK supplier of landing gear and other major subsystems to the international aerospace manufacturing industry. The company's Data Processing and Estimating departments are involved in the demonstrator application project, which aims to support the production of 'bid estimates' in the estimating department.

The academic collaborators of the project are the Loughborough University of Technology, Department of Computer Science, Computer–Human Interface Research Unit (LUTCHI), led by Professor Edmonds, in relation to user interface and human/social aspects of the expert system, and Brunel University, Centre for Information Technology, led by Professor Johnson, in relation to expert system architecture and knowledge acquisition aspects.

In mid-1986 the project's knowledge engineers conducted a wide-ranging survey of the user company's business operations, in the course of which the feasibility of several candidate IKBS applications was assessed. This resulted in the selection of 'bid estimation' as the most appropriate domain for the demonstrator application.

5.3.2 Bid estimation

As a result of the internationally competitive marketplace in which the company operates, it receives an ever-increasing number of invitations to tender or 'bid' for work on a wide variety of existing, new or experimental aircraft. Typically the deadline for submission of a bid gives the estimating department very little time to prepare an accurate estimate of the cost of manufacturing a complex and critical subsystem such as a set of landing gear or a hydraulic system.

Task analysis revealed that the majority of the time spent in preparing a bid estimate was devoted to preparing relatively detailed costings of the manufacture of each major component in the subsystem, such as the main fitting, the sliding member, and the torque links of landing gear. Thus it was decided to concentrate on this task in the expert system application.

Analysis of this task showed that it consisted of four main subtasks, namely (1) assessment of the component in question, based on a 'scheme drawing', (2) material specification, (3) operation layout: a manufacturing sequence to convert the raw material to a finished part is specified, and (4) time calculation: a setting time and base machining time.

5.3.3 Expert system: bid estimation support system

The first phase of the demonstrator system which had been completed in mid-1987 supports the complete range of tasks described above, although with extensive knowledge-based support primarily within the operation layout task. The problem of visual and spatial interpretation of engineering drawings is left with the estimator.

The user selects from concise, dynamically generated menus of suggestions, and/or adds his own inputs. The system checks the user's actions, commenting on any doubtful choices, and then goes into another round of suggestion. The user can also ask why a suggestion was made [13].

Certain factual knowledge is directly obtained from conventional databases, and conventionally programmed systems. Also, the expert systems communication with the outside world is purely in terms of Prolog structures.

The overall architecture of the Bid Estimation Support System is shown in Fig. 3. In this software architecture, the part which deals with presentation and dialogue managements is written in a pc-based Prolog and the main expert system resides on a mainframe under TOP-ONE.

6. CONCLUDING REMARKS

In this chapter, we described the relevant features of the on-line transaction-oriented Prolog of TOP-ONE, in particular, multi-user aspects and calling interfaces. We also described three types of commercial application of knowledge-based systems based on TOP-ONE, which reflect distinct characteristic types which are often identified in tp-oriented knowledge-based applications.

The first application, credit control, is an example of an embedded expert system within ordinary transactions, where procedural COBOL and rule-based Prolog coexist, complementing each other, in order to extend the scope of automation.

The second application, the underwriting information system, suggests a similar approach to implementing task-oriented intelligent front-ends to facilitate the use of other types of database, difficult application systems or complex software tools.

The third application, bid estimation, presents an example of, what we

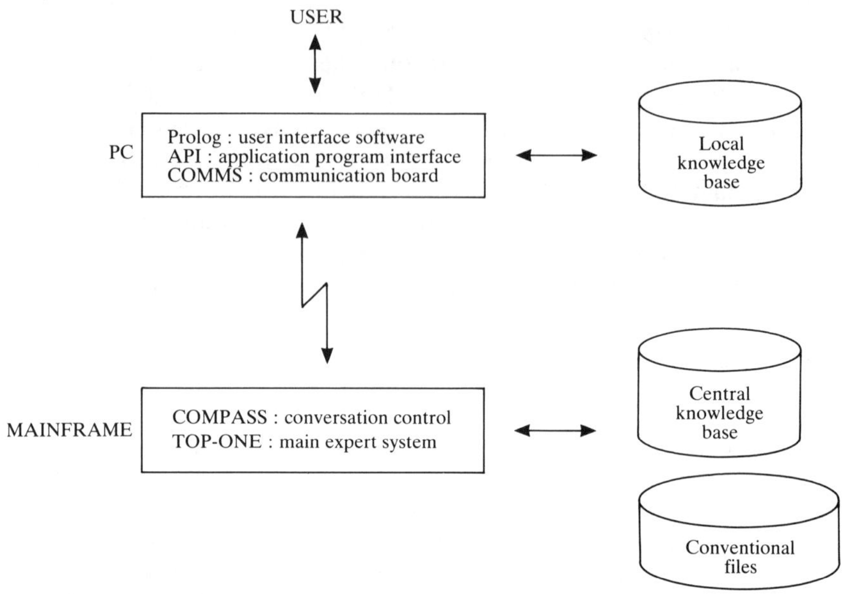

Fig. 3 — Overall architecture of bid estimation support system.

call, 'distributed problem solving', where a task is shared between two Prolog systems, one running on a pc or a powerful workstation, catering for single-user aspects of the task such as user interface and interaction, and the other running on a mainframe, taking advantage of true multi-user operations, on-line access to existing data and simple integration with conventional systems, the two parts of the task communicating by passing Prolog structures.

There are two common myths about expert or knowledge-based systems: that they are 'a solution looking for a problem' and 'inherently complex, risky and demanding'.

These are a direct consequence of the technology's origins in the outer regions of the academic world. The authors believe that problems for which the knowledge-based approach is the best or only solution are commonplace in the business world; that integration at the levels of corporate strategy, end-user working practice, existing manual and automated systems, and software engineering methodologies, is crucial to success; and that, given the will and the imagination, problems that defy conventional techniques can be solved quickly and cost-effectively using the knowledge-based approach, bringing major benefits in terms of costs or competitive advantage to the companies that take this technology seriously.

ACKNOWLEDGEMENTS

TOP-ONE development and applications have benefited from the contributions of many people over many years. The authors appreciate the efforts of their colleagues in Telecomputing whose ideas and hard work made these results possible. They would like to express their appreciation to Professors Edmonds and Johnson for their consistent support during the Alvey Project.

REFERENCES

[1] Brodie, M. L. and Jarke, M., On Integrating Logic Programming and Databases, in *Expert Databases Systems, Proc. First Int. Workshop*, ed. by Kerschberg, L., Benjamin/Cummings, 191–207, 1986.

[2] Brodie, M. L., Mylopoulos, J., and Schmidt, J. W., On Conceptual Modelling, Perspective from Artificial Intelligence, *Databases and Programming Languages*, ed. by Brodie, Mylopoulos and Schmidt, Springer-Verlag, 1984.

[3] Chan, P. and Shoshani, A., "SUBJECT": A Dictionary Driven System for organizing and Accessing Large Statistical Databases, *Proc. 7th Conf. on Very Large Database Systems,* 553–563, 1980.

[4] Clocksin, W. F. and Mellish, C. S., *Programming in Prolog*, 2nd edn., Springer-Verlag, New York, 1984.

[5] Date, C. J., *An Introduction to Database Systems,* Vol. I, Addison-Wesley, Reading, MA, 1983.

[6] Gray, J., The Transaction Concepts: Virtues and Limitations, *Proc. 7th Int. Conf. on very Large Data Bases*, 144–154, 1981.

[7] Jarke, M. and Vassilou, Y., Coupling Expert Systems with Database management Systems, in *Artificial Intelligence Applications for Business, Proc. NYU Symp.,* May, 1983, ed. W. Reitman, Norwood, Ablex Publishing Corporation, 65–85, 1984.

[8] Johnson, R. R., Modelling Summary Data, *Proc. ACM SIGMOD Int. Conf. on Management of Data*, 93–97, 1981.

[9] Johnson, T., *The Commercial Applications of Expert Systems Technology*, Ovum Ltd, 1984.

[10] Lunn, K. and Archibald, I. G., TREQL: An Intelligent Front-End to a Relational Database, see Chapter 3 of this book.

[11] Lunn, S. and Nomura, T., Prolog, Transaction Processing and Databases, in *Proc. SEAS Anniversary Meeting,* Edinburgh, 1305–1320, 1987.

[12] Nomura, T. and Lunn, S., Integration of Knowledge-Based Systems with Data Processing, Vol. 1, No. 1, *Knowledge-Based Systems,* Butterworth, Guildford, 24–31, 1987.

[13] Slatter, P., Nomura, T., and Lunn, S., A Representation for Manufacturing Sequencing Knowledge to Support Co-operative Problem Solving, in preparation.

[14] Stecher, P. and Hellemaa, P., An 'Intelligent' Extraction and Aggregation Tool for Company Data Bases, *Decision Support Systems,* **2**, 145–158, 1986.

[15] TOP-ONE Manuals: *The BIF Book, PACE User Guide, COMPASS User Guide, TOP-ONE/COBOL Interface Guide, Knowledge Base*

Administration's Guide, System Programmer's Manual, Language Manual, Reference Booklet, 1987.

18

The TRACE Club: expert systems and databases

Gareth Williams
Software Sciences Ltd, Macclesfield, Cheshire SK11 6SR, UK

ABSTRACT

This chapter is based on the experiences of using Prolog as a system development language in the Alvey awareness project TRACE, a project where an expert system was coupled to existing remote databases and where local databases were necessary to supplement the standard Prolog facilities.

The system was based on an IBM PC. This gave a particular flavour to many of the design issues we faced and introduced some problems into the Prolog area which would not be met in other environments. The project was implemented using a small toolkit called ROCKETT which was developed from earlier work by Software Sciences in its APSI programme. This toolkit combined the mechanisms of Prolog with structured objects and rules and low-level programming in C.

One of the (expected) lessons was that once you go beyond the straight-forward use of the Prolog database you need to get involved in low-level file/database design to get useful performance out of the system. The use of the right tools can help you to integrate the various methods, but some of the changes needed are in places where only the implementers of Prolog systems can help.

1. TRACE

The TRACE Club [1] was established during the latter half of 1985 and work commenced in earnest at the end of that year. The membership of the Club consisted of representatives of the Transport industry: in particular from the Public Transport and Holiday Travel sectors.

The initial feasility study found certain areas to be of especial importance and it was proposed to construct a system with these general characteristics:

- Its expert system component was to capture the skills of experienced enquiry personnel to provide a convenient computer-based aid to enquiry handling.

- Two prototypes were to be constructed: for package tour booking and for public transport enquiries.
- It would emphasize the role of the interface between the computer and the user in operational environments and contribute to the development of systems suitable for public use.
- The system would not be self-sufficient but would access remote databases for information.
- Such a system might provide help and assistance to the staff and give them access to a variety of data sources without their needing to know how to access them individually.

Enquiry handling was chosen as the common theme. On the holiday side this related to a situation where the salesperson and customer are normally face-to-face in a travel agency; on the public transport side, it related to the telephone enquiry service. The former therefore involved a more verbose style, with opportunities for sales messages to be presented by the system at suitable points in the consultation, whereas the latter was more geared to speed and to a terse style of interaction.

2. APSI

Software Sciences APSI research programme was concerned with the development, in Prolog, of varied reasoning mechanisms for use in Knowledge-based Systems. The first APSI was a forward-chaining production system with hierarchical rule structures. The second was a frame-and-rule-based system with a functional syntax for its expressions and a strategic goal mechanism. This tool had a high interpretation overhead and was fairly slow. Work on a compiled form of rules to give optimal Prolog access from nested expressions was therefore undertaken [2]. The flexibility of this system with its ability to combine any number of inference engines with free use of standard Prolog procedures seemed to be ideal for the sort of work to be undertaken on the TRACE Club. By the middle of the Club's lifetime the name ROCKETT†. had been coined.

3. ROCKETT

For TRACE we excluded the use of major toolkits on AI workstations as they were too expensive for the Club members to contemplate buying for initial exploratory work after the project; we were also unconvinced about the viability of porting from a toolkit to a small system on a PC after initial development. Also excluded were small expert system shells, as they had not enough power to handle complex problems. When we investigated the

† Representation of Club Knowledge for Expertise in Travel and Transport.

smaller tools at the end of 1985, we found them to be lacking in foreign language interfaces (so we could not, for instance, connect to existing databases or to modems) and in general flexibility (fixed reasoning methods, fixed MMI). In order to have sufficient flexibility to be able to attack a problem whose bounds we could not fully predict, we chose the development of a toolkit over which we could have control.

ROCKETT consists principally of an extension to Prolog which allows the representation of structured objects and supports access to them from within any Prolog procedure which has been passed through the ROCKETT compiler. Procedures which are so processed we refer to as extended procedures; they are in all other respects normal Prolog procedures.

We had originally thought to have the compiler present with the run-time system so that rapid updates might be made during testing. Shortage of space in the PC prevented this; we therefore had a separate compilation phase in which some degree of incremental development was possible. Our disappointment was not as great as it might have been, as we were rather opposed to the idea of changing the reasoning methods and continuing the run with possibly invalidated data.

The structured objects of ROCKETT were simplified in certain key areas to be more suited to the performance and capacity of a PC. Objects are of fixed type: once an object has been created as an instance of a type, its classification cannot be changed. Attributes are not in themselves objects in the way of some fuller frame-based systems such as DEKE [5]; types and the reasoning attached to them cannot be modified once any item has been defined which might depend on the information.

The compilation phase started as an efficiency mechanism for the extended Prolog syntax but developed further as a way of making the rules and frame accesses more readable to non-programmers as shown in an example in Fig. 1.

A significant feature of this translation is that the user-defined attributes become functors rather than being elements of some other structure such as **frame(person, jim, [son=fred, age=50]).** This has benefit in speed of access and clarity of transformation into Prolog but introduces some lack of control over user-defined names. We had many discussions over the semantic and implementation issues involved in altering the user-given names: strong candidates were the use of type and attribute names combined as in **person_age(jim,25)** (which was more restrictive when reasoning over types which had sub-types) and the use of internal names such as **%age.** As these would have made interfacing between handwritten and generated Prolog code harder to understand, it was decided to suffer the occasional attempts to define an attribute such as **name** which clashed with existing predicates.

The main chained reasoning of the system is implemented using extended Prolog procedures attached to attributes — the so-called type qualifiers or demons : *if needed* and *default* for backward chaining; *if-added* and *if-deleted* in the forward direction. Other qualifiers handle validation of attributes and objects.

Rules, of both the conventional if–then form and other related forms,

ˆjim(son ˆ(type person, gt age 25))
read as
"the object jim which has attribute son
whose value is an object of type person with age
attribute having a value greater than 25",
compiled to the optimal code
son(jim,A), person(A), age(A,X), X > 25
The language later became
jim with son = (person with age > 25)
with the same executed code.

Fig. 1 — Compilation example: 'Has jim a son who is older than 25 ?'

provide a strategic method of processing. The condition and action parts of rules are of the same form as extended Prolog procedures but, in the current implementation, the action parts do not backtrack. Rules are gathered into groups called Nodes which act as a focussing mechanism. Nodes specify goals for which the node might be useful, contexts under which they could validly be used and successor nodes which might be useful after the completion of the current node. Each node can specify the inference engine to be used to process it; in theory there could be a separate inference engine for each node but in practice only three engines were used significantly.

The application was highly non-monotonic in that the user was involved in the discussion and could change his mind about anything. The use of rules and nodes gave some control and consistency to the conversation as perceived by the user, leaving the automatically chained reasoning to the objects, their attributes and demons. One solution to this interactive aspect of the problem was the use a dependency directed backtracking where partial solutions were sought by different nodes, each controlled by an object which watched for circumstances where a reevaluation was necessary.

The MMI that we used for the project was heavily dependent on the windowing support available in PC-based Prolog implementations which we found to be very effective for our simple needs. The usual pop-up menus, questions and free text output were available.

Our implementation of *Help* invoked a separate instance of the reasoning system so that fully context sensitive help could be provided. *Explanation* was specialized to produce free text narrative on the reasoning so far — rather than explicitly detailing the reasoning after the style of a stack dump. Travel agents do not wish to know that **'By rule 21c I deduced that . . .'**. Both

Help and *Explanation* used separate files to hold the large bodies of text involved — these were called using the facilities built into the Prologs for accessing serial and direct-access files.

The final component of ROCKETT which was vital to the project was the ability to call up foreign code. This, allied to the need for a flexibility of reasoning, had been the main reason for developing a purpose-built shell.

4. DATABASES

In addition to the Prolog database and the conceptually separate storage for the attributes of objects, two main databases were accessed as part of the project.

Viewdata (Teletext) systems hold booking data and general information for the holiday travel industry. It was considered that these would be a useful example of a database to access. The systems were already in existence, permission to access certain parts of them was easily obtained and they represented the *de facto* standard for the industry.

On the public transport side the project created a set of timetables and imported a special-purpose timetable search algorithm developed by Wootton Jeffreys [2].

5. VIEWDATA

There are two main styles of Viewdata system: those which respond to requests to present pre-formatted pages of information and those which take data from the user for processing — in some senses 'passive' and 'active' systems. The passive systems are far easier to access for a number of reasons. There is less dependency on accurate transmission of data, there is less page interpretation to be performed, the data needed to access the passive systems are much more static — and fewer data are needed.

We confined the use of Viewdata systems to the holiday side of the project although there are also Viewdata pages available for public transport information — many thousands of Prestel pages exist, for instance, as summaries of important routes on British Rail. It was not considered worth while to repeat the explorations from the holiday side. Rather, we ensured that the low-level interface code would cope with all the different systems and wrote the higher level interfacing in Rule form and as Prolog procedures to make transfer easier.

Thomas Cook kindly agreed to let us use their systems, CARE and TIB, as examples, respectively, of active and passive Viewdata systems for demonstration purposes. There existed a training version of their booking system CARE which was therefore protected from (our) system errors. The Thomas Cook Information Bank (TIB) is a large repository of useful and detailed information about regions throughout the world: including climate, travel time from the airports, features of major resorts and visa requirements.

We discovered that we needed a very large amount of information held locally to access the booking system satisfactorily. The problem arose in two areas:

- the low-level data needed to check the formats of the Viewdata screens
- the low-level data for holidays (code numbers, pricing and date information) which form part of the basic information for handling a booking.

Representing this information in the Prolog database was too much for the Prolog systems we used.

Some of the holiday travel firms already use computers of the style of IBM PCs to help in the access of booking systems by analysing the screens — but they have the help of an auxiliary 32-bit processor to do the bulk of the processing. An active Viewdata system as seen after processing by such a front-end is more suited to processing by a knowledge-based system — the information has been condensed, validated and simplified. It has overcome, to some degree, the chief disadvantage of Viewdata in that it was intended for human reading. Without some assistance, Viewdata has several 'faults' when considered as a computer–computer communication protocol:

- Its data density is very low.
- It has many pages with meaningless data such as pictures in arbitrary positions.
- It depends on a human reader for its error checking with no checksum or other protocol in normal use.

We considered using an auxiliary database to assist the Prolog to store the information about holiday codes to support the booking system but we decided against it for two reasons : we were already intending to close-couple a database on the transport side and repetition within the project would be wasteful; we were also concerned that to write an adequate interface would absorb too much effort in low-level coding for an awareness project. It made more sense for our project to concentrate on the demonstration aspects of the connection, so the passive system TIB therefore became our main 'remote' demonstrator and in a quite well integrated way.

6. TIB ACCESSES

The *Help* system of ROCKETT invokes rules which have been specified as appropriate to the various stages in the processing. At some points, the appropriate activity was to dial out for information from TIB. Taking knowledge of the current regions and resorts of interest, and knowledge of the main indexing of TIB, the initial pages of the appropiate countries could be presented to the user in a help window — almost exactly as if an experienced user had called them up for himself. The rules of the system had by this point dialled the appropriate number on the built-in modem and sent the correct sequences of codes to log the user in. The only knowledge which we did not include in the knowledge base was the password to enable access — this had to be typed in each time. The knowledge-based components which assisted with the conversation with TIB were principally concerned with validation of user input against the current Viewdata screen and the mediation between the user and Viewdata when an error was detected (system not available, no dial tone detected, bad characters seen in key fields). At the end of use of the Viewdata system, the expert system would follow the correct procedures for logging off.

At the first level, the Viewdata transaction handler was an object with attributes such as error-message, dial-code, password and current-page. The demons of this object responded to various circumstances: on the receipt of an error message the system reported the problem to the user and asked whether he wished to log off or try again. The system used its knowledge of the sorts of messages which could appear on the error lines to avoid reporting prompts and confirmations to the user as errors. We tried to keep the user directly involved. Among other reasons, this avoided the starting of long activities when the user would rather abandon the attempt.

Behind the demons were a number of Prolog procedures which handled the main analysis and display of the text and carried out monitoring activities such as the spotting of error conditions. This area of the system showed the smooth transition from rule and demon to Prolog very well. Behind the Prolog procedures, in turn, were a number of C routines which handled the serial ports which controlled the modem and which were callable as Prolog predicates through the foreign language interface. The modem appeared to the expert system as a family of Prolog predicates such as

tr_dial(Number, Error_code)
tr_fetch(text, Screen_image, Error_code)
tr_send(Text, Error_code)

For the better handling of remote systems, one point we had to solve was the introduction of asynchronous processing under Prolog. Neither the PC under MSDOS nor the ordinary Prolog systems are renowned for their multiprocessing ability. While talking to the user, we might get further information from the Viewdata system — perhaps an error message — that we wanted to be able to process on the fly while, for instance, waiting for the user to respond to a question. We decided against the use of C-level interrupts as being a hard challenge, without knowledge of the internal processing of the Prolog system, and we implemented a rule-level interrupt mechanism — checking procedures which were invoked from the kernel of the inference engines if certain conditions were satisfied (in this case, if the Viewdata object had status attribute set to 'connected'). This was implemented in Prolog and gave us no problems at all, as we were not dealing with millisecond responses if the user was connected to the Viewdata browsing rules. The combination was very satisfactory and enhanced the system considerably.

7. RESORT INFORMATION DATABASE

The TIB system was also used in another way — for knowledge acquisition. One batch of information held on the system was that of the features of the various resorts such as beach quality, the level of night-life or the availability of horse-riding. These we were able to search to attempt to satisfy user requirements. Although this worked, it was very slow and obviously not practical. A swift analysis showed that the data were fairly compact and we would be able to transfer this knowledge into the knowledge base for matching using a local database. Prolog showed another of its strengths here, as we were able to capture the pages from the Viewdata system as text and convert them to suitable form using a rapidly developed Prolog 'compiler' to try out various representations of the data.

The data were stored in virtual memory, as it was quite large and it was later to become the prototype for the 'used methods' accesses described later. As an early attempt at improving performance of the accesses to this data we used a buffering technique.

In terms of Prolog clauses, this information was held by resort as key

where(place1, [feature1, feature2...])

so access to all places with a particular feature was a 'reversed' access. (We were heavily reliant on first argument indexing.) We felt that for a large number of clauses we could not implement a complete invert such as

what(feature1, [place1, place2..])

as there were about 400 places and 20 or so attributes for a fuller prototype system. We tried adding a 'cacheing' method to the object of type 'resort_information' so that requests of the form shown in Fig. 2 would be more efficient.

```
r1 :: curr_enquiry with
          possible_resort = R and
          user_feature_wanted = F ,
     R with not feature = F
  =>>
     enquiry called curr_enquiry to_have
          not possible_resort = R.

[ =>> is a 'forall' rule form ]
```

Fig. 2 — Rule which benefits from 'cacheing'.

If we received a request for information about one feature of a resort we could expect to receive others — the whole clause about the resort was therefore held in a 'currently-enquired-about-resort' clause in the (non-VM) Prolog database. This gave us some of the performance we wanted in the prototype but this information really has to go out to a non-Prolog database. It is not information which needs updating frequently and it handicaps the system to hold it in virtual memory.

Looking to improve the access further, it seemed more general to arrange the access methods so that for any attempted matching against a set of requirements, a well-chosen search was invoked — so, for instance, we avoid the cacheing overhead if there is only one element in the set of requirements. The method used was a prototype for a weighted evaluation where the requirements were ranked in order of importance with a scoring function to evaluate the degree of match.

In practice, having solved the problem of space for some of the data clauses, we were starting to run into problems storing the procedures to handle them: unexplained errors suddenly increased as the garbage collector was invoked. This effectively made our choices for us and limited our prototype. Knowing what we did later, we would have spent far less effort attempting to squeeze information into Prolog and gone straight for a simple use of indexed files of our own making.

8. TRANSPORT DATA

The public transport timetable and route search involved two main parts. The first was the finding of routes between two places by way of possible interchange points. The second was to find the fastest (and in other ways most suitable) of these routes.

We had hoped to prototype the whole of this in Prolog to give ourselves the flexibility to try out various scoring functions on the different partial routes. It was then the intention to harden up the winning strategy into C code where it was slow. To this end we encoded various standard algorithms to search for suitable routes — (depth/breadth/best) first and bounded search algorithms. These tests made the PC struggle severely and we decided to go straight to a conventionally coded algorithm. On the PC it does not seem to be possible to recursively process large lists of candidates — we had to iterate over the solution storing away partial solutions by asserting into virtual memory.

We used an enhancement of the *Travelguide* [3] algorithm with the expert system controlling the parameters of the search. This modified branch-and-bound search is specially geared to scanning this sort of timetable information. As it was written in C and accessed the disk directly, it took the pressure off Prolog and seemed to help it to work better in both direct (brute speed) and indirect (memory and garbage corruption†.) ways.

9. NAME TREES

A further form of database was used to access names of places. In our initial design it had been obvious that the user interface was going to need very

† A misprint for 'garbage collection' which is left, as it describes the system behaviour exactly.

special support where names of places and features were concerned. We therefore wrote a special-purpose database with its own updating and search. This was a multiway name tree prototyped in Prolog with automatic ambiguity resolving. For rule writers' convenience, this name-searching could be interposed between the question and the user so that any user errors were invisible to the rules.

We were going to convert this database to C but it ran very well in Prolog, so we left it. It was used from the user interface, so we only needed 'human' rather than 'computer' speeds. The main reason for rewriting it would not be for increased speed but to take pressure off the main Prolog memory and to reduce the space garbage-collected.

10. VIRTUAL MEMORY

It is also the case, in practice, that the Prolog database itself has to be considered in two parts. Under some implementations of Prolog, the virtual memory is not allowed to contain procedure bodies; on others, this does not work too well, even when allowed. Some implementations of Prolog divide the VM into 1 Mbyte chunks — this makes life difficult for the compiler writer in a system such as ours where the names of attributes were, for efficiency, the functors of clauses. Database design becomes a feature of ordinary Prolog accesses.

11. ADVANTAGES AND DISADVANTAGES OF THE PC

A PC is a very useful machine for an awareness project like TRACE. It is the right price for the Club members to continue using it after the project. It has a large range of add-ons such as the modem we used — and software comes at a reasonable price too. It is also in the right price-range to consider for the target application in retail operations where a large number of machines are required around the country as intelligent and multi-purpose terminals.

PC-based implementations of Prolog tend to have quite an attractive MMI although at least one did depend on external software for this. The two main Prolog implementations we used had MMI which was excellent for our purposes — one more flexible; the other easier to use. One of the hardest areas to face in moving to a larger machine without a close coupled screen would be the lack of simple, attractive MMI. The Prologs we used supplied easy file access facilities — the creation and access to random access files made light work of tasks which could be quite onerous on larger machine implementations.

The PC is, at heart, the wrong machine to run knowledge-based systems which are demanding of large amounts of memory. Under MS-DOS there is a total of 640 Kb of flat memory and, by clever access, a further few Megabytes can be made available. For efficiency, Prolog implementers have used a 64 Kb stack which disappears very rapidly unless everything is written carefully. Even then, recursive solutions are not viable for larger problems. The main heap is exhausted pretty rapidly by recursion involving big lists —

one of the reasons that our public transport search was so slow in Prolog was that we could not do a recursive search — we had to iterate and store the partial networks at each cycle. Once virtual memory is invoked, the slowdown is such that careful design is needed to ensure that key clauses are in the right place.

Later versions of MS-DOS have come to the rescue to a degree. It is allowed to plant the disk file which supports VM in high core memory above the 1 Mbyte boundary — this removes a lot of the speed loss. However, we have yet to time a PC-based Prolog garbage collecting over 6 Mb.

The PC is a very useful machine but unfortunately takes away much of the power of developing in Prolog — one has to think very hard at times about database design even within the built-in facilities — to the detriment of knowledge representation.

12. UNIFORMITY OF ACCESS AND POSSIBLE IMPROVEMENTS

Up to the latter part of the project, all accesses were to normal attributes. An access to an attribute was compiled as a triple as mentioned above. When a non-Prolog database access was to be used for a value, it was the *if_needed* clause which handled the access. Similarly, *if-added* and *if-deleted* access were coded to deal with the updating. This worked adequately but a more uniform method was sought. The compiler, which formed the triple access, now looks for specified families of user-written procedures which can be used for any number of attributes (Fig. 3).

This is a comfortable way of ordering matters, although there are still some deficiencies one would like to deal with. Where the relative volumes of data are fairly well known, it would be beneficial to have the compiler order the Prolog accesses for efficiency. We did not have much enthusiasm for the prospect of ordering queries at run-time, and there are many complex issues in this area — a useful starting point is found in [4]. With a division of labour between the Prolog and other databases, one of the main items we did not attempt was the automatic (compiler produced) or manual (specified in user methods) grouping of queries for presentation to an information retrieval service. While we made the interface uniform and fairly easy to use, we did not make it as efficient as it might have been.

Knowing that there are a very large number of persons and that fewer persons have programming expertise and that only type person has the attribute indicating programming expertise in a particular language, it would be useful to reorder so that

person called X with age= A and program_language= Value

becomes

program_language(X,Value), age(X,A)

rather than

person(X),age(X,A),program_language(X,Value)

```
type :: person => ... age,address...

type_qualifiers :: person.

  if_needed ::
  P with age = A =>
    P with date_of_birth = DoB,
    current_date(D),
    age_diff(D,DoB).

  use_method ::
  address => personnel_file.

  use_method ::
  name => personnel_file.

end_type.

/*  the user-method itself...  */
personnel_file(get,Type,Attr,Val) :-
     ....
personnel_file(put,Type,Attr,Val) :-
     ...
```

Fig. 3 — User-methods example.

Similarly, information which is in VM or on a non-Prolog database could be accessed in a better order.

Knowing that two attributes in a condition came from a particular record, it should be possible to achieve some automation of access to the compounded query. Reordering and regrouping of accesses, even if not made as a joined query, will have benefits if one assumes the presence of some form of underlying cacheing — two accesses to the same record for different data will be more efficient.†.

In writing the rules for the holiday system one (instinctively?) ordered conditions by increasing frequency and putting virtual memory items later. However, for the ease of manipulation it would be good to explore the

† I have to be a bit cautious here. I suggested to one Prolog vendor that having a single large buffer for his VM seemed wrong and I should like to see some sort of LRU algorithm — he tried it out for me and rather amusedly told me that it had slowed it down!

tradeoff between effort in compiler design, increased time of compilation and saving of storage and run-time by forcing the use of better ordered queries.

13. VOLATILITY

Many smaller expert systems are of the 'static network' variety. In such a system, there is a strong division between the knowledge represented by the rules (considered static) and the data brought to each consultation (considered transient). Once we use databases to enhance the process, and particularly when considering the use of compact knowledge as locally stored information, consideration of volatility becomes an important component of the design process of the system.

Taking the idea of distributed systems, with smaller machines acting as intelligent terminals accessing larger more centralized systems, one wishes to avoid excessive updating of the knowledge bases of large numbers of machines. The period of change can vary from minutes to years, and the impact of the changes can vary from being negligible to being financially damaging. It can also be impossible to know that one's current knowledge is correct without verifying it every time it is used.

Volatility can be thought of as a function of frequency of change, volume of changed data, significance of changed data and effort needed to obtain the correct version. By way of example, the data in Fig. 4 is in order of increasing volatility.

Spain is in Europe, Benidorm is in Spain.

Benidorm is a lively resort,
Benidorm is popular with young singles.

Thomsons do holidays in Benidorm.

Thomsons do holiday AAA123 in Benidorm.

AAA123 costs 250 pounds for a fortnight in mid-June.

AAA123 has 2 seats left in first week of June.

Fig. 4 — Examples of data of increasing volatility.

For the highest volatility we must use an access to the central database — however costly. All suggestions and decisions have to be based on assumptions up to that point — emulating the human sales person — and suitable information must be given to the client to avoid false expectations. At the next level of volatility, overnight updating over a network or postal delivery of updating diskettes may be in order.

None of this is new — it has been a problem for system designers for a number of years. It is now becoming an issue for the builders of knowledge-based systems. Once we start coupling to the real world to take advantage of its benefits, we have to take into account real-world problems as well.

14. PROLOG IMPLEMENTATIONS

This section should have been subtitled *The Good, the Bad and the Ugly*: a personal view of what is good about PC-based Prologs, what is bad about them, and what I would like to see in them.

We found the PC-based Prologs that we used to have excellent MMI for our purposes. Like much of PC-based software, they were provided with easy-to-use windows and facilities such as pop-up menus were easy to implement. Although MMI may not be the main goal of a Prolog implementation, implementors must not neglect the subject if Prolog is to be easy to use for an application where appearances are important. They must not neglect it if they are to sell Prolog systems to developers on as wide a basis as the language deserves.

Either easy-to-use windows should be supported or a simple interface to a recognized package should be provided. Similarly simple file I/O makes for rapid prototyping. Many of the facilities which we need to underpin systems are readily and rapidly developed (or at least prototyped) in Prolog, but screen and file I/O do not fall in this area. I do not need (and, it has been said, I do not always understand) six versions of **not,** but we do need easy access to the real world if we are to use Prolog for real systems. It is essential (and this applies to any system: not just Prolog and not just KBS) to have a foreign language interface that can be used without thinking too hard. We need both hammers and screwdrivers to build our systems — let us be able to use both in an integrated way; we do not want to have to hammer nails with our screwdriver.

Prologs are varied — too varied for comfort as yet. In this project alone we have used Prologs with and without strings and where operators were differently defined. The system was ported twice in the project and each time a substantial effort was needed on matters other than MMI (where one might expect individuality).

It is hard to obtain information about what is fast and what is bulky in a particular implementation. **repeat** ... can be dramatically better than recursion in one implementation and the reverse can be true in the next. First-argument indexing can cost a lot of valuable space — 10 bytes per clause is noticeable on a PC — and as it occupies real memory, it sets an upper limit on the faster parts of an application. Some implementations, such as Prolog/2, provide useful notes on this sort of topic.

On the PC the Virtual Memory issue looms large. Different Prologs have different mechanisms to deal with the problem. One implmentation has a 'flat' VM so that one only needs to say that a predicate is virtual for it to use that storage. This seems to be good until you see the effect on a simple-minded garbage collector. Another requires that a virtual predicate be declared within a module which is declared to be virtual — which seems good until you find that these modules have finite size. Yet another uses separate (B-tree) assert and retract mechanisms for its VM — a method which I have a liking for, as it separates the secondary storage very cleanly. Each of these mechanisms presents its own (very un-Prolog) problems to the system builder. We even had to consider, at times, whether the clauses of dynamically created procedures were stored consecutively or interleaved with the clauses of other procedures — this can cause a *large* time difference in access.

Prolog-level compilation is an issue affecting design. On one system, the compiled code was very fast but took an age to compile. On another, all code was compiled to threaded code very rapidly but made assert and retract much slower — a drawback for a system such as ours in which assert and retract are heavily used for updating the structured objects.

Where VM demanded that there be no body on a clause we had to 'Klein'†. our procedures and use **call**. On one implementation metacalled cuts were treated as equivalent to **true**. This did not help the logic of the system.

Because of the large amounts of information we were trying to cram into our system, we spent a lot of time falling down cracks. Garbage collectors which corrupted the system in exciting ways, such as uninstantiating variables, and debuggers, which changed the behaviour of the system, caused us a great deal of grief. I believe things are improving but that there are still elements of the expert system development technique known as 'slow prototyping' (or 'toothmarks in the desk') where one changes a design rapidly over a day and then spends a week of late nights finding out whether it is the programmer or the Prolog system which has erred. We were fortunate in using systems with UK-based support. We were pleased with the support we got — just that we would rather not have needed it! I think things are chainging — they had better, or one might even be tempted to use L***‡. for smaller systems next time.

Some applications would benefit if Prolog implementations were to provide access to other databases as a natural part of the language — *behind* the normal call access. Some Prologs are starting to supply interface modules to connect to utilities such as DBase3 — better might be the attachment of a specified access to different predicates after the style of the virtual declaration. It is how the 'user_method' would be if we could get under Prolog's skin. We would seem to get four benefits from this method:

- Speed — queries can be accessed optimally by existing algorithms and databases.

† My term. After the Klein bottle of topology where the body disappears inside the head.
‡ A List Processing language.

- RAM is not taken up with infrequently accessed data — and particularly by its indices.
- The Prolog garbage collection is not slowed down by the presence of lots of data into the Prolog system — especially important for demonstrations!

Set against this is the fact that such an interface can never be as simple as one would wish — practical considerations such as symbol tables seem to prevent the natural use of large numbers of databases as if they were just extensions of the Prolog database. To some extent, the wish-list is self-contradictory; I hope that an implementation can resolve the problem — perhaps by providing the tools for the developer to build appropriate specializations of the interfacing.

15. WHERE NEXT?

One of the main technical changes we see coming, for the larger knowledge-based system on a smaller machine, is the ability to use the 80386 chip — in particular we may be able to use large flat memory and multitasking on small commercial machines. This could make a large difference to implementers of commercial systems. It will move the boundary of the readily accessible memory an order of magnitude further away. That is not to say that the issues of connection to different sorts of data will go away — just that we might stand a fair chance of getting the system kernel into decent shape. If the lack of certainty over the future of OS/2 causes implementers to hold back on their investment in this area, then at least let us have Expanded Memory systems with more direct memory access to get an improvement over RAM–disk accesses where high memory is treated as a disk drive.

One of the main philosophical changes over the period of the TRACE project has been the acceptance of the naturalness of hybrid systems: that it is in some sense right to want to connect existing databases and conventional systems to expert systems. This idea was fairly new (apart from the 'intelligent front-end' work) when this project started. The ideas — and the wherewithal such as easy C interfaces — have now become readily available.

Our project choices and design were rooted in what was available in the latter half of 1985 — the world looks very different today. Unfortunately for those starting projects now, things are still in flux — does our crystal ball show something like good PS/2 Prologs in 12 months time — or do we still see a dichotomy between the 'workstation' developers and the 'commercials'?

REFERENCES

[1] The TRACE Club, Alvey Expert Systems Awareness Project IKBS 059.
[2] Hakami, B. and Williams, G., An Integration of Problem Solving Methods, in *Proc. AI and Advanced Computer Technology,* Wiesbaden, Sept 1985.

[3] *Travelguide,* A Route Enquiry System Available from Wootton Jeffreys Consultants Ltd.
[4] Smith, D. E. and Genesereth, M. R., Ordering Conjunctive Queries, in *Artificial Intelligence,* **26**, 171–215, 1985.
[5] DEKE, a Development Environment for Knowledge Engineering: An In-house Tool Developed and Used by Software Sciences.

19

A flexible Prolog-based lexical database system

William G. Imlah
Scicon Ltd
Bart Demoen
BIM

ABSTRACT

Natural language processing (NLP) systems often need large lexica, or dictionaries, better suited to secondary storage than to main memory. In ESPRIT project LOKI we are implementing a Prolog-based lexical database to support such a system. Our approach combines a relatively unstructured low-level database system supporting fast access via multiple access paths, with a Prolog-level management component which presents the NL system with the required view of the lexicon. Flexibility is an important asset: the design aims to keep the database system independent of language, application and even type of NLP system.

1. INTRODUCTION

This chapter discusses the implementation of a flexible Prolog-based lexical database. The work described here is being carried out in the LOKI project (ESPRIT ref 107) by BIM, Scicon Ltd, and the University of Hamburg. A major goal of project LOKI is to develop LOQUI, a natural language interface to databases. One of the problems we face is that for LOQUI, as for any serious attempt at providing a natural language interface, we must build up a large lexicon. The characteristics of such a database are clear: the lexicon will consist of a large number of unit clauses, too many to be usefully stored in memory, and, once entered, these data will be relatively static. On the other hand, the exact structure of the database is not so clear. In the course of the project it may be subject to change. This is common in natural language research, where changes to requirements may occur as new methods are applied.

2. PROBLEM STATEMENT

In the LOKI project we are developing a prototype for a German and English Natural Language Interface to relational databases. The system is capable of extended dialogues with the user and should have a realistic lexical coverage in each language. At the moment each lexicon has about a thousand entries. The next stage in the project involves lexicon expansion to at least five thousand entries in each language. These larger lexica are better suited to secondary storage than to main memory. For this we need a Prolog-coupled external database system supporting the following characteristics.

2.1 Fast retrieval

In a dialogue system, response time is crucial. If the user's interaction with LOQUI is to appear natural, the dialogue must take place in real time.

2.2 Multiple access paths

The LOQUI system can both analyse and generate text. These two processes use completely different access paths: character strings for analysis, semantic formulae for generation. For analysis there are two options: access on word forms or access on word stems. The database must be capable of supporting both. For generation we have also identified two access paths. Further system development, or changes to new application areas, may result in other access paths being identified.

2.3 Variable length entries

Some lexical entries have more data associated with them than others. During system development it is not easy to predict the size of entries. In Prolog this is no problem, because predicate arguments can be very complex structures of indefinite length. If our lexical database is to be at all flexible, it must support variable length entries.

2.4 Static data

Once the lexicon is fully developed it will remain static, with entries being created, removed or modified only as a result of transporting the lexicon to a new application domain, or to fix errors in the data. At system run-time we expect the data to be almost completely static.

2.5 Variable lexicon size

The database system must be flexible enough to perform well for databases of widely differing sizes. For instance, a fully developed lexicon may support hundreds of thousands of entries. At the other extreme, some applications may use a far smaller lexicon of, say, a few hundred words.

2.6 Generality

In the course of the development of our system we expect to add new features to the lexicon and, possibly, to access the data via new paths. Transporting the lexicon to a new application type can produce similar changes. Such requirements cannot always be foreseen. The lexical database system must be flexible enough to allow these changes to be made easily: to support new access paths and to restructure the data within the database. Ideally, our implementation should be independent of language, application and even type of NLP system.

3. THE DATABASE IMPLEMENTATION

Our approach to these problems involves a two-level implementation. A Prolog-coupled database system meets the general requirements of a fast-access, static database supporting multiple access paths. To complement this, a second level is defined in Prolog itself. This acts as a database management layer, imposing further structuring on the database records and presenting the NL system with a particular view of the lexicon.

3.1 Access mechanisms

There are two standard methods available for indexing on large volumes of data on secondary storage: hashing and B-trees.

Hashing performs extremely well when the database is static and the distribution of the key is known beforehand: in some extreme cases a perfect hash function can be defined which guarantees access to the data in a single logical disk access. Dynamic databases are rather difficult to maintain with hashing: the special case of database extension has only been handled successfully by extendible hashing [1,2]. In general, hashing is most appropriate when access time is critical and flexibility during exploitation is of a secondary concern.

B-trees are generalizations of an index to a sorted sequence of entities. An index contains a portion of the data and pointers to where chunks of information lying between two subsequent entities can be found (pages).

If one reduces the size of the pages, the index will grow considerably and one can think of indexing indices for example. This mechanism of multi-level index is also called a B-tree owing to its resemblance to binary search: after each step, search space is reduced by a constant factor and search time is proportional to the logarithm of the size of the database. A number of variants have been developed such as multi-dimensional B-trees, multi-level B-trees or B+ trees, but the general principle is the same: to allow reasonable behaviour in very dynamic conditions.

From the requirements of our lexical database as a static database demanding fast access hashing seems the best alternative. Below, we describe how the general principle of extendible hashing has been implemented to suit our needs.

3.1.1 Hashing

The hash function maps a variable length key (e.g. a word form) onto an index corresponding to an entry in the hash table. The latter consists of a certain number of slots, depending on the number of bits taken into account after application of the hashing function. The slots contain pointers to the physical location of the data to be retrieved. These data are organized in blocks (buckets), each containing a number of keys with their associated information.

Looking up a word in the lexicon thus comprises determining its place in the hash table by applying the hash function, fetching the associated bucket from the external database, and going through the bucket extracting entries with the required key. If the main hash table is stored in memory then only one logical disk access is needed to fetch the relevant bucket.

There are, however, a number of problems with this approach. First the hashing function returns a bit pattern of fixed length. This means that the number of slots in the hash table is limited and static, and a hard-wired number of slots would have to provide space for a very large lexicon, even if this were not needed in some applications. Moreover, different words will inevitably be associated with identical indices and, consequently, the same bucket on disk. This introduces the possibility of bucket overflow, where more entries map to a bucket than there is room for. Increasing the bucket size then removes the advantage of retrieval in a single disk access.

3.1.2 Extendible hashing

A more flexible solution, and the one adopted here, is extendible hashing. When bucket oveflow occurs, this mechanism automatically extends the bit pattern by one bit, thus causing the number of slots to double in size. There are now twice as many buckets available and the data are more evenly spread through them. The advantage to the lexicographer is that he can reorganize the lexicon as he wants. On changes to the data, the system's reorganization will be transparent to him.

3.1.3 Cache memory

To further enhance response time, an in-core database is maintained by the database system. This acts as a buffer between the secondary storage database and the Prolog system, storing frequently accessed entries. In each language there is a small set of words which are frequently used (e.g. 'the', 'is', 'of'). Moreover, for a particular application there is normally a small set of domain-specific words that occur frequently. When the database is first opened, these entries are loaded and kept in main memory. The database system looks up this internal database before deciding to go to the external database. To monitor the frequency of word use, the system keeps count of their frequency of retrieval. In this way the database subset in cache memory can be modified accordingly. A further possibility is total customization, where a table of word frequency is stored for each user or user group. This may prove practical in the case where user groups are interested in different subsets of information.

3.2 External database records

The external database system allows the definition of several record types, each entry of which is defined in two parts: a variable length key file and a variable length information field. Any number of record types can be defined. The information field contains a single Prolog structure, stored in the internal code of the Prolog system. The internal structuring of these fields is defined in the database management component defined in Prolog.

Each record can be retrieved in Prolog by a predicate call whose arguments are the name of the record, an instantiated key value, the data to be returned by the call, and a return status:

ldb_retrieve(⟨key⟩ , ⟨record type⟩ , ⟨status⟩)

Because the system is tightly coupled to Prolog, the information can be stored on disk in BIM_Prolog's internal representation. Access paths to the database always involve ground atomic keys. (Note that our examples use the default notation for BIM_Prolog variables, which is that they begin with an underscore.)

For our lexical database, all information on an entry is stored in a single entry, whose key is an arbitrary unique identifier, e.g.

REC TYPE	KEY	DATA
lexeme	LEAD1	[V,[INST,LEADING,[alpha,theta]], [[leads,V3], [lead,VBASE], [leading,VING], [led,VEN],[lead,VEN], [led,VPAST],[lead,VPAST]]]
lexeme	PERSON1	[N,[INST,PERSON,], [[person, N3PSG],[persons,N3PPL]]]
lexeme	LEADER1	[N,[VAL(1),LEADING,[alpha,theta]], [[leader,N3PSG], [leaders,N3PPL]]]

This means that all information about lexical entry can be retrieved by a single logical disk access.

But this record type only supports a single access path (its key), and we have already seen that the system must support access via several other paths. To overcome this we define further record types, one for each additional access path. Like the lexeme record, each of these has a single key field, but the data field in each of these does not contain a lexical entry. Instead it stores the key of the corresponding lexeme record:

REC TYPE	KEY	DATA
form	lead	LEAD1
form	leads	LEAD1
form	led	LEAD1
form	leading	LEAD1
form	leader	LEADER1
form	leaders	LEADER1
form	person	PERSON1
form	persons	PERSON1
semantics	LEADING	LEAD1
semantics	LEADING,alpha	LEADER1
semantics	PERSON	PERSON1

Access to any lexical entry then needs no more than two logical disk accesses: one to retrieve its lexeme-key, and one to look up the entry itself. If access is via lexeme-key then only one disk access is needed. For most lexicon lookups, the required entry will already be in cache memory, so that no external access will be required.

At this level of implementation, the internal structure of each lexical entry is largely undefined. The definition and management of lexical data structures is controlled by the Prolog-level interface between the database calls and the NLP system.

3.3 The Prolog-level interface

The Prolog-level interface manages the retrieval and updating of lexical data, and presents the NL application with the particular data structures it needs. Prolog is particularly suited for this because it allows the definition of rules which can be used to present views of the data.

For example, suppose we have the following external database records:

REC TYPE	KEY	DATA
lexeme	LEAD1	[V,[INST,LEADING,[alpha,theta]], [[leads,V3], [lead,VBASE], [leading,VING], [led,VEN],[lead,VEN], [led,VPAST],[lead,VPAST]]]
form	lead	LEAD1
form	leads	LEAD1
form	led	LEAD1
form	leading	LEAD1
saemantics	LEADING	LEAD1

The Prolog-level component can present the following 'structured' view of the data:

```
word_form(_Form, _Category, _Syntax, _Lexid, _Semantics):-
    lbd_retrieve(_Form,form,_Lexid),
    lbd_retrieve(_Lexid, lexeme, [_Category, _Semantics, _Formdata ]),
    member([_Form,_Syntax],_Formdata).
member(_H,[_H|_]).
member(_H,[_|_T]):-
    member(_H,_T).
```

This would present to the NL system the following sequence of facts:

```
word_form(lead,  V, VBASE, LEAD1, leading, [INST,LEADING,[alpha,theta]]).
word_form(lead,  V, VEN,   LEAD1, leading, [INST,LEADING,[alpha,theta]]).
word_form(lead,  V, VPAST, LEAD1, leading, [INST,LEADING,[alpha,theta]]).
```

```
word_form(leads,   V, V3,    LEAD1, leading, [INST,LEADING,[alpha,theta]]).
word_form(leading,V, VING,   LEAD1, leading, [INST,LEADING,[alpha,theta]]).
word_form(led,     V, VEN,   LEAD1, leading, [INST,LEADING,[alpha,theta]]).
word_form(led,     V, VPAST, LEAD1, leading, [INST,LEADING,[alpha,theta]]).
```

Using this method, the database information can be presented to NLP system in a highly structured form, disguising the fact that all the lexical data for entry LEAD1 are clustered on a single database record.

4. ADVANTAGES OF THE TWO-LEVEL APPROACH

This approach means that changes to the lexical database structure or to data representation can be carried out at the Prolog level, by rewriting the rules which specify the application's view of the database, and by updating the contents of the lexeme data fields on the database.

Secondly, changes in the type of information stored in the database are hidden from the database implementation level. The database can be updated via the Prolog interface without any change in the external database definition. This makes these types of changes simple and quick to make, and they do not need the user to have any knowledge of the database implementation itself, other than at the level of Prolog calls.

Thirdly, when a new access path is identified, the existing external database definition need not be modified, only augmented. A new record type is defined which relates the key of the access path to the lexical entry containing the data associated with it.

Lastly, the low-level implementation provides a general Prolog-based database system suitable for applications for which there is a large amount of static data requiring multiple access paths via ground values, and whose functional specification is liable to change.

5. SUMMARY

Lexical databases are characterized by large amounts of static data, better suited to disk storage than to memory. There is not yet a consensus as to what such a database should look like, or what or how many access paths it should support. At this stage in the development of NLP, what is needed is a general and flexible lexicon database, supporting fast access and multiple access paths while being flexible enough to allow changes to its access and structuring requirements to be made quickly and easily. The lexical database system we are developing in ESPRIT project LOKI is designed to meet these demands by using a two-level approach to database definition.

At the database-implementation level a theory-neutral, simply structured external database is being implemented. All lexical data are held in a single record, whose structure is defined and managed by a Prolog-level view of the data. Access is by ground atomic key value. Additional access paths are defined in separate record types, each relating one access path key to its lexical entry's key. Extendible hashing ensures that access to a lexical entry only involves one, or at most two, logical disk accesses, and a cache memory system means that the more commonly used words can be retrieved without going to disk. New access paths can be defined at the implementation level without affecting the existing database definition.

At the Prolog level, rules are defined to present a structured view of the lexical data. Prolog is ideally suited for this type of data manipulation. Having this part of the database definition in Prolog means that it is easy to adapt the definition to meet new requirements: the external database definition need not be changed, and in some cases neither do the stored data.

REFERENCES

[1] Larson, P., Linear Hashing with Partial Expansions, *6th International VLDB Conf.*, Montreal, 1980, 224–232.

[2] Fagin *et al.*, Extendible Hashing, *ACM-TODS,* **4**, 315–344, 1979.

20

Software configuration management using Prolog

Paul Singleton and **Colin D. Farris**
Computer Science Department, University of Keele,
Keele, Staffs, ST5 5BG

1. INTRODUCTION

This chapter describes the implementation of a logic-based software configuration management system using Quintus Prolog (QP) and a home-brewed tuple store, and asserts that, for serious applications, Prolog implementers need to borrow *indexing*, *query optimization* and *transaction management* techniques from database technology.

The authors are employed in an Alvey-funded project [1], building a knowledge-based software development environment, and are specifically concerned with logic-based management of evolving software configurations.

2. CONFIGURATION MANAGEMENT USING PROLOG

Software configuration management (CM) should perhaps record significant historical and semantic relationships between source files, compiled modules, libraries, headers, environmental features, etc., and all versions thereof so as to be able to answer any query, and perform any operation, for whose execution there is a logical basis. CM has, in the past, been tackled in three broad styles:

- *minimalist*: apart from luxuries such as compilers and editors, the programmer has been left to his/her own devices in recording (typically in human memory) the dependencies between files, and the definitions of deliverable configurations and sub-configurations. He/she may have written scripts to abbreviate some recurring operation, and used crude parameterization mechanisms (e.g. re-used filenames).
- *mechanized*: specialized programs, allied with ingeniously structured data files, have been devised to factor out some common 'system building' activities; for example, the UNIX *make* [2] tool accommodates user-defined rules about the automatic construction of files from other files

(e.g. programs from sources, libraries from components, etc.), although these rules are not susceptible to arbitrary queries such as 'which files are redundant?', 'Which products depend upon X but not upon Y?' even though they determine the answers to these (and many other) logical queries.

- *databased*: systems such as ECLIPSE [3] incorporate pre-defined schemas and a (otherwise) general-pupose database in order to support more controllably the traditional queries and operations.

We have chosen to use Prolog, in what we believe will introduce a new generation of CM systems. Our development strategy is evolutionary, and incorporates three experimental 'case studies', during the implementation of which we are always careful to adopt general, rather than application-specific, solutions.

Our three targets are:

- *Prolog itself*: we are generating substantial amounts of Prolog code, much of which is eminently reusable (due to the qualities of Prolog, as much as to our programming skills and powers of abstraction). We are therefore tackling the problems of constructing configurations of Prolog procedures out of shared libraries of generic routines, and providing ourselves with an evolving software development environment. Further details are given below in sections 3 and 8.
- *'C'*: our familiarity with UNIX programming tempted us to address the 'C' programming language (and its many allied tools). A substantial 'C' program configuration may be parametrized for many target software and hardware environments, for compatibility with alternative protocols, for export to different countries, for optional profiling, debugging, and for different levels of functionality. Reconstructable components should be managed intelligently, to minimize costs of a 'build', yet maintain enough space for each new activity.
- *Ada*: our third subject is the Ada programming system, which from its outset aimed to reduce the complexity of configurations (albeit by forbidding variation rather than by managing it).

A fourth target has been added recently:

- *documentation*: this too can benefit from logic-based CM (for example, to ensure that a released manual meets various specifications best expressed logically, such as full coverage of the product it describes, freedom from dangling references and version skew, correct identification, and consistent indexing).

3. WHY AND HOW WE ARE USING PROLOG

Prolog promises to support CM more powerfully than previous techniques. For example, we intend to be able to construct generic releases of software products, i.e. a partly reduced configuration of components within which some parametrization is yet to be resolved. This is closely analogous with an 'indefinite' proof (i.e. containing unbound variables) which a Prolog engine might return.

We deliberately avoid making any assumptions about specific functional dependencies within the possible relationships between components, as there is no merit in obstructing the representation of inconsistent states. Our approach to consistency within the CM database holds that:

- it is highly desirable;
- it is probably best defined by the user (or his manager);
- it is best achieved by allowing the inevitable occasional inconsistencies to be both representable and available for inference (to 'think the unthinkable').

We do not, for example, assume or require that there should be only one routine with any particular name, or that any symbolic constant should have only one defined value. An attempt to build a product of which some sub-component is multiply defined will yield multiple results, and this will be as true for an entire operating system release as it will be for a precompiled subroutine or formatted manual page. The user is encouraged (but not compelled) to provide disambiguating metadata in such circumstances (i.e. add facts and rules which qualify the validity of alternatives).

We allow any configuration component to be defined by rule instead of, or as well as, by fact.

We are not prepared to trade functionality off against performance, or against implementation simplicity. We want our CM system to be able to automatically answer any (non-deictic) query for which its knowledge contains the logical basis of a solution.

We regard the Prolog engine as a stateless mechanism for proving a theorem against a specified rulebase.

All important knowledge is recorded outside particular Prolog processes, in a shared conventional filestore. It is this filestore, not the Prolog interpreter, which constitutes the persistent part of our programming environment. We regard our Prolog interpreter as a 'proof window', and establish a new instance as we would a new 'shell' (we destroy them as casually, too).

We try to fit CM into the *proof* model: for example, building a release could be seen as proving that:

> '**A** contains **B**, where **A** is a magnetic tape, and **B** embodies level(2.0) of revision(B) of GIZMO, where **B** is appropriate for hardware configuration **C** . . .'

Unusual types such as *magtape*(**X**) and *a4*†(**Y**) are embedded as homogeneously as possible within the system.

† i.e. A4-sized hard-copy.

4. WHY WE ARE NEVERTHELESS INTERESTED IN DATABASE TECHNOLOGY

Our interest in database techniques stems from some shortcomings of our chosen (and not untypical) Prolog implementation.

We encountered, almost immediately, a need for a wider persistence than that provided by Quintus Prolog (QP) Release 1.6, our chosen implementation of Prolog. This was a unanimous and intuitive perception by the three active members of the development team, and was only rationalized in retrospect.

We identify three major reasons for wanting enhanced persistence:

- *shareability* of knowledge: there are three of us developing the configuration manager concurrently;
- *survivability* of knowledge: we want user-supplied knowledge to have a safer repository than that provided by the Prolog process;
- *enormity* of knowledge: the effective capacity of QP's database is well short of our requirements.

5. SHAREABILITY OF KNOWLEDGE

We intend that our delivered CM system will support a team of software engineers, not merely an individual, and consider it unacceptable that queries or other operations upon the CM knowledge base should have to be serialized (e.g. to a CM 'agent'). A typical Prolog interpreter can prove only one goal at a time, and cannot therefore be the sole repository of CM data without conflicting with our multi-user (*shareability*) requirement.

6. SURVIVABILITY OF KNOWLEDGE

We do not regard any single invocation of our Prolog system as a safe repository for newly provided knowledge, owing to the fragility of processes under UNIX. The mere act of asserting a clause into a particular Prolog rulebase does not ensure its long-term persistence, and we cannot rely on periodic 'backing-up' of these rulebases, since QP invocations may have to be destroyed at short notice for various reasons:

- QP will request additional virtual memory from UNIX as necessary, e.g. during a complex proof. It will subsequently offer surplus memory back to UNIX, which may [4] be incapable of using it again. We choose not to limit the maximum size for a QP instance, since this would restrict its capacity to construct useful proofs. We prefer to allow QP instances to grow without restriction, and kill them if they hog memory to the detriment of other processes.
- QP (in common with most other Prolog systems) does not recover the space taken up by redundant atom texts. Thus a QP process cannot, in general, run indefinitely, but must be killed before its performance deteriorates unacceptably. In one of our applications (a parser), atom

debris disabled the interpreter before any useful work had been done (the application had to be recoded — rather deviously — to work around this feature).

- QP instances may hang or crash owing to bugs in user-supplied 'foreign functions' or in the engine itself.

7. ENORMITY OF KNOWLEDGE

In an earlier project, we used C-Prolog on a PDP-11, and soon found the capacity of the (process-resident) rulebase to be inadequate. We expected this problem to disappear when we acquired computers with virtual memory (Sun 3s), but it reappeared almost immediately. Two facts combined to invalidate our optimism:

- QP performs poorly on a demand-paged machine (it appears not to take up Sun UNIX's invitation† to switch between the three available page-replacement algorithms according to the expected nature of its memory accesses).
- we could not (ever) afford enough main memory to accommodate all our clauses in resident pages.

In the course of formalizing the management of 'C' program configurations, we constructed a relation which summarized the contents of the 'C' libraries available on our system. This contained over 42 k tuples, and caused unacceptable degradation of QP performance when it was *compiled* or *consulted* into the QP rulebase (the 2 Mbytes of process space required for this single procedure stretches our QP processes to a size at which they 'page' heavily, and performance drops disastrously).

We investigated the alternative storage and access mechanisms available to us:

- the UNIX *dbm* library of 'database management routines' only handles key-content pairs, and not arbitrary relations. Other shortcomings will be described in section 11;
- we had a rather old version of the INGRES relational database with an 'embedded' interface to 'C' programs (and hence to QP): our observations are tabulated below;
- we developed our own scheme (Indexed External Relations — IER) which is described in section 11.

To be fair to QP and INGRES, their storage mechanisms support incremental assertion and retraction of tuples, although our 'C' library data was unchanging and hence benefited from the different design tradeoff adopted in IER.

† The *vadvise* system call.

storage scheme:	Mbytes occupied:	comments:
QP1.6 (*consulted*)	2.0 (process)	no indexing; heavy paging
QP1.6 (*compiled*)	1.9 (process)	first argument indexed; heavy paging
INGRES V6	1.7 (filestore)	first argument indexed; excessive I/O
INGRES V6	8.1 (filestore)	all four arguments indexed; excessive I/O
IER	2.9 (filestore)	all four arguments indexed

QP (*consulted*) serially matches a goal against every stored clause. The resultant heavy paging traffic can be reduced by selecting a 'sequential' page-replacement algorithm, but QP does not do this.

QP (*compiled*) stores clauses 'hashed' on their first argument. Goals with ground first arguments are matched fairly directly with candidates, but general goals must still be matched by serial search (as above).

INGRES (V6) stores tuples in a filestore-resident hashed or ISAM structure, indexed on one (user-nominated) argument. Retrievals are efficient where this argument is determined, but the serial searches necessary in other cases are very slow because of the (unnecessary) fetching of candidate tuples from disk.

INGRES (V6) permits 'secondary indices' on other arguments, or combinations of arguments. A goal in which two or more arguments are determined could be matched efficiently by intersecting the corresponding indices, but INGRES does not do this. Instead, it generates candidates on the basis of one argument value, then tests them against the values of the others.

IER stores the tuples in the filestore, and employs collapsed inverted indices on each argument position. These are intersected for general retrievals, minimizing the retrieval of spurious candidate tuples.

8. PROLOG + DATABASES: AN EXAMPLE

We now describe a specific aspect of our work in which, for various reasons, we needed an external database.

Our major software development tool is a QP saved state called *pcm*, which is primed with essential code for maintaining libraries. Our shared Prolog procedures (currently numbering 3000) are partitioned into libraries (currently numbering 40) for the usual reasons of managing complexity, containing combinatorial explosions, localizing inter-dependencies and generally keeping life bearable for the programmer.

Each Prolog procedure is held in a separate textfile (such fine granularity is necessary if we are to maintain versions of individual procedures), and each file can be parsed to identify:

- the name and arity of its principal functor, represented as a fact such as

  pcontents(argc/1).

- the names and arities of directly called procedures (disregarding the treatment of meta-predicates), represented as facts such as

pneeds(argc/1, environ/2).
pneeds(argc/1, term_chars/2).

One major query supported by these facts is the identification of those procedures which might be called (directly or indirectly) in the course of proving a particular goal. This is used in automatically loading the procedures necessary to generate the proofs, and is achieved by searching the (directed, and generally cyclic) graph defined by the *pneeds/4* facts (currently numbering 6000). (This automated loading helps support the illusion that the programmer is working in a filestore-resident environment of shared procedures, and that *pcm* is just a dispensable window onto that environment.)

Rather than always parse each procedure file anew, we aggregate the *pcontents/2* and *pneeds/4* facts into textfiles within each library directory, and update these summaries whenever a procedure is added or changed within a library. During software development (i.e. hacking), new procedures can be defined every few minutes (and by several programmers concurrently).

It is inappropriate to compile these facts into each *pcm*, as they soon become out of date. While it is feasible to recompile whenever necessary (such a technique is described, as *cached procedures*, in section 9), it is preferable to access these facts where they live, out in the shared filestore. Our mechanism to achieve this is described (as *external relations*) in sections 9 and 10.

9. HOW PROCEDURES ARE SHARED

We employ three distinct techniques for sharing procedures, each appropriate to different circumstances:

- *constant procedures*: these are procedures whose definitions we expect to remain unchanged, and which are simply compiled into *pcm*. Examples: code drawn from the QP library, or code implementing the essential functionality of *pcm*. In practice, these procedures occasionally have to be replaced (e.g. when a new release of the QP libraries is adopted, or when a bug is fixed), but we are content with traditional non-automatic solutions; typically, we reconstruct the 'binary' of the *pcm* program, and notify users that a new version has been made.
- *cached procedures*: these are general Prolog procedures, compiled or consulted into a *pcm* process before use, of which we require that they track any changes in their filestore-resident definition. An example: the *pcm* equivalent of UNIX *makefiles* are short procedures (*pmakefiles*) containing rules for the construction of documents and (sub-)configurations. Additions to shared *pmakefiles* should be visible to all *pcm* users, without requiring them to kill and reconstruct their *pcm* processes. This recompilation has been automated, by prepending (again, automatically) an extra clause to the procedure before compilation:

```
fred( _, _, _, _) :-
    abolish_and_recompile_if_changed( fred, 4),
    fail.
fred( A, B, C, D) :-
    % the regular clauses of fred/4 ...
```

This is a 'lazy' technique, which defers recompilation until a procedure is actually called in the course of proving a goal.

It is also naive, in that it requires a procedure to alter its own definition *while it is being called*. In general, a proof should be developed against the static set of procedure definitions prevailing at the moment it commenced, and should not take new definitions on board as it proceeds. Self-modifying code can have inscrutable semantics, and QP attempts to staticize a procedure once it is called. This unfortunately makes 'lazy' cacheing impossible, and we anyway have tentative plans to replace it with a more wholesome strategy.

- *external relations*: our third technique leaves a procedure's definition in the global filestore, and fetches its clauses whenever a goal is matched against that procedure's head. This scheme implements a special case of this, applicable to only those Prolog procedures whose clauses have:

  - no bodies;
  - no structured arguments;
  - no variable arguments.

This last, and severely restricted, model corresponds closely† to the concept of *relation* as understood by the database community, and our implementation, termed *external relations*, is described in the next section. Despite its restrictions, we have found several significant applications, and make heavy use of it within *pcm* itself.

- *indexed external relations*: these are *external relations* with collapsed and inverted secondary indices, which allow efficient access in the (general) case when one or more arguments of the goal are instantiated. Our implementation is described in section 11.
- *indexed external terms*: this scheme has been prototyped, and overcomes all the restrictions of *external relations*, in that we can store and retrieve general terms, with bodies and non-ground structured arguments; furthermore, we can index a set of terms so as to be able to retrieve (almost) only those which will unify with a given pattern. This work is still under way, and deserves a separate chapter.

† With two significant exceptions: Prolog clauses are always searched in the order in which they were defined, while relational databases may lose the entry order (e.g. in hashed storage structures); and duplicate clauses are allowed in Prolog, while a relational database may collapse duplicates (and perhaps should). In each respect, the functionality of Prolog subsumes that of the relational database.

10. AN IMPLEMENTATION OF 'EXTERNAL RELATIONS'

An external relation is a filestore-resident testfile mapped transparently onto a corresponding Prolog procedure 'facade' by a single general mechanism, which is implemented partly in Prolog and partly as a 'C' foreign procedure.

Consider, for example, the following tabulated textfile relation (it's the *pneeds/4* file mentioned earlier):

```
argc        1  environ    2
argc        1  term_atom  2
argv        2  argc       1
argv        2  arith      3
argv        2  environ    2
argv        2  nmember    3
argv        2  sum        3
argv        2  term_atom  2
bag_diffs   4  bag        3
bag_diffs   4  bag_diffs  9
etc...
```

which can be accessed from within *pcm* exactly as if the following procedure had been compiled or consulted:

```
pneeds( argc,       1, environ,    2).
pneeds( argc,       1, term_atom,  2).
pneeds( argv,       2, argc,       1).
pneeds( argv,       2, arith,      3).
pneeds( argv,       2, environ,    2).
pneeds( argv,       2, nmember,    3).
pneeds( argv,       2, sum,        3).
pneeds( argv,       2, term_atom,  2).
pneeds( bag_diffs,  4, bag,        3).
pneeds( bag_diffs,  4, bag_diffs,  9).
etc...
```

We have defined the structure of such a *textfile relation* as follows:

- an *attribute_value* is a string of ASCII characters (possibly empty);
- a *tuple* is a sequence of tab-separated attribute_values;
- a *relation* is a file of newline-terminated tuples.

Files with this structure are amenable to manipulation by many traditional UNIX tools, such as text editors, *sort*, *join*, *comm*, *wc*, etc., to which we have added *project*, *select*, *unite*, *unsort*, *flatten* among many.

By (local) convention, the successive tuples of a *textfile relation* are considered to be numbered from 1 upwards, as are the successive arguments (from left to right) of each tuple.

The implementation of *external relations* is described in five layers of code, embodied in procedures *er1*, *er2*, *er3*, *er4* and *er5*, progressively showing how the Prolog 'facade' is ultimately implemented in terms of primitive UNIX file operations.

The design objectives were (with some benefit from hindsight) that the mechanism should:

- be simple to employ (preferably automatically);
- accommodate any width (*degree*) of relation;
- accommodate any length (*cardinality*) of relation;
- accommodate any Prolog *constant* as an attribute value;
- be re-entrant (even with nested calls to the same relation);
- tidy up after cuts from Prolog when part-way through a relation;
- be efficient (so as to be usable, and to the satisfaction of the designers).

The five layers are presented next, starting with a specimen application: each quoted routine is followed by an explanation.

```
% pneeds( ?Arg1, ?Arg2, ?Arg3, ?Arg4) :-
%
%     behaves exactly as if there were a compiled or consulted
%     Prolog procedure of facts, one for each line of the
%     corresponding textfile relation.

pneeds( Arg1, Arg2, Arg3, Arg4) :-
      er1( '/usr/paul/pneeds', [Arg1, Arg2, Arg3, Arg4]).
```

This clause is all that has to be written to make **/usr/paul/pneeds** appear within *pcm*; the subsequent procedures (*er1–er5*) are built into *pcm*, and are shared by all *external relations*. Indeed, we can generate these 'interface' clauses automatically when attempting to 'load' an *external relation* into *pcm* (where 'load' is a generic operation which treats each class of procedure appropriately).

The first argument of *er1* is the full UNIX pathname by which the *textfile relation* is known. The second argument is a list of the variables in the head of the procedure (by this means, *er1* accommodates relations of any arity).

```
% er1(+Path, -Args) :-
%
%     the textfile relation at Path has a constituent tuple
%     with the attribute values within Args.

er1( Path, Args) :-
      er2( Path, 1, Values),
      Args = Values.
```

This stage retrieves (via *er2*) successive tuples from the named textfile, and unifies each returned list of attribute values with the arguments provided to the call (the second argument of *er2* is solely to serve *er2*'s self-recursion, as explained in the next section). If, for any tuple, this unification fails, then control will backtrack into *er2* for a further tuple. Note that the opportunity for accessing the relation more efficiently via an index is thrown away here, as we disregard any instantiated arguments which might constrain the search: we have, however, prototyped a scheme in which per-argument inverted indices are intersected to identify only those tuples which will unify with the supplied arguments.†

```
        % er2(+Path,+TupleNo, -Values) :-
%
%    the textfile relation at Path has a tuple
%    numbered TupleNo (or greater) whose attribute values
%    are those in Values

        er2( Path, TupleNo, Values) :-
            IF     er3( Path, TupleNo, 1, Values)
            THEN true
            ELSE  !,
                   fail
            FI.

        er2( Path, TupleNo, Values) :-
           NextTupleNo is TupleNo+1,
           er2( Path, NextTupleNo, Values).
```

The procedure *er2* succeeds for each tuple numbered *TupleNo* or higher: the *TupleNo* argument serves its recursive call of itself, and *er1* calls it with *1* in this position. It is *er2*, which allows *er1* to succeed multiply, by (recursively) calling the determinate procedure *er3*. Note that tail recursion optimization ensures that the cost of the recursion is of the same order as that of an iterative mechanism. (N.B. We exploit the symbol definitions

```
IF     ⇒ ((
THEN ⇒ )->(
ELSE  ⇒ );(
FI     ⇒ ))
```

by employing the 'C' preprocessor to convert Prolog source files containing these symbols into 'raw' Prolog source syntax. By making this 'local cut' easier to use, we are not necessarily condoning it.)

```
        % er3(+Path,+TupleNo,+ArgNo, -Values) :-
        %
        %    textfile relation Path has, in tuple numbered TupleNo,
        %    from argument ArgNo to the end of the tuple,
        %    the values Values.

        er3( Path, TupleNo, ArgNo, Values) :-
```

† With one exception: a goal with shared variables, e.g. pneeds(Name, Arity, Name, Arity), may match only a few of the tuples, but must be proven by retrieving **all** the tuples, and attempting the unification inside Prolog. Special indices for such retrievals are not obviously worth constructing.

```
IF     er4( Path, TupleNo, ArgNo, V)
THEN NextArgNo is ArgNo+1,
       er3( Path, TupleNo, NextArgNo, Vrest),
       Values=[V|Vrest]
ELSE Values=[]
FI.
```

This procedure implements the general treatment of all arities, by retrieving successive attribute values of the specified tuple for as long as there are more to be had. Our implementation is rather more complicated (although equivalent) for the sake of improved efficiency.

```
% er4(+Path,+TupleNo,+ArgNo, -Value) :-
%
%     the textfile relation at Path has,
%     in its tuple numbered TupleNo,
%     in its argument numbered ArgNo,
%     the value Value.

er4( Path, TupleNo, ArgNo, Value) :-
      er5( Path, TupleNo, ArgNo, Type, Atom, Integer, Float),
      er6( Type, Atom, Integer, Float, Value).
```

This determinate procedure fetches the value of an attribute specified by its TupleNo and ArgNo (*Y* and *X* coordinates respectively). It maps the traditional compile-time type determinacy of the 'C' foreign procedure *er5* onto the run-time type flexibility of Prolog.

```
% er6( Type, Atom, Integer, Float, Value) :-
%
%      given either an Atom, Integer or Float
%      (necessarily in its respective argument position),
%      and given an indication of its type in Type,
%      we return it as Value (this being Prolog).

er6(  1,    Atom,   _,         _,       Atom).
er6(  2,    _,      Integer,   _,       Integer).
er6(  3,    _,      _,         Float,   Float).
```

This procedure unifies its last argument with its second, third or fourth, according to the code passed in its first. The foreign procedure *er5*, being written in 'C', is (in principle, at least) unable freely to return an atom, integer or float in a single argument position.

```
er5( Path, TupleNo, ArgNo, Type, Atom, Int, Float)
char   *Path;
int    TupleNo;
int    ArgNo;
int    Type;
char   **Atom;
```

```
int     *Int;
float   *Float;
        {
        /* this is a C function */

        }
```

Before outlining the foreign procedure, it is necessary to present the rationale of the whole scheme. The introduction of *TupleNo* and *ArgNo* into the intermediate layers (*er2*, *er3* and *er4*) allows an entirely idempotent foreign procedure *er5* to be employed. Although *er5* could serve successive arguments in the manner of a traditional 'read' routine, it would need to retain non-trivial context to support this. True idempotency (by which we mean that a call to this procedure should always yield the same result regardless of history, or of context) is desirable because Prolog does not give foreign procedures any indication that a 'cut' has occurred within Prolog, and, whereas backtracking information within Prolog is tidied up after each cut, foreign procedures get no indication that they should do the same. When this state information includes open UNIX file descriptors, garbage collection becomes imperative lest the Prolog process becomes unable to open any more files (re-use of file descriptors is essential, since there is only a small number of them available).

To support this idempotency efficiently, the foreign procedure *er5* maintains a small cache of open file descriptors, and records sufficient information about each to enable re-use when appropriate. We may view these as Prolog facts of the form

context(Path, TupleNo, ArgNo, FileDescriptor).

where the *FileDescriptor* is understood to be pointing at the first character of the *ArgNo*th argument of the *TupleNo* th tuple of the textfile relation found at the end of *Path* (a full UNIX file pathname, since *pcm* may change its working directory).

After reading this argument, *context*(P, T, A, F) is replaced by *context*(P, T, A+1, F), or by *context*(P, T+1, 0, F) if the last argument of the tuple had been read.

If a call of *er5* specifies a tuple and an argument for which there is no current context, then a free file descriptor is obtained (if no genuinely free descriptor exists, then another context is destroyed and its file descriptor re-used). The specified file is opened, and the specified argument is reached by reading serially past as many tuples as is appropriate. Note that tuple addresses cannot be computed, since the relation is not an array, but a closely packed file of tuples of various (not variable!) lengths.

The efficiency of this scheme hinges on the (deliberate) fact that the Prolog procedures *er1* to *er4* eventually demand the arguments of any particular relation in strict left-to-right, top-to-bottom order through each textfile. The strategy for choosing a context to be destroyed is currently 'least-recently-used', but this may deserve further thought. Searches through the set of contexts start at the most-recently-used context, but, with only ten or so contexts retained, optimization of this aspect is not particularly important.

11. AN IMPLEMENTATION OF 'INDEXED EXTERNAL RELATIONS'

We have prototyped a scheme for efficient access to *external relations* via collapsed inverted indices to each attribute. While the techniques we use are common in database technology, our attempts to employ established database products for this purpose were unsuccessful.

Each tuple in a *textfile relation* is (implicitly) addressed by the file offset (its *tuple address*) at which its representation starts; e.g. for *pneeds/4*:

```
  0:   argc       1 environ    2
 17:   argc       1 term_atom  2
 36:   argv       2 argc       1
 50:   argv       2 arith      3
 65:   argv       2 environ    2
 82:   argv       2 nmember    3
 99:   argv       2 sum        3
112:   argv       2 term_atom  2
131:   bag_diffs  4 bag        3
149:   bag_diffs  4 bag_diffs  9
       etc...
```

For each attribute (1–4), an inverted index maps attribute values to *tuple addresses*, e.g. for the first attribute of *pneeds/4*:

```
argc         0
argc        17
argv        36
argv        50
argv        65
argv        82
argv        99
argv       112
bag_diffs  131
bag_diffs  149
etc...
```

and we can advantageously collapse this:

```
argc       0,17
argv       36,50,65,82,99,112
bag_diffs  131,149
etc...
```

Retrieval of tuples matching a general pattern (e.g. *pneeds(argv, X, Y, 3)*, where the first and fourth arguments are instantiated) can be performed efficiently by:

- (trivially) determining which arguments are instantiated, and which have logical variables;
- using the inverted indices, map any instantiated attribute values to their associated list of tuple addresses;
- retrieve those tuples whose addreses are common to all indicated lists (i.e. intersect the lists).

Some observations on the collapsed inverted indices follow.

- They can be regarded as relations of degree 2, but the *tuple address* list can be arbitrarily long (130 Kbytes in one application), and many relational storage schemes cannot cope with this (requiring, for example, that each tuple should fit into one filesystem block).
- Within each list, the *tuple addresses* are in ascending numeric order. This minimizes the cost of intersecting two or more lists (each need be traversed only once).
- The *tuple address* lists can be compressed, by storing incremental (rather than absolute) addresses, and reconstructing the absolute addresses as the list is traversed. This is advantageous only if a variable-length representation of integers is adopted.
- The cheapness with which a collapsed inverted index can have small updates performed in place (corresponding to the assertion or retraction of a tuple from the corresponding relation) depends upon the properties of the storage structure employed. Hashed schemes can be quite amenable to updates.

INGRES V6 supported the construction of secondary inverted indices for each argument, but it did not collapse them (hence used four times as much space as necessary). Nor did it intersect them on retrieval, but merely used the first instantiated argument as a key for indexed retrieval, and tested each 'hit' against the other instantiated arguments.

The UNIX *dbm*(3) library package can accommodate neither the uncollapsed form (it forbids multiple tuples with the same key values, i.e. it stores functions, not relations), nor the collapsed form (it has a 4096 byte limit on tuple size).

12. A PLANNED IMPLEMENTATION OF 'INDEXED INTERNAL TERMS'

We shall employ a general mechanism for storing arbitrary terms in the host filestore, such that any Prolog process can efficiently make a (heap-resident) copy of any term it requires. Typically, these terms will be *clauses*. Their representation will be tuned to favour copying into Prolog, on the assumption that (as in conventional filestore wisdom) 'reads' heavily outnumber 'writes'. A prefix flattening is probably optimum, but the usual replacement of atom texts by a vocabulary index is not necessarily helpful where

- several Prolog processes are developing their individual atom vocabularies;
- filestore space is cheaper than process space.

A compromise scheme nevertheless looks feasible.

13. CONCLUSIONS (AND SPECULATIONS): WHAT WE CAN ADOPT FROM DATABASE TECHNOLOGY

We consider six aspects of database technology in turn:

- *relational database theory*: since we choose not to impose constraints upon user-defined relations, we have little use for the theorems concerning functional dependencies and normal forms. We have, however, implemented mechanisms to search for incidental functional dependencies within user-defined relations, as their presence might be of interest to the user.
- *query optimization*: we intend to provide a query interface with as much of the power of first-order logic as possible. We know that optimization of these queries could be of great benefit, and aim to mechanize conversion of queries between Prolog, relational calculus and relational algebra forms, in order to exploit various well-known optimizations [5].
- *indexing techniques*: the performance gains to be had from thorough indexing of externally held clauses will be significant. We believe we have a technique for indexing terms on their unifiability.
- *transaction management*: concurrent access to a shared, evolving database will need some control. We favour optimistic concurrency techniques, as these sidestep the need for deadlock-breaking algorithms, and seem to fit well into the backtracking provided by Prolog.
- *formal treatment of time-variant knowledge*: we must retain the referential transparency of the knowledge in our database, while allowing old knowledge to be augmented or even contradicted. We shall need a disciplined approach to updates, and expect to have to associate timespans with each fact or rule. We want to be sure of getting the same answer to a query whenever it is given.
- *hypothetical knowledge bases*: the CM system must be able to answer hypothetical queries from, for example, the project manager, and must therefore support hypothetical knowledge bases. These are likely to be defined by qualifying or varying the 'common' knowledge base (if there is such a concept).

ACKNOWLEDGEMENTS

We gratefully acknowledge the support of the Alvey Directorate, and that of our colleagues in the ISM Project Consortium.

REFERENCES

[1] The ISM Project: Towards a Knowledge-based IPSE, ISM Project Consortium, 1986.

[2] Feldman, S. I., Make — A Program for Maintaining Computer Programs, *Software — Practice and Experience,* **9**, 255–265, 1979.
[3] Alderson, A., Bott, M. F., and Falla, M. E., An Overview of the ECLIPSE Project, in *Integrated Project Support Environments*, ed. J. McDermid, Peter Peregrinus, London, 1985.
[4] *Quintus Prolog System-dependent Features Manual*, *version 6*, Quintus Computer Systems Inc., 1986, p. 67.
[5] Gray, P., Query Transformation in Algebra and Calculus, in *Logic, Algebra and Databases*, Chapter 9, Ellis Horwood, Chichester, 1984, 176–199.

Index